The Art of Brian Friel

Neither Reality Nor Dreams

Elmer Andrews

Lecturer in English
University of Ulster

First published in Great Britain 1995 by
MACMILLAN PRESS LTD
Houndmills, Basingstoke, Hampshire RG21 6XS
and London
Companies and representatives
throughout the world

A catalogue record for this book is available
from the British Library.

ISBN 0-333-60075-4

 First published in the United States of America 1995 by
ST. MARTIN'S PRESS, INC.,
Scholarly and Reference Division,
175 Fifth Avenue,
New York, N.Y. 10010

ISBN 0-312-12046-X

Library of Congress Cataloging-in-Publication Data
Andrews, Elmer
The art of Brian Friel : neither reality nor dreams / Elmer
Andrews
p. cm.
ISBN 0-312-12046-X
1. Friel, Brian—Criticism and interpretation. 2. Northern
Ireland in literature. I. Title.
PR6056.R5Z57 1995
822'.914—dc20   93-39876
                                                                CIP

11 10 9 8 7 6 5
05 04 03 02 01

Printed in Great Britain by
Antony Rowe Ltd, Chippenham, Wiltshire

THE ART OF BRIAN FRIEL

Oh, the dreaming, the dreaming, the torturing heartscalding, never-satisfying dreaming . . . An Irishman's imagination never lets him alone, never convinces him, never satisfies him; but it makes him that he can't face reality nor deal with it nor handle it nor conquer it.

G. B. Shaw, *John Bull's Other Island*

Stop just licking your wounds. Start seeing things.

Seamus Heaney, *The Cure at Troy*

Contents

Acknowledgements

I wish to express my gratitude to the University of Ulster for study leave granted to me to complete this study.

Grateful acknowledgement is also made for permission to reprint the following copyright-material:

the extract from Elgy Gillespie's 'The Saturday Interview: Brian Friel' in *The Irish Times*, 5 September 1981, © 1981 *The Irish Times*;

the extract from an interview with Brian Friel in *The Irish Press*, 30 August 1981, © Irish Press Newspapers Ltd;

the extract from 'Irish Heroes Who Never Come to Life' by H. Kretzner in the *Daily Express*, 1 March 1973, © Express Newspapers plc;

the extract from 'How Poetry Joins Dramatic Action' by Fintan O'Toole, first published 29 November 1991 in *The Guardian*, © Fintan O'Toole, 1991;

the extract from 'Shock Play Hits at "Brutal" Soldiers' by T. Prentice in the *Daily Mail*, 21 February 1973, © *Daily Mail*/Solo;

the extract from a review of *Freedom of the City*, in *Belfast Newsletter*, 21 February 1973, © *Belfast Newsletter*;

the extract from a review of *The Three Sisters* in *The Irish Independent*, 10 September 1981, © *Irish Independent*;

the extracts from Frank Rich's review of *Dancing at Lughnasa* in the *New York Times*, 25 October 1991, copyright © 1991 by The New York Times Co.; reprinted by permission;

the extract from Milton Shulman's review of *Freedom of the City*, 'At the Royal Court' in *The Evening Standard*, 28 February 1973, © *Evening Standard*/Solo.

the extracts from Harold Pinter's speech to the Seventh National Student Drama Festival in Bristol, first published 4 March 1962 in *The Sunday Times*, © Harold Pinter.

Finally, my thanks to Brian Friel, for providing me with unpublished work and for the kindness and co-operation he has extended to me in preparing this book.

List of Abbreviations

The following abbreviations are used parenthetically in the text to identify either the collection of short stories in which a given short story appears, or the play, or the collection of plays in which a given play appears. Page references to the stories and plays, which are incorporated into the text, relate to the particular editions indicated below.

Short Stories

D   *The Diviner* (Dublin: The O'Brien Press; London: Allison and Busby, 1983).

GS   *The Gold in the Sea* (New York: Doubleday; London: Victor Gollancz, 1966).

SL   *The Saucer of Larks: Stories of Ireland* (London: Arrow Books, 1969).

Plays

CC   *The Communication Cord* (London: Faber and Faber, 1983).

CF   *Crystal and Fox* (Dublin: Gallery Press, 1984).

DL   *Dancing at Lughnasa* (London: Faber and Faber, 1990).

EW   *The Enemy Within* (Dublin: Gallery Press, 1979).

FS   *Fathers and Sons* (London: Faber and Faber, 1987).

GI   *The Gentle Island* (London: Davis-Poynter, 1973).

L   *Lovers* (Dublin: Gallery Press, 1969).

LCM   *The Loves of Cass McGuire* (Dublin: Gallery Press, 1984).

LV   *The London Vertigo* (Dublin: Gallery Press, 1990).

MC   *A Month in the Country* (Dublin: Gallery Press, 1992).

MH   *Making History* (London: Faber and Faber, 1989).

MS   *The Mundy Scheme*, in *Two Plays* (New York: Farrar, Straus and Giroux, 1970).

SP   *Selected Plays of Brian Friel*, ed. Seamus Deane (London: Faber and Faber, 1984).

TS   *The Three Sisters* (Dublin: Gallery Press, 1981).

V   *Volunteers* (London: Faber and Faber, 1979).

WT   *Wonderful Tennessee* (Dublin: Gallery Press, 1993).

1

Introduction

Background, Basic Premises, Early Work

Brian Friel was born in Omagh in Co. Tyrone in 1929, the son of a primary school principal. In the same year the family went to live in the Bogside in Derry. He spent five years at St Columb's College, Derry and, later, two-and-a-half years at St Patrick's College, Maynooth, the national seminary near Dublin. Instead of going on for the priesthood, he graduated with a BA and spent a year at St Joseph's Teacher Training College in Belfast. From 1950 until 1960 he taught in various schools around Derry. Since then he has been writing full-time. Though both he and his father were teachers, his grandparents, he tells us, were illiterate peasants from Co. Donegal whose first language was Irish not English. As Peter Breen notes (in 'Place and Displacement in the Work of Seamus Heaney and Brian Friel', unpublished Ph.D. thesis, Warwick University, 1993), Friel's own family background bears the marks of the historical divisions between traditional value and the processes of modernity which characterise the larger Irish and Ulster history.

The Derry in which he grew up, Friel explains, was 'a gentle and, in those days, sleepy town', but also 'a frustrating and frustrated town in which the majority of the people were disinherited. . . . Although the Civil Rights fires had been kindled in many places throughout the North, they burst into flames in Derry, because it was there the suppression was greatest.'[1] A member of the Nationalist Party in Derry for some years, he resigned in 1967 because he believed 'the party had lost initiative'.[2] Though most of his early life was lived in Derry, his roots, he always felt, lay in Co. Donegal. His mother's family came from near the village of Glenties in Co. Donegal and it was there that he spent part of his school holidays each year. Later, with the proceeds from his first big theatrical success, *Philadelphia, Here I Come!* (1964), he built a house in Muff, just across the border, 'partly to get into the countryside and partly to get into the Republic'.[3] The political situation in the North was a particular reason for moving: 'The sense of frustration which I felt under the tight and immovable Unionist regime became distasteful', he wrote, but, with a characteristic optimism, added: 'still, I don't think the gap is too wide to be breached. People are pliable and generous'.[4] The majority of his stories and plays are set, as Seamus Deane has noted, in 'that borderland of Derry, Donegal and Tyrone in which a largely Catholic community leads a reduced existence under the pressure of political and economic oppression'.[5] The border itself does not appear in Friel's work, but his characters are still radically marginalised or interstitial figures, members of Frank O'Connor's 'submerged population group', akin to Beckett's tramps and wanderers. Some are itinerants such as Frank Hardy (*Faith Healer*) and Gerry Evans (*Dancing at Lughnasa*), haunting the Celtic outback on the borders of civilised society; others, figureheads of their time such as Columba (*The Enemy Within*) or Hugh O'Neill (*Making History*), are nevertheless deeply divided individuals occupying historical positions of crisis and change, caught between the claims of different worlds; while still others such as Cass McGuire (*The Loves of Cass McGuire*), Skinner (*Freedom of the City*), Fox Melarkey (*Crystal and Fox*), Keeney and the other internees (*Volunteers*) are outlaws or deviants who refuse the roles prescribed by official society. In his latest play, *Wonderful Tennessee*, Friel situates his characters at the very edge of the known world: 'Next parish Boston, folks!' Reproducing the characteristic Irish modes of displacement, itineracy and exile, his work is the expression of an easily recognisable and deeply set border mentality.

In his 'Self-Portrait' of 1972, one of the few autobiographical statements which this shy and self-effacing man has allowed himself, he gives us the following insight into the private Brian Friel:

> I am married, have five children, live in the country, smoke too much, fish a bit, read a lot, worry a lot, get involved in sporadic causes and invariably regret the involvement, and hope that between now and my death I will have acquired a religion, a philosophy, a sense of life that will make the end less frightening than it appears to me at this moment.[6]

He presents himself as a man who can neither believe, nor be comfortable in his unbelief. Characteristically, he refuses to curb feeling and experience by the discipline of belief. He won't affirm faith when there is only a longing for faith. Politics, religion, philosophy mean discipline and are therefore alien to a sensibility always somewhat wilful, somewhat sceptical. Elusive, playful, he resists easy categorisation like a mischievous leprechaun:

> The interviewer's chestnut: When did you know you were going to be a writer? The answer is, I've no idea. What other writers influenced you most strongly? I've no idea. Which of your plays is your favourite? None of them. Which of your stories? Most of them embarrass me. Do you think the atmosphere in Ireland is hostile or friendly to the artist? I'm thinking of my lunch. Do you see any relationship between dwindling theatrical audiences all over the world and the fragmentation of what we might call the theatrical thrust into disparate movements like Theatre of Cruelty, Tactile Theatre, Nude Theatre, Theatre of Despair, etc., etc., Or would you say, Mr Friel, that the influence of Heidegger is only beginning to be felt in the drama and that Beckett and Pinter are John the Baptists of a great new movement? Well, in answer to that I'd say that – I'd say that I'm a middle-aged man and that I tire easily and that I'd like to go out for a walk now.[7]

One is reminded of lines of Emily Dickinson, another writer fiercely jealous of her privacy and equally suspicious of the reductive intellect: 'Surgeons must be very careful / When they take the knife. / Underneath their fine incisions / Stirs the culprit, life'[8]. In comparison with, say, Seamus Heaney, who has so successfully cultivated his public persona, Friel has shied away from both the analyst's knife and the publicist's hype. The plays evince a similar diffidence, a refusal to yield up clear and simple 'messages' or even single meaning. The presumption and the pretentiousness of the pattern-makers, the literary historians, the theorists and the chroniclers is a familiar dramatic theme, from the fairly light-hearted satire of the American historian Tom Hoffnung, in *Aristocrats*, to the more serious exposure of the official interpreters in *Freedom of the City* or of Hugh O'Neill's self-appointed chronicler, Archbishop Lombard, in *Making History*.

Friel is very conscious of the disappearance of the old certainties and of the disorienting influence of the spread of an international modernism: 'We are rapidly losing our identity as a people. . . . We are losing the specific national identity which has not been lost by the Dutch or the Belgians or the French or Italians. We are no longer

even West Britons; we are East Americans.'⁹ The great challenge
facing Irish men and women nowadays, he believes, is the task of
redefining their identity. Contrasting the present with the previous
generation of Irish writers, he states:

> For us today the situation is more complex. We are more con-
> cerned with defining our Irishness than with pursuing it. We
> want to know what the word native means, what the word for-
> eign means. We want to know have the words any meaning at all.
> And persistent considerations like these erode old certainties and
> help clear the building site.¹⁰

The 'building site' of Friel's stories and plays is alive with precisely
this kind of activity – demolishing the prison houses of old, dilap-
idated myths and stereotypes; refurbishing those traditional values
which are worth preserving; building anew on cleared ground. And
the 'building site' does indeed occupy a 'borderland', a 'borderland'
in the largest sense of the word – between home and exile, hope and
despair, *skepsis* and affirmation, tradition and modernism, tragedy
and comedy.

'The Man from God Knows Where' is the piquant title of an
interview which Friel gave Fintan O'Toole in 1982. In it Friel speaks
of 'a sense of rootlessness and impermanence' in his own life, which
he traces to 'the inheritance of being a member of the Northern
minority'.¹¹ Being at home is at one and the same time being in exile.
The difficulty in setting out to reclaim inheritance is knowing what
to reclaim: 'You can't deposit fealty to a situation like the Northern
situation that you don't believe in. Then you look south of the border
and that enterprise is in so many ways distasteful. And yet both
places are your home, so you are an exile in your home'.¹² Northern-
ers, Friel thinks, are offered the 'English home'; they are, he says,
'educated' and 'pigmented' by it to a much greater extent than
Southerners – 'And the rejection of all that, and the rejection into
what, is the big problem':

> You can't possibly – and don't even want to – jettison the whole
> English experience, but how to pick and choose what is valuable
> for us and what is health-giving for us, how to keep us from being
> a GAA republic, it's a very delicate tiptoeing enterprise.¹³

He acknowledges 'some kind of instinctive sense of home being central to life', but also a sense of 'home being a place of great stress and great alienation'. In Heaney's words, he feels 'lost / Unhappy, and at home'. The sense of exile, Friel goes on to suggest, brings with it 'some kind of eagerness and some kind of hunger . . . if you are in possession you can become maybe placid about things'.[14] His sense of exile as an Irishman, he speculates, may give him access as an artist to a more fundamental and widespread sense of alienation. This feeling of rootlessness and impermanence may not only be artistically enabling, it may also be the essence of the only authentic existence. Should he ever feel that he was settling into a comfortable 'home', he admits, he'd 'be off again'.[15]

The kind of art in which Friel specialises consistently acknowledges doubt, uncertainty and confusion. Hugh's line in *Translations* – 'Confusion is not an ignoble condition'[16] – could be Friel's own motto. It is an art which struggles to articulate the mystery of human life. Friel himself refers to 'the burden of the incommunicable'[17] which as an artist he feels he must communicate. Refusing to subordinate complex seeing to social or political demands, he warns himself against the temptation of allowing one aspect of personality to swamp other aspects. That, he insists, would be fatal to the artist in him because it would mean oversimplification and evasion of the full complexity of self and world. Instead, he speaks for a comprehensive, inclusive vision which takes account of as much of life as it can:

> We must synthesise in ourselves all those uneasy elements – father, lover, bread-winner, public man, private man – so that they constitute the determining artist. But if we attempt to give one element its head, what we do is bleed the artist in us of a necessary constituent, pander to an erratic appetite within us.[18]

The passage comes from his 'Sporadic Diary' which he kept during the writing of *Aristocrats* (1979). The gestatory problems he experienced with this play, he tells us, stemmed from a troublesome sense of political and social obligation which kept interfering with the free creative process. The play's 'true direction', he felt, was 'being thwarted by irrelevant politics, social issues, class'; but then, he says, came the liberating recognition that 'implicit in their (the characters') language, attitudes, style, will be all the "politics" I need'. He quotes Eugene O'Neill on O'Casey: 'but O'Casey is an artist and the soapbox is no place for his great talent. The hell of it seems to be when an artist starts saving the world, he starts losing himself. I know, having been bitten by the salvationist bug myself at times. But only momentarily . . .'. Conscious of the temptations of a salvationist glamour, Friel proclaims the primacy of the artistic vocation: 'We don't go to art for meaning', he writes, 'we go to it for perceptions of new adjustments and new arrangements'.[19] If we detect in this description of the artist as an 'arranger' an essentially musical concept of art, it is, we shall see, entirely relevant to Friel's dramatic practice.

Another basic premise of Friel's work is a notion of art as experiment, as a resistance to fixity and finality. To be an artist is to exercise creativity, and creativity is what ensures against any undue enslavement to the past or collaboration with the routine or the orthodox. To be creative is to transform the usual and received patterns of experience, to pursue the new and the 'strange'. Writing about the arts, Friel says:

> Flux is their only constant; the crossroads their only home; impermanence their only yardstick. . . . This is the only pattern of their existence: the persistence of the search; the discovery of a new concept; the analysis, exploration, exposition of that concept; the preaching of that gospel to reluctant ears; and then, when the first converts are made, the inevitable disillusion and dissatisfaction because the theory is already out of date or was simply a false dawn. And then the moving on; the continuing of the search; the flux. Impermanence is the only constant.[20]

Art is viewed as a constant process of defamiliarisation of the ordinary and Friel's emphasis on reworking received 'reality' is one of the things which gives his drama its wide appeal beyond an Irish audience. Friel's is a drama of 'rewriting' communal, national, and cultural origins and it is this dynamic which enables it to speak to other nations and cultures, as it has so successfully done, especially in Britain and America. Art is the place of experiment and risk; to write is to dare. This view of art as a laboratory is what informs Field Day, the theatre company which Friel helped to found in 1980. Field Day is expressly devoted to the search for 'a middle ground between the country's entrenched positions',[21] to opening up new possibilities so that Irish people may be allowed to consider new identities for themselves. The Field Day writers believed that Field Day could and should contribute to the solution of the present crisis by producing analyses of the established opinions, myths and stereotypes which had become both a symptom and a cause of the current situation. The collapse of constitutional and political arrangements and the recrudescence of the violence which they had been designed to repress or contain, made this a more urgent requirement in the North than in the Republic.[22]

Field Day, Friel said, grew out of 'that sense of impermanence, of people who feel themselves native to a province or certainly to an island but in some way feel that a disinheritance is offered to them'.[23]

The artist's constant search is the ground of hope, the guarantee of a future. Friel recognises that the modern dramatist disturbs us with 'his terrible, taunting questions', but also insists that when these dramatists 'depict in mean gruesome detail only one portion of our existence, perhaps in this generation the dominant portion, they are crying out for recognition of something less ignoble, something more worthy. They are asking us to realise that even in confusion and disillusion, strength and courage can exist, and that out of them can come a redemption of the human spirit'.[24] For Friel, then, art is a spontaneously revolutionary vocation, all the more so when the social conditions in which it must try and make its way are as excruciatingly rigidified as they would seem to be in Ireland. A major concern of this study will be to examine the kind of resistance which Friel's work offers to notions of social and historical determinism. Central to this investigation will be an analysis of Friel's concern with language, with the relationship between language and identity, language and reality. For he shows us how language can carry us out of ourselves, out of our usual habits of thought and feeling and proclaim our capacity to experiment, to invent and to move forward; but, equally, he wants us to recognise how it can seduce us with its consoling fictions into a dangerous alienation. Friel's is thus a deeply contradictory apprehension of the nature of language. Language has the power to create new imaginative worlds and open up new horizons of possibility, but it is also the means of conscious deception, evasion, illusion, rather than genuine communication or confrontation. Later chapters will consider the cultural and political implications of what Richard Kearney calls 'the problem of language'[25] and explore Friel's dramatic experiments with alternatives to linguistic communication. But we begin with the early short stories and unpublished plays which introduce the basic Frielian themes and preoccupations in the context of the more or less 'private' world of family and personal relationships.

THE SHORT STORIES

Friel's situation, it becomes clear, is in fact a good deal more complex than that indicated by Fintan O'Toole's description of him as 'The Man from God Knows Where'. As a writer, Friel is *both* inside and outside his society, the respectful and affectionate delineator of a recognisable landscape and community which he writes about from deep down in his environment and, at the same time, the critically detached observer, consciously setting out to loosen up, to interrogate and subvert the set patterns of thought and feeling, the fixed discourses, the stereotypes of routine perception. There were perhaps other reasons for his first being drawn to the short story than financial incentive and the relatively easy marketability of short stories, especially Irish stories in American magazines. ('The Widowhood System', 'The Death of a Scientific Humanist', 'The Gold in the Sea', 'Everything Neat and Tidy' and 'The Diviner' first appeared in *The New Yorker*; 'The Illusionists' and 'Ginger Hero' in *The Saturday Evening Post*; 'The Wee Lake Beyond', 'The Highwayman and the Saint', 'The Flower of Kiltymore' and 'The First of My Sins' in *Critic*.) Frank O'Connor has noted how the short-story writer's relation to society tends to be more strongly oppositional than the novelist's. In the short story, O'Connor suggests, we can see an attitude of mind that is attracted by

> submerged population groups, whatever these may be at any given time – tramps, artists, lonely idealists, dreamers, and spoiled priests. The novel can still adhere to the classical concept of civilized society, of man as an animal who lives in a community . . . but the short story remains by its very nature remote from the community – romantic, individualistic, and intransigent.[26]

The 'submerged population', O'Connor explains, 'changes its character from writer to writer, from generation to generation. It may be Gogol's officials, Turgenev's serfs, Maupassant's prostitutes, Chekhov's doctors and teachers, Sherwood Anderson's provincials, always dreaming of escape'.[27] To that list we might add all those characters of Friel's who are submerged by material considerations or the absence of spiritual ones and who are also dreaming of escape. 'Always in the short story', O'Connor declares, 'there is this sense of outlawed figures wandering about the fringes of society. . . . As a result there is in the short story . . . an intense awareness of human loneliness.'[28] This sums up admirably the mood of alienation in Friel's short stories. His sympathetic understanding of the estranged or the stranger is the understanding of one who himself feels astray in his own society. And O'Connor's remark that 'the strangeness of behaviour which is the very lifeblood of the short story is often an atavistic breaking out from some peculiar way of life, faraway and long ago'[29] precisely describes the situation that Friel explores in much of his work, from his early stories ('The Diviner', 'Among the Ruins', 'My True Kinsman' quickly come to mind) to his recent masterpiece *Dancing at Lughnasa*.

The novelist classically writes from the centre or at least with the benefit of a sense of a stable, hierarchical, well-established social structure behind him. Not so the short-story writer whose frame of reference can never be the totality of human life. The novelist's all-embracing view of many-faceted life and the multiplicity of actual experience contrasts with the short-story writer's emphasis on making the carefully chosen fragment resonate. As O'Connor puts it: 'a whole lifetime must be crowded into a few minutes, those minutes must be carefully chosen indeed and lit by an unearthly glow, one that enables us to distinguish present, past and future as though they were contemporaneous'.[30] Accordingly, O'Connor concludes, 'the storyteller differs from the novelist in this: he must be much more . . . of a dramatist'.[31] The short story, it would appear, thrives amid the breakdown of standards, conventions and values. Such a collapse, V. S. Pritchett observes, which has 'so bewildered the impersonal novelist' has been 'the making of the short story writer who can catch any piece of life as it flies and make his personal performance out of it'.[32] The short story is a more assertively personal ordering of the raw materials of life than the novel. In the words of another great practitioner of the form, Sean O'Faolain, the short story is an 'emphatically personal exposition', the 'personal and individual way of looking at things':

What one searches for and what one enjoys in a short story is a special distillation of personality, a unique sensibility which has recognized and selected at once a subject that, above all other subjects, is of value to the writer's temperament and to his alone – his counterpart, his perfect opportunity to project himself.[33]

O'Faolain suggests that this seeing things in a personal and original way, and with a disruptive passion, is peculiarly Irish and American rather than English. The English way of seeing, O'Faolain asserts, is much more social and much less personal and individual:

It is in the English tradition to nourish the fruits of good-humour and piety, in the civil and domestic sense, of the love of sport, the sense of decorum, the habit of respect, the absence of irony, the expansive tendency of the race, the emphasis on pragmatic action, all of which mitigate the Englishman's emotional tensions, irritations and nervous expectations.[34]

The colonial or postcolonial mind, grown sensitive to difference and less ready to accede to the notion of a monolithic cultural value system, O'Faolain suggests, finds its natural formal expression in the short story with its concern for authenticity, exploration, and the assertion of an individual vision, as opposed to the novel with its emphasis on tradition and shared values.

Characteristically, Friel opposes a bleak reality with the inspiriting possibilities of breaking out which are offered by the creative imagination. The perennial oppositions in his work are those between subject and object, rationalism and romance, reality and dream, intransigent individuality and the crushing weight of a hostile world. He is an expert at delineating oppressive, rigidified communities and the entrapped and frustrated lives that one finds there. The longing for freedom and regeneration is a familiar Irish theme, from Synge's *Playboy* to Joyce's urban version of entrapment in *Dubliners*. Friel is drawn not only to the 'emphatically personal exposition' of the short story as a form, but also to the highly individualistic character who embodies the creative and imaginative potential of the artist. As in the *Playboy*, his most frequently used pattern is that of introducing the romantic, mysterious, disruptive outsider who shatters the complacency of a closed system and opens up new horizons of possibility, more exciting vistas. Representatives of the 'Other' which is both threatening and excitingly attractive would be

Mr Sing ('Mr Sing My Heart's Delight'), M. L'Estelle ('The Illusionists'), Terry Bryson ('Straight from his Colonial Success'), Desmond
the new supply teacher ('My Father and the Sergeant'), Uncle Cormac
('The Death of a Scientific Humanist') and Grandfather ('My True
Kinsman'). Like Synge's Christy Mahon, the disruptive visitor is
often a great talker – Mr Sing, M. L'Estelle and Grandfather; but
sometimes, as in the case of the diviner (in 'The Diviner'), he is the
representative of wordless mystery. Friel explores the consequences
of too great an immersion in reality – boredom, drudgery, frustration, narrow materialism, spiritual and emotional deadness, moral
timidity; and of too much dreaming – foolish egotism, sterile escapism and dangerous unreality. Always, he implies the need for balance, for a dynamic dialectical rapport between subject and object,
dream and reality. His stories about animals, especially the training
of animals (cocks in 'Ginger Hero', dogs in 'The Fawn Pup', pigeons
in 'The Widowhood System'), are concerned with the attempt to
systematise behaviour, to make it predictable and efficient. This
impulse to control, we are shown, can lead to a brutal and antihuman
fanaticism. The dream of 'everything neat and tidy' (the title of
another story) is an impossible ideal. At the same time, the stories
celebrate noisy, unpredictable, swarming life: we impose systems on
it at the risk of destroying the wonder and excitement and joy –
precisely the values which Synge admired and affirmed in his Preface to the *Playboy* ('On the stage one must have reality, and one
must have joy . . . the rich joy found only in what is superb and wild
in reality'). Perhaps the bringer of wonder and excitement and joy in
'Mr Sing My Heart's Delight' is intended as an incarnation of
Mr Synge. More directly, the packman, who introduces himself as
'Singh' (*SL*, p. 67) but is thereafter referred to as 'Mr Sing' (*SL*, p. 67),
is associated with the freeing potential of singing, of the creative and
expressive powers in general.

'Mr Sing My Heart's Delight' is told from the point of view of a
nine year old boy who every year visits his Granny in a remote part
of Donegal while his grandfather goes off to work in Scotland.
Through the device of the boy narrator, which Friel commonly uses
right up to *Dancing at Lughnasa*, the writer establishes a point of view
that is fresh and innocent and sensitive to all that inspires joy and
wonderment. Granny lives a hard and lonely life: 'Even on the best
day in summer Mullaghduff is a desolate place' (*SL*, p. 59). Moreover, she is presented as the victim of a stern, patriarchal social
system which has condemned her to the margins:

It was a strange place to make a home but Grandfather was a dour, silent man and he probably felt that by marrying the girl of seventeen who had an infant daughter but no father to claim it, he had shown sufficient charity; the least she could do was accept the terms of his proposal. Or perhaps he was jealous of her vivacity and attractiveness and thought that the wide Atlantic behind her and a three-mile stretch of moor before her would be good deterrents to a roaming spirit.   (*SL*, pp. 59–60)

But Granny's spirit roams in other ways. She thrills to the tales of notably heroic women such as Florence Nightingale or Madam Curie that her grandson reads her and she conjures up elaborate stories of her own about the great 'lords and ladies' (*SL*, p. 61) who sail the great liners she watches out at sea. The grandson and she 'had riotous times together' (*SL*, p. 60), a particular source of their fun being Granny's English, for Gaelic was her first language and she never felt at ease in English. Despite the harsh conditions of her life, the grandson relishes his time with her as a great release from or expansion of his usual life: 'it suited me admirably too: I missed school for three months, I got away from strict parents and bothersome brothers and sisters . . . and in Granny's house I was cock-of-the-walk and everything I did was right' (*SL*, p. 58).

However, the story features an even more dramatic freeing. One night Granny and grandson have a most unlikely visitor, an Indian packman, Mr Sing, who, like Synge's Christy Mahon, first appears as a timid, delicate-looking, bedraggled little fellow arriving at the remote homestead out of the black and stormy night. Granny is the perfect audience for the packman. She is enchanted by her exotic visitor's dazzling display of brightly coloured wares and by his courtly speech. She responds to his charm with religious intensity: 'she dropped on the floor beside him and stretched her hands out as if in benediction over the goods . . . she went silent with awe' (*SL*, p. 64). The packman is a figure of the artist. Friel describes him 'painting the floor with yellows and greens and whites and blues' (*SL*, p. 63). The ritual of his display, his performance, it would seem, is more important to him than actually selling any of his wares. He leads Granny out of herself, beyond the rational world into a strange ecstasy that is very similar to that experienced by other Friel characters – the Mundy sisters in *Dancing at Lughnasa* or Lily in *Freedom of the City* – who likewise suddenly find themselves liberated from the usual confines of their life. Of Granny, we read:

Then suddenly she was on her feet, towering above us and leaping around the kitchen floor in a wild, mocking dance. . . . Then
she tried on a green hat and then white gloves and then a blue
cardigan and then a multicoloured apron, all the time singing or
dancing or waving her arms, all the time shaking her head like
mad, delighted, embarrassed, drunk with pleasure, completely
carried away. (*SL*, p. 65)

Her rhapsody, in which the sunny Punjab merges with the Garden
of Eden, until 'she was away from us as she spoke leaving us in the
drafty, flagged-floor kitchen' (*SL*, p. 68), is again an early version of
the rhapsodies in *Cass McGuire*, an assertion of the transcendent
power of imagination and story. Masquerade, play-acting, dancing,
singing, story, 'feast and festival' (*SL*, p. 67): these are the elements of
Granny's carnivalistic overthrow of the contingent world.

This huge imaginative vitality which Friel celebrates in the story
is the possession of a submerged class. It is in this respect that
Granny and the packman are fundamentally similar. Both are products of a colonial system, both are forced to communicate in a common language that is not their own and both have an uncertain and
idiosyncratic command of the 'master' language. Both take compensation for their dispossession in the collaborative dream of a lost
Eden. But neither they nor we are ever allowed to forget the wind
outside, the dark night, the struggle for survival, the impossibility of
total escape. Granny knows she could never afford what the packman
offers and at first this makes her angry. But the essential experience
which the story describes does not have a price tag. It has to do with
the freeing activity of the creative imagination, with release from
routine perception and with the empathy and understanding, the
simple kindness and good fellowship and mutual respect which
flow from this appreciation of the 'Other'. When the packman is
about to leave he declines to repay Granny's hospitality with what
he now calls his 'worthless goods' (*SL*, p. 70), which indeed they are
beside the great imaginative adventure they have all enjoyed. Instead, he gives her his ring which he places on her finger in a kind of
marriage rite signifying their spiritual bond. It is a beautiful ring, an
emblem of life's mystery, but also of its changeableness and a reminder, too, that Eden was also the home of the serpent. The grandson is transfixed by its 'miracles':

It was a gold ring, wrought in imitation of a snake which held between its mouth and tail a damson-coloured stone. As I watched it, the colour became vaporous, like smoke in a bottle, and seemed to writhe languidly in a coiling movement. Now it was purple, now rose, now black, now blood red, now blue, now the colour of sloes in the August sun. (*SL*, p. 63)

The great virtue of the story, as of all Friel's stories, is the author's freedom from any nervous compulsion to play the wise man of the tribe. His forte is the careful unfolding of the human situation he has chosen to explore without portentous generalisation.

In 'The Illusionists' it is M. L'Estelle, the illusionist who visits Beannafreaghan school every year, who offers momentary escape from drabness and decay, an imaginative release from the usual routines. Like Christy Mahon, M. L'Estelle is an irruption of the 'strange', the foreign and exciting into normal life. He is linked with the arrival of spring; he is a kind of fertility god. A 'free-wheeling' (*SL*, p. 220; *GS*, p. 31; *D*, p. 92) 'reckless' (*SL*, p. 221; *GS*, p. 31; *D*, p. 92) spirit, he is a distraction from rational process, a 'roguish' (*SL*, p. 224; *GS*, p. 35; *D*, p. 96) gallant, a disruptive influence who is adored but also resented and finally ejected from the midst of the community. He is, in fact, as ambiguous a figure as the faith healer Frank Hardy. He is 'the most wonderful man in the world' (*SL*, p. 220; *GS* p. 31; *D*, p. 92) but also 'a trickster' (*SL*, p. 221; *GS*, p. 32; *D*, p. 93) and 'trick-of-the-loop man' (*SL*, p. 221; *GS*, p. 32; *D*, p. 93) – the double image of the artist: sham or shaman?

The boy narrator, like the other schoolchildren, is enchanted by M. L'Estelle and wants to become his apprentice. Mother, on the other hand, is highly suspicious of him, recognising in him a threat to her domestic routines and traditional family values. Father welcomes him warmly but reacts with growing hostility when the illusionist stirs in him a troubling awareness of his failure and dissatisfaction with life. The two men's conversation soon degenerates into 'two monologues spoken simultaneously, each man remembering and speaking his memories aloud' (*SL*, p. 225; *GS*, p. 35; *D*, p. 96). We have here in germinal form the method which Friel uses in *Faith Healer* and in the closing section of *Making History* – intercut monologues conveying a fundamental isolation, retreat from the 'Other' into a solipsistic world, each character pursuing a dream of the past. Father's dream is of being a super-student, super-teacher and re-spected pillar of the community. Clearly, he is one of the illusionists included in the plural title. But Father's illusions are a good deal less exotic than those purveyed by the professional who boasts of how he was 'entrusted with the secret of this next act by the Sultan of Mysore' (*SL*, p. 227; *GS*, p. 38; *D*, p. 99) and of being 'Top of the bill in Leeds and Manchester and Glasgow and Brighton' (*SL*, p. 227; *GS*, p. 37; *D*, p. 98). As long as Father and M. L'Estelle are prepared to massage each other's egos by conniving in each other's illusions they get on fine together, but it is not long till Father's dream of rootedness is in open, violent competition with M. L'Estelle's dream of travel and adventure. Mother stresses the similarity between these two ferocious egotists. To her they are 'nothing but a pair of bletherskites' (*SL*, p. 225; *GS*, p. 36; *D*, p. 96), 'two drunk men' (*SL*, p. 228; *GS*, p. 38; *D*, p. 99).

After M. L'Estelle leaves, Father is keen to justify his actions to Mother, but all she wants now after listening to an evening of drunken, ugly argument is silence, an end to talk and useless dreaming: '"Shut up! Hasn't there been enough said for one night"' (*SL*, p. 230; *GS*, p. 40; *D*, p. 101). As in O'Casey, the bibulous vanity of the men is set against the level-headed, responsible practicality of the woman. However, before the story's end, Mother too reveals herself to be as much of an illusionist as the two men, though hers is an intensely felt dream of family life – of an idyllic summer day 'when the good weather comes' (*SL*, p. 233; *GS*, p. 44; *D*, p. 104) and she and her son will picnic in the meadow, play in the well and whitewash the byre. She imagines a perfect future for herself while the men imagine a perfect past: all the characters, it would seem, prefer to live in the past or the future rather than the present. Most notable of all, however, is the supportive and consoling nature of Mother's illusion as opposed to the childishly self-aggrandising fantasies of the two men.

The narrator's dream is to be squire to the illusionist's knight. At the end, he sees M. L'Estelle for what he really is, after the illusionist has fallen off his 'trusty steed' (*SL*, p. 231; *GS*, p. 41; *D*, p. 102) and is no longer the mysterious, god-like figure the boy had worshipped hitherto. It is a traumatic discovery for the boy, the moment of disillusionment. Friel displays great sensitivity and a sure, light touch in the way he conveys the boy's struggle to hold on to his dream, even while he is forced to acknowledge the reality. As his mother tries to comfort him with her own dream of the future, he arrives at his culminating insight that 'truth' isn't an absolute value, but a function of sincerity and conviction:

I stopped crying and smiled into her breast because every word she said was true. But it wasn't because I remembered that it was true that I believed her, but because she believed it herself, and because her certainty convinced me.   (*SL*, p. 233; *GS*, p. 44; *D*, p. 104)

After its savage mockery of Father's and M. L'Estelle's illusions and of the way they fight over them, the story finally comes round to this statement of compassionate understanding of the nature and function of illusion.

Another of Friel's several stories of fathers and sons is 'My father and the Sergeant'. Typically, this story is set in a narrow, parochial community presided over by a wily cleric (who in speech and manner might be seen as an early version of Archbishop Lombard in *Making History*) and a well-meaning, but uninspiring, distinctly Gradgrindian schoolteacher who is the narrator's father. Equally familiar, is the arrival into this small world of the romantic outsider, in this case a young painter from the big city, Mr Desmond, who at the beginning is hailed as 'an answer to prayer' (*SL*, p. 148) and a 'Godsend' (*SL*, p. 149) by Montseigneur Carroll because he has agreed to take over the school while Father recovers from pleurisy. Like Mr Sing, Mr Desmond introduces the possibility of imaginative transformation of a bleak reality: 'School became a new and astonishingly pleasant experience' (*SL*, p. 152). Desmond awakens the children's creative imagination. The narrator records enthusiastically how they worked with potter's clay, 'splashed hectic watercolours onto white sheets of paper' (*SL*, p. 152), read adventure stories, heard tales of life in Tangiers, Naples and Athens, sang songs about Dixie, Avignon and Skye, painted murals of Hannibal crossing the Alps and of a Viking ship landing in Ireland, and learnt about the miracles of nature: 'In short, he opened our eyes to the only wealth our dark hillside home had to offer us in abundance and for that I have always remembered him with affection' (*SL*, p. 153).

This bright interlude is suddenly ended when Desmond is accused of abusing his trust and kissing one of the girls in his class. The Montseigneur dismisses him and comes begging to Father to resume his duties. There are two sides, it would appear, to Paul Desmond. There are also two narrators, 'Plumb' (*SL*, p. 145) and 'Hargan' (*SL*, p. 145) – the beloved son and the pupil in the classroom who is treated just like any of the other pupils. And of course there are two sides to Father – his strict Public persona as the 'Sergeant' (*SL*, p. 145) in the classroom and the affectionate Private individual who is 'Plumb's' father. The other father in the story is also dichotomised. O'Flaherty beats his daughter viciously for flirting with Desmond, then buys her a gaudy gold necklace to atone for his violence. He is torn between moral outrage and paternal affection. In this story, Friel is experimenting with the idea of the split personality, the divided subject, Public and Private images, contradictory points of view, and highlights this central concern in the title he gives the piece. We are made aware of the hidden or repressed elements of identity which threaten to destabilise simple, neat categorisations.

The story ends ironically. The final scene has the narrator back at school, solving solvable problems:

> 'Hurry up! We haven't all day. Get a move on! Starting at question number 4. Read it out, Hargan, please.' I began falteringly but by the time I came to the words 'How long would it take 5 men working 8 hours a day to do the same job?' with Maire beside me and my father in front of me, my tone was calm and relaxed and confident. (*SL*, p. 162)

Composure is achieved by repressing the whole upsetting experience of Mr Desmond and returning to the *status quo*. The narrator prefers to take shelter in the illusory certainties of childhood, rejecting complexity, comforted by the voice of adult authority. Friel is as adept at handling this kind of ironic resolution as he is in tracing the process of the child's education in 'My True Kinsman' which brings troubling enlightenment, new insight and new experience, the recognition of contradictory impulses and the need to reconcile them.

In 'Straight from his Colonial Success', the exciting outsider is Terry Bryson, newly returned home from working as an Education Officer in Kenya. On his return, Bryson visits an old schoolfriend, Joe, who has become a country schoolteacher, and Joe's pregnant wife, the gravid, prematurely aging Catherine. Bryson awakens a sense of life's excitement and adventure, nostalgic desire to recover lost youth and lost possibilities, regret for lost freedoms. When Joe receives his cryptic telegram announcing his arrival, he behaves like a giddy schoolboy, excitedly describing Bryson to Catherine as 'a scream', 'the craziest, cleverest head-case in the country' (*SL*, p. 208). Bryson assumes legendary proportions in Joe's mind. He is a kind of comic-strip hero who signs his telegram 'Captain Kidd' (*SL*, p. 207). A fluid, Protean character of multiple identities, 'even in his finals he

signed all sorts of outlandish names on his papers – Gandhi, Little
Mo, Chaucer' (*SL*, p. 207). He is the archetypal joker, a mad, unpredictable playboy, a zany adventurer who speaks 'a sort of private
language' (*SL*, p. 208), but can absorb Joe completely with his exotic
tales out of Africa.

Catherine, however, refuses to be enchanted and is determined to
press the virtues of home and family, suggesting to Bryson that
perhaps he is missing out in not having a wife and family and living
in Kenya: 'There you are – twenty-four, twenty-five, whatever it is –
wasting your life out there, aimless, purposeless, unsettled' (*SL*,
p. 215). Earnest, practical Catherine urges responsibility and security. Bryson recognises that she is trying to 'trap' him into marriage:
'"These married women, they're all the same", he said to Joe. "Always trying to get single men trapped"' (*SL*, p. 214). Catherine can
see Bryson's potential to 'unsettle' (*SL*, p. 217) her husband and
admits that their charming visitor 'has got something' (*SL*, p. 218).
Joe is less honest. Unable to disguise his own feeling of entrapment
and envy of the adventurer, Joe, like Father in 'The Illusionists',
adopts a superior air, dismissing Bryson as 'a typical colonial bum'
(*SL*, p. 207). Then he falls asleep on Catherine's shoulder and the
story ends on this image of ironic retreat from self-confrontation, a
pathetic denial of experience as complete as Plumb Hargan's in 'My
Father and the Sergeant'. Once again, Friel displays his characteristic
lightness of touch in delineating the simultaneous feelings of envi-
ous longing for what might be or could be and the sad, bitter, even
relieved resignation to what is.

'The Diviner' features two mystery men neither of whom is entirely accepted by a repressed, highly conventionalised society presided over by the local priest. The first mystery man is Nelly's new
husband, Mr Doherty, who is 'from the West' (*SL*, p. 44; *GS*, p. 115;
D, p. 19) and about whom very little else is known. The object of
much curiosity and gossip in the community, Mr Doherty is noted
for his respectable appearance and for staying in the house all day
while Nelly goes out to work. When he is found mysteriously
drowned, the priest is quick to claim him as an exemplary son of the
Church. But even while this official version of Mr Doherty is being
formulated, it is being complicated, first by the discovery of two
bottles of whiskey on the drowned man's body then by some of the
locals' recollections of suspicious goings-on at Nellie's cottage since
her marriage to Mr Doherty – recollections of the sound of drunken

singing and of the doctor's frequent visits. As in 'My Father and the Sergeant', a gap opens between the Public and the Private reality.

The other mystery man is the diviner who is fetched from 'somewhere in County Mayo' (*SL*, p. 50; *GS*, p. 120; *D*, p. 24) to locate the drowned body at the bottom of the lake. The priest regards the diviner with particular disapproval because he sees him as a threat to his Christian authority and denounces him as 'A fake! A charlatan!' (*SL*, p. 54; *GS*, p. 124; *D*, p. 28). The diviner, like the faith healer of a later work, like the artist, is possessor of a mysterious gift, a man with seemingly magical powers, a vaguely disreputable figure capable of putting the people in touch with what lies hidden. In contrast to Frank Hardy, the diviner – nameless, silent – is a confident success and in a powerfully visual scene Friel describes how he unerringly locates the dead body by the light of the cars' headlights trained over the black waters of the lake. The diviner opens up a secret space beyond the rational mind, beyond words: 'No one spoke; no one dared speak' (*SL*, p. 54; *GS*, p. 125; *D*, p. 29). He represents an important element in Friel's own art, the element of the mysterious, the irrational, the pre-verbal that is set against the emphatically realistic evocation of a community and a landscape. It is out of this tension between mystery and realism, between the possibility of transformation on one hand and assertion of a deadening conventionalism on the other that much of Friel's best work emerges. By drawing us into the atmosphere of gossip and speculation (about Mr Doherty, about the diviner) and ironically undercutting so much idle or mistaken talk, he gives us a particularly strong, close sense of the elusiveness and instability of truth.

At the centre of both 'My True Kinsman' and 'The Death of a Scientific Humanist' lies the unknown and the forbidden. In the first story it is personified by Grandfather who is something of a mystery man, an outcast, a figure of suspicion, the representative of a transgressive energy that opens a breach in the monolith of respectable family life. The story begins with the narrator describing how as a child he and his two sisters played 'grandfather'. They 'invented' (*SL*, p. 112), 'created the myth' (*SL*, p. 111) of Grandfather, thereby playing with the idea of what was forbidden and taboo. Grandfather lives in the children's imaginations as an 'awesome' (*SL*, p. 112) figure and they have no chance of discovering the reality because Mother will not allow them to have anything to do with Grandfather. And so Grandfather is 'the dirty thing' (*SL*, p. 113), 'unkempt'

(*SL*, p. 113), wild, mocking, anti-religious, unlawful ('He had tussles with the police': *SL*, p. 113). The narrator remembers 'grouping him mentally with the unfamiliar and terrifying things which I encountered in the world beyond my immediate home area' (*SL*, p. 114). Grandfather is associated with such disquieting unknowns as 'the haunted house in the school field', 'old, demented Lizzy Quinn', 'Jack Taylor's cross terrier bitch' (*SL*, p. 114). The boy lives in fear of the day when Grandfather 'would get me and . . . devour me' (*SL*, p. 114).

The story tells of how Grandfather eventually did 'get' him. On the day of his tenth birthday the boy is sent to the village on his own on an errand for his mother and there he meets Grandfather. What takes place is a kind of rite of passage. The boy is hijacked by Grandfather whose endless talk soon disperses the boy's fear and arouses his curiosity instead. Grandfather grows into a figure of romance, a spirit of place and of adventure. Full of 'wonderful words' (*SL*, p. 118), he leads the boy away from the ordinary world into a realm of myth and legend, captivating him with his unpredictable excitements, his lonely pride in the past and in his own family. For the first time the boy is made to see the wonder of the ordinary. Reality becomes fabulous. Grandfather talks of Spanish galleons, of divers bringing back doubloons and moidores and sapphires and bijoux in their mouths and between their toes; of the slaughter of Cromwell's troops nearby, the site of the Druid temple, the caravan where the descendant of Cathair Mor lived, the place where Bloody Baldrick was kicked to death by a horse. Grandfather's rough vitality and spontaneity contrast with Mother's deadening calculations and regulations. Her strategy for increasing pleasure on a birthday by imposing a stricter regime than usual on the days leading up it only results in squabbling and tears.

But most important of all, the boy comes to see Grandfather as a real human being. The alien is humanised. At the end of the story, when Grandfather orders a drink in the pub, reality abruptly reasserts itself: Grandfather can't have a drink because he hasn't the money to pay for it. The boy's giving him the money is a sign of the value he now places on Grandfather and his stories. Rejected by the community and by his own family, Grandfather is finally accepted by his grandson, who thus qualifies as 'my true kinsman'. Grandfather succeeds in distracting the boy from his errand, but with the discovery of this new world opened up to him by his Grandfather, the boy gains the confidence to resist the stultifying pressures of family, of convention, of the routine, adult, practical world: 'I would have the courage to meet my mother and tell her the terrible news – that I had no iodine and no money and that Grandfather had got me' (*SL*, p. 121).

'The Death of a Scientific Humanist' is a criticism of Irish Catholic puritanism, of its rigid dogmatism and lack of generosity and understanding of the 'Other' or the alien. Uncle Cormac returns to Ireland after a long sojourn abroad only to suffer a heart attack in the Shamrock Bar on his first day home. On his deathbed in the Bethlehem Hospital he offends the nuns by roughly refusing the offer of a priest. Uncle Cormac dies, proclaiming himself a 'scientific humanist' (*SL*, p. 21; *GS*, p. 57). The nuns promptly set about turning him into a kind of bogey man, refusing him a Christian burial while affecting concern for his soul. Eventually, Mother arranges for him to be buried in a kind of no-man's land between the Protestant and Catholic sections of the graveyard. The eccentric Colonel Harrington officiates at the absurdly comical interment, at which he reads from Shelley:

> Nothing in the world is single;
> All the things, by a law divine
> In one another's being mingle.
> (*SL*, p. 30; *GS*, p. 66)

Friel is emphatically on the side of this credo. Shelley's lines about the mystic unity of all creation provide an ironic context in which the petty human wrangling must be judged. The rules and codes by which sects and societies organise themselves are viewed under the aspect of eternity. And what Friel stresses is the provisional, constantly evolving nature of the social order. The categories don't hold in place. So, after the Church has made such a fuss about refusing Cormac a Catholic burial, the place where he is eventually interred is later taken over by the Church which had rejected him in the first place. Mother is happy at the end because her brother has been reintegrated into the Catholic fold and the family name has been saved.

Language, too, is unstable. The term 'scientific humanist', for example, is subject to all kinds of misuse. Not even the travelled, worldly-wise Colonel Harrington knows what it means, while Mother does everything in her power to make it respectable by integrating it into traditional Catholic discourse. Rather than accept Cormac's differences she describes him as 'a very holy humanistic scientist' (*SL*, p. 26; *GS* p. 61), 'a devout scientific humanist' (*SL*, p. 28; *GS*, p. 63) and promises that 'he'll be buried as a good humanistic scientist should be buried' (*SL*, p. 24; *GS*, p. 60) – which to her means, in spite of Cormac's wishes, that there will be no omission of the Catholic observances before the grave is closed.

Mother's religion, we see, not only shuts her off to the 'Other' but threatens to destroy her own individuality. Under its oppressive and petrifying influence she is in danger of losing her own, personal language: 'the low-keyed, genteel presence of nuns smothered her native spirit and reduced her to a simpering, sighing caricature of herself' (*SL*, p. 20; *GS*, p. 56); 'For days she would rehearse the cutting remarks she intended making to the nuns, but once the huge oak doors of the convent closed behind us her resolution vanished and she lisped, "Yes, Sister" and "No, Sister" like a soapy schoolgirl' (*SL*, p. 20; *GS*, p. 56).

'The Queen of Troy Close' is another story about fear and suspicion of the 'Other – of riotous, warm-blooded life that ignores the social codes and offends genteel sensibility. Myrtle Finn is the Queen of Troy Close, 'Queen' because of her sense of self-importance and her dictatorial powers. This puffed-up do-gooder presides over Troy Close, 'Close' suggesting the narrow petit-bourgeois values of her suburban outlook, 'Troy' evoking thoughts of the city which fell to its ancient enemy when the Greeks smuggled themselves inside Troy's city walls. In Friel's story the enemy is the Duffys, the family of thirteen who have just taken possession of a house in Troy Close.

Myrtle sees the Duffys as an irruption of a wild lawlessness into the suburban quiet. The children are noisy and undisciplined; they eat outside on the well-groomed lawns of their new home; they are 'gipsies' (*GS*, p. 47) 'savages' (*GS*, p. 46). The other residents of Troy Close are 'stunned', 'irritated', 'outraged' (*GS*, p. 46) by the new arrivals. Myrtle cannot sleep any longer with the noise Mr Duffy makes coming home in the middle of the night on a crane or a mobile cement-mixer or a truck from the building site where he is a nightwatchman. Myrtle refers to the machinery as if it represented some kind of strange sexual force. She notices Mrs Duffy 'dance delightedly around' (*GS*, pp. 47–8) her frail little husband when he comes home from work and describes her as a 'slut' and 'unkempt' (*GS*, p. 47). Mrs Duffy personifies a kind of strange libidinal energy which contrasts with Myrtle's stiff propriety and passionless sexuality. The language she uses to describe her neighbours – 'latest ravages' (*GS*, p. 46), 'flaunting himself' (*GS*, p. 49), 'indecent' (*GS*, p. 49), 'this orgy every night' (*GS*, p. 49) – betrays her own sexual frustration and jealousy of the Duffys affectionate physicality. Where Mrs Duffy is a fecund, warm-blooded earth mother, Myrtle, we learn, is going through the menopause. The story emphasises the lack of communication between her and her husband: Myrtle doesn't tell him what the doctor's diagnosis really was; George doesn't tell her what really took place when he went to complain directly to Mr Duffy about the noise he made at night. The story ends with George and Myrtle lying in bed 'not touching' (*GS*, p. 53).

Myrtle's language is intended to demonise the Duffys, but when George approaches Mr Duffy in person he discovers that the reality is not at all what Myrtle had made it out to be. Mr Duffy is, in fact, more than understanding and apologetic and promises there will be no more noise. All that George and Myrtle manage to do in the end is suppress the life force. Insisting on silence, propriety, order – on everything neat and tidy – they have succeeded only in bringing about a kind of death. They end up longing for the noise of a crane or a bulldozer 'to charge the night with wonder and excitement and joy' (*GS*, p. 54). Life in all its noisy, unpredictable energy is a precious thing: we impose structures on it and 'tame' it or civilise it at the risk of destroying wonder and excitement and joy.

In 'The Flower of Kiltymore', the protagonist discovers a similar quietness and orderliness and embraces life in all its inclusiveness and unpredictability, delighting in process, tension and conflict as signs of continuing life, energy and a curious kind of freedom. At the centre of the story is the comic–pathetic figure of Sergeant Burke who has been henpecked by his wife, tormented by a local gang of yokels called the Blue Boys and is the butt of his colleague Finlan's barbed wit. The narrative voice, while not consistently or expressly the Sergeant's, is closest to his, thereby enlisting our sympathies on his side.

After his wife's death, the Sergeant experiences a strange peace. He is no longer 'flogged' (*GS*, p. 138) with her tongue nor tormented by the Blue Boys. But this 'peace' that he had once longed for turns out to be a painful 'vacuity' (*GS*, p. 138) that makes him physically ill. It is the dread of death, 'the unnatural tranquillity he had often heard about that frequently forebodes the end' (*GS*, p. 129). For the first time, he has the unsettling experience of 'this big bastard of nothing' (*GS*, p. 130). He can feel alive only amidst the daily struggles of ordinary life, when he feels exposed, under threat, forced to

face authority and the fact of death – only then does he have the
assurance that 'he was still in the centre of the pushing stream of life,
and not floating, as he had been since Lily's death on the peace and
calm of some stagnant backwater' (*GS*, p. 144). The proof of life is
pain, victimisation, struggle and those things become more valued
than the unreality of peace.

The story's ironies proliferate. In death, the local hooligans who
made the Sergeant's life a misery become 'the flower of Kiltymore'
(*GS*, p. 140). And the final irony is that Lily's companions in the new
cemetery where, she joked, she would be 'away from all the riff-raff'
(*GS*, p. 129), are two of the notorious Blue Boys who had been blown
up by a mine washed in from sea. Life is, ultimately, not amenable to
system or conscious understanding.

In the story entitled 'Everything Neat and Tidy', Johnny is the
systems man, admiring of all that is neat and tidy, a champion of
efficiency and rational order. Before he was married he lived in three
rooms 'as natty and precise as a doll's house' (*SL*, p. 104; *GS*, p. 150;
D, p. 150). Now, he has a 'neat' terrace house with a 'tiny, precise'
(*SL*, p. 101; *GS*, p. 147; *D*, p. 147) parlour. Johnny has long resented
his in-laws, the Macmenamins, for their wastefulness, their abuse of
privilege and neglect of their farm, and for the lack of interest in him
when he first came courting their daughter. Following the death of
her drunken and dissolute husband, Mrs Macmenamin suffers a
nervous breakdown and Joe takes her for her weekly electric shock
treatments at the County Psychiatric Clinic. While he waits for her,
he admires the Clinic's grounds, the 'trim paths and careful gardens', thinks complacently of his own 'compact, comfortable home'
(*SL*, p. 102; *GS*, p. 148; *D*, p. 148) and ponders on how he could have
transformed the ramshackle farm had he been able to take it over
instead of it falling to the bailiffs: 'The whole setup confused and
annoyed him, and yet fascinated him. When he was with them, he
was conscious only of impatience. What a business he would have
made of that place! How he could have run it!' (*SL*, p. 102; *GS*, p. 148;
D, p. 148). But Johnny's dream of order is frustrated, doomed to
remain incomplete.

Latterly, old 'Mrs Mac's' behaviour is a source of especial annoyance to Johnny, for the only effect her treatment seems to have is to
make her arrogant and overbearing, 'even more imperious than
Lady Hartnell of Killard' (*SL*, p. 102; *GS*, p. 148; *D*, p. 148). Johnny
has his revenge by taking advantage of Mrs Mac's temporarily im-
paired memory immediately following her treatments and encour-

aging her in her delusion that she is not only still in possession of the family farm but that it is a thriving commercial success. Ironically, this fiction means as much to Johnny as it does to Mrs Mac. Johnny, like Joe Brennan in 'Foundry House' or Eamon in *Aristocrats*, is secretly impressed and fascinated by the romance of privilege. He and his mother-in-law each satisfy a profound need in the other: he confirms her sense of social superiority; she keeps alive his dream of one day inheriting the farm. Mrs Mac's recovered stability is a 'personal disaster' (*SL*, p. 110; *GS*, p. 156; *D*, p. 155) to Johnny who cannot any longer play with the idea of transforming the decaying farm into an efficient business. His dream of everything neat and tidy is by that much diminished. The major focus of his desire and ambition in life is removed.

Friel is interested in revealing the secret depths of personality, the dark underside of consciousness, the hidden mystery of life. For twenty minutes after her treatments Mrs Mac shows a repressed, ugly side of her nature – her overweening desire to control and feel superior. At the same time, Johnny displays his cruel vindictiveness, his readiness to exploit the weak to satisfy his own ego. His wife, Mary, never knows the full truth of either her mother or her husband. To Mary, the former is simply a pathetic old woman, the latter a tenderly solicitous son-in-law and husband. Mrs Mac is in fact a 'split' or 'double' character, and so is Johnny, who is equally capable of demonstrating wildly contradictory behaviour. 'Doubleness' pervades the story, even in the image of the Country Psychiatric Clinic which, we read, 'was made up of buildings as contrasting as two figures in a parable' (*SL*, p. 100; *GS*, p. 146; *D*, p. 146). The disjunction between the Public and the Private realms generates a powerful irony, irony being a technique of rhetorical 'doubling'. Johnny, we are told, feels 'affection' for the old woman whom he also hates sufficiently to deceive ruthlessly and cruelly when she is mentally disturbed. And his particular brand of 'affection' springs from seeing her 'so helpless and so pale and so exposed' (*SL*, p. 102; *GS*, p. 148; *D*, p. 148), that is, it is related to his need for power rather than to any of his more tender feelings for her as a person. Friel relishes these curious paradoxes and ironies in human relationships and presents them with an admirable naturalness, without straining after effects.

In 'Everything Neat and Tidy' the past is not something that sustains (as it is in another story, 'Among the Ruins'), rather, it implies loss, wasted potential, unfulfilled opportunities. It is something frightening, a 'morass of memory' (*SL*, p. 110; *GS*, p. 155; *D*, p. 155) which drives Mrs Mac out of her mind and fills Johnny with melancholy, regret, resentment and guilt. The past is a disfiguring influence; it is a 'burden' which Mrs Mac manages to escape, but Johnny cannot, try as he does at the end: 'he drove faster and faster, as if he could escape the moment when he would take up the lonely burden of recollections that the dead had fled from and the living had forgotten' (*SL*, p. 110; *GS*, p. 156; *D*, p. 155). He is a man on the run, a fugitive from the past, demoralised by the realisation that everything cannot ever really be neat and tidy. Friel probes this point of crisis when the limits of the rational ideal become painfully apparent.

'The Widowhood System' is one of a number of very fine animal stories which deal with the attempt to impose scientific order upon brute nature. Harry, a pigeon fancier thinks he has devised a new system – the 'widowhood system' – to ensure his new pigeon will outrace all others. The first thing that is novel about Harry's system is that it is used with a male bird, not a female and, second, it exploits the bird's sexual rather than its nesting instinct. The assumption is that the mate rather than the nest is the stronger incentive. However, the 'widowhood system' fails to produce a winner. The cock doesn't behave in accordance with Harry's system in the mechanical way he expects it to behave. It returns all right, but in its own good time. At the same time, Harry makes the further discovery that his old flame, Judith, cannot be relied on either to act in a way that Harry has always expected her to act. Tired of waiting for Harry to marry her, Judith suddenly, mysteriously leaves home. Harry immediately jumps to the conclusion that she has at last given up waiting for him and gone off to live with her brother in Canada. He begins a frantic search for her, 'running in search for her "like a bloody pigeon"' (*SL*, p. 142; *GS*, p. 28; *D*, p. 63). Ironically, Harry himself, not the pigeon, conforms most strongly to the system he has devised. But Judith, having deliberately set out to use the 'widowhood system' against Harry, does not have his naïve faith in the validity of 'system' and 'science', loses her nerve and returns home.

The story is another ironic demonstration of the limits of the rational ideal (represented by the 'widowhood system') which seeks to eliminate the mystery of the world by making it measurable, knowable, predictable, thereby breeding complacency and blinding one to the unique quality of the 'Other'. Friel's fiction scorns crude system and fixity by eloquently underscoring individual uniqueness and unpredictability. He celebrates these liberating qualities formally. The ability to change key, to modulate from the tragic to the comic carries the story, which threatens to founder into loss and disappointment and discord, to a vibrantly humane, upbeat finale.

The cock returns and Harry and Judith are reunited. Harry experiences a new kind of intoxication that doesn't come from a bottle but from the transfiguring power of love openly declared. He enters strange new zones of being which he has never known before and for which he has no language: 'He knew that he had tried to answer her but he could only repeat that he had been running in search of her "like a bloody pigeon"' (*SL*, p. 142; *GS*, p. 28; *D*, p. 63); 'It was no time to talk of the race, he was aware of that, but that was what he talked of' (*SL*, p. 142; *GS*, p. 28; *D*, p. 63). Judith, too, is carried beyond rational language: 'He just closed his eyes and held her while she poured out a flow of gibberish' (*SL*, p. 142; *GS*, p. 28; *D*, p. 63). Transported beyond the calculus of the expected, beyond routine seeing, beyond mechanical theories and closed systems, Harry is aware as never before of how 'funny' and 'ludicrous' his old friends are, the endless futile talkers Handme and the Fusilier who have stepped straight out of the dramas of O'Casey. 'Now, for the first time, he saw them in another way' (*SL*, p. 142; *GS*, p. 28; *D*, p. 64), as he has been brought to see Judith and the heroic pigeon – indeed the whole of life – in a new way too. He discovers the freedom of laughter and crying all at once.

In all of this we read a metaphor of the creative act itself. Retrieval through language of what is lost or absent is the essence of art. Words stand in for what is absent. The story emphasises the dangerous presumption of attempting to impose too much scientific system, the need to remain open to fluid life and the bliss that comes from relaxing the rational, verbal controls and adopting the kind of susceptible, comic vision which Patrick Kavanagh advocated.

'Ginger Hero' is another animal story. Two friends, Billy and Tommy (who narrates the story), married to two sisters, fat, lovable Annie and shrewish Min, buy a cock – Ginger Hero – which becomes the champion cock-fighter in the country, destroying the Tawny Tiger owned by Captain Robson of Grasslough, though Ginger Hero eventually dies too from wounds it has sustained in the fight.

'Ginger Hero' is a powerful, painfully absorbing story, remarkable for its knowledge of both animal and human behaviour. Vivid, detailed description of cocks and cock-fighting is combined with psychological analysis of considerable depth and complexity. As in

'The Widowhood System', Friel is interested in 'systems' of control, in the rituals of preparation and training, and in the parallels (often ironic) between animal and human. Billy, small, muscular, remote, inscrutable, has many of Ginger Hero's qualities, including the cock's ginger colouring. He was even once a 'bantam-weight' (*SL*, p. 164; *GS*, p. 170; *D*, p. 106) boxer. His relationship with the cock realises a kind of sexual, masturbatory fantasy:

> He held it in his hands – it sat there, patient, docile – and under the ginger feathers and over the white transparent flesh his gentle fingers explored the breast and the back and the long neck, kneading, pressing, massaging, caressing slowly and with assurance, until the bird's eyes became drunken and its head rose and fell like an old man dozing before a fire. (*SL*, pp. 167–8; *GS*, p. 173; *D*, p. 109)

Childless Annie whose husband cannot give her a child has a more maternal touch:

> she would sweep it up into her arms, and it would rub its head against her face, and she would coo and whisper into its ear, and it would let itself be pressed against her big breasts, and she would fondle and caress it as if neither Billy nor I was present. (*SL*, p. 171; *GS*, p. 177; *D*, p. 113)

'Evil', as far as Tommy is concerned, is the mechanical savagery sponsored by the English Captain Robson in his own private cockpit where cock-fighting is no longer a public ritual, no longer a communal therapy for the expression of primitive energy, neither carnival nor transgression. At first Tommy is highly impressed by the way the Captain has made cock-fighting civilised. He feels encouraged not to think of it any more as a dangerous defiance of the law:

> He (the Captain) invited us into his house for drinks and discussed the fight – he called it 'the duel' – as briskly as if he were planning a day's harvesting; no winking, no nudging, no mumbling behind the backs of hands, no nervousness of a police raid. (*SL*, p. 177; *GS*, p. 182; *D*, pp. 117–18)

But as the fight continues in the eerie, echoing shed where, we might say, 'everything is neat and tidy', Tommy grows appalled by this kind of sanitised, 'English' barbarism:

> Until that moment I never knew how much I loved the familiar hissing and booing and cheering and squabbling and the vulgar comments and the swearing. This orderly, superior set-up was no sport. It was unnatural. (*SL*, p. 179; *GS*, p. 184; *D*, p. 119)

In the atmosphere of the Captain's shed, a strange change comes over Billy. Unlike Tommy and Annie he appears unaffected by the cruel destruction of Ginger Hero, and displays a ruthless, frighteningly inhuman fanaticism: 'I saw his lips moving and heard him breathe. "Yes. Yes. Yes. Yes. Yes. Yes . . .," without ceasing, almost inaudibly, as if he were praying devoutly' (*SL*, p. 179; *GS*, p. 184; *D*, p. 120). Annie pleads with him to stop the fight: like the cock, 'she clawed at his neck' (*SL*, p. 181; *GS*, p. 186; *D*, p.122) in desperation, until he viciously throws her from him and she retreats into Tommy's arms. Neither Tommy nor Annie is a real *aficianado* of cock-fighting: they represent a more truly and waywardly human, less rigidly and mechanically 'scientific' impulse. Leaving the self-absorbed Billy to his cock-fight, they make love in the van. Tommy hears some weeks later, after Billy and Annie have gone to live in England, that Annie is to have a child.

The story has a lovely shape, crafted to perfection with a deceptive ease and simplicity, its intricate pattern of ironies managed with a masterful control. It ends happily, while still giving us a strong sense of life as a fluid, unpredictable process in the way the tensions set up in the story work themselves out. Billy and Annie have the child they always wanted, but in a quite unexpected way. Although Min has never taken the slightest interest in the career of Ginger Hero, she benefits hugely from his death, for with the money Tommy has made out of his fighting cock, he finances a shop for his wife and offers her the freedom from home and children which she has been longing for. Phoenix-like, Ginger Hero rises again in the name which Min gives her shop. And in Ginger Hero's death, Tommy and Min's marriage, which had itself always been something of a cock-fight, an 'endless, ungenerous squabble' (*SL*, p. 173; *GS*, p. 179; *D*, p. 114), is transformed into an intimate, happy partnership.

'The Fawn Pup', the best of all the animal stories and the most amusing, concerns a schoolteacher, the 'Father' in the story, who is persuaded to enter his fawn pup in a local greyhound race after the animal has been duly trained by Lobster O'Brien, assisted by Dung Doherty 'the wind man', Fusilier Lynch 'the pad man', along with a 'diet man', a 'time man' and a 'pace man' (*SL*, p. 92), all of whom thrive on Father and Mother's hospitality while the long period of training is in progress. The pup, however, representing a natural, irrepressible, playful, unruly energy, is never entirely susceptible to the elaborate disciplines its trainers seek to impose on it. During the race 'it was obvious that he *wanted* to be overtaken and rolled over in boisterous play' (*SL*, p. 97). He keeps looking behind him 'not to measure his lead but to coax the others to shorten it' (*SL*, p. 97) and when he spots Father standing watching the race, he forgets all about 'the wonderful game he was having' (*SL*, p. 98) and bounds over to greet his master. The pup mocks all attempts to impose system on exuberant, youthful life.

Through greyhound-racing the boy narrator and his family are introduced to the dark, mysterious underside of society. The whole carnivalistic world of the race-track is quite alien to Father and Mother's genteel life-style. It is nothing at all like the elegant picture of 'Derby Day' that hung over their drawing-room mantelpiece, muses the narrator. In the penumbral world of the race-meeting, Mother and Father are comically inept and out of place. Mother asks if it is 'customary to clap' and Father guesses that it is, 'but only if the contestants have given of their best' (*SL*, p. 94). The educated formality of Father's 'I have placed a moderate wager on our entry. . . . Let us hope he does not disappoint us' (*SL*, p. 96) or 'Regard the second box. . . . Our good fortune depends on the initial burst' (*SL*, p. 97), contrasts sharply with the loud, raucous shouting of the other men, who have their own kind of secret language:

> Owners and backers shouted strange remarks to one another across the field, and these were greeted with bursts of laughter. 'Where's the turpentine, McBride?' 'Has the judge got his specs?' 'Ten to one on the bitch from Drumquin – if she's not too tired to run!' 'Stick to the rules, boys – teetotal dogs only allowed'. (*SL*, p. 96)

In this anarchic world of the race-track, the more spontaneous, vicious side of Father's personality comes out. When the fawn pup bounds over to him, Father's language is less than polite: '"The bastard!" breathed Father fervently, turning away from him. "The ungrateful bastard!"' (*SL*, p. 98).

We are made continually aware of language as the means whereby 'reality' is established. Lobster O'Brien and his men win Mother and Father's confidence through the language they use: 'They certainly did not look very expert, but they talked in a highly technical language' (*SL*, p. 92). Father seeks to 'naturalise' the 'Other' by integrating it into his usual discourse. Thus, he justifies his participation in the dubious world of the greyhound race-track by invoking 'lofty motives' and using 'expressions like "competitive spirit" and "natural grace of movement"' (*SL*, p. 93). After the humiliations of his day at the track he falls back on an old tactic – according exaggerated respect to anyone who was a past pupil of his school: 'Even the town's loafers were romanticized: "You should have heard Sweeney describe the six months he did in jail. Ah, he has a great command of language, that rascal! Always had"' (*SL*, p. 91). So, the bookie who took Father's money is not just one of the ugly demons haunting the edge of society and consciousness but, Father discovers, a 'past pupil', one of the conspicuous successes of the school who now has six offices in County Tyrone and is soon to open another in County Derry: '"He's going to go far that fellow!. . . . Always knew he would"' (*SL*, p. 99). In this way, Father assimilates into his value system the subculture of the race-track where he has been made to feel out of place and has been mocked and exploited.

By using a narrator, Friel foregrounds the production of his own narrative and we notice from the beginning that there is an unusual degree of self-consciousness about the construction and presentation of this narrative. On one level, it is a story *about* the attempt to impose some kind of order on unruly life which, like the fawn pup, always threatens to outrun and elude all efforts to control it. And so, the narrator begins by warning us and himself against the temptations of reductive stereotyping. Of his father, he states, 'there were anomalies in his make-up that left him larger than any pigeonhole' (*SL*, p. 89), one such 'anomaly' being his penchant for greyhounds. Similarly, the narrator reminds us of the fictionalising nature of memory: 'Memory is strange – and kind – in many ways. It will play back short, tantalizing sequences of the whole tape and then go silent' (*SL*, p. 90). That insight is to form the basis of much of Friel's work, from *Philadelphia, Here I Come!* (which ends with the same image of the tape of memory) to *Faith Healer, Translations* and *Danc-*

ing at Lughnasa. Friel acknowledges the instability of meaning, the selectiveness of memory, the limits of system – whether social, linguistic, religious, or political.

'The Barney Game' is another story celebrating swarming life and highlighting the dangers of explicit system which offends the natural order and evolution of things. The story emphasises the inchoate, unstructured reality of life and relationships and Friel's image for this is the field full of hares at the race-track to which Uncle Barney takes his nephew, Crispin, for an afternoon's outing. The field is 'alive with hares, a hundred of them, high, tensed, frenzied, stampeding up and down and across the enclosure, bounding over one another, colliding, hurling themselves against the mesh wire' (*GS*, p. 110). Seeming to 'palpitate and throb' (*GS*, p. 111), the field is like a heart, the centre of life itself.

Crispin, however, hasn't the patience to accept life that isn't shaped and made to answer plans and purposes. The 'Barney Game' – 'courting the old man for his money' (*GS*, p. 105) – has been going on for years, but now, urged on by his wife, Crispin wants clear answers, an end to uncertainty. On this particular visit to his uncle, he is determined to ask him outright for a substantial hand-out. In forcing the issue, he alienates the uncle:

'You would have got it all, for God's sake! he (Uncle Barney) blurted out in a sob. 'But why wouldn't you have waited? Why had you to ask, for God's sake? It was all yours, anyhow, all of it. But you should never have asked; it should never have been spoken; never!' (*GS*, p. 113)

The background to this confrontation between Crispin and Uncle Barney is the afternoon spent at the greyhound trials, another game of cat and mouse or rather greyhound and hare. Uncle Barney's zigzagging to escape Crispin's blunt request for money is a version of the hare running to avoid the dogs. Uncle Barney's prophetic comment on his own dog's attitude to his chickens – 'There's no badness in the pup, and he mightn't mean to touch them but he mightn't be able to help himself' (*GS*, p. 106) – is a shrewd insight into Crispin too. As for Crispin, he has no more stomach for pressing Uncle Barney for money than he has for watching the hare being mauled by the dog. Asking Uncle Barney outright for money is the point where the 'Barney Game' darkens into more serious blood sport.

In the end, however, Crispin knows that his uncle's anger and disappointment won't last. The story emphasises Crispin's genuine concern and affection for Uncle Barney. Crispin isn't simply interested in him for his money. The danger is that by asking for the money, his uncle will think that that is the only, or main, reason for his nephew's attentions. It isn't and Crispin realises at the end that Uncle Barney doesn't think so either. Friel expertly suggests the complexity of a person's motives and reveals the constant danger that words will cause misunderstanding, will oversimplify a complex reality. Crispin is irritated by his wife because she doesn't appreciate the feelings he has for his uncle. There's something cold-blooded about the term she has invented – the 'Barney Game':

> Every time she used it Crispin hated her with a quick, sharp hate, partly because she divined with such accuracy those thoughts of his that were so real and so uneasy, but more because she never even suspected that the affinity he felt for Barney could have been any more complex. (*GS*, p. 105)

A number of stories are concerned with pressing back against the walls of fact and opening up a lyrical space where one can experience freedom from rational constraints and normal perception, a secret place where the spirit can dilate. Such is the 'saucer of larks' (in the story of that name) set in the barren but beautiful Irish countryside which still bears the scars of war.

'The Saucer of Larks' tells of two representatives of the German War Graves Commission who are being taken by a local Gardai Sergeant and Guard Burke to the place where a German pilot had been shot down during the last war. The Sergeant thrills to the beauty of the Donegal countryside ('there were times when its beauty still shocked him' (*SL*, p. 196; *D*, p. 137)) and is filled with a Wordsworthian or Whitmanesque sense of the unity of all creation. His German visitors are, by contrast, stiff and formal, untouched by natural magic and concerned only with executing their task with maximum efficiency. Their destination is an enchanted place, 'Glennafuiseog' – the valley of the larks, a secluded and enchanted valley, wild and uncivilised, 'a saucer of green grass' (*SL*, p. 199; *D*, p. 140) that fills with the music of hundreds of invisible larks. Out of love and respect for the place, the Sergeant asks the Germans if they wouldn't leave it untouched, but they refuse to disobey the orders they have been given. There will be no deviation from duty. They complete the exhumation and leave for Dublin the same evening.

The story reworks a traditional theme, developing a contrast between Teutonic scientific efficiency and Celtic soul. In still broader terms, it is the conflict between natural law and civil law, between feeling and reason, system and individuality. These oppositions are reflected in the two kinds of language spoken in the story. German speech is stilted and practical, expressive of a utilitarian, Lockean view of life. The natives, on the other hand, speak a racy, flexible, idiomatic language expressive of a kind of Heideggerean soil mysticism.

The story depicts the Sergeant's comically ambivalent attitude to German efficiency. He cannot help but be impressed: '"It's no wonder they're a powerful nation. . . . Did you see the beat of them for efficiency?"' (*SL*, p. 204; *D*, p. 144). He feels embarrassed by his own sudden lapse from duty. Ironically, he feels uncomfortable for having demonstrated all that is best in him – his love of nature, his natural piety, his resistance to the depradations of a material world, his courage in suggesting that there is another, more fundamental order of being for which the impersonal state cannot legislate. His attempt to emulate German efficiency at the end in his dealings with Guard Burke only makes him a comic figure: 'The Sergeant turned and waddled back towards the building. For a man of his age and shape, he carried himself with considerable dignity' (*SL*, p. 205; *D*, p. 145).

In 'Aunt Maggie, the Strong One', the intractable real world has shrunk to a very small compass indeed. Gathered around Aunt Maggie's deathbed in St Joseph's Refuge, where Mother and nephew Bernard are keeping vigil, all eyes are fixed on the dying face, 'the figure in the bed, who lived only in the O of her mouth' (*SL*, p. 190). A kind of unreality surrounds the whole scene, the 'drugged atmosphere of the home and the sibilant hypnotism of the praying' (*SL*, p. 195), the prayers 'thickening the atmosphere, mesmerizing the senses' (*SL*, p. 186). The whole experience of the story is cocooned in the mesmerism of religious ritual.

Bernard's revery is what provides the countermovement, drawing us away from the dying face, from the Refuge, from this drugged atmosphere, to other times and places, to the Aunt of twenty years before 'who had run, laughed, sung, wrestled, fought, played with him' (*SL*, p. 186). Bernard's mind, we are told, 'had cut free' from 'the strange anaesthesia of prayers and warm odour and expectation of death' (*SL*, p. 186). The images that crowd his mind are of 'Aunt Maggie, the strong one', of her robust vitality, her defiant spirit and love of life. Recollecting the day he first took her to the Refuge, he remembers her words: '"They won't tame me, Bernard. They won't tame Maggie"' (*SL*, p. 188). She is kin to a later creation of Friel's, the insouciant Cass McGuire, another vital, sympathetic woman well stricken in years, consigned to a home and determined not to be 'tamed'. The contrast between Bernard's sharp, imaginative projections of Aunt Maggie, the strong one and the deadening liturgical incantations of the others grouped around her bedside also brings to mind the way Private Gar's vital imaginings of the young beautiful woman who was his mother are counterpointed with Public Gar's dull recital of the prayers for the dead in *Philadelphia, Here I Come!* In the story, memory and imagination have a triumphantly transcendent capability:

> Bernard felt himself soar higher and higher above them all, his brain throbbing with activity until he was sure someone must hear it hum. The noise of the praying and the shapes of the prayers were all one, an amorphous physical sound that writhed below him like smoke. (*SL*, p. 194)

Such feelings of elevation and free flying, however, cannot last. Bernard's impatience with reality, his desire for uninterrupted imaginative flight, is conveyed in the way he roughly tears his mother's hand away from his arm when she clings to him for comfort and support at the very moment of the final horror when Aunt Maggie dies. Once back in the real world, Bernard feels guilty. He determines to make up for his escapism by being 'much more considerate' of his bereaved mother (*SL*, p. 195).

The tension between the ideal and the real is again the theme of one of Friel's best-known and much-anthologised stories, 'The Potato Gatherers'. This is a story of great charm and tenderness, which memorably describes the feelings of pain and fatigue of back-breaking labour. It tells of twelve year old Philly's first day potato gathering with his brother, the slightly older, more experienced Joe. At first, in the early morning, Philly is exuberant, playful, full of hopeful anticipation and boyish fantasy thinking of all the wonderful things he could buy, all the exciting things he could do with the money he will earn. His playful self-dramatisation prefigures Gar O'Donnell's in *Philadelphia*:

'But a gaff, Joe, see? Old Philly down there beside the Black Pool. A big salmon. A beaut. Flat on my belly, and – *phwist!* – there he is on the bank, the gaff stuck in his guts.' He clasped his middle and writhed in agony, imitating the fish. Then his act switched suddenly back to cowboys and he drew from his holsters at a cat sneaking home along the hedge. 'Bang! Bang! That sure settled you, boy. Where *is* this potato territory, mistah? Ah want to show you hombres what work is. What's a-keeping this old tractor-buggy?'   (*SL*, p. 35; *D*, p. 67)

The other workers are sleepy and sullen and even Joe refuses to let himself be carried away by Philly's excitement. Nature itself is unpromising, refusing to inspire the dismal scene. A 'November frost had starched the country flat into silent rigidity' (*SL*, p. 33; *D*, p. 65); 'A pale sun appeared about eight-thirty. It was not strong enough to soften the earth' (*SL*, p. 37; *D*, p. 68); by noon 'the sun was high and brave but still of little use' (*SL*, p. 38; *D*, p. 70); 'The sun was a failure' (*SL*, p. 40; *D*, p. 71); by the end, the landscape is returned to nature's chilly grip: 'Darkness came quickly, and when the last trace of light disappeared the countryside became taut with frost' (*SL*, p. 42; *D*, p. 73).

Pain and tiredness put an end to Philly's expansive dreaming. The boys, like the countryside, are frozen into rigid postures. Their actions become a strange, mechanical routine:

They no longer straightened up; the world was their feet and the hard clay and the potatoes and their hands and the buckets and the sacks. . . . Their muscles had become adjusted to their stooped position, and as long as the boys kept within the established pattern of movement their arms and hands and legs and shoulders seemed to float as if they were free of gravity.   (*SL*, p. 40; *D*, pp. 71–2)

It is as if they were transfixed by a material world that is no longer amenable to the manipulations of imagination or, rather, that their minds are too tired to 'flux' an apparently intractable reality any more.

But though Philly is exhausted by the day's work and is flat out on his back, asleep with his head on his brother's lap as they are driven home in the back of the trailer, the other workers are only now beginning to come alive. Even Joe allows himself for the first time to indulge thoughts of what he will buy with his money. The other labourers are wrestling playfully with each other, laughing, talking of going to a dance that evening, singing, saluting 'extravagantly' (*SL*, p. 41; *D*, p. 73) people they meet along the way, threatening to fall over the side of the trailer with their wild behaviour. Philly's youthful dreams are defeated by the pressure of harsh reality, but these others – older and more experienced – have learnt how to negotiate with it. And so, the victory of life over death is assured.

Another of Friel's most popular stories is 'The Gold in the Sea'. This, too, is a story about dreaming and again demonstrates Friel's compassionate understanding of the need for illusion while recognising illusion for precisely what it is. During a night's fishing the irrepressible Con tries to keep his three crewmen's spirits up with stories of the past. One of these stories concerns a ship that went down just where they are fishing. Below them, says Con, lies a wealth of gold bullion. There is a direct relation between his story of the gold in the sea and the reality of failure and disappointment:

> The night was a failure. I was wet and hungry and miserable. 'At this very moment, friend', Con proclaimed suddenly, 'you're sitting on top of more gold than there is in the vaults of Fort Knox'. (*SL*, p. 254; *D*, p. 42)

Later, Con admits that Dutch salvage men had long ago retrieved whatever treasure there was, but he doesn't want his crew to know this: '"It's better for them to think it's still there. They're young men. . . . You see, friend, they never got much out of life. Not like me"' (*SL*, p. 256; *D*, p. 44). Con justifies illusion as compensation for the harshness of life, an idea to which Friel is frequently to return in later work such as *Philadelphia*, *The Loves of Cass McGuire*, *Aristocrats and Translations*. Con the story-teller wants to affirm hope and possibility ('"The fish is there", I say to them [his two crewmen, Philly and Lispy] when they lose heart' (*SL*, p. 256; *D*, p. 44)). He makes language serve an ulterior purpose to that of recording mere facts.

Friel uses a nameless narrator who is told that 'it's an education being out with Con' (*SL*, p. 244; *D*, p. 33) and the story is indeed concerned with the narrator's 'education'. One of the things he learns is the value of story. As Con ends his account of the Dutch salvage men with the request that the narrator doesn't tell Philly and Lispy about them, the narrator comments: 'I suddenly understood that he was asking me for something more important than money' (*SL*, p. 256; *D*, p. 44). The 'gold in the sea' assumes metaphorical significance. It is not just the bullion or the fish by which the three men make their living, but becomes symbolic of all the potential riches that life holds.

Earlier, there had been another insight for the narrator, one whereby he becomes more aware of the power, not of words, but of silence:

> For the next hour no one spoke, not even Con. . . . It was a strange sensation, floating in blackness across an unknown sea . . . in and around our floating arena there was a curious stillness. . . . And as time crept by, my senses sharpened and became responsive to a shift in the direction of the boat, to the slightest movement of a body, almost to the very presence of the fish beneath us. It was a strange, thrilling perceptivity, like playing blind man's buff for the first time as a child.   (*SL*, p. 250; *D*, pp. 38–9)

When language has left off the narrator feels at one with the mystery of the universe until the enchanted moment of heightened sensitivity and lyrical freedom is abruptly, violently broken by Con's resumption of speech and the endless stories spin on and on: '"It was in the winter of 1918", he said, "and I was assing about in the region of a town called Fort Good Hope on the Mackenzie River . . ."' (*SL*, p. 250; *D*, p. 39).

The tall tale on which Con embarks here concerns a scheme devised by the townspeople of Fort Good Hope to rid themselves of marauding wolves. A reward was offered for each dead wolf's head that was brought to the sheriff. In Con's story he cheats the sheriff by presenting the same wolves' heads over and over again to collect the reward. Con is something of a 'con-man' and proud of it. He is presently cheating the fishing authorities by fishing without a licence and attempts to cheat Philly and Lispy with his fantastical stories of the gold in the sea. Con the story-teller is a version of the artist and again we are offered the double image of one who is both 'educator' and 'con-man'.

Con ends his story about the wolves with words of admiration for the resourcefulness of the Canadian townsfolk: '"By God, sirs, you've got to hand it to them Canadians!"' (*SL*, p. 252; *D*, p. 40). Very similar words are used, refrain-like, to end the story as a whole – Con's praise for the Dutch salvage men who cleaned out the sunken ship with such efficiency: '"By God, sirs", he said, "You've got to hand it to them Dutchmen!"' (*SL*, p. 256; *D*, p. 44) – words of admiration which also echo those of the Sergeant who couldn't help but be impressed by German efficiency in 'The Saucer of Larks'. Con combines admiration of practical skill with a capacity to dream. In so many different ways Friel brings opposites into relationship with each other in an effort to give us a sense of life's rich, indivisible complexity. Con himself is both legendary hero and comically realistic – 'as bald and garrulous as Odysseus' (*SL*, p. 244; *D*, p. 33). The whole story is finely poised between myth and absurdity. Set on board the 'Regina Coelium', the boat's 'rheumaticky groans' (*SL*, p. 250; *D*, p. 38) dispel any romantic aura, and Lispy, who takes it upon himself to give the meaning of the Latin name, translates it wrongly. Con tries to put the mystery back into life, but through deliberate deception and illusion.

Though the story invites us to take a sympathetic view of illusion, Friel's pervasive irony and the self-consciousness of his narrative method keep the reader aware of the fictionality of the story itself – the story-teller's own illusion of reality – and inhibit our too close identification with it. Breaking the naturalistic surface of his story, he incorporates various poetic or musical devices. As well as the story's echoic and motivic quality, there is the way Lispy's speech, a series of proverbs 'that apparently had relevance only to private thoughts of his own' (*SL*, p. 246; *D*, p. 35), functions as a kind of non-naturalistic refrain. It is true, however, that in later work Friel will subject the claims of illusion to a much more exacting test than he does in this story, creating a complex and excruciating tension out of the conflict between the ideal and the real, radically problematising the status of the very narrative he offers us – indeed, problematising all narrative endeavour.

The past, of course, is always susceptible to the play of the selecting, editing, fictionalising memory. A number of stories – 'Foundry House', 'The Wee Lake Beyond', 'Among the Ruins' – explore the relationship between past and present. 'Foundry House' is a wonderfully dramatic, brilliantly observed story, the theatrical potential of which Friel was well aware of since he used its central situation as the basis of his play *Aristocrats*. In the story, Joe Brennan, who owns a music shop, lives with his wife, Rita, and their children in the Foundry House gate lodge which had once been Joe's childhood home. Like Eamon in *Aristocrats*, Joe idealises the Big House, 'founding' his own sense of identity, one might say, on Foundry House.

The red-brick factories are no longer in use, the gate lodge has fallen
into disrepair, the Hogans who own Foundry House are no longer
what they were – the past has disintegrated, but Joe clings to the
wreckage, refusing to acknowledge change.

Old Mrs Hogan asks Joe if he would mind coming to Foundry
House to help them operate a tape-recording machine so that she,
old Mr Hogan and their son, Father Declan, can hear a tape which
the daughter, Sister Claire, a missionary in Africa, has sent them.
Individual speech patterns swiftly, vividly, establish character – Joe's
craven respect for the Big House, Rita's sharp-tongued pragmatism,
Mrs Hogan's brittleness, Father Declan's platitudinous friendliness,
Sister Claire's alienation from reality. There is no free and easy
communication or movement whatever in the story. Everything has
seized up. Intercourse of any kind has become stilted, mechanical,
formal, artificial or blocked – Claire's voice on the tape which
'sounded more like reading than speaking' (*SL*, p. 84; *D*, p. 86);
Mr Hogan's slow and painful entrance, and his inability to make the
least intelligible verbal reply; Mrs Hogan's awkwardness – 'Now
that her request had been made and granted, Mrs Hogan stood
irresolutely between the white gaslight in the hall and the blackness
outside. Her mouth and lips still worked, although no sound came'
(*SL*, pp. 76–7; *D*, p. 79); Joe's stammering bashfulness when
Mrs Hogan calls to ask a favour (reminiscent of Gar O'Donnell
before Senator Doogan in *Philadelphia*) and his uncommunicativeness
when he returns home from Foundry House; Rita's readiness to turn
words into weapons – 'Rita . . . stood in the middle of the floor and
shouted unheeded instructions above the din. Joe's arrival drew her
temper to him' (*SL*, p. 86; *D*, p. 88); Father Declan's non-stop, empty
patter; the music on the tape recording which becomes a shriek. It is
the paradox of art that Friel's finely articulated and beautifully crafted
story can convey the breakdown and failure of communication,
the loss of coherence and fluidity, the sense of a pathetic, lonely
entrapment.

On his return from Foundry House, Joe's remoteness from his
wife is reminiscent of the situation in 'Among the Ruins', where
another Joe withdraws inside himself, much to his wife's annoyance,
after a day spent 'among the ruins' of his past. Joe in 'Foundry
House' struggles to retain his cherished image of the past in the face
of the afternoon's events: 'Mr Bernard . . . he's the same as ever.
Older, of course, but the same Mr Bernard' (*SL*, p. 87; *D*, p. 89).
Foundry House is 'the same as ever – no different' (*SL*, p. 88; *D*,

pp. 89–90). Joe's remarks about being 'forced . . . to have tea with them' (*SL*, p. 87; *D*, p. 89) when in fact they had apologised for not having anything to offer him is an effort to convince himself and Rita of the virtue of those whom he has chosen to idolise, in the same way as the boy's statement in 'The Illusionists' that M. L'Estelle had given him half a crown when he had really given him only a penny is an attempt to persuade his mother that M. L'Estelle was indeed a special person.

In both 'The Wee Lake Beyond' and 'Among the Ruins' Friel uses a Father narrator and continues his exploration of the relationship between fathers and sons as well as between past and present. In 'The Wee Lake Beyond', as the father makes his 'ritualistic preparations' (*GS*, p. 68) for a day's fishing with his son in a remote part of Donegal, his thoughts go back to his own childhood and to his relationship with his own father. One fishing trip with his father of many years ago stands out with particular vividness in his memory. He had quarrelled with his father and struck out on his own, discovering a 'private place' (*GS*, p. 74) of his very own. Now, he thinks, he could take full advantage of it and fish it 'with all the skill and craft and cunning and patience I acquired over the years' (*GS*, p. 74). He had opened up a free space for himself away from the influence of his father, 'the strong precursor' (to use Harold Bloom's phrase), but moved about in it in an inexperienced way:

> I leaped from rock to rock, scarcely waiting to play the flies on the surface of the water before I moved on, wishing to cover the whole shore at once, to be everywhere at the one time, to devour this private place of mine that no man – or at least my father – had ever fished. (*GS*, p. 74)

On his third attempt at fishing 'this wee lake beyond' he eventually achieves mastery. After the exhilaration of first freedom and the discovery of the 'private place' he recovers self-possession: 'this time there was no urgency, no compulsion to be on the point opposite, no force driving me on and on. This time I fished with almost lethargic deliberateness. This time I felt indomitable' (*GS*, p. 74).

The incantatory rhythms of Friel's writing here are reminiscent of Hemingway. Indeed, it is hard not to think of Hemingway's short story, 'Big Two-Hearted River' when reading Friel's. In both, the rituals of fishing are meticulously and lovingly delineated and possess a kind of magical, therapeutic power. In both, fishing is used as a metaphor for plumbing the secret depths of self. It becomes a tense struggle to resolve troublesome psychic conflicts, an effort to confront the past, the mystery of nature and assert an identity.

Friel's story concerns the difficult process of individualisation whereby the son asserts his own personality and distances himself from the influence of the father. That influence is imaged in the shadow which the great mountain casts over the lakes where they fish. The narrator remembers his own father as a strong, adept, kindly man who, nevertheless, could not conceal 'a note of relief' (*GS*, p. 75) in his voice when he learns that his wayward son had caught nothing while he had had a good day's fishing. Similarly, the narrator shows an obvious affection for his son, Frank, and tells of how he would like Frank to have some of the very same wonderful experiences he enjoyed as a boy, such as fishing Lough Anna. But he recognises that Frank 'might fish it a dozen times and see nothing' or – 'worse, a thousand times worse' – Frank might catch the big fish he didn't catch when he fished it as a boy, and that would be an insupportable 'disappointment' (*GS*, p. 74).

Friel emphasises cyclical pattern, a generational repetition, yet looming over all the events in the story is the shadow of imminent change. The narrator, who himself temporarily outgrew fishing holidays with his father at Meenbanid, knows that this may be the last time Frank will want to come on holiday with him, and is anxious therefore not to appear dictatorial nor patronising to his son. But he is also disarmingly honest about his own needs and weaknesses, admitting that while he wants to 'hold on' to his son, he could not bear the 'disappointment' of being outdone by him. Friel is an expert at revealing these subtle psychological tensions within a larger pattern of human recurrence, the interplay of the forces of change and those of continuity.

'Among the Ruins' tells of Joe's journey back to the past, to his childhood home accompanied by wife, Margo, and two children, Peter and Mary. Among the ruins of Corradinna, Joe demonstrates the power of mind to recreate what no longer exists. The past enters the present and takes on a life of its own, as the use of the present tense emphasises. Though the journey has been made at Margo's instigation, she begins to be as jealous of the past which gradually claims her husband and draws him away from her as Gabriel Conroy was of his wife Greta's past in Joyce's great story 'The Dead'. Margo demands to know what Joe and his sister were laughing at all those years ago when they hid in the 'bower' and feels relieved when Joe tries to explain though she tries to make Joe feel foolish by adopting a superior air. However, what Joe increasingly feels is that the past has gone for ever and can never be reclaimed: 'nothing came from the past – no voice, no cry, no laugh, not even the bark of a dog' (*SL*, p. 14; *D*, p. 132). As the car pulls away from his old home 'a sense of aloneness crept over him' and, glancing in the mirror, he sees that his old home is engulfed in the darkness. The past, he thinks, is 'a mirage – a soft illusion into which one steps in order to escape the present' (*SL*, p. 15; *D*, p. 133). He acknowledges the illusory nature of the images of the past which he has cherished and even tried to share with Margo. He even regrets having made the journey to his old home, for 'it had robbed him of a precious thing, his illusions of the past . . . in their place now was nothing – nothing at all but the truth' (*SL*, p. 16; *D*, p. 134).

The journey Joe makes, however, is a journey beyond illusion. As he thinks of his son's absorption, 'donging the tower' (*SL*, p. 17; *D*, pp. 135–6), playing as Joe himself might have played when he was a child, Joe recognises continuity as well as change. The story charts Joe's progress toward understanding what 'the past' is – 'neither reality nor dreams. . . . It was simply continuance, life repeating itself and surviving' (*SL*, p. 18; *D*, p. 136). It doesn't depend on any particular verbal formulation of it. In that phrase 'donging the tower' words aren't important as counters for naming things or experiences: they are a Heideggerian house of being. What matters is

> not the words, not the game, but the fact that he had seen his son, on the first good day of summer, busily, intently happy in solitude, donging the tower. The fact that Peter would never remember it was of no importance; it was his own possession now, his own happiness, this knowledge of a child's private joy. (*SL*, pp. 17–18; *D*, p. 136)

With this knowledge Joe achieves peace, a transcendence of the present moment of squabbling children and irritated wife.

What is evident throughout Friel's short stories is his acceptance of life's unruliness, its defiance of all our systems and expectations and plans, its ability continually to surprise. If language is the medium of consciousness, created to divide and distinguish, Friel sets out to use it in special ways – obliquely rather than explicitly, suggestively rather than merely discursively or descriptively, in order to get beyond division, to create a higher unity, to offer us an image of complex life in which division strives with fusion, order with disorder, certainty with uncertainty.

Chekhov is his chief mentor and spiritual precursor. He has Chekhov's ironic detachment, his immense reserve and objectivity, and demonstrates a similar hatred of nonsense, along with a similar insistence on an absolute personal freedom. Like Chekhov's stories, Friel's explore ordinary topics from life and are notable for their simplicity of narration and absence of effects and tricks. He draws his people with loving intimacy but keeps his distance from participation in their self-belief. His coolly objective eye gives his stories their intellectual veracity. For like Chekhov, Friel is no dreamer. His stories are concise, true to facts, clinically exact. He avoids sentimentality and cheap romanticism. But his is a fruitful realism in which external reality releases the imagination. He combines the objectivity of the naturalists with an impressionistic, suggestive, penetrative method. There is in every individual a sacred mystery to be plumbed. A favourite image with Friel, as with Heaney, is that of the diviner, the intermediary who puts the people in touch with what lies hidden, who mediates between the visible and the invisible worlds. Friel has the romantic sense of possibility, but persistently subjects the imagination to the evidence of the actual, a thorough and conscious principling which permeates his thought. There is a sense of space, but its delights and freedoms and illusions are always entertained under the aspect of Time, the Historical Sense, the Reality Principle, the awareness of change, of man in action. In short, his stories demonstrate a delicate balance of realism and romanticism that we find in Chekhov, an art that is 'neither reality nor dreams'.

UNPUBLISHED EARLY PLAYS

While establishing himself as a short-story writer, Friel began writing plays. His first two plays were radio plays – *A Sort of Freedom* (broadcast on BBC Northern Ireland Home Service, 16 January 1958) and *To This Hard House* (broadcast on BBC Northern Ireland Home Service, 24 April 1958). His next play was written for the stage and was produced at the Group Theatre, Belfast, in August 1960. Originally entitled *The Francophile*, it was adapted for radio, given a new title – *A Doubtful Paradise* – and broadcast on BBC Northern Ireland Home Service in 1962. Another play, *The Blind Mice*, was produced at the Eblana Theatre, Dublin, in February 1963. It, too, was 'translated' into radio and broadcast on 28 November 1963 on the BBC Northern Ireland Home Service.

The leap from short story to drama was perhaps not such a very big one in Friel's case. His stories often have strong dramatic elements and Friel himself would seem to have been well aware of their dramatic potential, judging by the way he goes back to them for situations which he reworks for the stage in his later plays. The dramatic sense, O'Connor stressed, is an essential element in short story writing ('the storyteller differs from the novelist in this: he must be much more . . . of a dramatist'): short-story writing requires careful selection and crafting so that the fragment can be invested with significance and resonance. On the other hand, early stage plays such as *The Loves of Cass McGuire* and later ones such as *Lovers, Faith Healer* or *Dancing at Lughnasa*, in their use of monologue and the central character as narrator, contain strong elements of the short story.

There were of course obvious financial reasons for Friel's attraction to writing plays, but no doubt there were also consciously held artistic and cultural reasons for shifting from the short story to drama. It might be seen as a move from what O'Faolain characterises as one of the most personal and private of literary forms (O'Faolain's 'emphatically personal exposition . . . the personal and individual way of looking at things') to what we might regard as one of the most objective and public. Impersonality, 'dramatisation', 'showing' rather than 'telling', are the essential principles of drama. In drama the author is displaced by the use of a range of characters whose discourse is deprived of the author's authority. Different characters are allowed to articulate different points of view – each of which may itself be in a state of internal conflict – without any of them ever being subordinated to the author's own speech. The move from the short story to drama may thus be seen to represent Friel's desire to withdraw his own ego, his own voice, and to foreground, exploit and celebrate the dialogic or polyphonic nature of language in living speech, that is, to include all voices. He tends towards the concept of truth expressed in Robert Frost's famous dictum 'all truth is dialogue'[35] and towards the view of the speech act theorists who have defined literary discourse in terms of the peculiarity of its elocutionary force. The great Soviet exponent of the 'dialogic' principle, Mikhail Bakhtin, believed that every 'authentically creative' writer was a 'playwright':

Isn't every writer (even the purest lyric poet) always a 'playwright' insofar as he distributes all the discourses among alien voices, including that of the 'image of the author' (as well as the author's other personae)? It may be that every single-voiced and nonobjectal discourse is naive and inappropriate to authentic creation. The authentically creative voice can only be a *second* voice in the discourse. Only the second voice – *pure relation*, can remain nonobjectal to the end and cast no substantial and phenomenal shadow. The writer is a person who knows how to work language while remaining outside of it; he has the gift of indirect speech.[36]

Bakhtin's priviliging of 'dialogic' (as opposed to 'monologic') discourse acknowledges multivocity and plurality; it resists reductive repression and all forms of transcendence, all attempts to unify. In the light of Bakhtinian theory, Friel's commitment to drama may thus be seen as reflecting his deliberate embracement of diversity, heterogeneity and 'difference'. Drama represents a dispersal of the unified self amongst a range of points of view and gives concrete embodiment to the active interrelations of both internally divergent selves and diverse socially situated voices.

The first of Friel's early unpublished plays was the radio play, *A Sort of Freedom*, the title, like that of another early play, *A Doubtful Paradise*, emphasising the note of doubt, qualifying straightforward assertion and signalling Friel's interest in exploring the possibilities of the ironic mode. *A Sort of Freedom* is a play about the nature of freedom and questions any simple arrogation of individual rights above social obligation and responsibility. It is also an exploration of the fatal consequences of personal inflexibility and lack of self-knowledge – a theme that is to pervade nearly all Friel's work. The play presents the challenge of adapting to new conditions when the old order is suddenly thrown into crisis. Frazer is a haulage contractor who refuses to accept change and the forces of modernisation represented by the Union. 'You know my attitude and if you know me, you know I won't change', Frazer boasts to Hamilton, the union organiser, when the latter appeals to Frazer to put pressure on one of his employees, Joe Reddin, to join the Union. Frazer deeply resents Hamilton's interference, regarding it as an attempt to compromise the rights of the individual, both his and Reddin's.

The subplot concerning Frazer's refusal to have his adopted son inoculated against TB amplifies Frazer's irrational and stubborn refusal to conform. Not only is he prepared to flout contracted agreements with the adoption agency and the health authorities and to resort to bribery to get his own way, but he is willing to risk the life of his adopted son whom he claims to be devoted to. His stand on individual rights is treated with heavy irony: he is exposed not only as a stubborn fool of a father but also as an unprincipled and untrustworthy employer. Though he assures Reddin that he will back him 'to the last ditch', he quickly deserts his old retainer and sacks him rather than face a strike amongst his other workers for employing a non-union man.

Two other characters help to unmask Frazer. The doctor whom Frazer has tried to bribe not to inoculate his son accuses him of lacking self-knowledge. Going behind Frazer's facade of respectability, the doctor sees he is 'worse than villainous', that he is 'depraved', 'callous and ruthless'. This sense of plural identity, the gap between Private and Public selves which the doctor opens up is to become another major theme of Friel's. The other person who challenges Frazer is his wife. Early on she demonstrates her independence when, instead of doing Frazer's bidding and looking after his broken-down lorry, she calls a taxi and goes off for a day's shopping in Belfast. At the end, she tries to make Frazer see his real reasons for adopting a son. She points out that it was no act of love, but an essentially selfish ploy whereby Frazer could perpetuate his name. 'There was never any humanity in you', she tells her husband and to the end he proves her true. Prompted by his wife to recompense Reddin financially for losing his job, Frazer is indignant at his wife's proposal of a pension of £400, agrees to £200 and ends up writing the cheque for £150.

Even more foolishly intractable is Joe Reddin who, for no discernible reason other than his own stubborn pride, is prepared to lose his job and subject his family to poverty and insecurity. His sort of freedom is a pig-headed, irrational, self-destructive refusal to compromise, even when it would be in his own practical interests as a worker to do so. With the slippery Frazer actually pleading with him to join the Union, Reddin still holds out and suffers the inevitable consequences. Like O'Casey, Friel questions the abstract 'principles' which his menfolk cling to and sets them against the common sense views of his women, Mrs Frazer and Mary Reddin. Mrs Frazer stands for human decency as well as common sense, wishing to make sure that Reddin is fairly compensated for his long and faithful service, but recognising that his dismissal is the only option Frazer is left with. Mary Reddin, like O'Casey's Juno, is the practical home-builder, scornful of Reddin's 'principles' and 'pride' and the sort of 'freedom' which he ultimately attains – the sort which condemns the family to the painful indignities of unemployment and poverty.

Neither Frazer nor Reddin is capable of self-discovery. Joe Reddin is never more than a stubborn, pathetic creature and, to the end, Frazer remains a self-centred, opportunistic, mean, manipulative, untrustworthy character, a thoroughly dislikeable individual, the living proof of the need for government control and Union organisation. These two characters take their place in a long line of failed fathers in Friel's work, from *Philadelphia* and *The Loves of Cass McGuire* to *Living-Quarters*, *Faith Healer* and *Fathers and Sons*. There are some effective twists and turns in the play (notably the ironic last scene when Reddin receives Frazer's cheque and is overcome with gratitude at his master's benevolence), but motivation is crudely handled (especially Reddin's inexplicable holding out against the Union and Frazer's manic opposition to having his adopted son inoculated against TB) and there is some rather clumsy and repetitive management of material.

The next radio play, *To This Hard House*, is a study of inflexible patriarchal authority represented by the schoolmaster Dan Stone. Not only is his name symbolic of his 'hardness', but he suffers from an eye disease, connoting his failure of both practical foresight and moral vision. He represents a crumbling old order: even his wife, Lily, remarks: 'Somehow he seems to be losing his grip this last year'. As in *A Sort of Freedom*, Friel takes as his central theme the challenge of adjusting to change, for Dan, like Frazer and Reddin, must come to terms with the modern world. He is faced with the problems created by the opening of a new school in the town which is attracting not only pupils from his own country school, but also his assistant teacher, Judy Flanagan, who obtains a post in the new institution. With falling rolls, Dan, after forty-two years teaching in Meenbanid school, which itself has been in existence for over two hundred years, faces the possibility of closure and redundancy. Dan sees 'ingratitude, treachery, meanness' all around him, even in his favourite child, Fiona, who tries to make him see sense. Out of hurt pride, Dan turns on Fiona, driving her away from the family home. She is the last of the Stone children to fly the nest and join the modern world, following the son, Walter, who has added to Dan's humiliation by accepting the post of principal of the rival school in town, and eldest daughter, Rita, who for some years has been living in London and, with the money Dan sent her to return home, has bought an air ticket to Canada.

Disappointed by Fiona and Walter, Dan deludes himself that his eldest daughter is the only child who really cares about him. Characteristically, Friel, seeking larger contexts for his play, loses no opportunity for 'intertextuality'. Dan's judgment is as misplaced as Lear's and indeed the Shakespearian parallel is made explicit in a rather heavy-handed way. As Dan waits for Rita, he has Lily recite Lear's lines: 'Come, let's away to prison; / We two will sing like birds i' the cage. . . .' Of course, Rita does not arrive and Dan, blinded by stubborn pride, doesn't realise that Fiona and Walter are the children who show love and concern for him. Friel enjoys playing with the complexity of motive: Fiona returns, but more because she has been let down by her boyfriend than because of family feeling; Lily welcomes Fiona home, without question, with open arms, but displays crass insensitivity to Fiona's feelings when her daughter confides that the real reason for her return home is her desertion by Sam Daly: 'That's the reason? What I always said: everything would turn out right in the end'; Dan, in the space of a short speech, moves from angry contempt at the news Fiona is home to ostensibly gracious welcome: 'But she's welcome, Lily. I forgive her. Tell her that her father bids her welcome and forgives her' – such largesse being an ironic inversion of Lear's speech where it is the old man who humbly asks forgiveness of the daughter he has cruelly wronged ('When thou dost ask me blessing, I'll kneel down, / And ask of thee forgiveness'). Lear's kind of seeing is not available to Dan – 'the doctors says that they have no hope for his sight'. Yet, paternal feeling is never totally eclipsed. There is 'welcome' for Fiona and eventually grudging support for Walter in his new job.

The play emphasises the need for compromise and negotiation, for rational judgment to temper traditional pieties and emotional attachments; for the capacity to adapt to changing conditions in the rapidly modernising Ireland of the 1950s – a world of new schools, fibre factories and milk bars. At the same time, Friel enforces a realistic, unsentimental view of the big world beyond Meenbanid: Walter becomes principal of the new town school but is harshly and humiliatingly treated by the school inspector for a minor slip-up; Fiona makes it to the freedom of London but quickly returns to the security of home; Rita, the most 'adventurous' of all the children, also seems to be the most restless and frustrated.

The next play, *A Doubtful Paradise*, begins, like *To This Hard House* and *The Blind Mice*, by establishing a family situation and then introducing the disruptive element that throws the domestic routine into crisis. In *To This Hard House* it is the arrival of the school inspector, Mr Blackley, the harbinger of modernity; in *The Blind Mice* it is the unsettling news of Father Chris's apostasy; in *A Doubtful Paradise* it is M. Georges Tournier who, though he never actually appears in the play, acts as the catalyst for the main action.

The Logue family consists of the father Willie, mother Maggie and the children – eldest daughter Una, now living in London; younger daughter Chris, who is being courted by the lodger, Gerald, an earnest, rather boring young man who works in a bank; and son Kevin, who has just arrived home having been suspended from the Bar for unprofessional conduct. Willie is a postal worker bent on self-improvement through studying mathematics and science, listening to opera and learning French. He writes terrible poetry for the local paper and looks forward to promotion (which he doesn't get) because of the opportunity it will give him to exercise 'a broadening effect' in the post office where he works. His speech contrasts with that of the other characters by its pseudocultured idiom, its unintentionally comic parade of knowledge, its Frenchified phrasing and numerous *faux pas*. Maggie is the stereotypical homely wife and mother, the cornerstone of the family, uncomprehending of and impatient with Willie's pretensions and ambitions. Her speech declares her lack of education and culture, but also recognition of her own limitations, a degree of self-awareness entirely absent in Willie. Maggie recognises the worth of Jack Graham who gets the promotion instead of Willie; to the end, she displays a kindly, caring attitude to the rejected lodger, Gerald; she sees the need for the whole family to take a more realistic approach to life; and like Lily, the mother in *The Blind Mice*, she realises the dangers of presumption and vanity and welcomes defeat as an opportunity to learn humility. Maggie admits she has secretly prayed for an end to her husband's vanity and a return to reality and humanity, just as Lily admits she has secretly welcomed her son's fall as the means whereby he may possibly become a true priest.

Tournier is the exotic outsider, an enchanter. First introduced as 'a traveller in French wines who just happens to be in town', the Frenchman has been invited to address the French class Willie attends. Willie only has to hear him speak and Tournier becomes 'A count. A full-blooded count! The owner of hundreds of acres of the best vine growing land south of Bordeaux . . . prince charming straight out of a fairy tale'. Like that other Frenchified illusionist, M. L'Estelle, in the story 'The Illusionists', Tournier stirs up discord in the family and attracts the particular resentment of the more realistic, level-headed mother. He causes Willie to make a fool of himself and thoughtlessly uses and then abandons Chris, as cruelly as Fiona Stone, that other runaway in *To This Hard House*, is abandoned by her faithless lover, Sam Daly.

Fiona's difficulties, like Kevin's and Una's, are all traceable, we are to believe, to the father. Kevin rancorously recalls how the two daughters, having been brought up to entertain exalted notions of themselves, were known locally as 'the Countesses'. Feeling oppressed by the burden of their father's expectations for them, Una has married a sixty year old man and fled the family to go and live in London without ever making the least effort to re-establish contact over the last four years; Chris, under her father's influence, is besotted by Tournier and gets involved in a disastrous relationship with her French playboy; Kevin, pushed by his father to become a barrister, eventually breaks under the strain and is disbarred. Kevin is the outspoken, rebellious son, loudly critical of his father's pretensions. In anticipation of Friel's much more complex study of the dangers and difficulties of exogamy in *Translations*, Kevin warns Chris against Tournier, believing she would be 'better off with someone of her own sort'. After Chris disappears with Tournier, Willie continues to idolise the French visitor, while Kevin berates his father for allowing himself to be 'bamboozled' by an imposter. Like Biff Loman in Miller's *Death of a Salesman*, Kevin strenuously tries to make his father confront the truth, accusing Willie of losing himself in 'a world of swotted facts and fake culture'. Willie Logue, however, is as incorrigible as Willie Loman.

Willie Logue, an absurd caricature of petit bourgeois pretension, is an early version of Mrs Diggerty who appears in Friel's recent play, *The London Vertigo*. Mrs Diggerty's Anglophilia is as ridiculous as Willie's Francophilia. Both characters aspire to the beau monde beyond the narrow confines of provincial Irish society. *A Doubtful Paradise* belongs with *The Communication Cord* and *The London Vertigo* as a lively satire of 'fake culture', of vulgar, sentimental aspiration and the self-hate that goes with it. Maggie accuses Willie of 'bringing this madness into the house, this madness about culture and learning and all that stuff away above and beyond us'. Her level-headedness produces unquestioning acceptance of the given reality: a conservative acquiescence in one's fate. By contrast, Willie's vertiginous aspirations reveal his discontent with the *status quo*, his wish for a fuller, richer life. Maggie resolutely refuses the delusion of 'dreams and images', retains compassionate understanding and practical common sense but, recognising only the domestic and familial, is also crucially limited in her perspectives on life. To her, as to O'Casey's women, the world beyond – the world of politics, education, science and art – is merely 'foolishness'. Where she is too deeply embedded in her world, Willie is driven by a naïve and unrealistic faith in the possibility of transforming it. Thus, he cannot see that Tournier is a cheat and a liar and that his own unreality is alienating his children. Willie never attains the moment of recognition, even to the minimal degree reached by Dan Stone in *To This Hard House*. Willie's recalcitrance, like Father Chris's in *The Blind Mice*, produces an excruciating irony, which Friel drives home in the last moments of each play. Thus, just when at the end we think Willie has learnt his lesson, he compounds his absurdity: 'I'll admit there was a mistake – an error of judgment. I took him (Tournier) for what he said he was . . . a count . . . and my pursuit of the language was not tempered by ordinary common sense. . . . But this time it will be above personalities . . . and above petty human schemings . . .'. The play ends with Willie's proclamation of his latest mad project: he is going to start learning the language of 'the brotherhood of man . . . the oneness, the family one-ness of creation. . . . Esperanto!'

Significantly, language is identified as the means of transformation. It is language which offers 'a kind of freedom'. Yet, the whole force of the play has been to show the deceptions and dangers of language, the unreality it can lead to. Listening to Kevin castigate his father's illusions, Maggie breaks in: 'Stop it! Stop it, both of you! D'you hear me. Stop it! I'm sick and tired of words and words and words', and reminds them of the immediate human problem facing them – the fate of the abandoned Chris. A little later, when Kevin again tries to bring Willie to face the truth, Maggie interposes, seeing the wounding words can cause: 'Let there be quiet for a while'. We can sympathise with Willie's longing for an ideal, transcendent language which would bring unity rather than division; but we laugh at his pathetic naivety.

Again, Friel clearly enjoys playing with ambiguity and irony, manipulating our responses. We laugh at Willie, we despise him; we admire him when he shows his appreciation of his workmate Charlie Bonner's gesture in calling to express the men's surprise at Willie's being passed over for promotion. But in the end we are exasperated by his incorrigible dreaming. Maggie is admirable for her good sense and compassion; but also irritating for the narrowness of her perspectives. Kevin is a cynical wastrel and sponger, but we can see why he is like that and he has insights the others haven't in suspecting Tournier from the start. He is perhaps the only one who learns, for at the end he swallows his pride to follow up Bonner's offer of a menial job in an office.

The central situation in Friel's next play, *The Blind Mice*, acquired an unexpected piquancy in the early 1990s with the experience of Brian Keenan, Terry Waite and others who had been accused of spying and held hostage by foreign powers being very much in the public mind. *The Blind Mice* concerns Father Chris Carroll who has been held prisoner for five years, accused of 'subversive activity' against the Chinese People's Republic. The opening scene intercuts three media versions of Father Chris's imprisonment and release: the first a radio announcement in Chinese/English accent from Peking, the second an American news broadcast and the third the Northern Ireland radio news. Immediately we are alerted to the question of point of view and the relativity of truth – a thematic concern which Friel develops in subsequent work, most notably in *Freedom of the City, Faith Healer* and *Making History*. Behind the media hype lies Father Chris's own version of what happened and the whole point about his story of events is its uncertainty. He is filled with doubt and anguish as he searches for the meaning of his own actions. Surrounding him are the other members and close friends of the family, as well as his clerical colleagues, all anxious to impose their own interpretations on Chris's experience.

Chris explains how, in his isolation, feeling that God had abandoned him, he sank into despair. Longing to confess this mortal sin he signed a document renouncing his faith in return for his freedom. 'Sign the document and you get to confession; don't sign and you go to hell': these were the stark alternatives as he saw them. Rejecting his popular elevation as the 'Hero of Thian-Hee', he anguishes over his apostasy. His brother, John, an ambitious Dublin doctor, is only concerned about what people will think of Chris and wants to hustle him out of the country to avoid a scandal. Similarly, Father Green, the Bishop's emissary, an unctuous diplomat, is anxious that Chris make it clear that he signed the document under duress, and grows increasingly impatient when Chris's insistence on the truth of his experience compromises his religious faith. Chris's sister, Ann, supports her brother, John, in urging Chris to flee to Dublin, but her boyfriend, Tom Bresland, who is a Union activist, believes: 'If he's a priest, if he's a man, he won't move'. Tom is one of the few who understand Chris and show sympathy towards him. The others are Father Rooney and Chris's mother.

Lily is another mother-figure in the O'Casey mould. Like Juno, she is the mainstay of the family, but with no more appreciation of the political world represented by Tom Bresland than Juno had of the strike action in the factory where her daughter Mary worked. Lily also finds it hard to accept poor Father Rooney: 'Offer him only one drink', she tells her daughter, 'I don't want the place being talked about'. Nevertheless, Lily displays a commendable insight in recognising early on the seeds of pride in Chris and hopes that his long imprisonment will have cured him. She accepts Chris's humanity, while John wants his brother perfect, mythologised in precisely the same way Archbishop Lombard in *Making History* wants O'Neill apotheosised in the popular consciousness.

Father Rooney, who himself knows misunderstanding and victimisation because of his alcoholism, also pleads for tolerance of human frailty. This little whiskey priest is both 'the best priest in the town' and the pathetic 'Wee Half One'. With both the characters of Father Rooney and Father Chris, Friel explores the contradictions between inner and outer that are to continue to absorb him in *Philadelphia* and other plays.

The Blind Mice ends ironically, with Chris recovering self-confidence and demonstrating that his five years' imprisonment have taught him nothing. He resumes his old affectations and vanities, showing himself to be as ambitious as his venal brother, just as keen to win approval and power. Lily closes the play in despair, fearing that once again she has lost her son to the world.

Father Chris, Father Green and Father Rooney are some of Friel's earliest studies of priests. Chris's self-division reappears in the characterisation of Columba in *The Enemy Within* and indeed Chris's 'enemy within' is the same as Columba's – pride and worldliness, the lust for power. However, Columba is a much more dramatically vital character, his internal conflict given precise and vivid embodiment where Father Chris's tends to be a matter of passive and retrospective brooding. Father Green's manipulativeness reappears in Archbishop Lombard, while the return of the disturbed, possibly lapsed priest, figures centrally in *Dancing at Lughnasa*. The people's disappointment and anger at the 'fake' priest in *The Blind Mice* links with the attitude of the people to the faith healer (in Friel's play of that name) when he fails to live up to their expectations and, of course, the people's turning on the unmasked 'hero' recalls the famous reversal in Synge's *Playboy*. In the popular Catholic mind Chris has betrayed his 'sacred Irish heritage': Friel's glancing treatment of this facile accusation initiates an extended critique of a sentimental, 'knee-jerk', fundamentally inhuman Catholic nationalism that is most fully developed in *The Communication Cord*.

None of this early unpublished work is in any way remarkable. There is no attempt to exploit or develop the medium of radio in the exciting and revolutionary ways that Beckett or Pinter did. It tends to be a drama of 'talking heads' in which character is always close to caricature, action to melodrama. But radio offered the opportunity for Friel to indulge his undoubted gift for dialogue, to gain experience in constructing character and structuring his material, and to develop his central thematic preoccupations – the conflict between fathers and children, the old and the new; the tension between dream and reality, public and private, inner and outer; the attractions of the exotic outsider to the inhabitants of a severely circumscribed world; the problematic of language and the relativity of truth. Radio and television plays satisfy a realistic criteria. The thing that marks Friel's later stage plays is a much greater ambition and willingness to extend the drama beyond a psychologically mimetic function. While still presenting substantially naturalistic characters and situations, he introduces mythic and parodic–travestying elements, mixing the modes of tragedy and comedy, 'high' and 'low'. Characters are constituted not only by their own linguistic registers and idiolects, but by all the discourses they quote or allude to. In short, Friel aims at a more comprehensive representation of reality than the purely realistic drama offers. Thus, his characters' speeches are often elaborate exercises in stylisation and parody, his characters often explicit about the problems and processes of narration. Often they are writers themselves, presented as makers of their own fictions, aware of the arbitrariness of their constructions.

The early (unpublished) stage plays, *A Doubtful Paradise* and *The Blind Mice*, were no more promising than the early radio plays, but with *The Enemy Within* and *Philadelphia* Friel wasn't long in demonstrating a much more considerable talent, developing a kind of stage drama which, curiously, lends itself particularly well to radio production. *The Enemy Within* and *Philadelphia* were both swiftly adapted for radio, the first broadcast on the BBC Third Programme in 1963, the second on the Third Programme in 1965. Another technically interesting and ambitious early play, *The Loves of Cass McGuire*, though now generally known as a stage play, actually started out as a radio play, broadcast on the Third Programme in 1961. The BBC Radios 3 and 4 Brian Friel Season of six plays (10 April–1 May 1989), spanning twenty-five years of his creative life, confirmed that Friel's writing is 'ideal for production on radio'.[37] The experience of listening to a radio play is akin to that of dreaming or day-dreaming. Radio is uniquely suited to presenting inner, subjective reality – which is very much the essence of a Friel play. In *Philadelphia*, for example, the 'blind' medium of radio comes into its own in representing the two sides of the one person – Private and Public Gar. The heavy materiality of two flesh-and-blood actors on a paint and canvas stage (or even on a film set, as in the clumsy 1970 film version of the play) is replaced by two disembodied voices. With its capacity for a much greater fluidity and swiftness of effect than the stage, radio can accomplish the complicated flashback transitions with a magical touch. Gar's mind itself, we are persuaded, is the stage on which the action takes place.

As a radio playwright, Friel owed much to the encouragement of the BBC Radio Drama Producer, Ronald Mason, who was eventually to become Head of BBC Radio Drama in 1977. From 1955 to 1966 Mason was a Drama Producer with BBC Northern Ireland in Belfast and it was he who commissioned Friel's first two plays. As a stage dramatist, Friel's major early shaping influence and inspiration was the work of the celebrated Irish director, Tyrone Guthrie who, though he had been responsible for establishing radio drama in Northern Ireland when he first joined the BBC in Belfast in 1924, was chiefly important to Friel for his work in the theatre.

INTRODUCING THE STAGE PLAYS: POSTMODERN HUMANISM

From April to May 1963 Friel was in America, observing Guthrie at work on *Hamlet* and *The Three Sisters*. These were the productions that were to launch Guthrie's new project, the Tyrone Guthrie Theatre in Minneapolis, America's first permanent regional theatre company. It was, said Friel, 'a courageous concept – an attempt to establish a classical theatre in what is traditionally considered the philistine Midwest'.[38] Guthrie, who had Irish connections (his family came from Co. Monaghan) and who had been an enthusiastic admirer and reviewer of Friel's short stories, was keen to encourage the new young playwright. An erstwhile administrator of the Old Vic and Sadler's Wells Opera, founder of the Shakespeare Festival Theatre in Stratford, Ontario, in 1952, a pioneer of radio drama with the BBC in Belfast in the 1920s, Guthrie was a creative, experimental and highly imaginative artist. He directed opera as well as drama, co-adapted Marlowe's *Tamburlaine*, wrote radio drama and produced a famous modern dress *Hamlet*. Seeking to break the conventional boundary between actor and spectator, he experimented with the thrust stage. His autobiography *A Life in the Theatre* ends by affirming a religious concept of theatre as ritual:

> I believe that the purpose of the theatre is to show mankind to himself, and thereby to show to man God's image.
>
> I believe that this purpose is ill served by *consciously* using the theatre as a moral, social or political platform. It cannot avoid being all three. Its ministers must not be so arrogant as to suppose that their work is to do good to their fellow men. . . .
>
> I believe that the theatre makes its effect not by means of illusion, but by ritual. . . .
>
> The theatre is the direct descendent of fertility rites, war dances and all the corporate ritual expressions by means of which our primitive ancestors, often wiser than we, sought to relate themselves to God, or the gods, the great abstract forces which cannot be apprehended by reason, but in whose existence reason compels us to have faith.[39]

Guthrie's credo bears on Friel's developing concern with incorporating into the theatrical presentation a primitive, non-rational, richly expressive discourse of music and dance capable of expressing simultaneously a sense of individual personality and a sense of community (in terms of both family and of race and ethnic origins) – and underlying both of these, an ontological sense of one's innermost Being-in-the-world.

Friel acknowledges that his trip to America marked a turning point in his career. Summarising the importance to him of the period he spent with Guthrie, he writes:

I learned about the physical elements of plays, how they are designed, built, landscaped.

I learned how actors thought, how they approached a text, their various ways of trying to realise it.

I learned a great deal about the iron discipline of theatre, and I discovered a dedication and nobility and selflessness that are associated with a theoretical priesthood. But much more important than all these, those months in America gave me a sense of liberation – remember this was my first parole from inbred claustrophobic Ireland – and that sense of liberation conferred on me a valuable self-confidence and a necessary perspective so that the first play I wrote immediately after I came home, *Philadelphia, Here I Come!* was a lot more assured than anything I had attempted before.[40]

While his plays after 1963 clearly continue themes and preoccupations of earlier work, they display a new sophistication and adventurousness in his formal means and an ability to take in a much wider cultural world than that of parochial Ireland where the plays are set. *Philadelphia*, the big hit of the 1964 Dublin Theatre Festival, *is* a remarkable *tour de force* and with it Friel routed all those critics who had tended to consider him only as a minor, parochial talent. It not only announced the playwright's greatly enlarged ambitions but also demonstrated a much more confident control than is to be found in previous plays. Having two actors play one person was a theatrical device every bit as daring as having one language play two in the much later *Translations*. The new work, exploiting a wide variety of theatrical resources, shows the influence of O'Neill, Williams and Miller in America and of Beckett and Pinter closer to home. In *Philadelphia*, for example, he moves naturally and effortlessly amongst a range of diverse languages (from contemporary Irish vernacular to American slang to the high style of Edmund Burke) and demonstrates an ability to unlock a wider variety of voices, to open up character in a greater variety of ways than ever before, his repertoire of technical means now extending from a minimal, Pinteresque use of language (as in the exchange between Canon and County Councillor) to deployment of the equally Pinteresque set-piece monologue (which becomes a major compositional feature of his next play, *The Loves of Cass McGuire* and, of course, the later *Faith Healer*).

But the most fundamental aspect of Friel's 'internationalisation' is his engagement with the problems of subjectivity, representation, history, and the body which have exercised many recent thinkers and literary theorists both in Europe and America over the last thirty years. The quadruple focus which I have adopted for the bulk of this study – Subject, Text, History and Body – would seem to correspond not only to the sequence of theoretical movements in recent years, but also to a progression of thematic emphasis in Friel's major work. If Friel's plays continue the native Irish tradition of 'verbal' theatre, they do so, as Richard Kearney observes, in 'a highly self-questioning mode'.[41] Friel stretches, questions and disrupts the procedures of 'classic realism', which Catherine Belsey defines as 'that form which is characterised by illusionism, narrative leading to closure, and a hierarchy of discourses which establish the "truth" of the story'.[42] Realism as a literary mode seeks to disguise the conditions of its production. Appearing to reflect accurately the world of external reality, a realist text aims to persuade us that it is a seamless and natural whole. In realist literature, as Peter Messent explains, 'attention is directed away from the instabilities of language and reference'. Language is a window onto a solid world. All stress is placed on referent. The text is, in Roland Barthes' terms, 'readerly' rather than 'writerly'. Realist, or 'readerly' writing, Messent says, is 'a form of writing that complies with our expectations, encouraging a sterile and passive consumption on the part of the reader or spectator .... The classic text can be seen as a "stable object" with a clearly indicated hierarchy of textual "levels". The literary work is thus contained within an "ideology of totality" which Barthes relates to what he sees as "the closure system of the West"'.[43] The 'writerly' text, on the other hand, encourages the reader or spectator to act as producer of meaning. It is open and 'plural'.[44] It allows the reader or spectator 'play' and 'pleasure'. In his own approach to Balzac's realist text, *Sarrasine* (1830), Barthes, says Messent, 'disrupts traditional unitary forms of criticism by refusing to look for any overall "singular, theological meaning" in the text, rather, ceaselessly breaking it up, "manhandling the text, interrupting it", showing both how the "reality effects" of the text are produced and how multiple these effects can be seen to be – once the text is unravelled, 'decomposed'. In doing this, Barthes shows how realism, is based on a fraud. He unravels the way meaning is produced in *Sarrasine* by illustrating how the apparently seamless textual surface, one which seems 'naturally' to depict and reflect the world it describes, is in fact composed of a network of overlapping codes'.[45]

Friel, too, starts from the premise that language is not a neutral, transparent medium for transcribing the world. As one of his characters, the linguist Tim in *The Communication Cord* says, communication is a process of encoding and decoding: 'All social behaviour, the entire social order, depends on our communicational structures, on words mutually agreed on and mutually understood. Without that agreement, without that shared code, you have chaos'.[46] Friel's own dramatic practice is one which foregrounds the constructed nature of the drama and of meaning by disrupting and defamiliarising habitual processes of perception. Thus, he breaks the illusion of reality by having two actors play the one character in *Philadelphia*, introducing characters such as the Brechtian 'Sir' in *Living Quarters*, intercutting the realistic level of action with the journalistic commentary of Man and Woman in *Winners*, employing a Morality play characterisation of types and abstractions and a cinematic structure of flashbacks and cross-cutting in *Freedom of the City*, and foregrounding music and movement as central theatrical elements in *Dancing at Lughnasa*. Rather than striving to maintain a consistent illusion of reality, Friel sets out with an opposite intention – to take the audience behind or beyond the world of familiar experience either by unmasking the constructed nature of reality and revealing the mechanisms whereby such illusions are created ('baring the device') so that the audience is encouraged to reflect critically on the action presented and to think about the ways it is constructed or by evolving a ritual, non-verbal drama of music and gesture to produce the epiphanic moment outside time when the division between subject and object, mind and body, is dissolved.

The Soviet critic, Mikhail Bakhtin's dialogic theory is helpful in throwing light on Friel's artistic enterprise because Bakhtin's theory places central attention on the importance of the actual historical situation in our construction of textual and social meaning. Bakhtin sees language as a site of conflict where different social groupings struggle for power. In Bakhtin's view, 'any single national language' is composed of a series of different 'languages' internally stratified into a series of complex and overlapping levels

> into social dialects, characteristic group behaviour, professional jargons, generic languages, languages of generations and age groups, tendentious languages, languages of the authorities, of

various circles and of passing fashions, languages that serve the specific sociopolitical purposes of the day, even of the hour.[47]

Friel's work is informed by a similar awareness of language as a register of social and historical diversity, of 'power relations and hierarchies' in the given culture. As a Northern Catholic with Nationalist sympathies, he was especially sensitive to the political reverberations of language. One of the problems in Ireland today, he comments, is that the two cultures 'are ostensibly speaking the same language but . . . in fact they are not'[48] and, as the linguist Tim insisted, 'without that shared code you have chaos'. As Friel sees it, the pressing need is for a new common language so that 'chaos' can be avoided. 'I think that the political problem of this island is going to be solved by language', he says, 'not only the language of negotiation across the table, but the recognition of what language means for us on this island'. The development of a new language, Friel hopes, 'should lead to a cultural state, not a political one . . . out of that cultural state, the possibility of a political state follows'.[49] The Field Day Theatre Company, was set up with precisely this objective in view: to provide a platform for alternative ways of looking at Irish society and history, in the hope that by revising and exploring established myths and language, a deeper understanding would follow, leading to reconciliation between the various factions in Irish life. Seamus Deane compares the role of Field Day to that of the early Abbey theatre in Dublin. In the programme note for Friel's *The Three Sisters*, Deane points out that Field Day is 'like the Abbey in origin, in that it has within it the idea of a culture which has not yet come to be in political terms. It is unlike the Abbey in that it can no longer subscribe to a single nationalistic basis for its existence'. Field Day, Deane implies, is designed to free Irish politics and literature from a single mode of thought; to acknowledge a more pluralistic society. Such a project clearly goes against the concept of a 'united Ireland' of Republican aspiration and rhetoric. Traditional Nationalist ideology enshrined the ideal of a fixed and coherent nation, a spiritual entity. It posited a self-sufficient, Catholic, rural society dedicated to the reunification of the island and committed to the revival of the Irish language. However, the social, economic, and linguistic development of Southern Ireland in the 1950s and 1960s represented a movement away from homogenisation as emigration continued and the process of modernisation gathered momentum. With the upsurge of sectarian violence in the late 1960s in the North, the issues of language and cultural/national identity became highly politicised and more contentious than ever. Fracture confirmed itself as the dominant Irish experience. Denis Donoghue in his book, *We Irish* (1986), attempts to give some sense of the extent of the divisions in Irish life:

> If there is a distinctive Irish experience, it is one of division, exacerbated by the fact that division in a country so small seems perverse. But the scale doesn't matter. At various times, the division has taken these forms: Catholic and Protestant, Nationalist and Unionist, Ireland and England, North and South, the country and the bloated city of Dublin, Gaelic Ireland and Anglo-Ireland, the comfortable and the poor, farmers and P.A.Y.E. workers, pro-Treaty and anti-Treaty, child and parents, the Irish and the English language, the visible Ireland and the hidden Ireland, landlord and tenant, the Big House and the hovel. To which it is now necessary to add: a defensive church and an increasingly secular state, Irish law and European law.[50]

In responding to this condition of fracture in Irish society, which is symptomatic of the larger crisis in the whole Western intellectual tradition, Friel is absorbed by many of the recognisable Postmodern concerns. There are of course many forms of Postmodernism, but the term is usually taken to refer to the sense of the bankruptcy of our inherited forms of knowledge and representation, a breakdown in traditional modes of cultural legitimisation, the feeling that we are now living in an age of irrationalism and impotence. Writers and thinkers such as Barthes, Bakhtin, Derrida, Foucault, Kristeva and Lyotard have demonstrated the radical indeterminacy of traditional meaning and dismantled the notion of 'foundationalism – the idea that there are absolute grounds of meaning and truth. The 'grand narratives' of Western history derived from Kantian thought have collapsed and with them has gone the idea of a correspondence between the structures of the mind and those of the world outside mind, between aesthetic form and that of the world outside the fiction. Without these 'meta-narratives' (God, Reason, Progress), history itself threatens to disintegrate into a plurality of discourses, hence, the dominant experience becomes one of multiplicity, fragmentation, instability of meaning, dissensus. With the breakdown of the grand orders of knowledge which legitimised foundationalist claims, security, knowledge and identity are available, if at all, only through the concrete, bodily, non-conceptualising modes of the aesthetic rather than those of pure reason.

Postmodernism's dangerous tendencies are readily apparent. The critique of 'meta-narratives' can lead to the claim that if truth is only an effect of rhetoric it is, therefore, simply a matter of power. If all truth is fiction, why should one fiction be any better or worse than another, one course of action any more or less ethical than another? What claims can literature make to be anything more than a playing off of alternative worlds in a game of pluralistic anarchy? What is there to prevent freedom to manipulate the world and create new identities for ourselves becoming an egotistical exploitation of the world?

Friel resists the apocalyptic tendencies of the Postmodern, advancing instead what we might call a 'New Humanism', an existentialist aesthetics which is critical of, as well as informed by, certain aspects of Postmodernism. For he is as much concerned with reconciliation, reintegration, synthesis, accommodation as with their impossibility. He views the fragmentation of value in the modern world and, specifically in Ireland, as creating the conditions where, far from destroying our powers of ethical self-determination, actually offers them new opportunities, new forms and contexts, new possibilities for reshaping the world and renegotiating identity in ways which, without completely abandoning traditional moral value, may release us from the prison houses of outworn myths and stereotypes. 'That stereotyping', writes Seamus Deane, one of Friel's co-founders of Field Day, 'has caused a long colonial concussion. It is about time we put aside the idea of essence – that hungry Hegelian ghost looking for a stereotype to live in'.[51] Though he does not claim any vantage point of truth outside of culture, Friel represents a more positive version of the Postmodern than many of his contemporary artists and intellectuals. He offers the possibility of redemption at a personal, social and political level.

In fact, the central tension in his work reproduces a major opposition in modern philosophical thought, one represented by the contrast between Heidegger and Nietzsche, both of whom are often invoked as precursors of the Postmodern. Both Heidegger and Nietzsche rejected the grand narratives of the past and their strict rational basis and both recentred the bodily and the material, priviliging the non-rational, non-conceptualising, concretely embodied modes of the aesthetic as a way of knowing and representing. But where Heidegger emphasised a radical situatedness or embeddedness in the world – what he called 'being-in-the-world' – Nietzsche emphasised the possibilities for aesthetic transformation of that world. The only means of transformation is through words, through linguistic manipulation of the available 'little narratives'. The question is: on what ethical basis should these manipulations be made?

Patricia Waugh, who has developed an account of the postmodern based on the Heideggerean–Nietzschean polarity in *Practising Postmodernism, Reading Postmodernism* (1992), quotes Jean-François Lyotard's insistence that we must accept that ethical decisions will always be context-specific. What is 'just' or 'true' within the terms of one language game may not be so in terms of another:

> Yes, there is first a multiplicity of justices, each one of them defined in relation to the rules specific to each game. These rules prescribe what must be done so that a denotative statement, or an interrogative one, or a prescriptive one, etc., is received as such and recognized as 'good' in accordance with the criteria of the game to which it belongs. Justice here does not consist merely in the observance of the rules; as in all the games, it consists in working at the limits of what the rules permit, in order to invent new moves, perhaps new rules and therefore new games.[52]

This is precisely what Friel is doing in, say, *Translations*, where he operates at the limits or point of intersection of various discourses (Gaelic and English, positivistic and ontological, Heideggerean and Nietzschean) and, while demonstrating the impossibility of producing a totalising discourse, is concerned with exploring new positions or spaces that may be occupied in the interstices of the existing discourses. The existing 'grand narratives' may be adapted rather than entirely displaced by the imposition of alternatives. Friel recognises the way myths survive and continue to inform human attitudes and behaviour: traditions persist unself-consciously as well as through being consciously articulated. He emphasises being-in-the-world, a sense of situatedness and embeddedness in a locale and a culture, which places limits on the extent to which we can simply manipulate our own language games and on the extent of our fragmentation and dispersal into the roles and rules of the different contexts in which we find ourselves. He shows us ways in which we can reconcile the need for continuity and the need for change. This he does by suggesting the political and ethical potential in his concept of translation.

Traditional nationalists denounced the idea of translation as an unacceptable dilution and disfigurement of an original energy. Here is Thomas Davis, founder of the *Nation* newspaper in 1842, writing in his essay 'Our National Language':

> The language, which grows up with a people, is conformed to their organs, descriptive of their climate, constitution, and manners, mingles inseparably with their history and their soil, fitted beyond any other language to express their prevalent thoughts in the most natural and efficient way.
>
> To impose another language on such a people is to send their history adrift among the accidents of translation – 'tis to tear their identity from all places – 'tis to substitute arbitrary signs for picturesque and suggestive names – 'tis to cut off the entail of feeling, and separate the people from their forefathers by a deep gulf – 'tis to corrupt their very organs, and abridge their power of expression.[53]

Friel, however, subscribes to a more modern concept of translation propounded by such thinkers as George Steiner (passages from whose book *After Babel: Aspects of Language and Translation* are echoed in Friel's play *Translations*[54]) which regards all communication – not just that between different nations, races or social groups, but also that between individuals – as an act of translation. Friel understands both the resistance to translation, and the consequences of a failure to translate. *Translations*, his great play of 1980 which launched the Field Day Theatre Company, emphasises how our perception of and attitude to the world we inhabit are crucially determined by the language that we use. Hugh, the old schoolmaster, explains to his English visitor, Lieutenant Yolland, the special quality of the Irish language: 'Yes, it is a rich language, Lieutenant, full of the mythologies of fantasy and hope and self-deception – a syntax opulent with tomorrows. It is our response to mud cabins and a diet of potatoes; our only method of replying to . . . inevitabilities'.[55] Hugh indicates the ironic disparity between the rich imagination of the Irish people and the poverty of their everyday lives, seeing the former as a means of compensating for the latter, a strategy for survival in difficult circumstances. He also recognises that the proclivity to fantasy and eloquence unfits Irish people for practical action, though the note of criticism is tempered with sympathetic understanding of the plight of his people and with affection and respect for the 'rich language' they have evolved. But he does not shrink from the awareness that as long as the people see their situation as 'inevitable' there is nothing to be done. Change is out of the question. Nostalgia for origins and uncritical embracement of what is dogmatically given guarantee the *status quo*. The best the people can do is reconcile themselves to their fate. What Friel wants to show, however, is that 'reality' is constructed, not 'given', and that there are different ways in which the world *can* be constructed. Hugh outlines one method of replying to 'inevitabilities', but the speech break before he utters the word 'inevitabilities' (the break functioning like quotation marks) acts to indicate his own resistance to the notion of 'inevitabilities'. Hugh, that is, speaks ironically. We can reply to 'inevitabilities' by no longer regarding them as 'inevitable' at all. We can refuse to be locked into the given order of things as if it were the 'only' or natural order. Friel plays with the possibility of critically reinterpreting or reframing the received reality, of 'translating' the past, so that the present can be positively transformed.

The concept of translation which informs the play represents an anti-authoritarian stance. Acknowledging the possible forms of co-operation, opposition and interaction between different communities of language and attitude, translation affirms both change and continuity. It is a means of acknowledging cultural implication without being transfixed by culture. The tradition cannot be denied utterly, but it can be reformulated, its elements creatively deformed and dissolved so that they can be recombined into new 'mythologies' and a new 'syntax'. Translation recognises the way in which the mind is structured through the languages of a cultural tradition, but equally implies that there should be no mindless acceptance of the past, no passive submission to the 'given' reality. It calls for active reworking of the established discourses, a sifting and selecting and rewriting so that what is useful may be retrieved and retained. The stability that comes from a sense of continuity or tradition is valued, but so is the capacity to adapt to new circumstances. Sentimental nostalgia for the idealised landscapes of the past is to be avoided every bit as much as a deadly kind of 'scorched-earth policy' which would obliterate all traces of previous landmarkings as part of a continual process of 'making it new'. Translation allows us not only to understand the past but to experience continuity of value even though we cannot escape our own historical condition into some neutral, 'disinterested', ideologically-free zone of being. It signifies Friel's belief in the urgent need to find a point of balance between respect for what is valuable in the collective historical experience on one hand and, on the other, the impulse to experiment, to play with and work upon the given reality in order to open up new possibilities of meaning. Translation is identification with critical distance. It traces difference through similarity. It acknowledges the inevitable institutionalisation of certain 'fictions', their elevation into 'truths', without forfeiting the possibilities of disruption from within. It is a form of simultaneously repeating and re-working the original text. If 'truth' can no longer be revealed, it may be positively renegotiated through a process of translation. If there is no longer a self-evident 'metanarrative' to ground ethical value, we must refashion the materials given to us in the world. As Waugh notes, we can no longer unself-consciously inhabit a single myth, but we may self-consciously manipulate the fragments of a diverse range of myths.[56]

Translations is such a self-conscious examination of the ethical implications of the loss of a grand narrative of history, in which Friel encourages us to manipulate the world, but also affirms the value of tradition. He offers us the challenge of shaping the new through a translation or reformulation of the old. In Friel's world we will not find absolute truth but neither will we be 'lost in the funhouse' of endless play and possibility. Identity involves free choice, but free choice constrained by recognition of others, by a sense of the collective historical experience, by complex emotional attachments, personal, religious and national. We are born into a network of relations in which past creations or 'fictions' place constraints on our own aesthetic creations. An authentic self can only be created in full acknowledgement of past actions and values. Friel seeks to rescue us from fragmentation without imprisoning us again in oppressive dogma. He recognises the potential of the aesthetic to negotiate between the two poles of Transformation and Being-in-the-world in order to achieve self-fulfilment. Cultural tradition provides some sense of that embeddedness which saves us from the agonies of disintegration, while the transformational capabilities of the individual imagination allows for a reshaping of the condition of being-in-the-world. Existence becomes a continuous process of 'translation' and renegotiation involving creative freedom but also recognition of limitation. Because the relationship between us and our world keeps changing, no statement of that relationship is final. There is always a range of possible perspectives; there are always many possible relations between man and his world. The need for belief has a repetitive pattern. Any particular 'fiction' can only be provisional and temporary. This means that we must maintain a constant dialectical rapport between the deconstructive activity of critical judgment (reason) which unveils the fiction's negative, alienating content, and the creative activity of our fiction-making powers (imagination) engaged in a process of symbolic transformation and answering our need for belief. Thus, Friel suggests ways in which Hegelian essentialism may be modified without collapsing entirely into ethical relativism (Lyotard's 'just gaming') or inert consensus (Richard Rorty's concept of truth as culturally and communally determined). He encourages the maturity of being able to live with ambiguity, contradiction, uncertainty and paradox and of still being capable of belief. He demonstrates an art of open dialogue between self and other. Autonomy is attainable, not through self-assertion and elimination of the 'Other', but through a close dialectical relationship between self and 'Other'.

In *Translations* the English visitor, Lieutenant Yolland, laments the fact that although he may learn 'the password of the tribe' he will never be able to penetrate to the 'private core' of Irishness.[57] Yolland expresses a Bergsonian notion of the self as an essential entity, an irreducible 'private core' distinct from the superficial 'public' personality which people see in the world. The 'private core' pre-exists divisions into body and mind and is so profoundly constituted that conceptual thought, the language of habit, must always betray it. Characteristically, Friel emphasises a sense of the intellect as something which, far from reflecting Platonic essences or pure structures of reason, is a pathetically inadequate means of formulating experience in order to establish a provisional working model of the world. The aesthetic, however, by breaking down routine habits of perception and offering itself as a form of non-conceptualising, sensuously embodied language, may be the means of discovery through creation. T. S. Eliot stated the idea thus:

> Poetry may help to break up the conventional modes of perception and valuation which are perpetually forming and make people see the world afresh, or some new part of it. It may make us from time to time a little more aware of the deeper unnamed feelings which form the substratum of our being, to which we rarely penetrate; for our lives are mostly a constant evasion of ourselves, and an evasion of the visible and sensible world.[58]

One's deepest emotional and personal life arises out of and is expressed through a sense of being-in-the-world which cannot be rationally formulated. In Heidegger, Eliot and Friel, the 'core' is always an embodied condition. But Friel also emphasises how such embodiment may mean alienation: tradition can be oppressive as well as nurturing. And when the bankruptcy of the old myths becomes apparent and our embeddedness degenerates into alienation we must draw upon the potential of the conscious mind to effect an emancipatory break with tradition. Tradition, which enables us to make sense of our world, is itself a product of a community's understanding of itself. This understanding is always being modified; it is never for 'always', as Hugh in *Translations* emphasises to Maire.[59] Past is continually shaped by present, present by past. The potential of the conscious mind to reshape traditional values is a necessary aspect of the project of articulating new emancipated identities. In Heideggerean or Bergsonian terms of sinking into an atavistic darkness, the individual may only end up becoming 'fossilised'.[60] The backward-looking, archaeological impulse may lead to an inert conservatism. If we fail to accept the challenge of authentic self-creation we are imprisoned in others' versions of the world. Equally, of course, the Nietzschean mode of self-creation, while offering the possibility of freedom from the narratives of others, can lead to radical denial of the 'Other', a nihilistic refusal of social responsibility, ethical obligation and personal relation which is ultimately self-consuming. Man can will nothingness: an individual, a nation, a culture deprived of positive goals destroys itself by willing the last thing left to it to will – its own destruction. We can see this kind of willing in action in plays such as *Crystal and Fox* and *Faith Healer* where the desire to penetrate to the 'private core' takes the form of a kind of negative capability which presses toward non-identity, non-being. In accepting the challenge of constructing their own 'fictions', Fox Melarkey and Frank Hardy turn their backs on their traditional obligations as husbands, fathers and employers, finally succumbing to an impious nihilism, a suicidal impulse, the desire for mergence and the peace of utter dissolution. If man does not learn to overcome this imperialist Nietzschean subjectivity he is doomed. Such learning means that he must return to the sources of his humanity and rethink the sense of Being. In *Crystal and Fox* and *Faith Healer*, the humility of Friel's dramatic form which so notably resists authoritarian closure, emphasises the futility of the central characters' quest and declares the impossibility of ever securely reaching the 'private core'.

How to reconcile the possibilities for aesthetic self-creation offered by modernity with ethical obligations which tie us to traditional fixed identities shaped and donated by others and lived out every moment in the body itself: this is the question all Friel's plays confront. In a modern world of proliferating, mutually contradictory language games, ancient grand narratives still provide some anchorage. Friel's dialectic of Transformation and Being-in-the-world offers a genuinely ethically motivated aestheticism. The great thing is to be able to escape what Harold Bloom calls 'the anxiety of influence', to avoid being imprisoned in others' patternings, in abstraction, and to be able to see the thing itself as it really is. This is Friel's big theme from *Freedom of the City* to *Translations*.

Friel's concept of 'translation' acknowledges the tension between what Bakhtin calls 'centripetal' and 'centrifugal' forces. Bakhtin sees the 'centripetal' as the way a culture and a language always work in the direction of the establishment of 'sociopolitical and cultural centralization'.[61] This movement, says Peter Messent, in *New Readings of the American Novel*, 'is in the direction of a closed system; the attempt to establish an officially recognised "unitary" or "monoglossic" language, a recognised cultural voice or literary language which goes hand in hand with an officially recognised set of national values'.[62] In dynamic tension with this is the 'centrifugal', 'the forces of disunification and decentralization endlessly developing new forms which parody, criticise and generally undermine the unitary ambitions of language. This model of language is chiefly characterised by its sense of struggle at the heart of existence. These opposed pressures keep language mobile and are responsible for its transformations'.[63] To the extent that Friel favours the 'centrifugal', he asserts his commitment to the pluralistic, to social diversity and change rather than to the hierarchical, the traditional or any idea of an absolute authority. The 'centrifugal' impulse, as Messent argues, 'ensures against a fixed, rigid, ordered concept of culture and emphasises, rather, its multilanguaged aspects, assigning qualities of health and vitality to those ongoing forces of decentralisation and disunification which the authorities and ruling classes of any group or society would try to deny'.[64] Thus, for example, Friel continues the hybrid tradition of tragicomedy, a form which is created out of the breakdown of the stable, traditional categories of pure tragedy and pure comedy.

Of course, comedy itself – and Friel's comedy in particular – has an obvious 'centrifugal' tendency, the function of humour being, as Bakhtin explains, to undermine authority:

It is precisely laughter ... that destroys any hierarchical distance. Laughter has a remarkable power of making an object come up close, of drawing it into a zone of crude contact where one can finger it familiarly on all sides, turn it upside down, inside out ... break open its external shell, look into its centre, doubt it, take it apart, dismember it. ... Laughter demolishes fear and piety before an object, before a world ... is a vital factor in laying down that prerequisite for fearlessness without which it would be impossible to approach the world realistically.[65]

Bakhtin transposes the model of carnival festivity into a literary context, using the term 'carnivalization' to refer to the process whereby conventional hierarchical barriers are removed, established order is dissolved, official systems are comically overturned or decentred and the body is liberated from puritanical oppressions. 'Carnival', as Messent notes, is associated with masquerade, the assumption of masks, false identities which blur any boundaries between high and low. It calls for a plot which will create 'meeting and contact-points for heterogeneous people'.[66] It is, above all, associated with laughter – a laughter 'directed toward something higher – toward a shift of authorities and truths'.[67] Obvious forms of Friel's 'carnivalistic' overthrow of the dominant discourse would be Private Gar's play-acting and parodying in *Philadelphia*, Shane's Dionysian influence in *The Gentle Island*, Skinner's irreverent 'parlour-games' in *Freedom of the City*, Fox's theatricalities in *Crystal and Fox*, Casimir's croquet-playing in *Aristocrats*, Frank Hardy's 'performance' in *Faith Healer*, Yolland and Maire's love duet in *Translations*, the dancing in *Dancing at Lughnasa*, which infiltrates even the strict, closed world of the sisters and represents the overturning of official systems of life by an unofficial folk culture and the energies associated with it.

It is Friel's emphasis on 'synthesising', 'negotiating' and 'translating' that signals his refusal to capitulate to the nihilistic implications of the 'Postmodern Apocalypse'. For Friel, the text is plural, but he does not give up entirely on an organicist conception of the drama. Plays such as *Faith Healer* and *Translations* forcefully demonstrate a 'polyphonic' rather than 'monologic' tendency in Friel's writing – the refusal to attempt to bind together the disparate voices and explicitly to counter the 'centrifugal' social and psychological forces and, yet, even if the dramatist is much less confident than in earlier times, even if he is no longer the God-like creator, he is still a crafty synthesizer of the forms of difference in the individual, in language and in society, capable of giving us the satisfying sense of an emotional working through, ultimately to arrive at some point of equilibrium. Orchestrating a range of diverse voices, he confronts members of each community of discourse with the diversity within their own voices as well as the divergences among the range of voices in the community, in the interests of promoting a mutually revealing responsiveness. In doing so, his plays represent neither a fluidity of indifferent acceptance nor a rigid dogmatism, but something in between – a strenuous, open-ended dialogism. The drama, as epitomised by _Translations_, one could say, expresses a morality of flexibility, resisting the stance of the pure relativist who asserts there is no truth to be found and, equally, that of the authoritarian who offers us definitive verdicts. It forces re-examination rather than outright rejection of the so-called 'humanist' concerns of traditional drama. Clearly addressing the Postmodern agenda, and using a variety of self-reflexive forms, it challenges political consensus, revises concepts of individual identity and history, and unmasks the hidden falsehoods in the official modes and processes of symbolic legitimation. The representational norms of the description of character, plot, history and morality still count, but so too does the newer concern with language, discourse and rhetoric that is more usually associated with poetic analysis. The theatre is no longer a theatre of ritual demonstration simply enacting an agreed Truth (as it was in medieval times or continues to be in Agit Prop theatre), but as a forum for presenting a plurality of fictions it can still provide an indispensible contribution to social and spiritual well-being. A principal part of Friel's dramatic enterprise is to expose the unexamined or corrupt myths that have animated Irish life for too long and, as the establishment of the Field Day Company would demonstrate, to affirm drama's place at the centre of Irish civilised life where, without surrendering the necessary modern independence of any doctrinal presuppositions, it can fulfil an important social mission. 'Poetry makes nothing happen',[68] says W. H. Auden: 'The fiction that we read affects our behaviour towards our fellow men, affects our patterns of ourselves',[69] says T. S. Eliot. Clearly the effects of poetry, fiction and drama can range from the direct to the indirect and highly mediated, but we have only to watch a child at play to recognise how human beings characteristically explore and gain mastery over their surroundings through complex imaginative strategies. Field Day is based on the belief that such imaginative strategies do 'make things happen', however indirectly, and that the public ritual of the theatre is one of the most potent, as well as one of the most sophisticated, ways we have of exploring imaginatively our social, cultural and emotional world. As the Field Day writers have emphasised, by enlarging our imaginative capacities and experiences, we may alter our understanding and capacity to act in the world.

Friel asserts imagination. Imagination is creative; it loves fiction, it runs beyond the empirical evidence. But for Friel imagination is also conscience; it has an ethical dimension. To deal with ordinary life imaginatively is to deal with it somewhat strictly, it is not a case of 'anything goes'. The essential quality of Friel's art is power: power that includes Appollonian mastery, control, carefully orchestrated effect as well as Dionysian passion, energy, imagination; the kind of power produced when thought and feeling are kept under the constant pressure of form. He resists finality, because finality (as Frank Hardy makes explicit in *Faith Healer*) is death. What I wish to show is that Friel values above any 'truth' or ideology the energy of conflict, the challenge of synthesis, which is the essence of drama. Denis Donoghue's description of Yeats in the Fontana Modern Masters Series, is equally relevant to Friel: 'His mind needs at least two terms, one hardly less compelling than the other: action and knowledge, essence and existence, power and wisdom, history and symbol, the word and the world, vision and reality, tradition and transformation. Any one of these may engage his feeling, but the feeling quickly wants to touch its opposite. The pairs are entertained for the tension – the drama – they engender, the energy they release.' It is foolish, then, to try and recruit Friel – at least Friel the artist – to a cause. He speaks through his characters, imagining feelings and situations different from his own. The remarkable omission from the Frielian calculus is the Ulster Protestant Unionist factor; this is the 'Other' which perhaps represents the ultimate challenge to his imaginative powers.

Barthes and Bakhtin, Heidegger and Nietzsche have been invoked for the ways in which they allow good critical access to certain aspects of Friel's work, but that work certainly does not represent any radical break with more traditional modes. Friel's interest in opening us to the dispersion of ideological forces, his carnivalising impulse with its antagonism to the blanket of holism can be seen to continue what the formalist tradition of Anglo-American literary criticism has repeatedly given us this century. I. A. Richards, in the early 1920s, recommended the use of irony as a means of making the artwork an alternative to action by 'bringing in . . . the opposite, the complementary impulse',[70] thereby neutralising the dominant impulse to act on a single side. Cleanth Brooks and the New Critics extended the paradoxical notion of a constant inconstancy, with its anti-ideological implications, to a more explicitly formalistic doctrine.[71] John Crowe Ransom was clearly aware of the political analogue of the antitotalising, anti-authoritarian character which he believed was special to poetry. The poem, he wrote, was 'like a democratic state, so to speak, which realizes the ends of a state without sacrificing the personal character of its citizens'.[72] It is 'democratic' because of the freedom of its elements to be independent, indeed 'irrelevant', as they hold out against the overriding structure. Though Ransom has lyric poetry in mind, the idea of the artwork as a space in which the attempt is made to confront the 'Other', to work with and organise a range of contending forces is relevant to Friel's concept of drama and it is relevant to Field Day and to Field Day's most ambitious project – the monumental anthology of Irish writing designed 'to introduce or reintroduce new or relatively ignored material', with the aim of 'revealing and confirming the existence of a continuous tradition, contributed to by all groups, sects and parties, in which the possibility of a more generous and hospitable notion of Ireland's cultural achievement will emerge as the basis for a more ecumenical and eirenic approach to the deep and apparently implacable problems which confront the island today'.[73] But if Friel continues the idea of art as a tension between opposing impulses enabling the audience to avoid a reductive opting for single meaning, the thing that keeps his drama so constantly challenging and invigorating is the scrupulous care he takes to guard against letting this ideological commitment to equipoise congeal into a set of unquestioned presuppositions. He refuses to turn the theatre into a 'closed' space: he relaxes the traditional emphasis on convergence within the text.

In what follows, I attempt to offer some placement of Friel's work in relation to both Postmodernism and traditional humanism: to demonstrate, finally, that while the forms of his dramatic statement may have a Postmodernist inflection, he is not essentially a Postmodern writer; to show that his affinity with the great liberal humanist tradition admits not the least complacency. The plays of the 1960s will be used to focus an investigation into his dismantling of the unified subject, while his plays of the 1970s will form the basis of a study of his disruptions of the unified text. These subversions are seen to allow for the reactivation of repressed forces in the self and the culture. Thus, after the emphasis on Friel's deconstructive tendencies in Chapters 2 and 3, Chapter 4 will examine the plays of the 1980s in the light of the Field Day concern with rewriting history and will highlight Friel's affinity with the great nineteenth century exponents of the liberal humanist tradition – Chekhov and Turgenev – whose work he has 'translated'. A concluding chapter will concentrate on his plays of the 1990s in which his probing of the problem of language gives way to some bold dramatic experiments based on a notion of the primacy of the unconscious, of the bodily and material, of desire, of libidinal impulses, and a concern to explore the possibilities of a non-rational, non-discursive and non-verbal communication – the possibility of a more authentic, less divisive expression before or beyond the duplicities of language. My contention is that Friel's art is an effort to reconcile the tensions between traditional value and Postmodern *skepsis*, between past and present, the ideal and the real, the 'centrifugal' and the 'centripetal', tragedy and comedy, the spiritual and the secular, memory and fact, music and language, between the rational, verbal world and the intuitive, preverbal world, in order to offer a truly comprehensive vision. In attempting to give an account of Friel's art as such a force field of powerful energies, I am left finally to admit the impossibility of pinning down this elusive, complex and fascinating talent.

2
Subject
Dismantling the Unified Subject: The Plays of the 1960s

THE SPLIT SUBJECT

In Friel's plays of the 1960s, we may examine the process whereby the playwright dismantles the unified subject, throwing it into confusion and contradiction – a disruption which is the source of meaning and action and of possible change. What Friel gives us is not merely character in a state of inner conflict, a common enough feature of classic realism, rather, the split subject is represented in a form of discourse which permits us to glimpse the concept of a division in subjectivity itself. The discontinuity of the ego and the explicit division of the subject become a structural principle of these plays. Friel wants to recentre that which is fantastic, subversive, antirational, transgressive, that which is disruptive of order, that which provokes a breach where we are forced to question ourselves and our world. By retrieving the *id* from the margins or depths of literary presentation, he reacts against culture's silencing of doubt and unreason. Such forces which threaten a tradition of rationalism have been apprehended as inimical to cultural order from at least as far back as Plato's *Republic*. Plato expelled from his ideal Republic all transgressive energies, which included fantasy, eroticism, violence, madness, laughter, nightmares and dreams, blasphemy, lamentation, uncertainty, female energy, excess. The *id* is made invisible in Plato's Republic and in the tradition of high rationalism which it fostered. All subversive social and psychological forces are expelled or censored in order to maintain the rational, unified state. Following Freud, Friel explores the dark, neglected recesses of consciousness, probing areas of activity, thought and feeling which are hidden from us in everyday life, but which contain a kind of ultimate reality – the unconscious: a region in which deep desires and fears are repressed and which manifest themselves in symbolic modes of

76

expression, such as dreaming. Friel is engaged in a quest for ways to embody these powerful repressed forces, to express the 'unsaid' of personality and culture.

Thus, in *Philadelphia, Here I Come!*, through the character of Private, Friel gives a voice to the *id*; in *The Enemy Within*, as the title implies, the irruption of submerged, unruly forces – the 'enemy within' – threatens St Columb's Christian mission in life; in *The Loves of Cass McGuire*, Cass herself, in the beginning at least, personifies the disruptive energy – the body which exists as a potent presence within Friel's concept of individualism – that the dominant culture wishes to marginalise, censor or silence; in *Crystal and Fox*, repressed desire results in a permanently split subject: Fox, like Gar or Columba or Cass, has a dark, subversive side to his nature which refuses to be bound by social convention and towards which Friel would seem to have deeply ambivalent feelings.

In Friel's analysis of the nature of the disruptive force, he shows that it is not simply negative and self-destructive, nor simply the source of confusion and contradiction: in giving voice to the suppressed contradictions in the subject, he also suggests a creative potential. Resistance to the dominant social values can lead to criminal deviance (Cass, Fox), but it also keeps open the possibility of triumphant self-discovery. Whichever, the subject is a process, not a fixity. In the plays of the 1960s, the emphasis falls on 'subjection' rather than 'transformation'. I have used the term 'subject', much favoured by modern theorists, in preference to 'individual' because notions of 'subjection' – both linguistic and social – are especially relevant to Friel's drama at this stage in his career. He is concerned with the way the individual's identity is substantially constructed from the range of languages available to him or her, just as the grammatical subject depends for its function and meaning on its relationship to the other words in the sentence. Allied to this is Friel's sense of the individual as subject to the forces of control in his or her society, just as the individual in a cultural and political sense is the subject of the political state and subject to its laws.

Traditional narrative often puts the unified subject to the test, threatening to split it apart, but traditional narrative eventually moves towards closure and the reinstatement of order, whether it be the old order restored or a new one installed. Decisive choices are made, identity is established, conflict removed and any threat to our own subjectivity removed. But in *Philadelphia*, for example, Friel refuses to smooth over contradiction to allow us as readers or audience a position which is unified and knowing. We are enlisted in the questioning process, alternately sympathising with and critically distanced from the central character. Friel's ironic 'resolutions' encourage us to live with contradiction and seek to make that kind of conclusion emotionally satisfying and artistically complete.

'If there is a characteristic image of Irish theatre in the last three decades, it is the image of the split personality',[1] writes Fintan O'Toole. He adduces the examples of Friel's Private Gar; Hugh Leonard's Charlie in *Da*, who is also played by two different actors, one to represent Charlie at seventeen, the other when he is forty-one; and Tom Kilroy's Brendan Bracken and his *alter ego* William Joyce in *Double Cross*, who are played by the same actor. There is a relation between the subject in crisis and crisis in the social formation. The glimpses Friel gives us in his discursive practice of the subject as a process rather than a fixity parallel the transformation taking place in Irish cultural life arising out of the tensions between tradition and modernity. As O'Toole also writes, the 'idea of a uniform society' in Ireland 'fell apart' in the late 1950s and early 1960s: 'We literally could not sustain the notion of a single Ireland, self-sufficient and bound in both its culture and economy.'[2]

THE ENEMY WITHIN

The Enemy Within (1962), was Friel's second performed stage play, but the first to receive a major production, when it was presented by the Abbey in August 1962. It was also the first of his plays that Friel was prepared to stand over: 'It's not good but it was a commendable sort of play. There's nothing very wrong with it and there's certainly nothing very good about it'.[3] The play was subsequently broadcast as a radio play in 1963 and nationally on television in 1965. It centres what is to become a major concept in Friel's drama – the 'enemy within', the submerged, 'private', unruly forces in personality and in culture, which threaten the established order.

Friel examines the figure of Columba, who was born in Gartan, Co. Donegal, c. 521 AD, founded monasteries in Derry, c. 546, Durrow, c. 556 and probably Kells, among them. In 563 he left Ireland for a 'bare, black exile' (*EW*, p. 21) on Iona, an island off the west coast of Scotland, where the play is set. Friel concentrates on the private man, a charismatic, worldly personality who struggles against 'the enemy within' to maintain a fearless commitment to his vocation. From the Christian point of view, the 'enemy within' is unregenerate 'violent Adam' (*EW*, p. 46), unruly self-will which refuses moderation, discipline and obedience. It is the instinct of '*Non serviam*'. Grillaan, Columba's 'spiritual director' (*EW*, p. 32), points out Columba's lack of 'prudence and moderation' (*EW*, p. 32), his 'excesses' which are 'surrenderings to this Adam' (*EW*, p. 47).

The play is based on the visits of three outsiders to the isolated island community, each of whom acts as a catalyst, stirring the enemy within Columba, putting him to the test. The first is Brian, on a recruiting campaign to secure Columba's support for his cousin, Hugh, whose kingdom in Ireland is threatened by certain greedy, murderous members of his own family. Brian is a clever manipulator and knows how to draw Columba into the political arena. He begins by appealing to Columba's family pride, his special relationship with Hugh, reminding Columba of a debt he owes his cousin, who has stood by him in the past. Another of Brian's tacks is that which demonises the enemy, the terrible Colman and the two Cumines. This ignoble confederacy has obtained the backing of the 'mad' monk Sirinus, under whose leadership they have managed to turn a family feud into a holy war against the 'irreligious' Hugh who is without any Christian sponsor. Columba is outraged by the gross injustice of the imputation that Hugh is a pagan ('Hugh is a Christian and a good one' (*EW*, p. 29)) and is increasingly worried about what will become of the fifteen churches that he founded in Tyrone and Tirconaill if they are left to the mercy of this emergent political order of murderers and madmen. Brian forces Columba to confront the question of whether or not a strict separation can or should be maintained between Church and State, between individual conscience and communal responsibility. 'A priest or politician – which?' (*EW*, p. 33) Grillaan asks, reminding Columba that his embroilment in Irish politics will disqualify him as a spiritual leader: 'He that loveth father or mother more than Me is not worthy of Me' (*EW*, p. 33). The terms of the argument are recognisably those which are carried forward into much of Friel's succeeding work: the protagonist (who is always, in important ways, a figure of the artist) is caught between conflicting loyalties: on one hand, the claims of the world, of social responsibility, politics, community, on the other, the quest for transcendence.

In the end, Columba cannot resist Brian's call to become a champion of his people and lead them against their earthly enemies.

Columba finally responds to the political imperative, not as 'a poor priest' (*EW*, p. 30), but as a proud leader of men: 'Royal blood that answers to the call of its people! Kings of Leinster and rulers of the land of Conall! (*EW*, p. 32). The 'enemy within' manifests itself as a lust for earthly glory, for adventure and excitement. When Columba returns to Iona, his account of his Irish expedition emphasises the excitements of the rout, the eating and drinking, seeing old friends; he even seems disappointed there wasn't more violence and blood-shed: 'There was no battle because the rats wouldn't stand for a battle' (*EW*, p. 39). The climax of the whole expedition is Hugh's impromptu marriage to a girl he abducted on his return from 'chasing the MacDiarmuid mob' (*EW*, p. 40). Everything Columba says unwittingly confirms the justice of Grillaan's earlier denunciation of the latest sordid Irish 'brawl' (*EW*, p. 32) in which Columba is proposing to involve himself. What finally brings Columba to his senses is the news of the death, in his absence, of the simple, faithful old scribe Caornan. While Caornan was dying on Iona, Columba was 'singing and feasting and laughing' (*EW*, p. 44) in Ireland. Recalling the earlier story of Columba's miraculous knowledge of the death of Finnian, another old friend, which came to him in a vision when he was in the chapel 'saying a mouthful of prayers' (*EW*, p. 18), we may judge the distance Columba has travelled from his religious vocation.

Columba's sense of guilt at failing in his religious duty provokes further violent behaviour. He asks Grillaan to impose 'the most severe penances you can think of' (*EW*, p. 46): 'Let me fast. Give me Caornan's chains. Forbid me my bed for five years. But conquer me, Grillaan! Crush this violent Adam into subjection!' (*EW*, p. 46). Grillaan points out that such masochistic excess is only another expression of unbridled self-will, another form of disobedience, and that Columba must learn to 'live the Rule of Iona to the letter' (*EW*, p. 47). With no relief from his guilt, Columba cannot bear to listen to Oswald's 'hero-worship' (*EW*, p. 50). Oswald, the English novice who has just arrived on Iona, is the second of the outsiders by whom Columba is tested. When Columba lashes out at him, destroying the young man's dreams, Oswald runs away and Columba exhibits even more extreme behaviour. In an effort to alleviate his guilt, he throws himself into a 'mad search' (*EW*, p. 54) for Oswald, which lasts for many weeks. During this time, he neglects his monastic responsibilities and Grillaan once again tries to recall him from private obsession to 'the wise discipline of the monastery' (*EW*,

p. 47): 'Give it up, Columba. Give it up. This obsession – it's bad for your body, it's bad for your soul. Oswald's gone. What matter? Not a month passes but a new student arrives. Forget him. We need you here, Columba. The monastery needs you. We all need you' (*EW*, p. 57).

Yet another aspect of 'the enemy within' can be seen in this passage:

> Out at the corn there, Cormac was cutting, and I was behind him tying, and the sun was warm on my back, and I was stooped over, so that this bare, black exile was shrunk to a circle around my feet. And I was back in Tirconaill; and Cormac was Eoghan, my brother, humming to himself; and the dog that was barking was Ailbe, our sheep-dog; and there were trees at the bottom of the field as long as I did not look; and the blue sky was quick with larks as long as I did not lift my head; and the white point of Errigal mountain was behind my shoulder as long as I kept my eyes on the ground. And when we got to the bottom of the field, Cormac called to me, 'Look what I found! A horse shoe! That's for luck!' But I did not look up because he was still Eoghan, my brother, and the earth was still Gartan earth; and the sound of the sea was the water of Gartan Lough; and any minute mother would come to the head of the hill and strike the iron triangle to summon us in for food. And when Cormac spoke I did not answer him because I could not leave them. (*EW*, p. 21)

Columba's speech has the rhythm of dreaming, of desire. What we see of Eoghan in person and what we hear of 'damned Ireland' (*EW*, p. 70) later in the play qualify the idealised vision of home and family evoked here. The tense and passionate lyricism, which is the expression of 'the inner man', 'the soul' (*EW*, p. 21), the voice of instinct and emotion struggling against the constraints of religious discipline, represents an extension of Friel's dramatic range beyond the native vigour of the domestic idiom reserved for the monastic community on Iona, and the barbarous plainness of the political mode of Brian and, later, of Eoghan and Aedh. Columba's escape from 'bare, black exile' is tinged with a residual paganism, a susceptibility to a kind of natural magic. He still responds to what Heaney calls 'the god in the tree'.[4] Columba resists the public myth of himself because it denies the free, natural, and, in Christian terms, unregenerate, compulsions of the self which he gives a voice to in this speech.

Columba is impatient with the kind of celebrity which he has achieved: 'As a builder of churches! As a builder of schools! As an organiser! But the inner man – the soul – chained irrevocably to the earth, to the green wooded earth of Ireland' (*EW*, p. 21). In a manner similar to Hugh O'Neill's refusal of Lombard's reductive categorisation in *Making History*, Columba enters a plea on behalf of his humanity. The myth of Columba denies the doubts and conflicts of the inner man, it suppresses complexity, condensing individual diversity into an inspirational model of wholeness. This is, of course, what Oswald idolises. Oswald sees only a hero, not the real man. In his story of the 'Flag of Columba' Columba mocks the myth-makers, those who have created the fiction of the slab of rock on which he once slept and which ever since is supposed to possess magical powers to cure the homesickness of the prospective emigrant who spends a night on it before leaving Ireland: 'I'll tell you the explanation', jokes Columba, 'the night on the rock paralyses them with rheumatism and when they do remember Tirconaill afterwards, they curse it to the depths of hell' (*EW*, p. 22).

The 'enemy within' is a force in Columba which resists Christian *disciplina*: it is also the mark of humanity, of sentient life. It is what denies monolith and stagnation. It is the irrepressible 'life-force' itself, the love of adventure and risk, relish of the physical world, the willingness to accept the 'challenge of a new territory':

> I know. I know. Prudence, you say, and patience, and counsel – the virtues of old men with wet chins and shapeless feet. But I cannot *feel* my sixty-six years, Grillaan. I am burdened with this strong, active body that responds to the whistle of movement, the fight of the sail, the swing of the axe, the warm breadth of a horse beneath it, the challenge of a new territory.   (*EW*, p. 46)

From the beginning, Friel emphasises Columba's massive vitality: 'Columba is 66 but looks a man 16 years younger. There is vitality, verve, almost youthfulness in every gesture. He has an open healthy face. He looks for no subservience from the community; they are like brothers together. When he comes on the atmosphere is breezy and vital' (*EW*, p. 16). It is Columba's religion which is called into question when it calls for the suppression of such attractive and vital, natural human energies. If politics is a dirty word in the play, the religious life is not beyond question either. Sanctity is questionable because it requires Columba's complete withdrawal from the world;

politics is questionable because it demands his complete immersion in the world; both are objectionable because they demand submission of the 'private' self to external, public pressures and expectations.

There are three main frames of reference in the play – the religious, the political and the personal, each in competition with the others, each with its own 'enemy within'. Friel refuses a single point of view and brings these three points of view into unresolved collision or contradiction. From the Christian point of view, the 'enemy within' is 'violent Adam', the force which diffuses the sense of vocation and sets Columba at odds with 'the rules of Iona'. From the political point of view, the 'enemy within' are those religious scruples which disallow Columba from involving himself in the affairs of his people; from yet another standpoint, the enemy is the perennial human susceptibility to any kind of salvationist glamour, whether religious or political, which elevates abstraction and system above concrete reality. In the dramatic kaleidoscope which Friel creates, Columba is thus variously seen: to Oswald he is 'a saint' (*EW*, p. 50), Eoghan leaves the monastery shouting 'Coward! Traitor!' (*EW*, p. 70) at him, to Grillaan he is unregenerate man, yet a loved and respected 'father' (*EW*, p. 47). As a composite of disparate urges and aspirations, Columba can find no point of balance between the various aspects of his personality and instead veers wildly from one extreme to another, one moment bowed and penitential, the next proud, reckless and violent.

Columba's third set of visitors from outside, his brother, Eoghan and nephew, Aedh, reiterate the political imperative, calling for Columba to lead an assault on a Pictish clan which has abducted Aidh's wife. The meeting with Brian consists largely of Columba's protests against the claims of politics and then, characteristically, a sudden reversal when actions contradict words and he starts preparing to leave for Ireland; in the interview with Eoghan and Aedh, which is a mirror image of the earlier scene with Brian, he seems to accept the inevitability of his political involvement, then, to his kinsmen's great surprise and disappointment, suddenly digs his heels in and refuses to cooperate: 'I'm not going' (*EW*, p. 68).

This decision, however, can hardly be seen to mark a resolution of the profound division in Columba. As soon as he has made it, his speech, more divided than ever, reaches a pitch of agonised lyricism:

Get out of my life! Go back to those damned mountains and seductive hills that have robbed me of my Christ! You soaked my

sweat! You sucked my blood! You stole my manhood, my best
years! What more do you demand of me, damned Ireland? My
soul? My immortal soul? Damned, damned, damned Ireland! –
(His voice breaks.) Soft, green Ireland – beautiful, green Ireland –
my lovely green Ireland. O my Ireland.   (*EW*, p. 70)

Having sent Eoghan and Aedh packing, Columba still cannot whole-
heartedly embrace the subject positions offered him by the religious
order and in consequence he is still not able to give meaning to his
world; he is still trapped in non-meaning. Seeking release from
division, he goes to the chapel to pray 'because I am empty' (*EW*,
p. 71). 'Confusion', as Hugh, the old schoolmaster, in *Translations*
says, 'is not an ignoble condition' (*SP*, p. 446): it can, however, as
Hugh also knows, be a source of great pain.

   Oswald reappears at the end, returning to the monastery 'because
I was hungry' (*EW*, p. 71). He is 'like something the sea washed up'
(*EW*, p. 71) and the resurrection motif is reinforced by Columba's
closing lines: 'We were . . . asleep. . . . But we are awake now and
ready to begin again – to begin again – to begin again' (*EW*, p. 72).
However, Columba's affirmations do not mean an end to contradiction. He is echoing an earlier speech of Grillaan's which denies
Columba the possibility of unity and consistency of character: 'In
some men . . . sanctity is a progression, a building of stone upon
stone, year after year, until the edifice is complete. In other men, it is
in the will and determination to start, and then to start again, and
then to start again, so that their life is a series of beginnings. You are
of the second kind, Columba' (*EW*, p. 47). Grillaan indicates a concept of the subject as continuously in the process of construction. He
reminds us of Brecht: 'The continuity of the ego is a myth. A man is
an atom that perpetually breaks up and forms anew'. In Friel's next
play, *Philadelphia, Here I Come!*, the discontinuity of the ego and the
division of the subject become even more explicitly a dominant
structural principle.

PHILADELPHIA, HERE I COME!

The Inside of His Skull, the title that Arthur Miller originally thought
of for his great play, *Death of a Salesman*, could just as aptly be used
for Friel's *Philadelphia, Here I Come!* In both plays, the stage on which

the action takes place is the stage of the protagonist's mind. Both Miller's and Friel's expressionistic techniques allow them to interweave fantasy and memory into the present emotional moment in order to widen it and deepen it. Expressionism enables them to take us beyond the banality of surface reality and to give us a closer, more penetrating and vivid apprehension of the contradictory impulses in the protagonists' minds. In *Philadelphia*, Friel strives for a free and fluid mode of presentation with an episodic structure, flexible set and special music and lighting effects to provide powerful atmospheric touches and emotional emphasis at key points. But the boldest device of all is having two actors play one character, so that the playwright can explore the frontier between Private Gar and Public Gar.

Private Gar is 'the unseen man, the man within, the conscience, the *alter ego*, the secret thoughts, the id . . . the spirit' (*SP*, p. 27). Again, Friel is interested in the 'unseen' of personality and culture, in that part which is obscured and locked away, buried as something inadmissible, unfamiliar, troublesome, disruptive of order. In giving a voice and a body to unreason, to otherness, to desire, Friel admits all that poses a threat to dominant structures. Private Gar is a device to prise open the usual categorisations of experience, to dismantle the 'real', to mock and parody a blind faith in psychological coherence, in a unified, stable 'ego'. Through Private, Friel seeks to make the heart's darkness visible, its silence articulate. We are denied a unified and unifying perspective on the events of the play.

There would seem to be a direct relation between cultural repression and its generation of unruly, oppositional energies which dissolve the unitary self. As Hélène Cixous writes: 'The machine of repression has always had the same accomplices; homogenising, reductive, unifying reason has always allied itself to the Master, to the single, stable, socializable subject, represented by its types or characters'.[5] Gar's plural identity demonstrates Friel's resistance to such reduction, his desire for something excluded from cultural order and its usual forms of representation. The character of Private allows him to give expression to all that is opposed to the small-town, highly conventionalised social order of Ballybeg. One of the notable things about Friel's drama of desire is the central position occupied by the representatives of the Law. In *Philadelphia* alone we have a Senator, a Master, a Canon and a County Councillor. *Freedom of the City* features an array of Judges, Brigadiers, Professors, Constables and Priests, all seeking to establish their particular version of

events; *Aristocrats* depicts the decline of an old family of Catholic
Judges; the action of *Living Quarters* is controlled by Sir and, again,
deals with the break-up of an old order which had been presided
over by Commandant Frank Butler; in *The Communication Cord*, the
principal dupe is Senator Donovan; *Making History* dramatises Archbishop Lombard's nationalistic bid for the control of meaning of
Hugh O'Neill's life and career. In all these plays, Friel satirises
'official' Ireland. His 1968 lecture, 'The Theatre of Hope and Despair', reflects on the failure of the 'traditional social structure' in
Ireland:

> The world, according to the dramatists, is divided into two cat-
> egories. There are the rulers – the establishment – who pretend to
> believe in a traditional social structure that is Christian in origin,
> that is now seen to be false but which they still pretend to believe
> in in order to give them the authority they require. And there are
> simply the rest – individuals, isolated, separated, sick and disillu-
> sioned with their inheritance, existing in the void created by their
> rejection, waiting without hope for a new social structure that will
> give a meaning to their lives.[6]

This sums up pretty well the limbo in which Gar finds himself,
following upon the recognition of the bankruptcy of traditional values and the inadequacy of the present 'rulers'. Master Boyle is a
deluded, alcoholic failure continually at odds with his superiors in
Ballybeg; Senator Doogan is a terrific social snob; Canon O'Byrne is
an ineffectual religious leader; County Councillor 'Screwballs'
O'Donnell is 'a responsible, respectable citizen' (*SP*, p. 34), but in-
capable of communicating with his son or showing any affection.
Gar's imaginative and emotional needs, as reflected in his fecundly
human private language, are not even recognised: 'Private Gar, the
spirit, is invisible to everybody, always' (*SP*, p. 27).

Baile Beag, the Irish form of Ballybeg, means 'small town', and
small-town Ireland is portrayed as an unpromising environment,
emotionally repressed and economically and culturally starved. Gar
chafes under its joyless puritanism, but home is where the heart is,
and however much he fulminates against Ballybeg, he is tied to it by
bonds of sentiment not even he understands. On one hand, he is
bound by traditional value which, however unsatisfactory, still constitutes a safe, known world, and, on the other hand, he is attracted
by the adventure and excitement which the modern world promises.

'This place would drive anybody crazy!', Public says of Ballybeg; 'Look around you for God's sake! Look at Master Boyle! Look at my father! Look at the Canon! Look at the boys! Asylum cases, the whole bloody lot of them' (*SP*, pp. 78–9). Echoing Master Boyle, he denounces 'all this sentimental rubbish about "homeland" and "birthplace". Impermanency – anonymity – that's what I'm looking for; a vast restless place that doesn't give a damn about the past. To hell with Ballybeg, that's what I say' (*SP*, p. 79). The irony is that to the very end Gar is constantly collecting 'memories and images and impressions' (*SP*, p. 58) of Ballybeg. The bitter frustration of Public Gar's wild denunciation of Ballybeg to his ex-girlfriend, Katie Doogan, reverberates against Private's wistful ruminations towards the end: 'Four more hours. This is the last time you'll look at that pattern (on the floor), the last time you'll listen to the silence of Ballybeg . . .' (*SP*, p. 91). Hardly the behaviour one would expect of a man who really valued impermanence and anonymity, whose ideal home truly was 'a vast restless place that doesn't give a damn about the past'.

Memory, Friel wants us to see, is a creative faculty. Ballybeg may be 'a bloody quagmire, a backwater, a dead-end' (*SP*, p. 79) and Gar's friends, 'the boys', may be 'louts, ignorant bloody louts' (*SP*, p. 77), but Gar knows the tricks the mind can play with facts and that once in Philadelphia, memories of his home and the people he was close to will come to plague him, for then those memories will be distilled of all their coarseness and what will be left will be 'precious, precious gold' (*SP*, p. 79). Friel emphasises the mind's seemingly endless powers for recasting the actualities of life in images capable of satisfying deep, personal needs. This fantasising impulse, he insists, is universal. Master Boyle is in reality a wreck of a man and as frustrated in Ballybeg as Gar is. Like Gar he, too, dreams of escaping to America and his talk of the job he has been offered in a Boston university is as childish as any of Gar's fantasies. 'The boys'' stories of sexual conquest and physical prowess are a cover for loneliness, boredom and sexual frustration. They avoid talking about Gar's impending departure, for they don't want to have to question the realities of their own lives. Only fantasy can make life bearable in the real world of Ballybeg.

Gar's, of course, are the most extravagant fantasies of all. Gar, like the others, uses language to compensate for failure in the real world. Thus, he imagines himself a conductor and soloist, a famous footballer 'taking a slow, calculating look at the goal' (*SP*, p. 31), a pilot with his 'competent fingers poised over the controls' (*SP*, p. 31) – all

fantasies of expertise and control. The language is active and positive, and contrasts with the reality of being unable to order a dozen
loaves without his father's say-so, forgetting where he put the fence
posts or spending the evening shuffling around the gable of the
hotel. Gar's endless role-playing offers graphic depiction of a subject
in process, suggesting possibilities of innumerable other selves, different histories, different bodies. Thus, Friel's concept of character
threatens to dissolve the symbolic order of linguistic and social
control. Fantasies image the possibility of radical transformation –
cultural as well as personal – by refusing the boundary lines and
categories of the rational mind and conventional codification. Gar's
extravaganzas of variousness, his carnivals of metamorphosis represent a valuable personal and cultural potential. Friel's aesthetic of
inconstancy can produce dynamic newness – both for drama
and life; but we also see that it is expressive of a fragmented
and confused cultural inheritance, the sign of a profound crisis of
identity.

At the beginning of the play, Gar escapes from the stultifying
conditions of life in his father's shop by transporting himself in
imagination to vast open spaces where he roams as 'Garry the Kid':
'Let's git packin' boy. Let's git that l'il ole saddle bag opened and
let's git packin' (*SP*, p. 36). Gar identifies with the cowboys, with the
American myth of freedom, the pioneering spirit, the forces that
sought to open up a new world. He can, however, just as readily
respond to the high art of the European tradition. His enjoyment of
Mendelssohn indicates his aspirations to a wider cultural context
than that of provincial, Catholic Ballybeg. Yet, the indigenous culture is never far away. When he is thinking of his dead mother he
recites the prayers for the dead; in a fit of exuberance he dances to
ceilidh music; after a half-hearted rendition of 'Philadelphia, Here I
Come' at the end of Episode 1, he opens Episode 2 by pensively
singing the traditional Irish air 'She Moved Through the Fair'. Gar's
brilliantly funny announcement of the fantasy performance of
Mendelssohn's violin concerto encodes, in its conglomeration of
classical European, parochial Irish and popular American idioms,
the range and conflict of cultural influence acting upon him:

> The main item in tonight's concert is the first movement of the
> violin concerto in E minor, opus 64, by Jacob Ludwig Felix
> Mendelssohn. The orchestra is conducted by Gareth O'Donnell
> and the soloist is the Ballybeg half-back Gareth O'Donnell. Music

critics throughout the world claim that O'Donnell's simultaneous wielding of baton and bow is the greatest thing since Leather Ass died. Mendelssohn's violin concerto, First Movement. (*SP*, p. 36)

Yet another of Gar's voices is the one borrowed from Edmund Burke, the great conservative Anglo-Irishman, who invoked an ide-alised past and propounded a romantic fiction of the French monar-chy and of Marie Antoinette against the radical, impatient, aggres-sive, Jacobinism of his day. Throughout the play, Gar quotes the opening lines of Burke's famous pamphlet *Reflections on the Revolu-tion in France* – 'It is now sixteen or seventeen years since I saw the Queen of France, then the Dauphiness, at Versailles' – as a kind of talismanic release from his own thoughts or memories when they threaten to overwhelm him. Like Eamon in the later play, *Aristocrats*, Gar responds to an aristocratic dream of continuity and human excellence in a present of staggering uncertainty.

Philadelphia is firmly in the native Irish tradition of verbal theatre, the high point of which was Synge's *Playboy*, where Christy Mahon remakes himself by 'the power of a lie'. The *Playboy* ends with a transformed Christy and a transformed relationship between Christy and his father, both finally rededicating themselves to a fictionalis-ing language: 'but my son and myself will be going our own way, and we'll have great times from this out telling stories of the villainy of Mayo and the fools is here'.[7] No such self-discovery, no such progression, no such resolution of identity, are available in *Philadel-phia*. Gar is the same gormless ninny at the end as he was at the beginning – divided, emotionally immature, evasive, incomplete. Although he relives the events of his life in a critical and analytical fashion he does not gain from that experience. He is full of 'fine talk', but it takes him nowhere. He is unable to establish or maintain meaningful relationships with others, especially his father and his girlfriend; and he is unable to express his own deepest feelings, despite the presence of Private. He longs for intimacy with S. B. but admits that both of them would only be embarrassed by it. Gar is the product of an entire community that is unable to communicate. Dialogue has degenerated to clichéd, evasive non-communication. The Canon fails in his role as 'translator' (*SP*, p. 88). Private screams at his father: 'Screwballs, say something! Say something, Father!' (*SP*, p. 80). He wishes S. B. would 'make one unpredictable remark' (*SP*, p. 49) that would break the usual routines, prove that he has feelings, a Private life and can talk of something other than rat-traps, barbed wire and his bowels. The play ends on a resonant image of this lack of communication: each of the three main characters, Gar, S. B. and Madge, is absorbed in his or her own thoughts, oblivious to or misunderstanding the others. Madge's prophecy that Gar will end up just like his father indicates an endless cycle of disappointed relationships and non-communication. For all Private's ebullience, he is unable to force meaningful confrontation. Under pressure he loses control of language, as at the end of Episode 2 when, after Katie leaves, Private's speech degenerates into a fragmented and near-hysterical rewinding of past speeches: 'We'll go now, right away, and tell them – Mammy and Daddy – they're at home tonight – now, Gar, now – it must be now – remember, it's up to you – gut and salt them fish – and they're going to call this one Madge, at least so she *says* – ' (*SP*, p. 80). Private taunts Public with his failures, but acts to distract him from facing up to reality: 'An' you jist keep atalkin to you'self all the time, Mistah, 'cos once you stop atalkin' to you'self ah reckon then you jist begin to think kinda crazy things' (*SP*, p. 38).

Speech, as Harold Pinter has said, can be 'a stratagem to cover nakedness': 'There are two silences,' says Pinter, 'One when no word is spoken. The other when perhaps a torrent of language is employed. This speech is speaking of a language locked beneath it. That is its continual reference. The speech we hear is an indication of that we don't hear. It is a necessary avoidance, a violent, sly, anguished or mocking smokescreen which keeps the other in its place. When true silence falls we are still left with echo but are nearer nakedness. One way of looking at speech is to say it is a constant stratagem to cover nakedness'.[8] Like Pinter, Friel sets out to devise a special kind of dramatic language, one which, as Pinter put it, we are aware that 'under what is said, another language is being said'.[9] In a later play, *The Communication Cord*, Friel toys with the idea that maybe silence is preferable to 'the torrent of language': 'Maybe silence is the perfect discourse' (*CC*, p. 86), the linguist, Tim, opines. But in *Philadelphia* silence is what must be avoided at all costs – 'To hell with all strong, silent men!' (*SP*, p. 89), Private shouts at S. B. and the Canon.

Friel emphasises the death-in-life that comes from fixity and routine, but he also insists upon the unhappy consequences of fluidity when it means merely formlessness rather than freedom. Gar's speech is wonderfully vigorous and playful, the expression of an unquenchable human spirit, but it continually proclaims its own inadequacy. There is, we see, a multiplicity of languages available to him over which he demonstrates an impressive command; but he has no language of his own. There is no sustained sense of self, no centre, no stability of meaning following upon the disruption of the old ortho-doxies. Gar's continual role-playing is a stratagem to avoid self-confrontation. Words compensate for failure to act decisively and meaningfully. In this, Gar is no different from 'the boys'. His atti-tudes are very similar to theirs: 'What 'ya say l'il chick, you and me – you know – I'll spell it out for ya ifya like [*Winks, and clicks his tongue*]' (*SP*, p. 46). As with 'the boys', Gar's macho bravado is the mask of loneliness and frustration. He may deride their fantasies, but his own images of America are no less juvenile. He is only a slightly less serious case of arrested development. The only differ-ence between them is that Gar has more insight and awareness than 'the boys' and he has a more vital imagination than they have: his fantasy women are much more exotic creatures than their squint-eyed Annie McFaddens.

Without any secure identity, Gar is vulnerable to hostile forces from society. His verbal prowess deserts him in a crisis, as when Senator Doogan, whom Gar visits to ask for Katie's hand in mar-riage, reduces him to gibbering idiocy. Like Sarah in *Translations*, Gar becomes a non-entity when he loses his language. Language is power. The only way Gar can compensate for his hurt and humilia-tion is through Private language and an elaborate revenge fantasy: 'you know, too, that in his spare time he (Senator Doogan) travels for maternity corsets; and that he's a double spy for the Knights and the Masons; and that he takes pornographic photographs of Mrs D, and sends them anonymously to reverend mothers' (*SP*, p. 35); 'Did your investigators not discover that Senator Doogan is the grandfather of fourteen unborn illegitimate children? That he sold his daughter to the king of the fairies for a crock of gold?' (*SP*, p. 53).

However, Friel includes in the play a kind of remembering which signifies the individual's genuine desire and effort to define himself and his world. When Gar tries to 're-member' his dead mother or when he seeks confirmation of a childhood fishing trip with his father, he is trying to discover or confirm some kind of 'core' per-sonal identity in the process of 'distilling' the past. These are points in the play of particular emotional intensity where Friel initiates what is to become a long experiment (culminating in *Dancing at Lughnasa* (1991)) with the possibility of expressing the deep rhythms of personality through music and/or musical language. In the scene where Gar evokes the memory of his dead mother, Public's recitation of the set prayers for the dead is juxtaposed with Private's intensely poetic improvisation of the warm, vivacious, unspoiled young girl who was his mother. In imagination, she becomes a luminous, enchanting symbol of youth, beauty, vitality and freedom: 'She was small, Madge says, and wild and young, Madge says, from a place called Bailtefree beyond the mountains, and her eyes were bright and her hair was loose' (*SP*, p. 37). Friel perhaps intends an ironic contrast between vital imagination and the deadening forms of conventional religion (as, later, he contrasts the Canon's and S. B.'s demoralising platitudes with Private's imaginative and verbal vitality). Significantly, Private's rhapsody on his dead mother is accompanied by the plangent tones of Mendelssohn's Violin Concerto. The music serves to heighten the lyrical power of the language, which reaches an unusual pitch of intensity and pathos and becomes freer and less constricted by logical and grammatical structures. The speech, giving a voice to semi-fictional, highly sensuous, dream-like recollection, itself approaches the condition of music.

Music is evocative not only of a lost relationship between mother and son, but of a possible non-verbal bond between father and son:

> but between us at that moment there was this great happiness, this great joy – you must have felt it too – although nothing was being said . . . and then, then for no reason at all except that you were happy too, you began to sing.   (*SP*, p. 83)

Gar explicitly draws attention to the evocative power of music:

> Listen! Listen! Listen! D'you hear it? D'you know what that music says? It says that once upon a time a boy and his father sat in a blue boat on a lake in an afternoon in May, and on that afternoon a great beauty happened, a beauty that has haunted the boy ever since because he wonders now did it really take place or did he imagine it.   (*SP*, p. 89)

Music fills the silence between father and son, past and present, helping to evoke that lost past, to express unrealised or latent possibility, a 'great beauty'. It enables the character to go back in time, to dissolve the intractable present, and recreate the world. 'It's not the literal past, the "facts" of history which shape us, but the images of the past embodied in language', Hugh says in *Translations*, identifying the past as a linguistic construct and opening the possibility of interpretative transformation. Gar lays claim to this possibility for his own life, hoping to prove that the world is not the unbreachable monolith it might seem to be. The music not only indicates the limitations of language, but affirms the possibility of transcendence and harmony. It doesn't yet function as a viable alternative form of communication in itself, but helps to effect the shift from one form of consciousness (that of the rational, public world) into another form (that of the private, subjective world of memory).

Music facilitates the expression of irrational memory, and irrational, fictionalising memory need not simply mean escapism and avoidance of confrontation. Rather, it can play a valid and vital part in the construction of 'truth' and identity, as Synge demonstrated in *The Playboy* and as Friel insists in an autobiographical anecdote which obviously forms the basis of Gar's memory of the fishing trip with his father:

> What I want to talk about now is a particular memory of a particular day. There's no doubt in my mind about this – it's here now before my eyes as I speak. The boy I see is about nine years old and my father would have been in his early forties. We are walking home from a lake with our fishing rods across our shoulders. It has been raining all day long; it is now late evening; and we are soaked to the skin. But for some reason – perhaps the fishing was good – I don't remember – my father is in great spirits and is singing a song and I am singing with him.
> And there we are, the two of us, soaking wet, splashing along a muddy road that comes in at right-angles to Glenties main street, singing about how my boat can safely float through the teeth of wind and weather. That's the memory. That's what happened. A trivial episode without importance to anyone but me, just a moment of happiness caught in an album. But wait. There's something wrong here. I'm conscious of a dissonance, an unease. What is it? Yes, I know what it is: there is no lake along that muddy road. And since there is no lake my father and I never walked back from it in the rain with our rods across our shoulders. The fact is a fiction. Have I imagined the scene then? Or is it a composite of two or three different episodes? The point is – I don't think it matters. What matters is that for some reason . . . this vivid memory is there in the storehouse of the mind. For some reason the mind has shuffled the pieces of verifiable truth and composed a truth of its own. For me it is a truth. And because I

acknowledge its peculiar veracity, it becomes a layer in my sub-
soil; it becomes a part of me; ultimately it becomes me.[10]

Poised before his leap into the unknown ('a vast, restless' America),
Gar's sense of himself, of his whole culture, focuses on a moment of
communication and wholeness between himself and the father who
has been struck dumb by his culture. He attempts to excavate around
this shard of the past, but the attempt fails. S. B. is unable to confirm
Gar's memories. With a beautifully modulated dramatic irony, however, the silent father finds his voice when Gar is out of hearing. He
shows himself to be just as susceptible to fictionalising the past. With
a lyrical intensity that is really quite surprising coming from him,
S. B. recalls to Madge a time of great happiness when he took Gar,
dressed in a sailor suit, to school. Madge, however, points out that
Gar never had a sailor suit. Whether or not S. B.'s memory is accurate
is, in some sense, less important than the fact that he has exhibited an
aspect of his personality that Gar has had the greatest difficulty even
imagining ('God – maybe – Screwballs – behind those dead eyes and
that flat face are there memories of precious moments in the past?
My God, have I been unfair to you?': *SP*, p. 82). Ironically, S. B.
reveals his Private side to Madge only, never to Gar, who thus
misses the evidence of the one thing that might hold him in Ballybeg.
Gar's and S. B.'s memories proclaim the love that each has for the
other, but there is a failure to make a connection between the two
images, to negotiate a shared past. Though music allows Gar some
form of expression of irrational memory, it is too introverted and
subjective an expression to be communicable to others. There is no
dialogue between father and son and the result is paralysis, ossifica-
tion, epitomised by the last line of the play: 'I don't know' (*SP*, p. 99).
By the time we come to *Faith Healer*, Friel's dramatic structure doesn't
allow even for the possibility of dialogue between the characters.

Even though no new order of felicity evolves in the course of the
play, Friel has not given up hope. He shows his characters in all their
weakness, but his faith in human nature is never shaken. He affirms
not only an unruly energy which works against stagnation and
inertia, but also gentle concern, affection, dignity, which by the end
have replaced pretence and buffoonery: Gar asks Madge to make
sure and let him know if anything happens to his father; S. B. has
been listening to the weather forecast; he is so preoccupied by Gar's
departure that he doesn't realise he is holding his newspaper upside
down; unable to sleep, he sits in the kitchen in the small hours of the

morning gazing at Gar's packed cases, touching his son's coat, staring at his bedroom door; Madge invites 'the boys' round to say goodbye to Gar and hides money and food in his coat – the last of her many little secret acts of kindness. Madge's realistic acceptance of the world, her forthright honesty, along with Gar's willingness to play and experiment, constitute a faith for the future, the basis of a reply to inevitabilities. Even in the midst of disillusion and confusion, strength and courage and resourcefulness continue to exist. The means of transformation are there and so are the human qualities which would ensure a transformation for the better. As the title of Friel's lecture has it, this is theatre of despair AND of hope.

THE LOVES OF CASS McGUIRE

Between 1962 and the foundation of the Field Day Theatre Company in 1980, all of Friel's stage plays were premiered in Dublin, except for *The Loves of Cass McGuire* and *Faith Healer*, both of which opened on Broadway, the first at the Helen Hayes' Theatre in October 1966, the second at the Longacre Theatre in April 1979. A radio version of *The Loves of Cass McGuire*, broadcast by the BBC Third Programme in 1966 actually preceded the opening of the stage play and was the last play of Friel's to be written originally for radio.

In *The Loves of Cass McGuire*, a 'sister' play to *Philadelphia*, Friel continues his exploration of the themes of 'home' and 'homecomings', of the relationship between the individual and the community. Cass is, in some sense, an older Gar. Where *Philadelphia* dramatises the moment when youthful innocence, hope and idealism reach out for New World fulfilment, *The Loves of Cass McGuire* reveals the failure of that promise. Cass McGuire is a seventy year old spinster recently returned to her brother's home in Ireland from an American exile of fifty-two years working 'one block away from Skid Row' (*LCM*, p. 19) on the lower East Side of New York. In an ironic reversal of the popular sentimental story of the returned exile's welcome back into the bosom of the family in 'the old country', Cass is promptly rejected by brother Harry and his wife, Alice, and packed off to old people's home. Cass finds herself stateless, left in a limbo between a country which rejects her because she is old and useless and a community which no longer recognizes her. Rejected by her family, she is thrown back on her own resources to create a 'home' for herself and this she does by constructing a compensatory fiction of her life. Her multiple disappointments have not eradicated desire, which is now the yearning to reclaim in imagination a lost personal Golden Time.

Loud, bawdy, impulsive, drunken and foul-mouthed, Cass is the personification of a repressed, disruptive force which frightens and shocks the established order. The play, which Friel calls 'a concerto in which Cass McGuire is the soloist', is very deliberately conceived as a play of voices and in the opening section Friel establishes sharply and economically the range of languages out of which it is composed. Harry and Alice are traditional, middle-class Catholics, and Cass's colourful vernacular coming straight off the mean streets of New York sounds comically out of place in the genteel setting of their home. Grandma, 'deaf and doting' (*LCM*, p. 11), has ceased to communicate meaningfully, though she tries to maintain an air of authority by speaking as if she were still addressing the schoolchildren she used to teach. Her grandson, Dom, can talk dirty like Cass, but is careful to do so only when his parents aren't around. Grandma's deafness symbolises a pervasive isolation, for all the characters are locked into their own solipsistic worlds, talking out of their own obsessions, talking past each other, unable to engage the 'Other'. It is only a small step from this kind of disjointed dialogue, sometimes intercutting speeches from widely different points in space and time, to the 'rhapsodies' that are the play's most boldly experimental feature. The fluid, dream-like world of the play operates on several levels of reality simultaneously, including the one on which Cass periodically addresses the audience directly.

We hear a good deal about Cass before she ever appears in person. Dom first mentions her name and as soon as he does, Alice quickly tries to diffuse any discussion of Cass. When Harry enters, his questions further intensify Cass's mystery, confirming her as a violent, anti-social, lawless force, someone who is, significantly, besmirched with the primeval 'clay' (*LCM*, p. 14) and whom the police have been called in to suppress:

ALICE: Did you find out where she was? What happened?
HARRY: Where was she not. I called in Sweeney's pub on the way home and paid for the breakages. Apparently every table in the lounge was an antique.
ALICE: And the police?
HARRY: The sergeant was with me. I squared that. Dom!

ALICE: And the clay on her shoes – how did she get it?

(*LCM*, p. 14)

'I squared that', says Harry the accountant, meaning that he has paid for Cass's breakages (the result of a vandalisation of traditional values, as the 'antique' reference implies), but also indicating the attempt to impose geometric order upon the wild, inchoate energy embodied by Cass. Cass's presence is an assertion of the body which offends the traditional discourses of family and religion. Disgorged from the social world, within which she exists as a potentially destructive element, she 'charges on stage (either from the wings or from the auditorium) shouting in her raucous Irish–American voice' (*LCM*, p. 14). This violent, anarchic irruption shatters 'the subdued domestic atmosphere': 'Everyone on stage freezes' (*LCM*, p. 14). 'Gaudy', 'voluminous', 'loud', 'coarse', 'ravaged', 'strong', 'resilient' are the words Friel uses in his opening description of her.

The play becomes a battle to establish dominance of a particular point of view, a particular version of things. Whose language, and whose reality', will prevail, Cass's or Harry's?

CASS: I go to the ur-eye-nal for five minutes and they try to pull a quick one on me.

HARRY: The story has begun, Cass.

CASS: The story begins when I say it begins, and I say it begins with me stuck in the goddamn workhouse! So you can all get the hell outta here!

HARRY: The story begins in the living-room of my home, a week after your return to Ireland.

(*LCM*, p. 15)

Cass's direct address to the audience (whom she treats as 'her friends', *LCM*, p. 17) has the effect of getting us on her side. She speaks for the submerged, unruly, female energies that the mainstream culture, represented by Harry, wishes to censor, marginalise or silence. Cass sees her removal to the old people's home as a betrayal. She refutes Harry's statement that she 'went' to the Home: 'I didn't go, Harry boy, I was stuck in!' (*LCM*, p. 15). And she has no illusions about why she is being suppressed and rejected. As she says to Dom: 'The less you see of your old Auntie Cass the better, because she ain't got no money, and we suspect she doesn't go to church, and we're not too sure if she's a maiden aunt at all' (*LCM*, p. 16). Harry exclaims the official definitions: 'Eden House is a rest home for the elderly' (*LCM*, p. 16), but to Cass, it is a 'workhouse' (*LCM*, p. 16). Harry wants an opportunity to explain why Cass has ended up in the home and so he insists that the story should be told 'in proper sequence' (*LCM*, p. 16). Cass, however, is not interested in Harry's rationalisations and wants the story to start with her betrayal already a *fait accompli*: 'We're going to skip all that early stuff, all the explanations, all the excuses' (*LCM*, p. 16). By dint of the sheer force of her personality, Cass succeeds in seizing the story from Harry: 'they'll see what happens in the order *I* want them to see it' (*LCM*, p. 16).

Thus, Harry's plea for a rational, chronological order is subordinated to the demands of a psychological, poetic narrative. Where Harry, like Sir in *Living Quarters*, insists upon a fixed, chronological version of the past, Cass's past is impressionistic, its evocation following an emotional and associative logic, rather than a strictly rational economy of cause and effect. Frequently, Cass insists that she is only concerned with present reality, not the past: 'there will be no going back into the past' (*LCM*, p. 16); 'And I don't go in for the fond memory racket!' (*LCM*, p. 19); 'I live in the present, Harry boy! Right here and now! (*LCM*, p. 49). In fact, however, she is continually going back into the past, indulging memories of Jeff Olsen, her one-legged employer whom she loved; of Joe Bolowski, one of her drunken customers; of Con Crowley whom she had had her eye on before she went to the States; of her father. She tries to keep these memories at bay by talking to the audience, but 'some are so potent that she is seduced into re-living them' (*LCM*, p. 18). These memories, however, are quite different from the extravagant idealisations of Ingram and Trilbe, the two 'gooks' she meets in Eden House. As the vitality of her language indicates, Cass still maintains a normal healthy friction with reality and, of all the characters in the play, she is the one (at the beginning, at least) with the sharpest, least illusioned insight.

Cass's narrative is concerned with the longing for love, for a home and for a father. In Eden House, she encounters a curious strategy for dealing with the failures and disappointments of life. Where up to this point she has answered a harsh reality with the raucous vitality of her own defiant will she now discovers the enchantment of illusion. At first she finds herself as out of place, socially and linguistically, as she was in Harry's house. Her earthy, slangy speech jars with the lyricism of Mr Ingram's and Trilbe Costello's fantasies, or their everyday genteel speech. Trilbe and Ingram have created a 'private world' which they 'take refuge in occasionally' (*LCM*, p. 28) and for which they invoke a Yeatsian sanction:

> INGRAM: 'But I, being poor, have only my dreams – '
> TRILBE: 'I have spread my dreams under your feet – '
> INGRAM: 'Tread softly because you tread on my dreams'.
> TRILBE: Our truth.
>
> (*LCM*, p. 46)

Theirs is the plight of the romantic in an unromantic world. From the 'big, winged armchair', each of them takes flight from a disappointing reality. Dreaming is compensation for failure and betrayal, a means of avoiding self-contempt and despair, a protest against determinism, a strategy for survival. Friel continues the concern of the Irish drama of Synge and O'Casey with the tension between a reality of crisis and the eloquence of the characters, which is a way of avoiding facing up to crisis. Language is detached from reality; it becomes preferable to direct action, to reality, to genuine engagement; it becomes a mask. The lyricism achieves the status of a performance. Language becomes 'rhapsody'.

Friel's 'rhapsodies' are strongly reminiscent of Eugene O'Neill's 'arias' in *Long Day's Journey into Night*. Indeed, the celebratory tone Friel adopts when he is describing the 'rhapsodies' in his 'Author's Note' would seem to take him a step beyond the qualified, but still compassionate, justification of illusion which we find in the tradition of O'Neill and Tennessee Williams. Friel describes each of the three 'rhapsodies' as a triumph of language, a marvellous act of translation in which each character 'takes the shabby and unpromising threads of his or her past life and weaves it into a hymn of joy, a gay and rapturous and exaggerated celebration of a beauty that might have been'. Wagner's music is to provide a 'potent crutch' to help the actors achieve 'grace and dignity' and invest their soliloquies with 'cantabile magic'. The choice of Wagner is quite deliberate, for Wagner's theories, expounded in *The Art-Work of the Future* (1849), *Opera and Drama* (1851) and *The Purpose of the Opera* (1871), have a relevance not only to this play but to Friel's whole dramatic development. Wagner championed a theory of 'music drama' based on Schopenhauer and German metaphysics. He believed language could be extended by sound to create a fuller emotional expression. His ideal art – the 'total artwork' – would bring together dance, poetry and music, in a way they had not been unified since Greek tragedy. He wanted to combine the movement of the body and the sound of the voice, to reclaim the expression of some pre-rational time when both dance and poetry had their beginning – to 'emotionalize the intellect'.

Trilbe is the first of Friel's three 'rhapsodists'. Like Williams's Blanche Du Bois in *A Streetcar Named Desire*, Trilbe is one of the 'soft people', the artistic spirits, the sensitive souls, the fugitive kind, struggling to survive in a harsh, materialistic world by retreating behind illusions. Her dream, backed by the rich, majestic music of Wagner's 'Venusberg' from *Tannhauser*, is a dream of love in exotic places, designed to mask the reality of spinsterhood, of trying to make ends meet as an elocution teacher, of a drunken father who always wore wellingtons and a greasy bowler hat and worked as a caretaker at a greyhound track. The accompanying music has a thematic relevance, the 'Venusberg' (Mountain of Venus) motif alluding to Tannhauser's vision of Venus which tempts him from Christianity. He must resist this seduction if he wishes to save his soul. At this stage, Cass reacts to Trilbe's elaborate fantasy with 'naked astonishment' (*LCM*, p. 17) and, shocked and not a little frightened by Trilbe's performance, renews her resolve to 'ride this gook joint' (*LCM*, p. 33) and fight off the temptations of illusion.

Ingram's 'rhapsody', accompanied by Wagner's 'Magic Fire' music from *The Valkyrie*, is a joyful celebration of his life with Stella, his young, dancer bride. In imagination, Ingram converts the reality of betrayal and desertion into a dream of love abruptly ended by Stella's tragic drowning. The interweaving of fact and fantasy produces an absurdly lyricised language:

> INGRAM: – because my prize was a young prize, with hair golden as
> ripe wheat, and there was music in my ears, throbbing, heady,
> Godly music . . .
> TRILBE: Away, away to the end of the promontory.
> INGRAM: Where we kissed and danced and loved . . .
> TRILBE: Poised above the waves –
> INGRAM: And then –
> TRILBE: And then –
> INGRAM: And then, one day, running before me, calling to me, she
> slipped . . .
>
> (*LCM*, p. 41)

The repetitive dialogue, with its antiphonal arrangement and hieratic expressiveness is highly musical. Again, the accompanying music helps to amplify the theme, emphasising 'both the isolated nature of the world Cass enters and its undeniable seductiveness', as Julia Cruickshank points out in 'Brian Friel: Language, Music and Dance' (unpublished MA dissertation, University of Ulster, 1991). The 'Magic Fire' motif, 'Cruckshank explains, alludes to the circle of fire in which the sleeping goddess Brunhilde is imprisoned. The circle can only be broken by Siegfried, the warrior sent to save the gods. As a punishment for earlier misdeeds, Brunhilde will lose her immortal status when the ring of fire is broken. The fire thus becomes a symbol both of protection and imprisonment. It allows Brunhilde to live forever, but condemns her to complete isolation'.

Listening to Ingram's 'rhapsody', Cass's reaction this time is 'not too violent. She is more perplexed, more puzzled' (*LCM*, p. 46). She is finding it more difficult not to surrender to the past, not to give in to illusion and she responds with typically fighting talk: 'They (Trilbe and Ingram) think they're going to run me back into the past but by Gawd they're not. . . . I live in the present. . . . Go away! Go away! Gooks . . . real gooks living in the past, but not Cass McGuire' (*LCM*, p. 49).

At first, Cass is like the superior, significantly named Mrs Butcher, the newcomer to Eden Home at the end, and considers herself above fantasy. But gradually she surrenders to the consoling world of illusion into which she is initiated by Ingram and Trilbe. Tell-tale signs of her own susceptibility are visible early on, such as her assertion that she is only a 'temporary' (*LCM*, p. 20) resident in Eden House. She becomes more and more detached from the reality around her, reaching the point where she no longer recognises the 'Other' – the audience whom she has addressed directly throughout the play. Cass's 'rhapsody' is backed by the 'Liebestod' from Wagner's *Tristan and Isolde*, which begins in a discordant, minor key, reflecting Cass's agitation when she suddenly realises that she is inventing and re-arranging the facts of her past. As the 'Liebestod' grows into a confident, vibrant march so Cass becomes more confident of her own creative powers. 'Liebestod' means 'love-death' and the story of Tristan and Isolde is a story of love's victory over death. As Cruickshank further notes, 'love is ultimately fulfilled in death, therefore the death of both characters at the end of the opera is willing, almost suicidal'. In the same way as Isolde submerges her will to live beneath her desire for Tristan, Cass sheds realistic controls and succumbs to a world where all her unrequited or frustrated loves are fulfilled: 'Connie and father and Harry and Jeff and the four kids and Joe and Slinger . . . and I love them all so much, and they love me so much; we're so lucky, so lucky in our love' (*LCM*, p. 66). Cass ends by repeating '"I have spread my dreams under your feet"' (*LCM*, p. 66), finally joining Ingram and Trilbe to assert 'our truth' – a subjectively conceived reality over and above the 'truth' of the public, 'objective' world.

In the chronic, turbulent need to transform a sordid, painful past into a romantic fiction all three of these characters become experts in rewriting history. They depend on each other to construct and maintain their fantasies. Ingram encourages Trilbe and Cass with his readings from *Tristan and Isolde*, while Trilbe acts as a one-woman chorus to Ingram's fantasy. They know to tread softly, because they are treading on each other's dreams. Like the deadbeats and dropouts isolated from the world in Harry Hope's Last Chance Saloon in O'Neill's *The Iceman Cometh*, the residents in Eden House retain their dignity and identity through the mutual understanding and support of each other's dream. Even Cass (whose memories of living down and out in New York make the comparison with *The Iceman Cometh* almost unavoidable) learns compassionate tolerance for the dreams and hopes of others – and not just for Ingram's and Trilbe's. She plays along with Alice's image of her father as a 'gentleman', 'dignified, and scholarly, and courteous' (*LCM*, p. 47), rather than force her to confront the fact that he was a dirty old man; and she tries desperately to restrain herself from destroying Alice's illusion of a happy, united family, when, in truth, Harry and Alice have been rejected by their children, who hardly ever even visit them now. Again, when Tessa, the maid, shows her her engagement ring at the end, Cass acquiesces in Tessa's dreams of the future. Ironically, it is in these desperate conspiracies of untruth that the human capacity for imaginative sympathy most conspicuously reveals itself. The voice of 'reality', the play's equivalent of the 'iceman' Hickey, is Pat Quinn, a malicious, treacherous little weasel who delights in the misery of others.

The play, however, need not be seen simply as an endorsement of illusion. Trilbe and Ingram, for all their fantasising, still pass most of their day in complete boredom, engaged in pointless conversation. The culminating irony is that Cass's 'rhapsody' is a dream of respectability, security, propriety and centres on the family. She ends by

embracing the values which Harry asserts against her at the beginning. But she does so at a grievous price. As she becomes absorbed
in her 'rhapsody', her language is sanitised, her vibrant humour
disappears. Her retreat from reality to 'rhapsody' renders the frightening, submerged forces of personality no longer threatening to
institutionalised order. They are now formalised, tamed, 'civilised'.
She has surrendered her own rebellious will and defiant individualism and assimilated Harry's values. She can join Trilbe and Ingram's
dream club only when she renounces her unruly instincts. Her survival is, in fact, a defeat. She is like Jeff's dog which has been 'desexed'
and 'debarked'. All that would seem to be left for Cass, too, is to
'dee-cease' (*LCM*, p. 19). Having asserted her right to order history
as she had asserted her right to a language outside the norm, her
eventual capitulation to myth, to 'our truth', is accompanied not
only by a retreat to 'normal', non-profane language, but also by
a surrender to Chronos, symbolised by Cass's preoccupation
with the Christmas presents at the end and by Liz Butcher's arrival
which signals a recommencing of the cycle. Cass's attempt to arrest
history and force it to obey her own narrative fails. Her loss of
narrative control and of an original, vital language and her adoption
of an artificial, 'civilised' alternative, pre-figure Friel's concern in
Translations, where dispossession acquires cultural and political
dimensions.

The 'cantabile magic' of the three 'rhapsodies' co-exists uneasily
with Friel's ironic recognition of illusion as no more than a disguised
negation of life. Through the windows along the back of the stage we
see into the garden of Eden House where a Cupid statue is 'frozen in
an absurd and impossible contortion' – a symbol of the absurdity
and impossibility of the characters' illusions of love. Cass may find
an expression for the tenderness which she feels toward Harry, her
father and Jeff Olsen, but in the process she has given up her long
struggle to remain in active contact with present actuality. At the
end, Cass, in a drunken stupor, doesn't even recognise Harry or
Alice and talks only to herself. Gar's rhapsodies on his mother or on
the fishing trip with his father differ fundamentally from Cass's
because his 're-memberings' still recognise the pressure of reality
and are motivated by a desire to discover a 'core' identity and
enough self-confidence to *leave* home. Cass, on the other hand, having to face what she fears most – homelessness – after she is rejected
by Harry and his family, gives up on reality altogether. Her closing
line is the play's climactic, resonating irony: 'Home at last. Gee, but

it's a good thing to be home' (*LCM*, p. 69). The whole play has been concerned with Cass's struggle to rediscover the home she has dreamt of all her life: 'That's what it's all about, isn't it – coming home' (*LCM*, p. 43). Or as Trilbe has it in the words of her little poem: '"We puff over meadows and rivers and streams / Till we come, puffing gaily, to the land of our dreams; / and there we are happy to wander and roam / For we feel so content in this land that is Home"' (*LCM*, p. 60). Friel's family homes (in *The Loves of Cass McGuire, Philadelphia, Lovers, Crystal and Fox, The Gentle Island, Living Quarters, Aristocrats* or *Dancing at Lughnasa*) are always either broken or in the throes of breakdown and certainly no longer able to sustain; his images of tradition, the past, the homeland (in *Translations* or *The Communication Cord*) likewise emphasise crisis and disruption and material exploitation rather than spiritual anchorage; the pre-lapsarian bliss promised by 'Eden House' is as blatant an irony as the traditional rural idyll signalled by 'the gentle island' ('My God, this is heaven': *GI*, p. 18). For Cass, 'home' is in the private core of mind, hermetically sealed off from the external world. It is a necessary illusion.

The search for love and for home is connected with the search for the father. Fathers figure prominently in the play. One of the first things Cass does on her return to Ireland is to visit the grave of the father whom she loved and remembers as a protector, hiding her away in the signal box of the railway station where he worked. But she is also haunted by the knowledge that he deserted his children and lived for twenty years as a bigamist in a doss house in Glasgow. All of the fathers in the play are failures and disappointments; the children are in search of the stabilising authority of a new 'father': Alice wants to replace a father who was a child molester; Trilbe longs for a more noble father than a greasy little drunk; Ingram dreams of a father who was a bright young lawyer. In psychoanalytical terms, the play enacts the longing for a transformation of the dominant, patriarchal order. Cass's harrassments and disruptions of the Law of the father (now championed by Harry, himself a failed father who has been rejected by his own children) provokes frightening retaliatory action that leads to the suppression of her unique human quality and her total disengagement from the external world.

Friel's feelings about illusion are complex and he hasn't quite found the form which will allow him to express that complexity coherently. Starting off by satirising the rigidity and narrowness of dominant structures, he asserts powerful repressed forces of personality which threaten to split apart the recéived social order dominated by the Law which the father embodies. These vital forces, motivating the transformative powers of the imagination, represent a liberating potential. Friel wants to celebrate the freeing activity of imagination, the magic of language which can create new worlds; at the same time he wants to keep us uncomfortably aware of the dangers of dissociation from reality. He treats those whose survival seems to depend on illusion with understanding and compassion, but he also wants to expose their folly and absurdity. The difficulty of reconciling these incompatible elements – the exhilaration of freedom and flight on one hand and a sense of obligation to the 'reality principle' on the other – is to remain a central theme in his work.

CRYSTAL AND FOX

Crystal and Fox was first produced at the Gaiety Theatre, Dublin, in November 1968 and received its first American production at the Mark Taper Forum, Los Angeles, in 1970. The play concerns a run-down travelling show headed by the eponymous Crystal and Fox Melarkey. As the surname implies, this is a couple whose business is entertainment, fun and games, fantasy transformations, play of all kinds. Fox exercises god-like powers. He is an impresario of other worlds, a truly mythic ringmaster. The rest of the troupe depend on him, follow him, serve him faithfully, are subject to his whims. He manipulates their identities, dictating the roles they will play in his show. There was a time when 'he had the country in the palm of his hand' (*CF*, p. 22). However, over the last five tears, there has been a mysterious degeneration in Fox. 'Things start to go well,' says his long-suffering wife, Crystal 'and you begin to make plans; and then he has to go and make trouble. . . . Eight – ten years ago – my God he was on top of his form then! Cracking jokes, striding about, giving orders like a king' (*CF*, p. 22). Just as the ruination of the ancient Fisher King brought about the ruin of his kingdom, so Fox's degeneration has led to the breaking up and the demoralisation of his troupe. His retinue is already dwindling and in the course of the play he drives El Cid and Tanya away, poisons Pedro's beloved performing dog, Gringo, and seems to have lost all interest in the show. Instead of entertaining the world, he now thinks of himself 'fighting the world' (*CF*, p. 33). He despises his audience, mocking their illiteracy and their vulgar taste and he cynically cheats them with his fixed raffle. He is obsessed by the thought of 'something better' in life: 'Once, maybe twice in your life, the fog lifts, and you get a glimpse, an intuition; and suddenly you know that this can't be all there is – there has to be something better than this' (*CF*, p. 47). He knows, however, that 'something better' may only be an illusion: 'afterwards all you're left with is a vague memory of what you thought you saw; and that's what you hold on to – the good thing you think you saw' (*CF*, p. 48). Fox's agony thus stems from his suspicion that there are no grounds for hope and faith and it is the desperate effort to realise what he knows may only be illusion which produces his perverse, ruthless, ultimately self-consuming behaviour.

Crystal remembers the time when Fox's decline first became apparent: 'Just before Gabriel went away; that's when it began' (*CF*, p. 22). It would seem that in casting out his son, Gabriel (his name associating him with the angelic messenger who brought the good news of Christ's birth), Fox has cast out all hope and possibility of renewal. Now, Gabriel's sudden reappearance has a religious force:

> [*Crystal turns round and stares incredulously.*]
> CRYSTAL: Gabriel? . . . O my God – Gabriel! It's Gabriel – O my God!
> . . .
> FOX: [*Now he sees Gabriel*] – it's not . . .?
> GABRIEL: The prodigal son, Fox.
> FOX: Jaysus!
> CRYSTAL: I told him you'd be –
> FOX: Gabriel! . . . . He's looking . . . divine.
>
> (*CF*, pp. 32–3)

With Gabriel's return, Crystal and Pedro see new hope for the future. 'It's like old times again', says Pedro as he prepares to celebrate another 'Christmas' (*CF*, p. 35). Similarly, Crystal believes 'we're round the corner now' (*CF*, p. 35). But Gabriel, bearing mortality's inevitable taint, has no redemptive powers. He tells how he has been diagnosed 'autistic – "unable to respond emotionally to people"' (*CF*, p. 37). He is as manipulative, sly and restless as his father and, like his father, he takes advantage of people who know and trust him. He is on the run because he battered almost to death an old lady who caught him stealing from her till. Gabriel is unable to arrest the course of doom and is, in fact, sacrificed himself.

Crystal and Fox is another story of 'the enemy within', of repressed desire which results in a permanently split subject. Fox, like Gar or Columba or Cass, has an unruly, rebellious side to his personality which refuses to be bound by social convention. Private Gar was a marvellously comic creation, but with Fox Friel explores depths of the Private self which are dark and dangerous. Like Gar, Fox longs for release from the demoralising routines of his everyday life. As he remarks to Pedro: 'Round and round in circles. Same conversations, same jokes, same yahoo audiences; just like your Gringo, eh?' (*CF*, p. 23). For Fox, as for Frank Hardy, Fox's reincarnation in *Faith Healer*, death is the ultimate freedom. There is a demonic aspect to both these characters. Included in the Melarkey repertoire is 'The Doctor's Story', a drama about Christian missionaries in the African jungle, and Fox takes a savage delight in mocking the Christian message of resignation and the ideal of service which the playlet celebrates: 'Contentment lies in total obedience – St Paul's epistle to the South Africans' (*CF*, p. 24), he jokes grimly. Fox has greater affinity with another drama to which he alludes – the story of Faust, the man who refused to obey, who refused to accept his place in the divinely ordered scheme of things and lost his soul as a consequence of his overreaching pride.

Like Faust, Fox commands our sympathy as well as our disapproval. His perversity, we can see, is the result of a frustrated idealism:

> FOX: Weary of all this . . . this making do, of conning people that know they're being conned. Sick of it all. Not sick so much as desperate; desperate for something that . . . that has nothing to do with all this. Restless, Gabby boy, restless. And a man with a restlessness is a savage bugger.
>
> GABRIEL: What do you want?
>
> FOX: What do I want? I want. . . . I want a dream I think I've had to come true. I want to live like a child. I want to die and wake up in heaven with Crystal.
>
> (*CF*, p. 36)

In the disjointed, incantatory rhythms and repetitions of this speech Fox expresses his desire to step out of the world of flux and change and restlessness into a timeless heaven. Like Fitzgerald's Gatsby, another mystery man possessed of and betrayed by a dream, Fox wants the impossible; he wants to turn the clock back. But unlike Gatsby, Fox admits the unreality of the vision which motivates his whole life ('a dream I think I've had'). The 'dream' is a myth of the past, composed out of fragmented images of the day Fox first met Crystal or of a time when they waded through streams filled with fish. Just as Daisy was installed as the object of Gatsby's vast desire, so Crystal is always at the centre of Fox's dream. The past, recreated in imagination, becomes fairy-tale:

> And the Fox was cycling out to make his fortune in the world with nothing but his accordion and his rickety wheel and his glib tongue, when what did he spy at the edge of the road but three snow-white horses and three golden vans. . . . And there was no one in the first golden van. And there was no one in the second golden van. But beside the third and last golden van there was Papa rubbing down a snow-white mare. And beside him a princess. (*CF*, pp. 24–5)

Fox is engaged in a process of codification, schematisation and ritualisation, a process which stereotypes and mystifies the past and permits him to justify his actions in the present in terms of this sanctified inaugural experience, this sacred Beginning. The claims of myth having outstripped respect for fact and reason, Fox's recollections are no more reliable than S. B.'s or Gar's memories of precious moments in their personal pasts. Friel wants us to see Fox not only as tortured romantic hero, but as the exponent of a deadly kind of idealism which, in fleeing the pressure of reality, of the present, of social responsibility, is ultimately self-defeating. Fox's dream, we are made to see, betrays him into solipsistic isolation, into what Gabriel calls 'hate' ('You're full of hate – that's what's wrong with you – you hate everybody!' (*CF*, p. 48)). In his monomaniac pursuit of his dream, Fox sheds all encumbrances, callously casting off his faithful retainers, his son and in the end the wife whom he loves, 'the best part of me' (*CF*, p. 64). Fox's story is of a gradual paring down ('The Doctor's Story' miniaturising the pattern of leaving and loss at the heart of the play) until he reaches his final, lonely stasis. He struggles to reclaim a sense of identity, a purpose, a 'home', but the nostalgic yearning for the lost Eden only generates fatally destructive fantasy and leads to the basest treachery and betrayal. Later plays such as *Volunteers*, *Translations* and *The Communication Cord*, explore a similar theme of archaeological unveiling in a historical and political context.

Episode 6, the final section of the play, opens with Fox and Crystal, having sold their travelling show, standing like Beckettian tramps at a crossroads in open country, with nothing but a couple of suitcases, the rickety wheel, an accordion and a stove. They are drunk, and giddy with the thought that 'we're going to spend the rest of our lives in the middle of nowhere' (*CF*, p. 56). Shedding social constraint, they have regressed to childhood: 'They make so much noise – chattering, laughing, whooping, singing – that one would expect to see a dozen happy children appear' (*CF*, p. 55). Fox is more exuberantly playful than ever, 'eejitin about' in a manner highly reminiscent of Gar O'Donnell, entertaining a delighted Crystal by switching from one role to another, in a hectic, virtuoso display of his skills as an impersonator. As far as Fox is concerned, 'heaven's just round the corner' (*CF*, p. 55). But Fox's dream remains as elusive as Gatsby's. The excitement is shadowed by despair. In the midst of his 'exultation', Fox 'is aware – and Crystal is not – that it has also a cold brittle quality, an edge of menace' (*CF*, p. 58). The play's final twist is Fox's destroying the thing that means most of all to him, his relationship with Crystal. In the grip of a destroying force that he can neither explain nor control – 'I tried to stop myself but I couldn't' (*CF*, p. 64) – he wrecks the one illusion he has left, the illusion of love. He can't stop himself destroying his only chance of happiness, his dream of the past. He does so by telling Crystal that he has informed on their son for the reward money. With this perverse confession Fox puts Crystal to the ultimate test to see if she really would 'go to hell' with him (*CF*, p. 61). Up to this point, she has connived in Fox's ruthless, selfish actions: 'I didn't give a damn about any of them, God forgive me, not even Pedro, not so long as you didn't turn on me. That's all I cared about' (*CF*, p. 60). But now Fox is simply 'evil'. Confronted with the dark Unknown of personality, Crystal recoils from her playboy in fear and loathing: 'It's too much. . . . I don't know you. . . . Don't know you at all. . . . Never knew . . . never . . .' (*CF*, p. 63). Like Frank Hardy, the faith healer in the play of that name, Fox longs for transcendence, which is a death-wish as well as a desperate hope. He yearns for silence and an end to division.

There is a sense of inevitability about the course of Fox's career. Early on, El Cid predicts that Fox will come to a bad end: 'But I know him . . . twisted, that's what he is. . . . And I'll tell you something more about him: he's not going to stop until he's ratted on everybody! I know that character' (*CF*, p. 19). Gabriel, too, forsees the course of Fox's life: 'You hate everybody: . . . Even Crystal . . . she'll be the next. You'll ditch her too' (*CF*, p. 48). Fox sings 'A-hunting you will go / You'll catch no fox and put him in a a box' (*CF*, p. 64), but he does so 'lamely', with no more enthusiasm than Gar could muster when he tried to reassure himself by singing 'Philadelphia, Here I Come'. The irony of Fox's bid for freedom is that underlying it is his deeply pessimistic conviction that his life is already 'fixed'. Convinced of this, he acts to bring about his own self-ordained defeat. In the role of a fairground barker, he spins the rickety wheel and addresses an imaginary crowd:

> You pays your money and you takes your choice, not that it makes a damn bit of difference because the whole thing's fixed, my love, fixed – fixed – fixed; (almost gently) but who am I to cloud your bright eyes or kill your belief that love is all. A penny a time and you think you'll be happy for life.   (*CF*, p. 65)

In the middle of the speech Fox retreats from despair and, with surprising humility and kindness, reinstates the value of illusion. The shaman/artist's job, he implies, is to provide reinforcement of the illusions of love and hope, and distraction from the bleak 'secrets of the universe' (*CF*, p. 65) to which he is privy. That knowledge, after all, has only left him immobilised and alone. Tortured by a sense of the ironic futility of life, he at last subsides into a posture of quiescent acceptance. Having destroyed love, his dissociation from the world is complete. All he is left with is his rickety wheel – blind chance: 'A car passes. He does not hear it. He closes his eyes, puts his arm over the rickety wheel, and quickly buries his face in his arm' (*CF*, p. 65).

Friel's ending is characteristically Beckettian. In *Act Without Words* the solitary actor who struggles vainly from start to finish against unseen forces is seen at the end on his side, staring before him and refusing to move. At the close of *Waiting for Godot* Vladimir and Estragon 'do not move'[11] and Hamm brings *Endgame* to an end when 'he covers his face with handkerchief, lowers his arms to armrests, and remains motionless'.[12] Friel's picture of unaccommodated man stripped to the bare essentials of life, confronting the basic questions of existence, situated in an unspecified, empty landscape (at 'a signpost pointing in four directions' (*CF*, p. 55)), subject to a slow, inexorable decline and ultimately relapsing into silence and immobility inevitably evokes Beckett's tramps and clowns. They, too, are dichotomised creatures, split, like Friel's, into the essential Self and the apparent Self. Krapp, for example, vainly seeks to discover his true identity by reliving various periods of his past life. But if Krapp fails to find the 'end', there remains the memory of an ephemeral, irrational, tenderness beyond words which, despite its evident futility, still suffuses the whole background of *Krapp's Last Tape*. Fox, however, has gone beyond even this minimal idealism of a communication achieved through love. Beckett's purgatorial vision has deepened in *Crystal and Fox* into a parable of a truly demonic possession.

In Friel's play, the future belongs to the symbolically named Dick Prospect, the man with the 'big red face' and 'big bull head' (*CF*, p. 21) – a very different kind of 'animal' (*CF*, p. 59) from Fox. He never actually appears on stage, but from the outset he is established as Fox's antagonist. He is the one who gives employment to the performers who leave Fox, it is he who buys Fox out at the end and there is the suggestion that at one time his acquisitive designs even stretched as far as Crystal. In his world, both life and art are reduced to business, and the loud-mouthed vulgarity and brash pragmatism with which he conducts his business make him an unappealing prospect for the future.

LOVERS

Lovers, consisting of two complementry plays, *Winners* and *Losers*, was first produced at the Gate Theatre, Dublin, in July 1967. The play received its first American production at the Vivian Beaumont Theatre, New York, in 1968 and its first London production at the Fortune Theatre, in 1969. The two plays are ironically titled: Joe and Mag in the more lyrically pitched first play are 'winners' in drowning before they are destroyed by marriage; Andy and Hanna in the more broadly comical second play are 'losers' because their eventual marriage brings, not fulfilment and happiness, but entrapment and subjection. In both plays Friel evinces an interest in exploring a kind of 'supra-naturalism'[13] in the use of the chorus-like commentators in *Winners* and of the Beckettian monologues in *Losers*. Perhaps it is in recognition of the new technical and imaginative freedoms that he learnt from Tyrone Guthrie that he has dedicated *Lovers* to his fellow Ulsterman, friend and mentor.

In *Winners*, the lovers are two seventeen year olds, Joe and Mag, who meet to spend a sunny summer morning studying for their final school examinations on Ardnageeha, a hill overlooking the town of Ballymore where they live. Mag is pregnant and the two youngsters are to be married in three weeks' time. We are again made aware of a disruptive or destroying force that exists both within and without the human subject. It is the consciousness of this force submerged in both character and situation that controls the entire action. The subject is not only a centre of initiatives, author of and responsible for its actions, but also a subjected being who submits to the authority of Society and of Fate. In *Winners* the decisive enemy happens to come from without. At the same time, we are made continually aware of the division within the self, of the unconscious as a constant source of potential disruption, of 'the enemy within'. We suspect that if Mag and Joe had not drowned their future life together would very likely become a slow, miserable death-in-life. The bitter irony of the title is that Mag and Joe are 'winners' because their premature deaths have saved them from the protracted and inevitable misery of marriage to each other.

Though Joe and Mag show a determination to be positive and optimistic about their future, especially towards the end of the play, their reply to inevitabilities is uncertain and ambivalent. Joe has agreed to marriage, but he regards it as a threat to his plans to go to university and become a maths teacher. His feeling of entrapment breeds bitter resentment against Mag and the resentment leads to frighteningly insensitive behaviour towards her. Mag has every reason to wonder if there will be much room left for her in Joe's life after they are married. She pleads for reassurance: 'After we're married we'll have lots of laughs together, Joe, won't we? [*She begins to cry inaudibly*] Joe, I'm nervous; I'm frightened, Joe; I'm terrified' (*L*, p. 28). But Joe is too self-engrossed to respond to the needs of the other. The gap between them is graphically represented by the contrast between his silent absorption in his books and her craving for attention and endless chatter. Mag pours out her doubts and fears about the future and reaffirms her love for Joe, but he is deaf to all of this and shows little appreciation of what Mag is feeling:

(Joe flings his book from him in exasperation. Speaks very articulately) You – are – a – bloody – pain – in the – neck! (Quickly) You haven't shut up for five consecutive minutes since we've got here! You have done no work yourself and you have wasted my morning too!   (*L*, p. 30)

Mag's talk is a venting of unstructured, free-wheeling energy and emotion – the equivalent of her exam technique which is 'to write down everything you know – no matter what the question is' (*L*, p. 27). In contrast, mathematical Joe likes order and discipline. Mag's scattiness infuriates him. She reacts by name-calling: 'Stewbag! Stewbag!' (*L*, p. 31).

At times the tensions reach breaking point. One of Mag's fears that recurrently preys on her mind is that in marriage she will simply have consigned herself to the role of wife and mother and will have forfeited any life of her own. She doesn't want to become like Bridie Brogan – 'she developed pernicious microbia' (*L*, p. 41). When Joe refuses to take these fears of Mag's seriously, she betrays her latent class prejudice in a frustrated outburst against him:

JOE: Pernicious what?
MAG: You're too ignorant to have heard of it. My father came across frequent cases of it. I don't suppose your parents ever heard of it.

(*L*, p. 41)

The insult elicits the vicious retort:

JOE: Well, let me tell you, madam, that my father may be temporarily unemployed, but he pays his bills; and *my* mother may be a charwoman but she isn't running out to the mental hospital for treatment every couple of months. And if you think the Brennans aren't swanky enough for you, then by God you shouldn't be in such a hurry to marry one of them!

(*L*, p. 42)

The slanging-match reveals deep prejudices that earlier Joe and Mag had made a point of covering up by professing an exaggerated respect for each other's parents. Mag refuses to speak to Joe any more and he is left to try and retrieve the situation by acting the clown. Instead of confronting their problems, he simply takes evasive action. Drawing on his repertoire of impersonations of local people, he seeks to restore a more relaxed and playful mood. This facility for mimicry and fantasy is one of several characteristics Joe shares with that other exuberant playboy, Gar O'Donnell. Like Gar, Joe has a father who is uncommunicative and scared of showing his feelings and like Gar, Joe, too, can be 'kinda cold'. Like Gar, Joe longs for escape from his constricting background and displays not only a similar imaginative vitality but a similar naivety and immaturity in his avoidance of reality. Only the reality – the horror – of the body (pregnancy pains, Caesarian birth) seems capable of shaking Joe out of self-engrossment or fantasy and recalling him to actuality and responsibility.

We also see Joe and Mag's effort to resist panic and despair. There are times when the future seems hopeless: 'It's no good' (*L*, p. 33), says Mag sadly, in reply to Joe's charge that she has trapped him into marriage. But the dark mood doesn't last and a few moments later 'they both howl with spontaneous, helpless laughter' (*L*, p. 34) at Joe's play-acting. The spectres of misery and defeat surround them, but Mag, especially, maintains a touching youthful optimism: 'I think sometimes that happiness, real happiness, was never discovered until we discovered it. Isn't that silly?' (*L*, p. 22); 'And when I look around me – at Papa and Mother and the O'Haras – I think: by God we'll never become like that, because – don't laugh at me, Joe – because I think we're unique!' (*L*, p. 30) – a faith which is ironically qualified by Joe's exasperated outburst which immediately follows. The culminating irony is that in the last scene in which we see Mag and Joe, the lift towards a transcendent optimism, their new-found eagerness to embrace the future, comes just at the point where their final obliteration is most imminent.

What Friel wants to show in this play is not only the precariousness of conscious subjectivity, but also the plurality of meaning which is a necessary consequence of the fracturing of human consciousness. Representation, like the self, is not single. Events can no longer be presented from a specific and unified point of view. Thus, the story of Mag and Joe is told on two levels: interspersed throughout the vividly realised moments of Mag and Joe's day is Man and Woman's account, such as one might read in a newspaper, of the circumstances surrounding the youngsters' deaths. Mag and Joe's story quickly assumes the status of memory (we know before the end of Episode 1 what the outcome of the story will be). The drama of their relationship is, from an early point, tinged with a fatalistic sense of their necessary and imminent end. Dispensing with the conventional dramatic elements of narrative and suspense, Friel turns his play into a gradual unfolding of a complex poetic image. The abrupt juxtapositions of the Private and Public languages give the sense of a deliberate temporal and spatial dislocation. The intrusions of Man and Woman's objective narration dispels, at least momentarily, the illusion of reality and complicates a simple empathy by enlarging our perspectives and forcing us to stand back and view Mag and Joe under the aspect of eternity.

Man and Woman's speeches are read from a book: 'Their reading is impersonal, completely without emotion: their function is to give information. At no time must they reveal an attitude to their material' (*L*, p. 11). Their speech belongs to the same order of discourse as the 'play' inscribed in the 'ledger' held by Sir in *Living Quarters*. Like Sir, Man and Woman are the custodians of the facts of history and their version of events foregrounds a mechanistic, linear process of cause and effect, suppressing expressive personality and concrete relation. Men and Women are, in effect, the chill voice of doom.

Several details in the play serve to situate Mag and Joe in the constant presence of death and defeat: Mag watches a funeral in the streets below; their love-nest is located right at the very edge of the slaughterhouse yard; in the lives of their own parents, whether rich or poor, they can see the hand of the destroying force. But it is through Man and Woman's post-mortem interruptions that Friel most forcefully emphasises a demoralising fatalism, a sense of the ironic futility of all human effort. *Winners* is the reply to inevitabilities of the perpetual loser, of the disintegrated personality that has been robbed of its confidence in the possibilities of change and reconstruction.

Losers is no more optimistic. In this, the companion play, a reworking of the early short story 'The Highwayman and the Saint', the two middle-aged lovers are 'losers' because they fail to make good their chance of fulfilment together. Despite an initial spirited defiance, Hanna and Andy eventually fall back into the old nets of family and religion. *Losers* is an elegy to lost possibility. Where Joe and Mag were at least engaged to the very end in a battle – albeit a losing battle – for a future together of love and hope, Hanna and Andy reply to inevitabilities by simply capitulating – Hanna first and then, rather more recalcitrantly, Andy too. Joe and Mag are ultimately defeated by forces beyond their control, but in *Losers* Friel concentrates on the lack of courage equal to desire, on Hanna and Andy's individual weakness which stops them from creating a more congenial life for themselves.

Andy and Hanna, at mid-life, discover passion. Romance dissolves fixity and routine. Of Hanna, we are told: 'this sudden injection of romance into a life that seemed to be rigidly and permanently patterned has transformed a very plain spinster into an almost attractive woman' (*L*, p. 53). Andy recalls a time of great excitement when 'the aul' legs would damn near buckle under me' (*L*, p. 53), a time of belated promise and new beginnings, of rebelliousness against the traditional pieties insisted upon by Hanna's mother, the shrivelled but still fiercely demanding old invalid, Mrs Wilson. The submerged sexual energy which Hanna and Andy liberate in each other is seen as a threat to the strict domestic and religious order presided over by Mrs Wilson from the throne room of her upstairs bedroom. Opposing and disrupting the dominant discourse, which enshrines the values of family and Church, is the discourse of the Body – Andy and Hanna's passionate, wordless body language. It contrasts with both Andy's recitation of Gray's 'Elegy' which serves to mask the sounds of love-making and the equally mechanical nightly ritual of Mrs Wilson's saying the rosary. In both cases, language has congealed into formulae. Of Cissie Cassidy, Mrs Wilson's friend and neighbour who joins the invalid for the nightly prayers, Friel writes: 'A lifetime spent lisping pious platitudes has robbed them of all meaning. The sickly piousity she exudes is patently false' (*L*, p. 61). Cissie reacts as strongly as Mrs Wilson against the threat posed by the Body: to Cissie, Andy is just a 'dirty animal' (*L*, p. 72).

At the beginning of her romance, Hanna bitterly resents her mother's disapproval and Andy remarks on how revitalising the spirit of revolt had been: 'By God, she had spunk in those days, eh? Suited her, too: gave her face a bit of colour and made her eyes dance' (*L*, p. 59). But Hanna is not ruthless enough to resist her mother's influence. Andy laments Hanna's failure: 'But whatever it was that happened to her . . . to see a woman that had plenty of spark in her at one time and then to see her turn before your very eyes into a younger image of her mother, by God it's strange' (*L*, p. 59). After Hanna and Andy get married, Hanna's combativeness disappears, as Andy notes with detached and philosophic resignation: 'Like, you know before we got married, she was full of fight there: let the aul' woman step out of line or say something sharp to me and by God she jumped at her like a cock at a gooseberry. But somehow the spirit seemed to drain out of her from the beginning' (*L*, p. 68).

Andy, who sees himself engaged in a battle of wills with

Mrs Wilson, can't help but admire the old woman's craftiness. After the honeymoon, he and Hanna even find themselves living with the mother, though Andy takes a stand on the 'rosary caper' (L, p. 59), knowing that if he didn't he would appear to accede to the mother's belief that 'the family that prays together stays together' (L, p. 60). The Vatican announcement that all Roman Catholics must discontinue devotions to St Philomena (the saint to whom Mrs Wilson always prays) 'because there is little or no evidence that such a person ever existed' (L, p. 70) provides the opportunity for Andy's last desperate gesture of revolt. However, his coarse, drunken outburst against family piety only succeeds in consolidating mother's position and finally alienating Hanna. The three women – Mrs Wilson, Cissie and eventually Hanna – close ranks against the drunken Andy, against the Body, against the freedom of the individual. Even when the dominant mythology has been unmasked its exponents, in order to maintain their balance of power, quickly recollect themselves in terms of an even more fiercely prosecuted mystification, one which seeks to place itself beyond rational critique altogether:

> CISSIE: We've no statue, true enough; but we have a saint in our mind even though we've no figure for it. . . .
> ANDY: What saint?
> CISSIE: Aha, that's something you'll never know, Andrew Tracey! Wild horses wouldn't drag that out of us. You robbed us of St Philomena but you'll never rob us of this one, for you'll never be told who it is!
>
> (L, p. 76)

At the end, Andy and Hanna are still living with mother. We learn that Andy now joins in the nightly rosary and that Hanna sleeps in her mother's room: 'Well, I mean to say, anything for a quiet life' (L, p. 75). The play ends by returning to the nihilistic, Beckettian image with which it began – Andy 'staring fixedly through a pair of binoculars at the grey stone wall, which is only a few yards from where he is sitting. It becomes obvious that he is watching nothing: there is nothing to watch' (L, p. 51) – an image which mirrors Mrs Wilson's fixed gaze upon the saint who doesn't exist. Nevertheless, Mrs Wilson is the one who is the winner in the play's power struggle. Along with Cissie, she has succeeded in dispelling the movement toward change, freedom and passionate life which Hanna and Andy's relationship

at first promised. Hanna and Andy are the losers because they have
allowed themselves to settle for a life without any future, a life of
subjection to an old, repressive, life-denying order. Friel touches on
a distinctively Irish theme: the willingness to acquiesce fatalistically
in one's own enslavement; the tendency to reply to 'inevitabilities'
by passively accepting that they are inevitabilities; the inability to
say 'Non serviam' and to accept the challenge of evolving a new
order. The structure of the play emphasises both the point of view of
the victim and the fixation with the past. Andy, who is both inside
the action (as participant) and outside (as narrator), controls the
shape of the play because the events which we witness are his
recollections of past failure, viewed with a mixture of regret, resignation and fascination. He lets us into various points in his past life
over the previous four years, beginning and ending in the hopeless
present. The whole play is a kind of secret confession, a further
transgression, a private statement lodged in defiance of the dominant public discourse:

> when he (Andy) becomes aware of the audience, he lowers the
> glasses slowly, looks at the audience, glances cautiously over his
> shoulder at the kitchen to make sure that no one in the house
> overhears him, and then speaks directly and confidentially down
> to the auditorium.   (*L*, p. 51)

The play's chief merit is its subtle combination of elegy and indigna-
tion, comedy and tragedy, its ability to enlist our sympathy for the
victim and at the same time reveal the absurdity which results from
human weakness and failure.

THE MUNDY SCHEME

The Mundy Scheme is rather different from anything Friel had done
before, a kind of satirical *jeu d'ésprit* which, he tells us, he submitted
to the Abbey 'with the greatest misgivings and little enthusiasm'.
The Abbey turned the play down on the grounds that it was too
controversial, but it was produced at the Olympia Theatre, Dublin,
in 1969 and opened at the Royal Theatre, New York in the same year.

   The Mundy Scheme sets out to debunk the fiction of romantic
Ireland, an endeavour which is continued most notably in *The Gentle*

Island and *The Communication Cord*. 'Ireland', Friel wrote in 1973, 'is becoming a shabby imitation of a third-rate American state. This is what *The Mundy Scheme* is about.'[14] Desmond Maxwell summarizes those 'sore spots' which Friel wishes to interrogate: 'shoneenism, xenophobia, time-serving religion, even the Irish death-wish – characteristics that invert the stereotypes of tourist brochures'.[15]

The most obvious target of Friel's satire is the country's political leadership (which, ironically, Friel himself was to join, at least symbolically, with his acceptance of the nomination to the Irish Senate in 1987). *The Mundy Scheme* is another play filled with authority figures – the taoiseach, F. X. Ryan and the government ministers who preside over the newly formed Irish state. Friel protests against the lack of integrity in public life, highlighting the gap between inner reality and outer appearance. Ryan, for example, is a ruthless Machiavellian in the public sphere, yet pathetically dependent on his 'mammie' in private life. And all of Friel's public figures, while striving to maintain an estimable public image, are revealed as essentially creatures of outrageous, hopeless, comprehensive depravity. The public image is a transparent mask, a carefully engineered effect. What this means is that the split subject has been simplified into a crude, monochromatic type or abstraction. Fully rounded, complex characterisation which explored internal contradiction and division would only inhibit the message Friel wants to convey.

Like many other of Friel's plays, this one focuses on a point of crisis, when momentous decisions have to be made. The country is in a bad way, on the brink of bankruptcy and unable to secure financial support from the international community. The Minister of Finance, Boyle, has just returned empty-handed from Zurich and the offer from the US Defense Department to buy a nuclear submarine base in Cork or Galway has proved unacceptable, not, finally, for reasons of principle but because none of the Irish ports would be big enough to satisfy American needs. The country's present condition is a demoralising disappointment in light of the dreams of 1916. The Voice which opens the play states the question: 'What happens to an emerging country after it has emerged?' (*Ms*, p. 157). Ireland is the country which was 'occupied and oppressed by the English who treated the natives as serfs and who even tried to supplant the Catholic religion' (*MS*, p. 158). What quickly becomes clear is that the new, post-colonial order is not any more satisfactory. The country is in the hands of ruthless predators, unprincipled politicos, venal materialists, dangerous opportunists. The man at the helm, the despicable Ryan, is, we learn, afflicted by the symbolically named 'labyrinthitis . . . sudden bouts of dizziness and nausea' (*MS*, p. 160). In the opening scene his Private Secretary, Nash, is attending to Ryan's correspondence, demonstrating a comic virtuosity and fluency, in mimicking the range of styles employed by the taoiseach: the nature of the language of politics is thus forcefully and amusingly foregrounded.

'Decay or development' (*MS*, p. 200), as Michael Moloney, Minister for External Affairs, puts it, are the stark alternatives. Like Hugh in *Translations*, Moloney argues for the need to adapt to new circumstances and avoid fossilisation. But the kind of development Moloney champions – backing a Texan–Irish entrepreneur, the Mundy of the title, who has a scheme to turn the west of Ireland into a gigantic cemetery for the world's dead – is, like Swift's 'modest proposal',[16] the focus of the writer's excoriating social criticism. Friel's satiric whip is directed against those who would do anything for power and money, even sell their inheritance. The scheme represents an extension of and capitalises on a well-known unhealthy tendency in the Irish psyche – the Irish addiction to death. As Boyle recognises: 'A lot of our literature, our music, our legends, the whole emphasis of our religion – all revolve around death and the dead . . . you will end up with a nation of chronic necrophiliacs' (*MS*, p. 220). Nevertheless, it is the gruesome 'Mundy Scheme' that is hailed as the solution to Ireland's ills. The play's subtitle – '*May We Write Your Epitaph Now, Mr Emmet?* – is an allusion to the words of Robert Emmet in 1803, on the eve of his execution, when he requested that no epitaph should be written for him until the time 'when my country takes her place among the nations of the earth'.[17] Moloney, Ryan and the rest of the Irish government ministers eventually conclude that their 'Mundy Scheme' will enable them to fulfil the heroic patriot's wish for his country.

Moloney and Ryan succeed in obtaining support for the preposterous plan by emphasising what each member of the Cabinet stands to gain personally from its implementation. 'Profit' is the magic word and the abuse of power and privilege is the order of the day. Religion is invoked to justify political decisions, as when Ryan claims in a television broadcast that the 'Mundy Scheme' is 'an opportunity for the Church to show that Irish Christianity once more leads the world in ecumenism and charity' (*MS*, p. 273). Ryan's public language, formal and archaic, with its religious colouring and rational tone, masks voracious greed and the basest treachery. As soon as he sees that the scheme is going to be adopted by government, he starts buying up land cheaply, knowing that he will be able to resell at inflated prices to the Americans. When Nash threatens his plans, he simply frames him and has him arrested for drug-trafficking. Rather than share the profits from his land deals with his old friend and instigator of the scheme, he sets about removing Moloney from office by bringing to public attention Moloney's affair with the Albanian Ambassador's wife. There is no honour amongst these thieves.

The play ends with Ryan, his political position now thoroughly consolidated, watching television coverage of work which has just begun on the new cemetery. It is a bleak view of human nature which the play reflects, for there is not a single character capable of representing an alternative to the ubiquitous greed and duplicity. In reverting to a concept of character as a fixed essence, Friel withholds the possibility of change and development. Yet, in compelling us to face the consequences of constructing the world in this way, the play itself may be seen to initiate certain imaginative positives in reply to 'inevitabilities'.

3

Text

Disrupting the Unified Text: The Plays of the 1970s

Everything is fiction. There is no such thing as reality, only versions of reality. Science is fiction, politics is fiction, history is fiction. So runs a line of potentially demoralising postmodernist thinking. The Modernist saw the world as chaotic yet believed the artist still retained power to convert disorder into the perfect order of art. But where does postmodernism leave art? If there is nothing to reveal but fiction, how can fiction tell us about anything other than itself?

Friel takes up many of the postmodernist concerns. He offers us drama as self-conscious fiction which draws attention to the fact that it is fiction. The conjuror, it would seem, can no longer perform the trick without declaring that it is a trick. The trick is narrative and the problematics of narrative intrigue Friel. His plays are full of narrators, writers, chroniclers, history-men, stage directors, translators and artists of one kind or another whom we watch in the very process of constructing their narratives. Representation is no longer single or unified, but fragments into a range of competing discourses and languages, none of which is clearly privileged. It is in acknowledgement of the constructed, linguistic aspect of Friel's drama that I have used the term 'text' rather than the more traditional 'work'. The term 'text' is used to draw attention to the fact that what we are dealing with is a network of meaning, an interweaving of various discourses. (Roland Barthes is fond of metaphors of 'weaving', 'tissue', 'texture', 'strands' and 'filiation' when describing the structure of texts.) The text is multilayered and plural and its multiplicity cannot be reduced to a single, neat, fixed meaning. Thus, Friel's drama might be seen to act out Jean-François Lyotard's rejection of the idea of 'meta-narratives' in order to indulge 'little stories'[1] or

Mikhail Bakhtin's notion of the 'carnivalesque,' of dialogistic subversion and plurivocity. In challenging and subverting 'monologic' and authoritarian discourse by including other kinds of language which parody or deflate the central, official language and values, Friel follows Bakhtin in seeking to suspend the 'hierarchical structure and all the forms of terror, reverence, piety and etiquette connected with it'.[2] The 'carnivalesque' lets loose antitotalising disruptions of the dominant ideology to the extent that it pre-figures alien and unforseen possibilities and allows new relations to emerge.

In these plays of the 1970s we shall find that Friel is more interested in exploring the conditions of 'truth' than in propagating any particular 'truth'. He is suspicious of completion and a singularity of experience which would prove definitional. By refusing single meaning he refuses conformity and seeks to encourage complex seeing in the audience. His endings are characteristically 'open', unresolved or ambiguous, confirming the playwright's relinquishment of a too authoritarian control over his material. This suggestion of 'play' in the construction of the text is also found at the level of character, in Friel's use of the Protean Playboy as a central figure – the neurotic, restless individual (Shane in *The Gentle Island*, Skinner in *Freedom of the City*, Casimir in *Aristocrats*, Keeney in *Volunteers*, Frank Hardy in *Faith Healer*) whose acts of transformation, like the playwright's art, are a means of survival, an assertion and celebration of the resistant spirit.

Yet, however fragmented and problematic reality may be for Friel, plot and character are not entirely done for in his plays. The plurality of meaning does not simply become a matter of infinite play, an anarchic scepticism, the celebration of undecidability as an end in itself. Friel warns of all the impostures of narrative, but insists we are still watching a group of human beings or a window on time. The conviction that everything is fiction, that truth is forever elusive, can produce a pessimistic resignation, a sterile conservatism, but for Friel it is when we think of reality as fixed and final, when we forget that meanings are produced and that they serve the interests of particular groups, it is then that we begin to 'fossilise'. Art does not match life, but for Friel that does not have to be the only subject matter. The virtue of fiction lies in what its detractors so often accuse it of doing: it tells us entertaining lies, it stimulates us with things that are not, then and there, literally true, it exercises our imaginations. Play and story are the best ways we have of doing that. If play and story did not convey meaning there would be no urgent need, a need as old as Plato, to expose their insanity. But nobody need suppose they were ever fact.

Friel emphasises the social context for meaning – what Seamus Deane refers to as 'the politics of language, the language of politics and their relation to the language of poetry and drama.[3] The relation between meaning and power becomes a central theme in plays such as *Freedom of the City*, which is strongly influenced by the French philosopher, Michel Foucault's view of language as a form of political and social control in which 'truth' becomes more relative and pragmatic rather than absolute and ideal, functioning only in a specific historical context. We cannot exercise power, Foucault says, except through the reproduction of 'truth':

> Western history cannot be dissociated from the way 'truth' is produced and inscribes its effects. We live in a society which to a large extent marches in time with truth – what I mean by that is that ours is a society which produces and circulates discourse with a truth function, discourse which passes for the truth and holds specific powers.[4]

With reference to the plays of the 1970s, this chapter continues the discussion of Friel's investigation into the artificial nature of reality and considers his analysis of the social contestation of meaning and value. His own plays are viewed as arenas for negotiation between different discourses, the crucial question being: what, for Friel, passes for the truth? Fiction/theatre inhabits the gap between the real and the ideal, mediating between what is and what might be. The authentic fiction, we are shown, must keep the ideal and the real in close and creative relationship and it must know itself to be fiction, not literal fact. Only by so doing can fiction avoid 'fossilisation' and remain constantly open to change.

THE GENTLE ISLAND

The Gentle Island was first produced at the Olympia Theatre, Dublin, in November 1971 and then at the Lyric Theatre, Belfast, the following year. In this play, as in many other of his plays, Friel focuses on a small group of individuals surrounded by a disintegrating world. He homes in on the point of crisis, the point at which an old order is on the verge of collapse and choices have to be made. The central problem which Friel faces, along with a good many other Irish writers, is how to negotiate between the past and the future, how to reconcile traditional value and the search for individual freedom and authenticity, how to avoid the danger of fossilisation on one hand and the danger of postmodern dehumanisation on the other. What transpires on the ironically named 'gentle island' epitomises the crisis of culture in the larger island of Ireland: the unresolved conflict between Tradition and Modernity. It's an old theme of Friel's, taking us back to *Philadelphia* (1964) and Gar O'Donnell, who must make up his mind between staying at home in the repressed, small-town backwater of Ballybeg and jetting out to the excitements of the New World. In that play, the modern world has tragically failed to satisfy Aunt Lizzie's emotional needs and Ballybeg, for all its limitations, still exerts a powerful hold on the restless Gar. 'Ireland – America – what's the difference?' (*SP*, p. 64) remarks Ben Burton, extending a culturally inflected dilemma into a universal malaise. In *The Gentle Island* the choices are as finely balanced, but grimmer than ever. The departing islanders face an uncertain future in the urban gehenna where work will be hard, families will be split up and the old stabilising certainties will no longer hold. Those who remain will continue to face physical hardship and deprivation, the intense and claustrophobic conditions of their island home breeding the most shocking violence and the most ruthless treachery.

The play is, in fact, a bitterly ironical reworking of certain romantic fictions of the past. This island is home to no rural idyll. Though its 'gentleness' is what first impresses Peter's urban sensibility, it turns out to be a place seething with frustration and violence and blighted by an ancient 'curse'. Its inhabitants, devious, desperate and vicious, are lurid contradictions of the popular fiction of the Noble Peasant. Ironically, the only positive human values come from the city: it is Peter who brings sympathy and understanding into the violent amorality of Friel's antipastoral and it is Peter's friend, Shane, who turns the cold douche of common sense on Manus's fervid pieties and Peter's touristic enthusiasms alike. Peter is one of a line of outsiders in Friel's plays whose enchantment proves deceptive. Yolland, the English officer in *Translations*, for example, is mocked for his romantic views of Ireland ('For God's sake! The first hot summer in fifty years and you think it's Eden. Don't be such a bloody romantic. You wouldn't survive a mild winter here': *SP*, p. 414), and in both *The Mundy Scheme* and

The Communication Cord Friel takes a ferocious delight in overturning the romantic myths on which a false and sentimental nationalism rests.

Most ironic of all is Friel's treatment of the family, that traditional bastion of moral value. Family life in *The Gentle Island* is a hotbed of ugly passions, unspoken rivalries, guilty secrets and unresolved mystery. We never know exactly what happens on the island. There is a range of competing versions of events, but Friel declines to exercise his authorial privilege to fix and finalise. Rather, he exploits uncertainty and ambiguity. As Manus says: 'There's ways and ways of telling every story. Every story has seven faces' (*GI*, p. 56). The episode where Manus and his daughter-in-law Sarah exchange accounts of how Manus lost his arm is one of Friel's early Pinteresque experiments in the use of contrapuntal narratives as a means of strict psychological notation. Manus, seeking a strong self-image, boasts he lost his arm in a mining accident in Butte, Montana. Sarah tells us he lost it in a sordid fight on the island when he was attacked by two men whose niece he had got pregnant. According to Sarah, Manus is a reactionary old dinosaur whose brutishness has made it impossible for his son, Philly, to relate naturally to a woman. Manus, however, presents himself as a devoted husband. Sarah says the only reason he has remained on the island is that there were no jobs for one-armed labourers in America or England: Manus, on his account, repeatedly champions an atavistic law of 'belonging' and the sanctity of roots:

> They belong here and they'll never belong anywhere else! Never! D'you know where they're going to? I do. I know. To back rooms in the back streets of London and Manchester and Glasgow. I've lived in them. I know. (*GI*, p. 10)

Manus's island images tend to float free of reality altogether and assume an independent, talismanic force. He well knows the power of story. Story-telling is a kind of magical ceremony and requires certain objective conditions for its magic to work. Thus, Manus refuses to tell Peter the story of the Monks: 'Some night I'll tell you. No man can tell a story in the middle of the day' (*GI*, p. 26). To Shane, Manus's version of the island is both false and dangerous. Shane knows that he and Peter

give support to his (Manus's) illusion that the place isn't a cemetery. But it is. And he knows it. The place and his way of life and everything he believes in and all he touches – dead, finished, spent. And when he finally faces that, he's liable to become dangerous. (*GI*, p. 37)

The romance of primitivism is another joke ('Look at the act I have – the simple upright, hardworking island peasant holding on manfully to the *real* values in life, sustained by a thousand year-old culture, preserving for my people a really worthwhile inheritance': (*GI*, p. 37), as is the mystique of eloquence which keeps the old values alive ('And now, as a di-varsion, I'll tell youse the old tale of the white-haired harper from the townland of Ballymaglin in the barony of Kildare': *GI*, p. 37).

Shane is the only one who acknowledges the fictional nature of reality. He speaks of life as a story, a game or a play and expresses himself in a highly self-conscious manner, deliberately mixing idioms, breaking the rules, refusing the magical function of story which Manus so passionately affirms. He is a chameleon-like, truly ambiguous character, the ambiguity extending even to his sexuality. He is the antithesis of Peter who wants 'the calm, the stability, the self-possession . . . no panics, no feverish gropings. A dependable routine' (*GI*, p. 52). In the end, the playboy Shane's antics are as intolerable to the natives of the 'Gentle Island' as Christy Mahon's are to the Mayo peasants. Shane's behaviour is an affront to ancient piety, and deep springs of violence are activated by his transgressive, Dionysiac behaviour. When the others come upon him singing and dancing frenziedly to a gramophone record of 'Oh, Susanna' in mock celebration of 'a memorable holiday I once had on a heavenly island one divine summer' (*GI*, p. 40), Sarah slaps his face 'viciously' (*GI*, p. 42) and Joe and Philly punch him to the ground. In the end he has to be executed. The attempted murder is justified by hearsay only. Manus is apparently prepared to commit murder with no more evidence than the testimony of a woman who has consistently been his chief adversary up to this point. Sarah's version of what happened in the boat-house sets in motion a jealous woman's deadly plan of revenge against the man who had rejected her earlier advances and stolen her husband. Deeply resenting Manus's patriarchal law, under which she has been made to feel a failure because she has not borne a child, Sarah cunningly manipulates the old man, leading him to make a scapegoat out of Shane: Shane has to be punished for seducing Philly from his sacred duty of siring Manus's grandchildren and bringing back life to the island graveyard. Stories, we see, are constructed to satisfy particular needs, not some standard of objective truth. Stories give shape and utterance to our deep wishes and fears: they stir us to our most feverish gestures, sacrifices and betrayals.

The world of the play is a demoralised version of the absurdist vision. Friel puts greater emphasis on the absurdists' concern with the irrationality of life than their affirmation of human resourcefulness and resilience. Something of the playfulness of Vladimir and Estragon is present in Shane, but generally Friel's is a dark and nihilistic view of human relations, showing more interest in the demons within than in the potentially liberating human qualities. He offers no hope for the future, no possibility of fundamental change. This is what comes, Friel shows, of assuming an unchanging, essential human nature. No history, no politics. Instead, a notion of eternal recurrence: Manus is a Sweeney, a version of the ancient Sweeney who was caught between two worlds, the ancient and the modern. The island exodus strikes one of the émigrés as another 'Flight of the Earls' (*GI*, p. 4). Yet another paradigm is suggested by the story of 'the Monks' which tells of two young monks who were turned to stone because they fell in love with the old monk's niece and tried to escape with her from the island. The story establishes the ritual pattern, the key elements of which – youth's disruptive sexuality, conflict between old and young, the need to escape, the evil curse which negates the effort to escape – have their obvious contemporary parallels. The stories of the niggerman's torture, of the war dead who fell burning from the skies or were washed in by the tide, of Manus's horrific mutilation, of the sickening end of Mary's little dog, of the many storms and wrecks along the coast – these are all further instances of an endless, dark necessity.

In this play we see Friel struggling to find a form which would allow him to dramatise this supernatural world-view and at the same time incorporate a judgement of it. The play, in fact, epitomises the problem which we find Friel struggling with throughout the 1970s: how to satisfy the demands of both realistic enactment and rational critique. In *The Gentle Island* we constantly feel the pressure of the schematic parable behind the ostensibly realistic speech and situations. It is, in the end, a rather schematic play working to overturn the schema of conventional expectation and traditional value.

THE FREEDOM OF THE CITY

Friel's next play, *The Freedom of the City*, was first produced at the Abbey Theatre, Dublin, on 20 February 1973. A week later it was given its first English production when it opened at the Royal Court Theatre, London. Clearly, the play is, in some measure, a response to the events of Bloody Sunday (30 January 1972), when thirteen civil rights marchers in Derry were shot dead by British troops, and to the ensuing Widgery tribunal which, in exonerating the British army, served to exacerbate the shock and outrage felt by many Irish civil rights supporters. Establishment opinion in both England and Northern Ireland reacted strongly against Friel's play. Ulf Dantanus summarizes:

> most English newspapers were predictably hostile to its (the play's) political content, and some sort of defence had to be made: 'an entertaining piece of unconvincing propaganda' (*Daily Telegraph*); 'its bias against the English robs it of its potential power' (*Sunday Express*); the play 'suffers fatally from this overzealous determination to discredit the means and the motives of the English in the present Ulster crisis' and the writer 'is also engaged on a Celtic propaganda exercise' (*Evening Standard*); 'Friel's case is too loaded to encourage much intelligent sympathy' (*Daily Express*). These views were corroborated by the *Belfast Newsletter* which called the play 'a cheap cry' and described it as 'mawkish propaganda'. The *Daily Mail*, finally, told its readers that 'the play has angered senior Army officers in Ulster'.[5]

What none of these commentators acknowledges is the way Friel's theatre space is always at some remove from, or angle to, the temporal narrative, just as Ballybeg is a parish slightly outside, though not unaffected by history. Dantanus offers the following corrective observation on *Freedom of the City*: 'In order to relieve the play of the possibly limiting effects of too narrow an association with Bloody Sunday and in order to neutralize some of his own personal involvement in the issues, Friel used various distancing effects. The first of these was to set the play in 1970'.[6]

Most of Friel's plays are history plays or memory plays, working on (reworking) either public events (Columba on Iona, Bloody Sunday, the Ordnance Survey of 1833) or private traumas, but always on the moment of crisis, the Fall, the moment which is taken to be the origin of and key to all subsequent moments. In turning to Bloody Sunday in *The Freedom of the City*, he turned to an episode in the recent Irish past which quickly and deeply embedded itself in the ideology of republicanism, assuming the status of a mythic reiteration of earlier sacred foundational acts (in, say, 1798 and 1916), the recollection of which serves the purpose of integrating and justifying Republican consciousness. Thus, one option for the artist was to use his art to contribute to the common fund of hallowed traditions, orthodox pieties and idealised self-images whereby one particular social group maintains its sense of identity. At the other extreme, however, he could resist the process of stereotyping social formation and social action; instead of repeating the regressive movement which always fixates on the past, he could open up a progressive movement toward new meaning. And, indeed, what we actually find in *Freedom* is not a justification of terrorist violence, but an exposure of the bogus language of the corrupt state authority *and* of the equally bogus language of traditional Nationalist mythology. Public language, like Private language, is subject to and has to be rescued from, the distorting strategies of a false idealisation.

Friel's play, as Heaney has said of his own poetry, bears the 'watermarks and colourings'[7] of a Northern, Catholic, Nationalist sensibility. But without denying the implications of his own background and experience, Friel aims for depth and completeness in his depiction of the rebellious oppressed, so that between author and audience common recognition will emerge, a supervening bond above and beyond ideas. Thus, Friel's civil rights marchers are not Republican mouthpieces nor committed revolutionaries, but very ordinary people whose ambitions are remarkable for their innocence, that is, for being so stringently depoliticised and non-sectarian.

The three central characters represent working-class, Catholic Derry. Suffering from the effects of CS gas during a banned civil rights march, they seek refuge in Derry's Guildhall, a symbolic bastion of British imperialism. Michael doesn't want to change the system at all, only his place within it. He has all the respectable middle-class susceptibilities, including an exaggerated respect for authority. He is the least talkative of the central trio and his language tends to be a humourless, platitudinous, rather stilted recital of standard bourgeois attitudes:

It was a good, disciplined, responsible march. And that's what we must show them – that we're responsible and respectable; and they'll come to respect what we're campaigning for. (*SP*, pp. 128–9)

Michael's speech lacks the vigour of the class he wishes to leave, but has none of the confidence of the one to which he aspires. Of the three central characters, it is he who is treated with sharpest irony. Upwardly mobile as he would like to think of himself, both he and his father have lost their jobs; he and his fiancée are on the brink of marriage without even a place of their own to live in; and Michael, the most law-abiding of the unfortunate trio, is the one who at the end is charged with firing a weapon.

Skinner, the aimless ne'er-do-well, homeless and jobless, has more insight, recognising that the plight of Derry Catholics should be seen in the wider context of a world-wide struggle for civil rights. The civil rights movement, he believes, is the poor 'stirring in our sleep' (*SP*, p. 154), that is, it represents a primitive, pre-verbal energy which long precedes the ideologues. But, like Gar O'Donnell, Skinner represents eloquence without power. Not having any of the discipline nor commitment of a true revolutionary, he retreats behind a mask of 'defensive flippancy' (*SP*, p. 150).

The third marcher trapped in the Guildhall is warm, garrulous, resilient, endearing, amusing Lily. Lily's concerns are always personal – her family, children, neighbours, Michael's fiancée – never political. Politically unawakened, she accepts her lot in life, a passive victim of an unjust economic system, as she is now of the military and judicial authorities. Her intuitively flexible, idiomatic speech exhibits an imaginative energy and emotional robustness, an unquenchable human spirit that survives despite the life of grinding poverty to which she has been condemned. Inside the Guildhall, within the imposed ideological and linguistic structures, is a flow of signification, closely connected to femininity, setting up a play of unconscious or only half-conscious drives that counterpoint the received social meanings. Lily's speech represents a kind of pleasurable excess over precise, crystalline meaning, an opposition to all transcendental significations:

At this minute Mickey Teague, the milkman, is shouting up from the road, 'I know you're there, Lily Doherty. Come down and pay

me for the six weeks you owe me.' And the chairman's sitting at
the fire like a wee thin saint with his finger in his mouth and the
comics up to his nose and hoping to God I'll remember to bring
him home five fags. And below us Celia Cunningham's about
half-full now and crying about the sweepstake ticket she bought
and lost when she was fifteen. And above us Dickie Devine's
groping under the bed for his trombone and he doesn't know that
Annie pawned it on Wednesday for the wanes' bus fares and he's
going to beat the tar out of her when she tells him. And down the
passage aul Andy Boyle's lying in bed because he has no coat.   (*SP*,
p. 141)

Composed of a series of swift and vivid vignettes of individuals she
knows intimately, Lily's speech has an immediacy and particularity
which contrast sharply with Dr Dodds' sociological stereotyping
and with the abstract, theoretical language of the other public officials. The simple, declarative sentences and the cumulative, coordi-
nate structure suggest that the images are being given to us directly
as they occur in Lily's mind, without the intervention of a selecting,
discriminating, organising intellect. Only at the end of the speech
does a vague, moralising judgment, the most basic of deductions,
struggle into words: 'I'll tell you something, Skinner: it's a very
unfair world' (*SP*, p. 141). For the most part, Lily represents that
stage – 'before we were educated out of our emotions' – wistfully
described by Eamon in *Aristocrats*. Her speech, an instinctual, un-
educated, unself-conscious response to immediate circumstances,
comes closest to the unmediated and, therefore, relatively uncon-
taminated, expression – the 'Response Cries' – which are the subject
of Tim's thesis in *The Communication Cord*.

   Lily's expression, in all its vitality and spontaneity, represents a
valuable human potential and renders her the most dramatically
appealing character in the play, but it is also shown to be disas-
trously limiting. It makes it impossible for her either to articulate
strong personal feeling or to conceptualise the world. Lily says she
marches for her mongol son, Declan, which is 'the stupidest thing'
her husband has ever heard of – 'That's what the chairman said
when I – you know – when I tried to tell him what I was thinking. He
never talks about him . . .' (*SP*, p. 155). There is no language for
powerful, private feeling. Husband and wife are no more able to
communicate about their son than Gar could communicate with his

own father in *Philadelphia*. And Lily's speech, completely taken up with her sense of domestic responsibility, shows her inability to think beyond the family and the neighbourhood where she lives. Hugh in *Translations* recognizes how the *'desiderium nostrorum* – the need of our own' (*SP*, p. 445) has interfered with his own ability to engage with the issues of the wider world, but Lily is much more seriously incapacitated than Hugh for she is unable even to begin to conceptualise her situation, either personal or political. She strikes a key note of the play towards the end when she realises that never once in her life 'had an event . . . been isolated, and assessed and articulated' (*SP*, p. 150). Her failure to articulate means that she 'died of grief'. This emphasis is the opposite to the one we find in, say, *Dancing at Lughnasa*: where *Dancing at Lughnasa* celebrates the recovery of free, instinctual expression and release from the constraints of rational order, Lily longs for rationality and articulation. The desire for true articulation, for self-expression, is a desire to have some control over one's life. Ironically, the medium of this self-expression – language – is the very thing that imprisons, oppresses, falsifies.

Increasingly, Friel's dissatisfaction with language as a means of communication leads him to experiment with other expressive means, particularly with the possibilities offered by music and dancing. From *The Enemy Within* through *Living Quarters, Aristocrats, Translations* to *Dancing at Lughnasa*, history provides both a containing frame *and* a space for lyricism. In *Freedom of the City* that lyrical moment is profoundly innocent. In the mayor's parlour Lily and Skinner momentarily achieve a powerful communion through their dressing up and play-acting, their drinking and laughter. Skinner is the anarchic, Dionysiac spirit who leads Lily beyond social constraint. For a moment she is unburdened of her manifold responsibilities and freed into a dimension of pure play. The endless, human capacity for play, we see, is the means whereby the determinism of the universe may be held at bay. In emphasising this kind of broadly human rather than a strictly political potential, Friel suggests a natural, universal impulse from which no creed or class need feel excluded. (He could hardly have chosen a more 'Orange' name for one of his characters than Lily!) Friel's agitators are redeemed of all doctrinal prejudice, racist nationalism, class oppression and totalitarian ambition. He distinguishes between causes and results and shows more interest in probing the deep and simple causes of revolt in the private lives of individuals than in involving himself in an adjudication between different ideological positions (which would be to concentrate on results, not causes of the people's 'stirring'). The play ends in death, but the possibility of fluidity and experiment has also been affirmed.

Friel's problem is that while using such partial or limited ('innocent') characters as Michael, Skinner and Lily, he must find a dramatic structure which will allow him to bring out the implications of their particularised experience. There are plenty of interpreters on hand, but all unreliable. The interpretation of events by the representatives of the public world, from both sides of the sectarian divide, is a travesty of the real experience of the central trio. The opposition between Public and Private languages established in the short stories and central to *Philadelphia*, also forms the substance of *Freedom of the City*. Language is now seen as the vehicle not only of personal illusion but of public misrepresentation of the facts. The language of institutions, like the language of individuals, displays a similar fictive tendency. Moreover, Friel delineates the relationship between meaning and power: the control of meanings – of democracy, freedom, justice, etc. – is political power. Language is not only the means of constructing 'reality', but an instrument of oppression or containment within society. Thus, the Judge constitutes the terms of the inquiry into the shootings in such a way that the trio is already pre-judged:

> It is essentially a fact-finding exercise; and our concern and our only concern is with that period of time when these three people came together, seized possession of a civic building, and openly defied the security forces. The facts we garner over the coming days may indicate that the deceased were callous terrorists who had planned to seize the Guildhall weeks before the events of February 10th; or the facts may indicate that the misguided scheme occurred to them on that very day while they listened to revolutionary speeches. (*SP*, pp. 109–10)

The language of the public officials serves the interests of class or ideological domination by propagating a false consciousness of historical reality. The language of politics becomes synonymous with lies, manipulation and indiscriminate force. The witnesses are credible because they speak a controlled, educated, technical language and their pronunciation is of the received standard variety – the type of voices Lily and Skinner try to mimic in their parlour games.

The Catholic Church is represented by Father Brosnan whose name, roughly translating from the Irish as 'a man of sticks', suggests the brittleness and insubstantiality of the response of the Catholic hierarchy to social crisis. The play opens with the priest mumbling prayers in the ears of the already dead trio. This 'mumbling' (*SP*, p. 107) is dignified by the priest as 'administering the last rites' (*SP*, p. 124) in his Act 1 address, wherein he proceeds to ascribe heroic motives to the dead three. His Act 2 sermon begins by repeating the opening lines of his Act 1 address, but his earlier solidarity with the victims is now replaced by a much more critical attitude. Presumably acting under instructions from his superiors and living up to his name, he denounces the civil rights movement as an instrument of 'Godless communism' (*SP*, p. 156) and reminds the congregation of Christ's exhortation to be accepting and passive: '"Blessed are the meek for they shall possess the land"' (*SP*, p. 156).

The Nationalist Balladeer is no more interested in what really happened than any of the others. His primary concern is with elaborating and perpetuating a myth of heroic rebellion and martyrdom. Friel's depiction of the Balladeer is a criticism of imaginative inflexibility and balances the earlier critique of imperialistic Kipling's 'If' in Act 1. The RTE commentator, like the Balladeer, circulates untruths, which in this case actually jeopardise innocent lives. The rhetoric of the Media, like that of the State, the Church, and Academia reverberates with bitter irony against the brutal reality of the three dead bodies. In the final funeral scene, the dead are shamefully marginalised, the pressman even forgetting Skinner's name, in a commentary which shows much more interest in the various dignatories and politicians who attended the funeral than in the pathetic victims. Dr Dodds, the American sociologist with a special interest in the 'subculture of poverty', does consciously attempt to maintain an academic neutrality, but his sociological jargon, like the language of the priest or the press, distances us from the reality of poverty.

Freedom of the City is a play of voices – a clamant, confusing babel of voices, none of which can offer an adequate or reliable account of the story of Lily, Skinner and Michael. The confrontation of ideals with reality is the central theme and Friel exalts the present physical experience over the static iconography of the mythical. The play is on the side of the concrete and specific: abstraction is the real enemy. Friel's concept of individualism challenges the dominant social and linguistic codes by reclaiming the body (*Dancing at Lughnasa* being the culmination of this concern, a triumphant vindication of the body). The investment in the immediacy of the present experience is reflected in the discourse of the spontaneous and the physical which the central trio, but especially the two social outsiders, the female Lily and the playboy Skinner, represent. This living body is expressed by a naturalistic presentation, as opposed to the symbolic mode used in the depiction of the official world. The Judges, Press Officers, Policemen, Professors, Priests and Balladeers are remote and dehumanised, bereft of any of the compelling human characteristics so sensitively and lovingly delineated in the central trio. The public world, though it quite literally calls the shots, is emphatically less real, its meanings proliferating in violent disregard of the intimate, private reality which alone can justify them and on the side of which we are aligned from the start. The depiction of the central trio we are to take as an irreducible, incontestable 'truth' or 'reality'.

Without system or pattern, as Lily was dimly aware, there is no control, or, as Skinner put it, we are as if asleep, yet once we start imposing patterns we run the risk of trapping ourselves within a particular version of reality, which is inevitably, to some degree, falsifying. In the end, Friel is determined that the story of Michael, Skinner and Lily should disclose abstractable meanings after all and that we should recognise that the naturalistic presentation of his central characters is every bit as much of a fiction as the typological notation he uses to represent the public world. Thus, in the manner of Brecht's 'alienation' technique, he has the three characters, before they die, slip out of the flexible, idiomatic, private language he has so brilliantly devised for them, into the abstract and impersonal language of the public world:

> MICHAEL: I knew they weren't going to shoot. Shooting belonged to a totally different order of things. And then the Guildhall Square exploded and I knew a terrible mistake had been made. And I became very agitated, not because I was dying, but that this terrible mistake be recognized and acknowledged . . .
>
> LILY: And in the silence before my body disintegrated in a purple convulsion, I thought I glimpsed a tiny truth: that life had eluded me because never once in my forty-three years had an experience, an event, even a small unimportant happening been isolated, and assessed, and articulated . . .
>
> SKINNER: And as we stood on the Guildhall steps, two thoughts raced through my mind: how seriously they took us and how

unpardonably casual we were about them; and that to match
their seriousness would demand a total dedication . . .

(*SP*, pp. 149–50)

The fate of the three characters is directly related to social forces,
but social forces construed, apparently, as the instruments of an
inexorable fate. The social formation in *Freedom* would seem to have
precisely the same determining function as the 'curse' in *The Gentle
Island*. *Freedom* ends with the soldiers' burst of automatic fire – at the
split second before the point where the play began – with the three
dead bodies on the stage. Is Friel then colluding with a magical view
of reality, removing Lily, Skinner and Michael out of history and
converting their deaths into myth, forcing them to conform to the old
story of Irish political failure and martyrdom? Surely not. The play,
I would wish to argue, demonstrates empathy with the mentality of
powerlessness, but also represents what Heaney calls 'a coming to
consciousness',[8] an objectification of a certain, negative, alienating
habit of mind. Friel's framing technique (a more skilfully deployed
break with the conventions of naturalism than the sudden
polemicisation of Michael's, Skinner's and Lily's speech) serves the
purpose of foregrounding a particular way of viewing history – one
which, in fact, brings history to a standstill and promotes the recog-
nizably Gaelic, Catholic, Nationalist idioms of myth, tradition, piety
and martyrdom. Such a way of viewing history may have the purpose of both integrating and justifying a social group, but it may also
condemn that group to a demoralising cycle of recurrence and
eternal defeat. History is no longer an open-ended process of transformation: action must always ultimately conform to the terms established by the foundational act or 'curse'. What Friel suggests is a
relation between the object of perception and the mode of perception. In choosing to foreground a particular form of imaginative
projection in a context of tragic waste, he is warning against, not
reinforcing, a group's predisposition to recollect itself in terms of
such gambits of despair. But ultimately he declines to complete the
circle. The situation at the end is *not* an exact replication of that at the
beginning: after the Judge's final pronouncement and the burst of
gunfire 'the three stand as before, staring out, their hands above
their heads' (*SP*, p. 169). Friel refuses to freeze experience into unchanging repetition.

Philadelphia ended with Gar's image of the film which he will run
over and over again: 'Watch her carefully, every movement, every

gesture, every little particularity; keep the camera whirring; for this is a film you'll run over and over again – Madge Going to Bed On My Last Night At Home' (*SP*, p. 99). One thinks of Sartre's *Huis Clos* (translated as *No Exit* or *In Camera*). The film imagery is also relevant to *Freedom*, with its cinematic structure of rewindings, cuts, dissolves and flashbacks, but what this play suggests is that we need not simply replay the old scenarios over and over again. *Freedom* creates the conditions for a re-editing or rewriting of history. Instead of consigning the story of Lily, Skinner and Michael to the realm of the eternal and the timeless, Friel suggests the possibility of breaking with established patterns, of reinterpreting and thereby taking control of a changing world. Friel chooses to end his play by issuing a challenge to his audience to 'break the barbarous cycle' (to use Derek Mahon's phrase in 'The Last of the Fire Kings'). Occupying a space between the ideal and the real, he manages to affirm a minimal optimism in the face of the determining forces, a faith in the unquenchable human spirit, which has been so memorably and vividly personified for us in the character of Lily.

LIVING QUARTERS

Living Quarters was first produced by the Abbey Theatre, Dublin, on 24 March 1977. Friel follows Seneca, Racine, Robinson Jeffers, Robert Lowell and the film director Jules Dessin in finding the Hippolytus story relevant to his own artistic purposes. *Living Quarters* is written 'after Hippolytus', Friel's characters, like those in classical Greek tragedy, acting as if in fulfilment of an ancient curse. In Euripides' play, Hippolytus is a noble young man vowed to chastity. Phaedra is his father's young wife who falls in love with him. Hippolytus rejects her and Phaedra in passionate despair kills herself. Theseus, on returning home from a year of voluntary exile, and believing himself to have been shamed by both wife and son, hurls against Hippolytus a curse which is quickly fulfilled.

Friel's play concerns Commandant Frank Butler who, returning home from five months' service with the UN in the Middle East to discover that his young wife, Anna, has had an affair with his son Ben, shoots himself. In Friel's version, Ben is neither so noble nor so priggish as Hippolytus and it is not the guilty young wife who kills herself but the innocent husband.

Philip Vellacott, in his introduction to his Penguin translation of Euripides' play tells us that 'the "tragic agent" is divine, and the human characters are all primarily the innocent victims of Aphrodite. The question of their guilt is secondary'.[9] After all, Aphrodite claims in her prologue to have willed the events which we are about to watch. She shows herself as cruel and as vindictive (the way she is usually seen in antiquity) and destroys not just Hippolytus for his rejection of sex, but three people, two of them innocent of any insult to her. Divine beings behave with disastrous insensitivity to those mortals who must allow them into their lives. They are not clearly on the side of goodness. Moreover, they are in competition with each other (in following Artemis, Hippolytus is cut down by Aphrodite for presumption) and they are the justification for all kinds of excess (Phaedra is driven to lustful longing by Aphrodite; Hippolytus' cold rejection of Phaedra, his misogyny, his failure of sympathy, all stem from his devotion to Artemis).

However, we cannot escape recognition of another kind of 'tragic agent'. Robert Bagg, in his introduction to his translation of the play, shifts the emphasis from a divine to a human principle of causation: 'Alert readers of the play have always remarked how redundant the literal intervention of Aphrodite is. Everything could happen without her . . . events are perfectly intelligible as products of interacting human wills'.[10] Bagg emphasises how it is the failure of the characters to perceive each other's true nature which leads ultimately to disaster. (The Nurse doesn't understand Phaedra's agony and is unable to help her; Hippolytus, being ignorant of passion, cannot understand Phaedra's desire nor her longing for purity and he doesn't see why his father should be so violently desolated by Phaedra's suicide and by her accusations; Theseus's worldliness disables him from appreciating his son's claims to innocence.) In seeking to connect the nature of Aphrodite and the other divinities with the 'seemingly autonomous plot', Bagg asks us to think of the divine as the creation of the human rather than the human as determined by the divine:

> Euripides seems to have a wonderful awareness that if divinities such as Aphrodite, Artemis, Dionysos, *et al.* naturally form part of his culture's (and *mutatis mutandis*, our culture's) imaginative mythology, men will tend to perceive and to act out their destinies within the myths of one or more divinities, and that such a process, though it has its rewards and powers, will both oversim-

plify the individual's comprehension of reality and delude him
into transposing the behaviour of others into the terms of his own
myth – with disastrous results. This oversimplification and trans-
position – Hippolytos does it to women, Theseus to his son –
occurs nearly unconsciously, unless one is shocked awake as one
should be at a play like the one at hand.

Euripides confronts us with our narrow habits by making the
gods, even while he sings their power and grandeur, appear as
the emblems and creators of our failure to perceive; emblems,
even, of the stupidity of human life.[11]

Bagg's redefinition of the relationship of the human and the divine is relevant to what Friel is doing in his version of the Hippolytus
story. Friel presents characters who perceive and act out their desti-
nies in accordance with a preordained structure of reality and he,
too, wants us to be 'shocked awake' to the reality of his characters'
inner lives. He doesn't have gods, but he has 'Sir', who is the 'emblem' and 'creator' of his characters' failures and stupidities. In
opposition to a fatalistic acceptance of the incalculable forces, Friel
suggests another truth: 'You have chosen to be what you are',[12]
words of Sartre's which he quotes in his 'Sporadic Diary' which he
kept during the writing of his next play, *Aristocrats*.

The action of *Living Quarters* takes the form of a re-enactment of
past events as they are set down in the 'ledger' which Sir holds. The
play dramatises the characters' enchantment with the moment of
failure, betrayal or defeat in the past. The past absorbs them more
completely than the need to confront the present. At a time when it
behoves them to find some new principle of order, when some new
creative charge is needed to rescue them from total disintegration,
they have all retreated from the challenge of reality into a lost time
before the Fall, a time when they could still enjoy a sense of 'belonging', a shared system of value. With the bankruptcy of the old structures they have refused the responsibility of choice. Since their present
is regarded as devoid of possibility, the characters have all fallen into
a state of Joycean paralysis. To confirm their hopelessness they have
invented Sir.

Sir remarks that it is 'out of some deep psychic necessity' (*SP*,
p. 177) that they have invented him, a meticulous enforcer of the
literal facts. He allows only one version of the past, that which
faithfully reflects the chronological order of events. All that is latent,

all that is excluded from the dominant discourse (but which still has a kind of limbo existence between reality and ideality) does not count with him. He is the champion of rational empiricism and common sense. For him the outcome of events is more important than the precise nature of the events: the end determines the means; process is subordinated to the need for closure. The characters relive the past 'as if its existence must afford them their justification, as if in some tiny, forgotten detail buried there – a smile, a hesitation, a tentative gesture – if only it could be found and recalled – in it must lie the key to an understanding of *all* that happened' (*SP*, p. 177). However, Sir's primary function is to ensure that no new meaning *does* emerge. He acknowledges that his version *is* a version ('What I would like to do is organise those recollections for you, impose a structure on them, just to give them a form of sorts' (*SP*, p. 178)), but the other characters show no more than a token resistance to Sir's version in which they are inscribed: courage not equal to desire. Just before they reach 'the point of no return' (*SP*, p. 206), Sir reviews the options open to them in the past: 'Because at the point we've arrived at now, many different conclusions would have been possible if certain things had been done or left unsaid and undone' (*SP*, p. 206). Anna could have held her tongue and saved Frank's life; Helen could have spent the night with Charlie and Miriam, avoided the trauma of that evening and perhaps spared herself mental break-down; Ben could have joined his friends on the salmon boat; Frank need not have shot himself. What all the characters show, however, is a desire not to examine the alternatives too closely.

From time to time, some of them toy with the idea of mutiny, tantalising or tormenting themselves with alternatives, involving themselves in a Pirandellian search for an Author. Father Tom imagines for himself a more intimate role than that of 'outsider' (*SP*, p. 185) in which he is cast; Charlie wants to play a more important part; Helen protests that the 'atmosphere' isn't right: 'There was unease – I remember – there were shadows – we've got to acknow-ledge them!' (*SP*, p. 188); Ben wonders if there isn't another way to tell the story altogether: 'With our bloody boring reminiscences and our bloody awareness and our bloody quivering sensibilities. There must be another way of ordering close relationships, mustn't there? (*Shouts*) Mustn't there?' (*SP*, p. 229). At the beginning of Act II, Sir is not on stage and they have their chance to seize their momentary freedom and redirect the course of events. This is their chance to rewrite history. 'Throughout this sequence', the stage directions read, 'none of the characters obeys the conventions of the set' (*SP*, p. 217): possibility becomes, for a moment, unfixed and fluid; 'a gaiety . . . a giddiness' (*SP*, p. 210) permeate the scene. But the opportunity is lost. As Sir, in his usual patronising tone, confides to Charlie later, 'they're always being true to themselves. And even if they've juggled the time a bit, they're doing no harm' (*SP*, p. 225).

Frank is the one who, despite his protests against the injustice of his fate, is especially eager to follow Sir's lead. Indeed, like Fox Melarkey in *Crystal and Fox* or Frank Hardy in *Faith Healer*, he is impatient for Apocalypse:

> SIR: At this point, indeed at any point, you could well have –
> FRANK: Please – please. I did what I had to do. There was no alternative for me. None. What I had to do was absolutely clear-cut. There was never any doubt in my mind.
> SIR: I'm afraid that's true, Frank.
> FRANK: So carry on as you think best, Sir. I'm in your hands.
>
> (*SP*, p. 207)

For the most part, the characters refuse to contemplate difference. Each is 'encased in his privacy' (*SP*, p. 208); they are 'all isolated, all cocooned in their private thoughts' (*SP*, p. 241). Only Father Tom insists on hope and change:

> I've got to speak what I know to be true, and that is that grace is available to each and every one of us if we just ask God for it . . . which is really the Christian way of saying that our options are *always* open. Because that is the enormous gift that Christ purchased for us – the availability of choice and our freedom to choose. (*SP*, p. 208)

The priest, however, is as ineffectual as the Canon in *Philadelphia*. When Frank, after he hears of his wife's infidelity, turns to Father Tom for help, the drunken priest is pathetically unable to respond to Frank's despair and stop him taking his own life. Later, Father Tom, 'now sober' (*SP*, p. 241), challenges Sir's despotism, but is sharply rebuked for presuming to protest after the event, having failed so despicably to take decisive action when it counted. Determinism, we see, can simply be an excuse for avoiding responsibility:

SIR: Sit down and keep quiet.

TOM: I will not sit down and I will not keep quiet! My friend,
Frank, had gone into that back room and not one of you is
going to –

SIR: Shut up! Now!

TIM: I will –

SIR: You had your opportunities and you squandered them.

TOM: I never had –

SIR: Many opportunities, many times. You should have spoken
then. We'll have none of your spurious concern now that it's all
over.

(SP, p. 242)

Sir fulfils the dual role of both creature and master of the other
characters: 'And yet no sooner do they conceive me with my authority and my knowledge, than they begin flirting with the idea of
circumventing me' (*SP*, p. 178). Ironically, the play itself emphasises
not the invention and change of which Sir complains, but impotence
and passivity – the schoolboyish deference to authority suggested by
Sir's name. Sir is there as the sign of man's powers of invention, but
paradoxically those very powers of resourcefulness and ingenuity
are placed in the service of myths which incarcerate rather than
liberate. Only Ben seems to acknowledge the dangers of 'fossilization', the self-destructive behaviour in the name of false myths of the
past – the 'hitting out, smashing back, not at what's there but at what
you think you remember' (*SP*, p. 212).

Friel acknowledges that man and society are alterable and emphasises the disastrous consequences of always living in the past.
But, absorbed by the psychology of defeat and the point of view of
the victim, with its opportunities for both nostalgia and melodrama,
he declines incorporating any realisation of new freedoms. The focus
is consistently on the past: there is no strong sense of the present, nor
of the futural dimension of experience. Motivation begins to sound
very like mystification: the characters keep returning to the past 'out
of some deep psychic necessity' (*SP*, p. 177). Not only are all the
characters subject to exactly the same compulsion to live in the past,
but the past is seen in essentially the same way by each of them. This
homogenisation of memory may be seen as yet another distorting
strategy of reactionary domination, another instance of Friel's ironic
connivance in his characters' denial of change and possibility.

VOLUNTEERS

Volunteers, first produced at the Abbey Theatre, Dublin, on 5 March 1975 is, like *Freedom*, based on contemporary events, this time in the Republic of Ireland – the destruction by Dublin City Council of some of the most important Viking archaeological sites in Europe to make way for new commercial developments in the Wood Quay district of Dublin. The play concerns a group of political internees who for the last five months have been on a daily parole to assist in the excavation of a Viking site in Dublin that is soon to be buried under a multistorey hotel. The volunteers are subversives, political activists who have been 'interned . . . because of attitudes that might be inimical to public safety' (*V*, p. 46). Lily, Michael and Skinner in *Freedom*, we may recall, were also described by the Balladeer as 'volunteers' (*SP*, p. 148). In *Volunteers*, Friel is once again dramatically centring that which has been socially marginalised and psychologically and culturally repressed. The volunteers work beneath the surface of the city. They are quite literally underground men, victims not only of the dominant society but, as we discover, of their own comrades back in prison who regard them as traitors and collaborators and who are going to kill them when the dig is completed. Ultimately, the volunteers are to be seen, like the characters in *Freedom*, *Living Quarters* or *The Gentle Island*, as prisoners of fate.

The Viking parallel heightens the suggestion of determinism. One way of viewing the volunteers' plight and, beyond that, the whole violent history of modern Ireland (to which the action is related by the term 'volunteers', with its connotations of both Republican and Loyalist paramilitarism), is to see them as part of a timeless continuum of sacrifice and martyrdom rather than the product of a specific network of social relations. One of the diggers, Keeney, while pondering the circumstances of the ancient Leif's death, unmasks the mythology of martyrdom:

> Maybe this poor hoor considered it an honour to die – maybe he volunteered? Take this neck, this life, for the god or the cause or whatever . . . he was – to coin a phrase – a victim of his society . . . Maybe he was a casualty of language. Damnit, George, which of us here isn't? (*V*, p. 26)

In the light of this speech, it is difficult to see the play as George O'Brien sees it, as 'an image that honours the values of voluntarism'. Whatever Keeney's own motives may have been for joining the 'movement', he speaks now with scant respect for the willing victim. He also takes us to the heart of Friel's theme by seeing the individual's relation to his society as fundamentally a matter of language, of which 'story' he happens to believe. Keeney, like Hugh in *Translations*, knows that the individual can become imprisoned in 'a linguistic contour which no longer matches the landscape of fact' (*SP*, p. 419). The volunteer, Keeney suggests, can be just as fixed and narrow in his views as the system he is committed to subverting.

Keeney himself takes his place as the latest in a line of fiction-specialists, impressarios, symbol-conscious commentators, obsessive role-players, Protean spirits, anguished doubters, dreamers with an almost compulsive resourcefulness. He leads the dialogue, which is notable for its sudden, unpredictable shifts of subject and tone. Keeney is 'quick-witted, quick-tongued, and never for a second unaware. Years of practice have made the public mask of the joker almost perfect' (*V*, p. 18). The exuberant playfulness of his speech is an expression of freedom, of his refusal to be demoralised, a defiance of the system and of fate. Like Hamlet he adopts an 'antic disposition' to enable him to cope with difficult circumstances. As Heaney comments, Keeney is 'a Hamlet who is gay, not with tragic Yeatsian joy but as a means of deploying and maintaining his anger'.

Assisted by his vaudevillian feed man Pyke, Keeney offers a series of stories to explain Leif's death, continually probing the significance and value of the mind's inventive power while apparently remaining outside any particular version or story himself. The stories tend towards parable and allegory and Keeney is always there to spell out their secret meanings ('So that what you have around you is encapsulated history, a tangible précis of the story of Irish man' (*V*, p. 31)). The unfortunate effect of this is that Friel's talent for rendering individual speech realistically is compromised by the literary quality of the dialogue. We feel the strain between inner and outer, enactment and assessment, the particular and the general, and we are aware once again of Friel's difficulty to find a form which will embody the private reality and at the same time accommodate larger insights than those which any of his limited and partial characters are capable of.

Pyne's story of Leif's death is of a punishment killing for Leif's exogamous relationship with an American Indian woman. The story is a version of what Heaney calls the tribe's 'exact and intimate revenge'[13] against the man who dares to transgress traditional pieties.

Keeney, like Manus in *The Gentle Island*, is concerned that Pyke tells his story to best effect ('"Once upon a time" – keep up the protection of the myth' (*V*, p. 51)) and congratulates him on his performance at the end ('Not bad, Pyne, fairly trite melody but an interesting sub-theme' (*V*, p. 52)). Compulsive story-teller that he is, Keeney takes it upon himself to speak for the recalcitrant Knox. In this version, Leif was a man who for money and companionship carried messages between two groups of 'subversives' (*V*, p. 57). Keeney apparently tells the story against Knox for it prompts the latter to an angry outburst. Butt also has a version – or rather, several versions – of Leif's death, all of which Keeney can predict. To each of the stories of dispossession and deprivation recited by Keeney Butt assents with a resounding 'Yes' (*V*, p. 58). Keeney, however, though he can reel off the stories without even having to think, cannot subscribe to any of them. 'I'm sure of nothing now' (*V*, p. 58), he says. He finds the greatest difficulty in sustaining faith or even interest in any particular fiction. He no longer has 'a confident intellect': 'my paltry flirtations are just . . . fireworks, fireworks that are sparked occasionally by an antic disposition' (*V*, p. 57). Keeney is the disillusioned volunteer, demoralised by the elusiveness of certainty, yet, in the vitality and playfulness of his language, continuing to embody unquenchable, if unruly, human spirit. All that is left him are imaginings, questionings, endless questionings: 'Was Hamlet really mad?' (*V*, p. 66) he keeps asking, the query echoing through the play like the quotation from Burke in *Philadelphia*. Keeney would understand Heaney's self-criticism in *North*: 'skull-handler, parablist / smeller of rot in the state, infused / with its poisons, / pinioned by ghosts / and affections, / murders and pieties'.[14] Keeney's dilemma is that he wants to break out of passivity and acceptance, but he is inhibited from doing so by an overwhelming sense of futility and despair. As a result, he represents a diffuse, anarchic energy that has no positive or constructive ambition. George the foreman recognises in Keeney the most 'dangerous' kind of subversion of all: 'But Keeney – a danger-man, Butt, a real danger-man. No loyalty to anyone or anything' (*V*, p. 63).

What prompts Keeney's most ferocious outburst is the reception the pathetic Smiler receives when he returns after his attempted escape. He is fussed over, given tea and one of Knox's best cigarettes, while Butt 'drapes a very large sack round Smiler's shoulders. It is so long that it hangs down his sides and looks like a ritualistic robe, an ecclesiastical cape' (*V*, p. 59). Keeney savagely mocks this idolisation of the victim:

> He's an imbecile! He's a stupid, pig-headed imbecile! He was an imbecile the moment he walked out of this quarry! And that's why he came back here – because he's an imbecile like the rest of us! Go ahead – flutter about him – fatten him up – imbecile acolytes fluttering about a pig-headed victim. For Christ's sake is there no end to it?   (*V*, p. 60)

The real object of Keeney's disgust is the incorrigible Irish respect for sacrificial immolation, the notorious martyr complex which inhibits realistic, forward-looking action.

Leif is installed in the same idolising discourse:

> PYNE: Never harmed man nor beast.
> KEENEY: And generous – give you the shirt off his back.
> PYNE: The bite out of his mouth.
> KEENEY: One of nature's gentlemen.
> PYNE: A great husband – a great father.
> KEENEY: May the hard-core rest light on him.
> PYNE: We'll never see the likes again.
>
> (*V*, pp. 66–7)

But, again, Keeney insists on generating another, less innocent, less reassuring, version of Leif, associating him with the 'tight and bitter', 'notionate', grudge-bearing 'Boyces of Ballybeg' (*V*, p. 67). Through Keeney, Friel draws attention to the masks of illusion and questions the idols of false consciousness. Keeney stops short of initiating any progressive movement towards the emergence of new meaning, but his *skepsis* may be the prerequisite to the opening onto other possible worlds which transcend the narrow limits of the play's fictional world.

It is the experience of difference and division which, above all, characterises the world of Friel's play. The internees are separated from the rest of society; the diggers are ostracised by their comrades back in prison and divided amongst themselves. The dominant order is no monolithic unity either, but riven by class divisions. Friel's main interest is in the way meanings maintain themselves or are fought for in a world bereft of consensus. Art has a particularly hard

time of it, as the story of the priceless jug would illustrate. George
has pieced and glued the jug together from fragments unearthed by
Smiler: 'A little patience – a little art – and there he is in all his
pristine dignity' (V, p. 15). It is not long, however, till the ostensibly
self-sufficient art object is at the centre of a fierce dispute: Where
does it belong? Whose is it? What does it signify? To the diggers it is
a symbol of Smiler: 'This is Smiler, George; Smiler restored; Smiler
full, free and integrated' (V, p. 46). George wants to remove the jug
from society altogether and preserve it as a sacred thing in a mu-
seum. The others object to such mystification. At the end, Butt, who
has worked so hard on restoring the jug, rejects the establishment
values George has been trying to inculcate in him and turns out
instead to be a convert of Keeney's. Butt drops the jug and smashes
it rather than let George and Professor King become the custodians
and designators of its meaning. The anarchic refusal of any meaning
(symbolised by the breaking of the jug) is preferable to what Butt
regards as the false image of perfection represented by George's
well-wrought urn. Butt's action signifies his new-found resistance to
fixed, transcendent meanings; it is the only action left him when he
sees that the interpretive process is being foreclosed.

The play itself embodies the principle of openness, an acceptance
of mystery and uncertainty, a suspicion of simple answers and of
clear or predictable definitions. At the centre of the play are the
symbols of Leif and the jug: they are the focus of a constant play of
meanings, generating endless interpretation and imagining – like the
question of Hamlet's madness which Keeney keeps raising (absurdly)
in conversation. *Volunteers* is an example of what Catherine Belsey
would call an 'interrogative text'.[15] The great challenge, Friel implies,
is to find a way to preserve the sceptical habit of mind without being
driven into self-denying, self-destructive negativity. It is one thing to
deconstruct the alienating content of inheritance, to smash the old
idols of false consciousness: another is to be able to enjoy the gift of
the past, to be able to recognise and to hold on to what is valuable in
inheritance.

ARISTOCRATS

Aristocrats was first produced at the Abbey Theatre, Dublin, on 8
March 1979. The setting – a Big House in Ballybeg, its interior and

gardens – is very Chekhovian and a Chekhovian 'dying fall', sometimes bordering on pastiche, suffuses the action. Curiously, *Aristocrats* is concerned with the middle class – actually, a family of
middle-class Catholics. It is as if Friel was dressing up the Catholic
middle class in the borrowed robes of the Ascendancy, which itself
was, as Seamus Deane points out, 'a predominantly bourgeois social
formation' transformed by Yeats and other Ascendancy writers into
'an almost comically absurd historical fiction'[16] of Irish Protestant
Aristocracy.

In *Aristocrats*, as in *Living Quarters* or *The Gentle Island*, an old
order is disintegrating. At this critical juncture questions are precipi-
tated about the real value of this hitherto privileged centre of meaning and identity, and a younger generation is faced with the
challenge of finding the means to make shift in a less congenial
world. The play dramatises their struggle to come to terms with an
oppressive, patriarchal authority which has controlled their personal and collective histories. That authority has been principally
vested in Father, the master of Ballybeg Hall. However, the former is
now fallen into decrepitude, the latter into a state of terminal decay.
'It's as if the Hall didn't exist without him' (*SP*, p. 311), the son,
Casimir, remarks after his father's death. All his life Father has stood
for a sterile conservatism, an aristocracy 'without passion, without
loyalty, without commitments . . . ignored by its Protestant counterparts, isolated from the mere Irish, existing only in its concept of
itself, brushing against reality occasionally' (*SP*, p. 294). Within his
own family circle, Father has exerted a chilling authority, his strict-
ness inhibiting the least possibility of intimacy with his wife and
children. Indeed, his presence is associated with an oppressive silence. Mother, not being quite respectable, was 'absorbed into the
great silence' (*SP*, p. 295) after her death and Eamon describes Ballybeg
Hall as 'a house of silence, of things unspoken' (*SP*, p. 279). Now,
even though Father has degenerated into a state of incontinent and
utterly dependent senility, he still clings to a pathetic semblance of
authority. Alice is perturbed by her father's helplessness because for
the first time in her life she 'felt so equal to him' (*SP*, p. 290).
Nevertheless, he continues to exert a strange power, his voice still
able to 'create a stillness, almost an unease' (*SP*, p. 289). With a stroke
of savage humour, Friel reduces traditional authority to a disembodied voice through a baby alarm. Yet, the very sound of that voice is
enough still to terrify Casimir and make Eamon wonder 'who's
spying on whom?' (*SP*, p. 279)

Father's disorientation is most powerfully and memorably drama-tised at the end of Act 2. Hearing the sound of his daughter Anna's voice on the tape recorder, he makes his way downstairs and enters the room where the tape is playing, 'trying to locate where Anna's voice is coming from' (*SP*, p. 304). This scene reverberates ironically against the one at the end of Act 1, where Casimir jumps to attention at the sound of his father's voice over the baby alarm, then 'realizes that the voice was from the speaker' (*SP*, p. 282). Act 1 ends with a demonstration of the effect of Father's authority: Casimir falls to his knees crying 'I'm sorry – I'm sorry' and sister Judith takes him in her arms and rocks him 'as if he were a baby'. Act 2 closes with Father's 'almost animal-like roar' – 'Annnaaaaaaa' – overlapping with the tape's 'scream' when Judith accidentally turns the volume up in-stead of down. The frightening sounds of Father's voice over the intercom earlier and then this shocking single appearance just before his death, are like violent irruptions of the uncensored, unnegotiated past punctuating the present. The raw sound of authority frustrated beyond endurance finally subsides in Father's apoplectic collapse. It is a highly dramatic moment, fusing memory (of a lost daughter), music (Anna's violin playing on the tape) and direct, powerful self-expression. The verbal tension that has been built up in the course of the Act through the bickering and teasing of the other characters is suddenly, heart-stoppingly, shattered. Friel was clearly deeply inter-ested in this scene, for it also forms the climax of his short story, 'Foundry House', an early version of the situation which he explores in *Aristocrats*. The full dramatic potential of the scene, he saw, could only be realised by translating the combination of screaming tape, violin music and Father's roar from written text to theatrical per-formance.

The question is how this 'aristocracy' is to be remembered, and what of the future? Tom Hoffnung (his name, as Casimir reminds us, being the German word for 'hope') is the American academic over to write the official history of the Irish aristocracy. His field of interest – 'Recurring cultural, political and social modes in the upper strata of Roman Catholic society in rural Ireland since the Act of Catholic Emancipation' (*SP*, p. 265) – complements Dr Dodds' study into the subculture of poverty in contemporary, Catholic, urban, working-class Ireland in *Freedom*. Tom finds himself in a situation where truth has become intensely problematic and where he must adjudicate between conflicting versions of this fading dynasty. As Alice says:

'God help the poor man if he thinks he's heard one word of truth
since he came here. . . . All you're hearing is lies, my friend – lies, lies,
lies' (*SP*, p. 284). Tom, like Sir, is the proponent of an empirical kind
of truth. Eamon knows what the conventional assessment would be:

> What political clout did they wield? (Considers. Then sadly shakes
> his head.) What economic help were they to their co-religionists?
> (Considers. Then sadly shakes his head.) What cultural effect did
> they have on the local peasantry? Alice? (Considers. Then sadly
> shakes his head.) We agree, I'm afraid. Sorry, Professor. Bogus
> thesis. No book.

But Eamon also believes that the true meaning of the aristocracy
cannot be assessed in these terms only. He objects to Tom's project
because he assumes that the outsider could not possibly appreciate
Ballybeg Hall's symbolic worth. It is Eamon, the boy from the village
who married into 'aristocracy', who has the most to lose if the family
home is sold, or if the chronicler does not represent it fairly. With
disarming candour, Eamon acknowledges the appeal of 'aristocracy'
to 'all that is fawning and forelock-touching and Paddy and shabby
and greasy peasant in the Irish character' (*SP*, p. 318). To such, the
Big House is 'irresistible' because it represents 'aspiration' (*SP*,
p. 319). This, Eamon believes, Tom could never understand: 'There
are certain things, certain truths . . . that are beyond Tom's kind of
scrutiny' (*SP*, pp. 309–10). Eamon's devotion to his aristocratic dream
is nowhere more strongly felt than at the end of Act 2 when Father
finally collapses: Eamon 'runs to Father and catches him as he collapses so that they both sink to the ground together. . . . Eamon
screams . . . as if his own life depended on it' (*SP*, p. 305).

Eamon endorses Hugh's insight in *Translations* that 'it is not the
literal past, the "facts" of history, that shape us, but images of the
past embodied in language' (*SP*, p. 445). Recognising both the symbolic importance of the Catholic Big House and its reality, Eamon's
is the most complex of all the versions of 'aristocracy' in the play, a
mixture of admiration and contempt, idealism and irony. He is
capable of casting a cold eye on the dying dynasty and still remain
alive to its 'romantic possibilities' (*SP*, p. 294). Contradictory character that he is, he can espouse an aristocratic dream of traditional,
hierarchical value and at the same time embrace revolution and the
struggle for human self-determination in the civil rights movement

– the kind of activity which would have appalled Father, only it was
'away in the North' (*SP*, p. 272). Eamon is a knowing devotee, both
inside and outside the Big House civilisation, simultaneously enchanted and cynically aware: 'I know more about this place, in-
finitely more . . . than they (the O'Donnell family) know' (*SP*, p. 277).
Witty, perceptive, self-aware, linguistically confident, he is nevertheless a failure as far as his own personal life is concerned. He
doesn't see the illusory quality of his feelings for Judith, though his
wife Alice does: 'you think you love her . . . and that's even more
disturbing for you' (*SP*, p. 324); and the breakdown of his marriage
is accompanied by violence.

Contrasting with Eamon is the figure of Casimir, the one who is
the most obvious casualty of Father's oppressive influence and who
even now is struck into quivering silence by the very sound of
Father's voice. Casimir is pathetically lacking in self-confidence and
his language is erratic, confusing and hesitant. His communicational
difficulties are epitomised by his muddled attempts to place a long-
distance telephone call and by the fact that he doesn't even speak the
same language as his wife and children. What he shares with Eamon
and indeed nearly all the other characters in the play, is a propensity
for fantasy. In fact, Casimir is a veritable impresario of fictions – the
instigator of the game of fantasy croquet, the 'master of ceremonies'
(*SP*, p. 302) who entertains the rest of the family with the tape that
sister Anna has sent from Africa and, of course, the ridiculous fantasist
of Ballybeg Hall. He doesn't remember the old family retainer Willie
Diver, nor *actual* childhood events, but recalls in incredible detail
visits to Ballybeg Hall from the celebrated writers and intellectuals
of the day – Yeats, Hopkins, Daniel O'Connell, Hilaire Belloc, George
Moore, Tom Moore. Not surprisingly, his stories confound the factual chronicler (Tom) who is left floundering in his efforts to make
sense of them, while Eamon, who regards Casimir as an absurd
ingenu, treats his stories with scornful mockery. Thus, in a virtuoso
display of his own verbal prowess, Eamon parodies Casimir's wild
fancifulness, using the style of Flann O'Brien to recount the meeting
between Mother and O'Casey:

And O'Casey – haven't they told you that one? – poor O'Casey
out here one day ploughterin' after tennis balls and spoutin'
about the workin'-man when she appeared in the doorway in
there and the poor creatur' made such a ramstam to get to her that

he tripped over the Pope or Plato or Shirley Temple or somebody
and smashed his bloody glasses! (*SP*, p. 295)

Tom's uncertainty is further increased by Eamon's jokes that Helga
and the children whom Casimir is always telephoning may only
have a phantom existence in Casimir's imagination:

EAMON: Cassimir pretending he's calling Helga the Hun. All a
game. All a fiction.
ALICE: Oh shut up!
EAMON: No one has ever seen her. We're convinced he's invented
her.
(*Tom laughs uncertainly*)
TOM: Is he serious, Claire?
EAMON: And the three boys – Herbert, Hans and Heinrich. And the
dachshund called Dietrich. And his job in the sausage factory.
It has the ring of phoney fiction, hasn't it?
CLAIRE: Don't listen to him, Tom.

(*SP*, p. 278)

The deliquescence of Casimir's world, we come to see, is the
condition of his survival in diminished circumstances. His game of
imaginary croquet offers a salutary reminder of the limits of fact as
well as fantasy. Down-to-earth Willie is drawn into the game initiated by Casimir and imagines himself to be winning: 'His elation is
genuine – not part of the make-believe. And his triumph has given
him a confidence' (*SP*, p. 300). These stage directions emphasise the
positive effects of play. By breaking with the normal rules and routines, by our willingness to experiment, we can open up lost or
buried channels of feeling. Through play we can experience a freeing
of self and glimpse the means of a future transformation of our
condition. Encouraged by Eamon to 'submit to the baptism' (*SP*, p.
297) into idealism, Willie has proved that he is 'a real insider now'
(*SP*, p. 300). Eamon's language suggests ritual initiation into the
aristocratic dream. To Eamon, this is something which is possible for
the local boy, Willie, while Tom, of course, remains the 'stranger'
(*SP*, p. 313) for whom, as Yolland in *Translations* puts it, 'the private
core will always be . . . hermetic' (*SP*, p. 416). However, the croquet-
playing episode concludes by emphasising the limits of play. When
Willie, flushed with his success, goes to have a drink of wine, only to

find the bottle empty, Eamon comments: 'Imagine it's full. Use your peasant talent for fantasy, man' (*SP*, p. 301) – another of Eamon's ironic slightings of the ubiquitous peasant propensity to dream as compensation for deprivation and failure. Willie, however, has no intention of allowing any peasant talent for fantasy to control his life: despite his almost servile attitude towards Judith, he has no desire to follow in Eamon's footsteps by marrying into the Big House. The romance of 'aristocracy' cannot compete with Willie's flair for business and, as well, he simply doesn't want to be burdened with responsibility for Judith's child.

It is Casimir's playfulness that is continually emphasised – whether in his playing imaginary croquet or in his musical guessing games with Claire. With Casimir nothing is fixed and final. Though more of an *ingenu* than Shane or Skinner, he is still kin to those other Protean playful spirits. He survives because of his playfulness and his constant readiness to adjust to change: but also because of his recognition of his own limitations:

> I made a great discovery when I was nine. . . . I suddenly realised I was different from other boys. . . . That was a very important and a very difficult discovery for me . . . but it brought certain recognitions, certain compensatory recognitions. Because once I recognized – once I acknowledged that the larger areas were not accessible to me, I discovered – I had to discover smaller, much smaller areas that were. (*SP*, p. 310)

Casimir's fictionalising memory is both an avoidance of reality and a creation of identity. As with Gar O'Donnell or Cass McGuire, it is a way of reforming one's own past, a means of survival. But Casimir is no mere illusionist. There is something of the wise fool about him. His play is not a sterile escapism, but the means of self-discovery, allowing him to create new boundaries, new histories for himself, 'smaller areas' in which, nevertheless, he may discover some security and retain some measure of dignity which had previously been denied him. Through his fictions he opens up a space where he can exist on his own terms and demonstrate a kind of mastery. His childhood idyll, we understand, is an effort to compensate for a deep sense of inadequacy bred in him by his father; a determination to resist the 'silence' to which his mother has been condemned and which threatens to 'absorb' (*SP*, p. 310) him also. It is expressive of a longing for 'home', for a sense of belonging.

As in *Philadelphia* or *Cass McGuire*, the fictionalising memory is associated with music. Casimir's romantic evocation of 'home' is always accompanied by Claire's playing Chopin: 'When I think of Ballybeg Hall, it's always like this: the sun shining, the doors and windows open, the place filled with music' (*SP*, p. 256). Chopin's intensely romantic, nostalgic music evokes the past, but also insinuates a break with historical reality, a lyrical moment which is not subject to rational or linguistic frameworks. Himself bearing a Polish name (meaning 'proclamation of peace'), Casimir is associated with Chopin, who was Polish and an exile: 'Chopin died in Paris, you know, and when they were burying him they sprinkled Polish soil on his grave. (Pause) Because he was Polish' (*SP*, p. 307). The connection with Chopin is, of course, partly ironic, for Casimir's romantic dream is continually being punctured by Father's commands, Eamon's parodies and Tom's sceptical questions.

Casimir has his own idiosyncratic method of replying to inevitabilities. Anna and Father are the play's 'fossils' – the two most conspicuous failures at coping with the debased modern world of civil rights, sausage factories, slot-machines and plastic bananas. Father's first debilitating stroke actually coincided with his becoming aware of his daughter Judith's betrayal of the old values by participating in the civil rights campaign. Eldest sister Judith's hard-headed realism forms the basis of yet another kind of adaptation. Her method of occupying the 'smaller areas' has been to lead a life of strict routine and to blot out of consciousness any thought of larger possibilities or grander aspirations. Countering Eamon's idealisms, Judith speaks for the reality of decline, poverty and sickness. She is the one who has taken responsibility for Father and for looking after Ballybeg Hall. To Judith, the old order is simply not worth preserving. She, it appears, has for long been in revolt against her class. In remaining 'indifferent' to the violence in the North and in regarding politics as 'vulgar', the Catholic 'aristocracy' has, in her view, rendered itself socially irrelevant. For the first time Friel includes a serious countermovement which opposes itself to defeat and inevitability. The possibility of renewal and continuance – even heroism – is affirmed. The future, we see, depends on Judith's determination that she and her family confront reality and come to terms with their diminished circumstances; on Casimir's recognition of both possibility and limitation, his ability to make the best of 'smaller areas'; on the family's toughness, resilience and tenacity, its 'greed for survival' (*SP*, p. 294), which so impress Eamon; on the younger genera-

tion's awareness that any adequate version of reality cannot consist
entirely of either Tom's mechanical facts or Eamon's romantic va-
pours; on the adaptability which Claire, the youngest sister, shows
in marrying the local greengrocer. Father's funeral and Claire's impending marriage, along with the decision to sell Ballybeg Hall and
move on are the principle markers of the family's rite of passage.
Judith's child comes out of the orphanage; and Uncle George whom
Alice and Eamon generously invite into their home, speaks for the
first time in years: the 'silence' imposed by Father is lifted. Dumb
Uncle George, like dumb Sarah in *Translations*, is one of Friel's odd,
waif-like characters who, because they are without language, are
continually in danger of being written out of the social reckoning
altogether. Both Sarah and Uncle George respond to the 'warmth'
and 'concern' of others. Sarah learns to speak with Manus's help and
encouragement and is frightened into dumbness again by Lancey's
rough interrogation. Uncle George, seeing the heroic effort going on
around him to resist 'fossilisation', is finally touched into life and
language by Alice's kindness and concern.

The play as a whole may be seen as a giving voice to the suppressed forces for change in society and the individual. It is a play
about survival, and survival, we are shown, depends on the ability
to subsume respect for the past within a dynamic sense of the future.
The play ends on the very moment of transition (which, in Friel's
great play of 1980, is also the moment of 'translation'). That moment
is elevated to become life's eternal moment. Knowledge of life as a
perpetual process is the prerequisite of authentic existence. Uncle
George enters:

> He puts his small case on the ground and his coat across a chair
> and sits with his hands on his lap. He has all the patience in the
> world. As he sings Cassimir glances over the house. Claire begins
> to hum. One has the impression that this afternoon – easy, re-
> laxed, relaxing – may go on indefinitely.   (*SP*, p. 326)

The play not only affirms Becoming over Being, but emphasises
irrepressible human spirit in the face of the brute facts of death and
defeat. That energy pervades the play in the non-discursive form of
Chopin's music which drifts in and out of the action and in the
popular song which eventually replaces Chopin. In Act 3 Claire
vows never to play Chopin again and Casimir for the first time fails
to recognise the piece she is playing. Thereafter, the music of high

culture is replaced by the popular song, 'Sweet Alice'. The play's music changes from highly individual self-expression, as it was for Casimir, to the democratic music of the folk-song. The movement from classical, elitist music to the more popular melody underscores the decline of the Big House and its social pretensions and snobbish isolationism, and the acceptance of diminished realities and a more 'plebeian' future. Having been 'educated out of their emotions', as Eamon put it, the family is perhaps at the end rediscovering them in the haunting folk-tune they all join in singing. Their singing is a final gesture of defiance against the old order of the deceased Father who had violently objected to the singing of such 'vulgar rubbish' (*SP*, p. 308), as he had objected to Claire's musical ambitions: 'Oh, I'm afraid he was adept at stifling things' (*SP*, p. 307), Casimir remarks. 'Sweet Alice' was, in fact, Mother's song, so that singing it at the end also recentres Mother's ghostly, transgressive presence, the memory of which has been suppressed in the official family myth because of her dubious origins as an actress (she is, significantly, another exponent of 'play') and her equally dubious end.

The song tells of the burial of 'Sweet Alice' under 'granite so grey', intimating, like Melville's song, 'Billy in the Darbies', at the end of *Billy Budd* or Carson McCullers' song of the chain-gang with which she concludes *The Ballad of the Sad Café*, that even when the artist's version of events may seem pessimistic and despairing we can still be invigorated and extended by the energy of perception and invention which went into the making of the version and without which there would be no plays, no games and no songs. The play is, finally, a celebration of the human impulse to turn the negative aspects of everyday life into positive form: translation.

At the heart of the play, Friel said, lies 'the burden of the incommunicable'.[17] He was unsure, he tells us, 'whether to reveal slowly and painstakingly with almost realised tedium the workings of the family or with some kind of supra-realism, epiphanies, in some way to make real the essences of these men and women by side-stepping or leaping the boredom of their small talk'.[18] The burden of communication is continually foregrounded. Various artificial aids to communication are featured – telephone, baby alarm and tape recorder. Casimir's attempts to communicate with Helga are farcical, the disembodied voice of sister Anna on the tape recording from Zambia or Father on the baby alarm from upstairs indicates a total dissociation from reality. In the end, Friel broke with a strict naturalistic notation to develop what we might call a musical form for his drama. Music has a central role to play because of its ability to evoke and express irrational memory. In the play's carefully orchestrated pattern of various sounds, of mechanical and natural speech, of speech and music, of silence and music, we recognise the effort to communicate the uncommunicable.

FAITH HEALER

Faith Healer was first produced at the Longacre Theatre, New York, on 5 April 1979, where the play, consisting of four extended monologues, was not well received in the commercialised Broadway theatre. Nor did it make much impact when it was produced at the Royal Court Theatre, London, in 1981. However, the Abbey Theatre's memorable production of 1982 confirmed that the play did indeed represent a major extension of Friel's talent.

Faith Healer is another memory play, a set of recreations of the past from three different points of view. But where the memory of all the characters in *Living Quarters* was contained within the same dramatic structure, *Faith Healer* is divided into four distinct parts. There is no Sir and no ledger to ensure that the representation follows a pre-ordained plain: each character is freer to construct his or her own version of the past. Thus, there is no single event which forms the undisputed common point of reference for all other events in the lives of the three characters. Each character, that is, has a different centre of meaning and so produces a different version of the past.

The four monologues are spoken by Frank, the faith healer (he has two of the monologues), Grace his wife (or is she his mistress?) and Teddy, Frank's business manager. Each character gives his or her version of what is essentially the same story. But there are stories and there are stories. The past lives on in three different versions of it, in each of which certain details are repressed or displaced, others highlighted or exaggerated, according to personal need and emotion. The characters never interact directly with one another: each is locked into the solitary confinement of his or her own version of things. Being is a fundamentally private affair. Our concentration is fixed entirely on the three voices, on the very process whereby they encode a consoling or justifying fiction, on the deep rhythms of personality to which they give utterance.

Frank's speeches concentrate on his troublesome gift, as he debates its nature, recollects his successes and failures. Friel, we soon come to understand, is exploring the dubious nature of his own art. Faith healing is a metaphor for the art of writing. The origins of drama, after all, lie in primitive and religious ritual. Theatre, like religion, answers a deep human need for magic and transformation. But as well as presenting himself as priest or votarist or Messiah, Frank is aware that there is a strong element of the cheap trickster about him. Sham or shaman: not even Frank himself can be sure which he is. He is burdened with questions and doubts:

> Was it all chance? – or skill? or illusion? – or delusion? Precisely what power did I possess? Could I summon it? When and how? Was I its servant? Did it reside in my ability to invest someone with faith in me or did I evoke from him a healing faith in himself? Could my healing be effected without faith?   (*SP*, p. 334)

Yet, however much of a charlatan he may feel himself to be at times, he is confident that his art responds to a profound human need for healing and transformation.

Grace's monologue emphasises the personal life and betrays her deep and manifold resentments of Frank, of his gift which removes him from the world of ordinary feeling and relation and makes him seem inhuman. To Grace, Kinlochbervie is the place 'where the baby's buried' (*SP*, p. 344): Frank, however, only remembers what is relevant to his life as a faith healer and so to him Kinlochbervie is simply 'a picturesque little place' where 'we were enjoying a few days' rest' (*SP*, p. 337). He has obliterated from memory all thought of his stillborn child. Grace resents the way Frank has freely adapted the facts of her life, even changing her name, her birthplace, how they first met, etc., to suit his own narrative purposes. She recognises that 'it was some compulsion he had to adjust, to refashion, to recreate everything around him' (*SP*, p. 345) and that he was motivated by a desire to redeem life: 'it was always an excellence, a perfection, that was the cause of his restlessness' (*SP*, p. 346). If Frank cured a man, we are told, that man became for him 'a successful fiction' (*SP*, p. 345). Grace recognises that she, too, is one of Frank's 'fictions': 'O my God I'm one of his fictions too, but I need him to sustain me in that existence – O my God I don't know if I can go on without his sustenance' (*SP*, p. 353). And, indeed, when Frank's 'authorship' terminates with his death, she falls apart completely and takes her own life by overdosing on sleeping pills.

Frank's supreme fiction, of course, is his own death which, exhausted and impotent, he plots at the hands of his own people. Looking forward to his homecoming as 'a restoration ... an integration, a full blossoming' (*SP*, p. 372), he presents himself in biblical and apocalyptic terms. As he walks towards his executioners, it was 'as if he were entering a church'; he is 'both awed and elated' (*SP*, p. 376). The material world dissolves 'and had become mere imaginings' (*SP*, p. 376).

Teddy is described by Grace as 'a dedicated acolyte to the holy man' (*SP*, p. 345), while Frank recognises Teddy's satisfaction in being 'associated with something . . . spiritual' (*SP*, p. 334). But Teddy is also the comic cockney entrepreneur who still speaks of Frank and his miraculous gift in much the same jaunty way as he does of other 'artists' he has handled – Miss Mulatto and Her Pigeons or Rob Roy, the Piping Dog. To Teddy, they are all 'bloody artists!' with unruly temperaments which continually elude and defy normal expectation and his own efforts at rational control. Brilliance of performance, Teddy notes, does not depend on the artist's conscious awareness of what he is doing. Indeed, Frank seems to be inhibited as an artist by his compulsion to analyse his gift: he is, says Teddy, 'castrated' and 'knackered' (*SP*, p. 363) by his desire to know. He gives his best performances when he is least self-conscious. Teddy is intrigued by the difference between what the artist is capable of as an artist, and what he is like as a man. He sees that Frank can do 'Fantastic things' (*SP*, p. 359), but that he also was 'a bastard in many ways' (*SP*, p. 363). Though Teddy recommends a strictly 'professional relationship' – equivalent of Frank's artistic detachment – he himself cannot avoid personal feeling and relationship. His recognisable human feeling, his warmth and compassion, make a striking contrast with Frank's cold detachment and self-absorption. Outraged by Frank's treatment of Grace, Teddy is the one who stands by her when she is most in need of comfort and support.

Faith Healer carries forward Friel's investigation into the self-destructive impulses of the artist obsessed with his own art, which had been the subject of *Crystal and Fox*. Frank Hardy is the fiction-maker who has sacrificed life to fiction and finds that he is the creature as well as the creator of his own fiction. Friel offers a troubled critique of the artist's transformative powers, emphasising the human cost of the pursuit of perfection. Yet there is certainly no simple condemnation of the imaginative and aesthetic life: one time in ten Frank *did* succeed; and he was prepared to lay down his life for his faith. He may not always be successful, but as long as he is sometimes successful there is warrant for dismissing the idea of a deterministic universe. The faith healer/artist occupies a borderland between hope and despair. He makes it impossible for his people to settle for either – or for any fixed meaning or attitude. As Frank says, he denies the people who come to him 'the content of a finality' (*SP*, p. 337). He even considers that 'it would have been a kindness to them not to go near them' (*SP*, p. 337). Frank's agony, too, stems from not having 'the content of a finality'; only in death is there an end to uncertainty, peace: 'then for the first time there was no atro-phying terror; and the maddening questions were silent. At long last I was renouncing chance' (*SP*, p. 337).

In this, the most disrupted, the most stylised and unconventional of all Friel's plays, music and 'musical' language again prove useful in developing a non-rational theatre. All three characters begin their monologues with their eyes closed, Teddy listening to 'The Way You Look Tonight', Frank and Grace reciting the Scottish and Welsh place-names. Teddy, like Gerry in *Dancing at Lughnasa*, is associated with Fred Astaire music, his jaunty cockney manner contrasting with the brooding Celtic melancholy of Frank and Grace, as Gerry's insouciant manner contrasts with the anguished spiritual depths of the Mundy sisters. No music accompanies Frank's or Grace's mono-logue, but each of them at times abandons rational communication for the comfort of ritual. Grace tries to keep her thoughts of Kinlochbervie and her dead child at bay by rhyming off the place-names; Frank chants the names 'just for the mesmerism, the seda-tion, of the incantation' (*SP*, p. 332), seeking escape from the maddening questions which torment him. Their recitations of the place-names, like Gar O'Donnell's quotations from Burke, are ex-pressive of the longing for transcendence, for a break with historical reality, a lyric space.

The strikingly unusual form which Friel has devised for his play enacts the maddening questions which afflict not only Frank but Grace and Teddy too, for all of these monologues are characterised by worry, bafflement and endless questioning. Friel's form enforces the denial of the satisfactions of completion, closure and full know-ledge. The play proclaims its own impotence by continually contra-dicting itself and countering any notion of finality and fixity. We find ourselves not a little bewildered amongst a variety of competing versions of what happened because Friel makes no effort to provide a hierarchical index to the conflicting discourses. Instead, he dramatises the abolition of a centre, of a given and accepted authority. History is a jigsaw of self-contradictions, of extra pieces and missing pieces. The individuality of the histories presented allows for no dialogue: each of the speakers becomes 'fossilised' in his or her version of events. Failure is imminent in the attempt to turn the theatre into a stage for short stories. If the theatre is to transcend contingency, if it is to offer healing potential, wholeness, renewal, a sense of the fluidity of history, then its ultimate aim should be dialogue.

Yet, while breaking down conventional forms of communication, Friel isn't involved in a project of callously and cynically demolishing all meaning and hope and presenting a completely arbitrary world. He doesn't plunge us into the abyss so much as lead us to the heart of mystery beyond or beneath the rational strategies of language. There is still enough coherence to keep alive the traditional humanist concerns that depend on our identification with the characters and our involvement in their moral life. The play celebrates the resistant spirit, the possibilities for transformation. There isn't dialogue, but there are story-telling and moral questioning, and story-telling and moral-questioning are positive acts. The very fact that a story is told suggests that something has been overcome; it is a sign of hope. Of the Irish language, Hugh in Friel's next great play, *Translations*, says: 'Yes, it is a rich language, full of mythologies, of fantasy and hope and self-deception. . . . It is our response to mud cabins and a diet of potatoes; our only method of replying to . . . inevitabilities' (*SP*, pp. 418–19). Language and fiction inhabit the gap between the real and the ideal, mediating between what is and what might be: the great task is to create an authentic fiction, a workable model of wholeness, a responsible reply to 'inevitabilities'. And that, Friel shows us, requires an end to solipsism, a readiness to expose the self to the 'Other', to the challenge of reality, through dialogue.

Faith Healer declares the paradox of Friel's wanting to be an artist without making us feel we are being trapped into one particular version of things. While constantly pursuing its own kind of sense, the play disrupts the forms of conventional drama – illusionism, narrative leading to closure, and a hierarchical arrangement of discourses – so that Friel can demonstrate his own freedom from control. The theatre space he creates is one where he can explore ambiguity and uncertainty, where he can refuse authoritarianism and demonstrate simultaneously his scepticism *and* his creativity, the limits of his art *and* its possibilities. The greatness of the play lies in his ability to turn these difficult oppositions into a sustained and emotionally satisfying drama. Refusing to propagate any particular 'truth', he explores in these plays of the 1970s the conditions under which 'truth' may be established.

4

History

Rewriting History: The Plays of the 1980s

THE FIFTH PROVINCE

If the individual and the world are substantially (though not entirely) constituted through language and if, therefore, 'identity' and 'reality' are fictional constructs which continually elude full representation, then there is always the possibility that both the individual and the social reality in which he is inscribed can be reinvented. To effect such a re-creation was precisely the challenge taken up by the Field Day Theatre Company. Field Day was born in 1980 in the depressed city of Derry, from the conviction that the political crisis in the North and its reverberations in the Republic made the necessity of a reappraisal of Ireland's political and cultural situation explicit and urgent. 'Everything, including our politics and our literature, has to be re-written – i.e. re-read',[1] announced Seamus Deane, one of the founding directors. Field Day set out to 'contribute to the solution of the present crisis by producing analyses of the established opinions, myths and stereotypes which had become both a symptom and a cause of the current situation'.[2] The initial moving force behind the formation of the company was the Belfast actor, Stephen Rea who, despite his success on television and the London stage, wished to return to Ireland to contribute to cultural life there. He approached Brian Friel whose play *The Freedom of the City*, Rea had acted in at the Royal Court. Friel happened to have just completed *Translations* and, anxious to escape the professional theatre in London and Dublin, was wondering about the possibility of an independent production of his new play. Field Day grew out of their decision to put the play on in Derry and then tour it around Ireland. In order to achieve charitable status, four more directors were appointed: Seamus Heaney, Tom Paulin, Seamus Deane and David Hammond. (They were later joined by Thomas Kilroy.)

Field Day asks us to unlearn the Ireland that we know, the received ways of thinking about it and to learn new ones. One of the central Field Day concepts is that of the 'Fifth Province', a notion originally explored by Richard Kearney and Mark Hederman in the first issue of *Crane Bag* in 1977. Noting that the Irish word for province was 'coiced', literally a fifth, they proposed the idea of a fifth province of the mind – 'the secret centre . . . where all oppositions were resolved. . . . The constitution of such a place would require that each person discover it for himself within himself'.[3] Friel suggests that the 'Fifth Province' 'may well be a province of mind through which we hope to devise another way of looking at Ireland, or another possible Ireland'.[4] It is, he says, 'a place for dissenters, traitors to the prevailing mythologies in the other four provinces'.[5] Friel is speaking of a neutral realm of the imagination where the symbol may mediate between subject and object, where actualities need not be so terribly insisted upon as they normally are in Ireland.

Field Day has no 'core' company but uses largely expatriate Irish actors. It has produced work by non-Irish dramatists and used non-Irish directors. It does not have any fixed base. Friel has stated that 'we want to be transient in the aesthetic sense as well as in the practical sense, which gives us independence'.[6] He is anxious to avoid neat artistic or political categorisation. Field Day, he believes, 'should lead to a cultural state, not a political state. And I think out of that cultural state, a possibility of a political state follows' – but swiftly, and characteristically, qualifies any doctrinaire tendencies: 'It's very grandiose this, and I want to make notice of abdication quickly. You have got to retain some strong element of cynicism about the whole thing'.[7]

Since its inception, Field Day has sponsored not only theatre, but a series of pamphlets addressing the major cultural issues, embracing such topics as 'The Protestant Idea of Liberty' and extending the debate about the interdependence of culture and politics beyond Ireland to draw on writers such as the Palestinian Edward Said and the American Frederick Jameson. The most ambitious publishing venture is the *Field Day Anthology of Irish Writing* (in both languages), edited by Seamus Deane, which is 'the first comprehensive exhibition of the wealth and diversity of Irish literature from 550 AD through to the present day'. Dealing with Irish writing – literary, philosophical, political, social and scientific – 'from every tradition', the aim was to provide a view of 'the continuity and coherence of the Irish achievement in letters . . . to provide a sense or vision of the island's cultural integrity which would operate as a basis for an enduring and enriching political settlement'.[8]

TRANSLATIONS

Translations, according to Deane, is Field Day's 'central text'.[9] The play was premiered on 23 September 1980 in Derry's Guildhall, the symbol of Unionist domination in *The Freedom of the City*. The central dramatic conflict arises when a platoon of Royal Engineers of an Ordnance Survey arrive in a rural, Irish-speaking community in County Donegal in 1833 to map the country and translate Irish place-names into English equivalents. *Translations* is another play centring on a point of crisis and, as in *Freedom of the City*, the crisis is one of special relevance to the nationalist community in the North of Ireland. As well as the arrival of the English soldiery, the play refers to the imminent abolition of the hedge school which has been supported by the local people and its replacement by the new state-run national school in which the teaching will be in English, not Irish.

Though enthusiastically received by all sections of the community when first performed, both *Translations* and Field Day have proved highly controversial. The influential Belfast critic, Edna Longley, charged Friel with simply reiterating old myths of dispossession and oppression rather than interrogating them. Welcoming the notion of the 'fifth province', Longley nevertheless believed that the Field Day enterprise was a prisoner of is own Catholic, Nationalist bias. Friel was accused of avoiding a complex contemporary reality and retreating into 'a mythic landscape of beauty and plenitude that is pre-Partition, pre-Civil War, pre-famine, pre-plantation and pre-Tudor',[10] a Hibernian pastoral that is destroyed by the incursions of British colonialism.

Longley's concern was shared by Brian McAvera. Complaining about the play's political implications, McAvera believed that 'traditional nationalist myths were being given credence' and that 'a dangerous myth' was being shored up – that of 'cultural dispossession by the British'. McAvera sees Friel's awareness as being one-sided: 'The "shape" observed is a Nationalist one – and a limited partial view at that'.[11] The play's Nationalist perspective, these critics argue, leads to an exaggeration of the repressiveness of the British military and a suppression of the facts of Republican violence. The officers of the Ordnance Survey, they point out, did not carry bayonets and did not assist in evictions. Drawing on J. H. Andrews, the leading historian of the Ordinance Survey, McAvera accuses Friel of transposing 'Cromwellian notions into a nineteenth century framework'.[12]

Another critic, Sean Connolly, complains about the way the decline of Irish is presented as, crucially, a despoilation by conquerors: Friel, Connolly asserts, emphasises external pressure and does not give enough weight to the fact that the decline 'resulted from forces within the Irish community itself'.[13] The Ordnance Survey, Connolly informs us, enlisted the expertise of eminent Irish scholars, poets and antiquarians of the day – men such as John O'Donovan, Eugene O'Curry, George Petrie and James Clarence Mangan. There are no historical grounds, Connolly insists, for presenting the whole enterprise 'as having been undertaken in the "Sanders of the River" spirit of colonial paternalism portrayed by Friel'.[14] Similarly, the national school system, Connolly further explains, was not the insensitive imposition of central government that Friel makes it out to be, but 'a massive state subsidy to an existing system of elementary education',[15] merely continuing the work of the independent pay schools for which there had been a huge increase in demand. In teaching through English, Connolly claims, the national schools were simply responding to the needs of the times, when English was the language of the law, of the employing and landowning classes, of commerce, of the towns, of the Catholic Church and of O'Connell's politics.

The play, Connolly concludes, is based on 'an artificial contrast between the hopelessly idealised and the hopelessly debased'.[16] Friel draws on a fairly blatant kind of popular Nationalist sentiment, Connolly argues, by presenting the Irish as poor but impossibly well-educated and the English as crass, materialistic and uncultured. Captain Lancey, for example, cannot tell the difference between Latin and Irish. Lieutenant Yolland is lost in admiration of a culture so much richer than his own, one which is self-sufficient and organically complete – in Yolland's own words, 'a consciousness that wasn't striving nor agitated, but at its ease and with its own conviction and assurance' (*SP*, p. 416). The play, in Connolly's view, is 'a crude portrayal of cultural and military imperialism visited on passive victims . . . substituting caricature and political cliché'.[17]

The historian, J. H. Andrews, was one of those who defended Friel's handling of the facts, not because the playwright was always historically accurate, but because he was interested in another kind of truth than the merely factual. Andrews found the play 'an extremely subtle blend of historical truth – and some other kind of truth'.[18] He saw the play 'as a set of images that might have been painted on screens, each depicting some passage from Irish history, ancient or modern, the screens placed one behind the other in a tunnel with a light at one end of the tunnel and the audience at the other, so that it is only the strongest colours and the boldest lines that appear in the composite picture exhibited on the stage. On this reading Captain Lancey's brutal threats would be justified as projections perhaps backwards, perhaps forwards, from some quite different period'.[19] What Andrews correctly recognises here is that Friel's chief interest is not in chronicling the literal facts of history, but examining a mythology of dispossession and oppression which even today shapes the Northern Catholic psyche. As Friel's old hedge schoolmaster, Hugh, says: 'it is not the literal past, the "facts" of history, that shape us, but images of the past embodied in language' (*SP*, p. 445).

Friel himself seems to have come to doubt the play's political connotations. The irreverent farce of his next play, *The Communication Cord*, he tells us, was deliberately designed as an 'antidote' to any possible sentimentalism in *Translations*. It was no part of his intention, he declared, simply to evoke nostalgic yearning for a lost Gaelic Eden. *Translations*, he said, 'was offered pieties that I didn't intend for it'.[20] His main concern, he stressed, was with language:

> I don't want to write a play about Irish peasants being suppressed by English sappers. . . . The play has to do with language and only language.[21]

At the same time, he did not want 'to write a threnody on the death of the Irish language'.[22] As Friel explains in his 'Sporadic Diary' which he kept during the time he was writing *Translations*:

> One of the mistakes of the direction in which the play is presently pulling is the almost wholly *public* concern. . . . Public questions; issues for politicians: and that's what's wrong with the play now. The play must concern itself only with the confrontation of the dark and private places of the individual soul.[23]

In fact, it may be said that Friel succeeds in dissolving the distinction between political theatre which concerns itself with big 'public' themes and psychological drama which sounds the depths of the individual mind. His main concern is with the difficulties of 'interpreting between privacies' (*SP*, p. 446), these words of Hugh's suggesting that a process of interpretative transfer characterises not only translations between languages but also communications within a single language. The idea and even the phrasing derive from George Steiner, for whom all communication is an act of translation and interpretation because it always implies the loss of an original plenitude and is never complete. Thus, authenticity lies in 'the dark and private places of the individual soul', in an essential privacy, which can never be fully expressed in Irish nor in English. Friel explores the dreadful silences, cultural and personal, lying underneath the surfaces of language.

The play opens with a young man (the hedge schoolmaster's son, Manus) encouraging a young woman (Sarah) who 'has been considered locally to be dumb and . . . (who) has accepted this' (SP, p. 383) to say her own name. The scene distils the substance of the whole play: the struggle for utterance, for expression of an identity, for the means and the confidence to say who you are. Interspersed with Manus's efforts to encourage Sarah are Jimmy Jack's readings of Homer's story of how Pallas Athene made 'a tramp' (SP, p. 385) out of Ulysses, a story of the perennial desire to dominate. Sarah's struggle for language is related to the struggle for power. She herself seems to acquire presence through language and, later, when the English soldier, Captain Lancey, frightens her into silence again, she is described as 'more waiflike than ever' (SP, p. 430), as if her physical presence has been weakened by her loss of language. A thing is brought into existence by naming it: as Owen says, 'We name a thing and – bang! – it leaps into existence' (SP, p. 422). Conversely, without language a thing or person has no meaningful existence, identity or presence. Sarah's difficulties in stating 'My name is Sarah' are matched by Owen's inability to state 'My name is not Roland!' (SP, p. 421). Where Sarah is silenced and deprived of her own language by the colonist, Owen asserts not simply his own name but also his resistance to the colonising process. He argues and will fight. The simple act of naming becomes a claiming and revising of history.

In Translations, the act of naming, of enclosing, of trying to encapsulate or own a concept, of historifying, is fragmented. The play examines the difficulties of translating from one naming system, one language, one culture, to another. The theme of naming occurs in many different forms. For most of the time, Hugh absents himself to attend the 'ritual of naming' (SP, p. 397) Nellie Rudh's baby. The two principal English characters are introduced as Captain Lancey and Lieutenant Yolland, their titles immediately identifying their function within a military hierarchy. The Irish names indicate a very different order of being, a closely-knit, family-based society. Maire Chatach and Nellie Ruadh are so named because of attributes of their family's hair. Jimmy Jack Cassie, Sarah John Sally and Doalty Dan Doalty refer to three generations in their names. The ritual of naming, the *caerimonia nominationis* – whether of people or places – involves generations of associations which will be lost if English standard practices are adopted. A history, a culture, an identity, are threatened when a language is threatened.

Friel keeps us vitally aware of how translation can involve loss as well as gain, how being adaptable can result in the erosion of a particular history and identity. The name 'Tobair Vree' is to be anglicized as 'The Cross' or 'The Crossroads'. Only Owen remembers the derivation of the name. There used to be a well at the Tobair Vree crossroads ('Tobair' means a well in Irish), and a hundred and fifty years ago a man called Brian sought healing from the waters of the well, until one day he was found drowned in it. Ever since, the crossroads has been called 'Tobair Vree' ('Vree' being a corruption of the Irish 'Bhrian'), even though the well has long since dried up and nobody but Owen remembers the old story. What that story illustrates is that language *is* rooted in extra-linguistic reality and has been shaped by it, though it does not passively reflect pre-linguistic or even physical reality. There is no isomorphic mapping between word and world, yet precise reference and accurate description are a normal part of everyday life. No 'natural' correspondence exists between 'Tobair Vree' and the crossroads it names, but for Owen at least the sign is not arbitrary nor merely conventional. Language, Friel shows, may not be a simple mirror or window on the world, but neither is it a completely arbitrary and relative Saussurian system of signs with no positive terms.

The play, as Richard Kearney has shown, dramatises two conflicting models of naming, symptomatic of fundamental philosophical and ideological differences.[24] The 'Gaelic' view of language sees it as the means to express an essential privacy, the hermetic core of being, to divine origins and etymologies, thus enabling a community to recollect itself in terms of its past. It is opposed by the technological, 'English' view of language, which sees it as a system of signs for representing, mapping and categorising – for 'colonising' the chaos of reality. Where the 'Gaelic' view embodies a logocentric notion of cultural rootedness and centredness, the utilitarian 'English' view has no time for the etymologist's reverence for language as a remembrance of the hidden origins of meaning or community. The danger with the 'Gaelic' model is that it can imprison a community in the past and lead to political stagnation; on the other hand, the 'English' model, taken to the extreme, reduces language to a mechanistic, totalised and ontologically depthless system of arbitrary signs (a map) for the attainment of certain and certifiable knowledge.

Friel, however, complicates any simple binary opposition between 'English' and 'Gaelic'. The serpent has already entered the Gaelic Eden before the arrival of Lancey and his men. Maire, the principal female character, is anxious to learn English to further her hopes of leaving Baile Beag and going to America and she adduces the teachings of Daniel O'Connell in her support. Owen at first believes that there seems little point in preserving some of the original place-names because even the local people no longer know why the places are so called.

Any straightforward Nationalist appeal the play might have is further complicated by the central action, involving the English soldier, Yolland, who falls in love with Ireland, the Irish language and with the local girl, Maire. Yolland is a striking contradiction of the myth of the marauding English colonist. He is a soldier by accident, finding himself in Ireland because he missed the boat to India. Yet he asks us to consider the colonial mentality in a positive and sympathetic light, emphasising its spirit of adventure, its optimism and expansiveness, its 'energy', 'coherence' and 'belief'. Speaking of his father, he expresses a dynamic continuity between the revolutionary and the colonial spirit:

Born in 1789 – the very day the Bastille fell. I've often thought maybe that gave his whole life its character. Do you think it could? He inherited a new world the day he was born – The Year One. Ancient time was at an end. The world had cast off its old skin. There were no longer any frontiers to man's potential. Possibilities were endless and exciting. He still believes that. The Apocalypse is just about to happen . . . I'm afraid I'm a great disappointment to him. I've neither his energy, nor his coherence, nor his belief'. (*SP*, p. 416)

'The Year One': here Yolland indicates another pure source, the imperial equivalent of the Gaelic Utopia. And both, we are shown, require the constant vigilance of critical evaluation to ensure that the original energy does not succumb to stagnation or be perverted into a reactionary domination.

1789 is a year endowed with different significance by different people. It is remembered by Yolland as the year of the fall of the Bastille; by Hugh and Jimmy Jack as a time of brief heroics and meaningful homecoming. Just so will the day of the final scene of the play be remembered by some as the day of the burning of the English camp, by others as the day of joining the freedom fighters and by others as the day on which Nellie Ruadh's baby died. Friel's history is a frame for individual stories, alternative narratives.

Regretting that he does not possess the purposeful colonial personality, Yolland eventually discovers that Ireland is his spiritual home: 'It wasn't an awareness of *direction* being changed but of experience being of a totally different order' (*SP*, p. 416). It is he who realises, long before Owen, that an 'eviction' is taking place and it is he who insists that Tobair Vree be allowed to keep its name (though, ironically, the name he wants retained is itself an Anglicisation). He can see the loss as well as the gain in translation and mapping, and suspects that even if he learns to speak Irish 'the language of the tribe' (*SP*, p. 416) will always elude him. That is, he recognises and respects difference, while affirming the possibility of communication. Total communication, even between people using the same language, is a mirage, but the fact that there can be no final certainty doesn't prevent us from understanding *something.*

In the love scene between Yolland and Maire, their comic protestations of incomprehension, even as they both express themselves in perfectly comprehensible English, would seem to mock the idea of an insuperable barrier between different languages and cultures. The love scene, like the scenes between Skinner and Lily in the Mayor's parlour in *Freedom of the City* or between the members of the Butler family when Sir is away in *Living Quarters* or the dancing in *Dancing at Lughnasa*, opens up a lyrical space which presses back against history. It represents a momentary break from historical reality, from the troublesome projects of naming and enclosing in the public world. It is a moment of healing. Earlier, with Owen as translator, Yolland and Maire had not found it possible to make contact. Alone, their speech becomes incantation – pure sound and rhythm, divested of conceptual meaning and value judgement. Reciting the Irish place-names creates an intoxication that brings them closer together than any of their earlier attempts to communicate discursively in English. Their speech and actions deny the border between them, transcending the conventional divisions and classifications. Here, Friel pursues his experiment with non-rational communication, an experiment that he carries significantly further in succeeding plays, with the final kiss in *The Communication Cord* and the music and dancing in *Dancing at Lughnasa* – forms of communication which are free of the social contaminations of ordinary language and allow for fuller expression of 'pure' internal experience.

Friel certainly cannot be said to underestimate the difficulties of translating between cultures or interpreting between privacies. Owen's blithe reassurance to Yolland, 'You can learn to decode us' (*SP*, p. 416), is the decultured collaborator speaking and his practical optimism must be placed beside Jimmy Jack's more seasoned final adjudication that 'you don't cross these borders casually' (*SP*, p. 446). What Yolland learns, as Michael Toolan succinctly puts it, is 'the possibility of communication without unification'.[25] But that is a momentous recognition. The 'Other' can be enriching, rather than something to be feared and abominated or brought under control by being 'colonised'. A new political agenda suggests itself, for to be able to see the 'Other' as attractive rather than something to be distrusted is to escape the conventional, ethnocentric pieties and open up the possibility of a rejuvenating pluralism.

Maire shares Yolland's openness to the 'Other'. Reciting the place-names of Yolland's native Norfolk, she concludes: 'Strange sounds, aren't they? But nice sounds' (*SP*, p. 438). Maire's desire for openness and change, however, entails a more outright rejection of roots than we find in the classical balance of Hugh's achieved position. She is the character who most strongly and consistently questions the traditional 'Irish' habits of mind, the conventional ethic of 'belonging', the primacy of 'nation'. The Irish, Maire complains, have connived in their own victimisation and she attacks their seemingly endless susceptibility to fatalistic resignation. The people, she says, are always complaining, always expecting the worst. Like the 'Gentle Islanders' in the earlier play, the Irish imagine they live under a 'curse' – symbolised in *Translations* by the pervasive sweet smell (of rotting potatoes) – and their actions and attitudes are all determined by this constant sense of doom which inhibits forward-looking, dynamic action:

Sweet smell! Sweet smell! Every year at this time somebody comes back with stories of the sweet smell. Sweet God, did the potatoes ever fail in Baile Beag? Well, did they ever – ever? Never! There was never a blight here. Never. Never. But we're always sniffing about for it, aren't we? – looking for disaster. The rents are going to go up again – the harvest's going to be lost – the herring have gone away for ever – there's going to be evictions. Honest to God, some of you people aren't happy unless you're miserable and you'll not be right content until you're dead.   (*SP*, p. 395)

Again, Friel's irony is never far away: history contradicts Maire. In the next decade famine reduced the population of Ireland as a whole by one-quarter, either through death or emigration.

Nevertheless, Maire is the play's principal spokesperson of the forces of modernisation. Reacting against the shared norms, she wants to see English replace Gaelic. She sees knowledge of the English language as a means of escape from limited perspectives. Hugh speaks of how Gaelic is 'our response to mud cabins and a diet of potatoes' (*SP*, p. 418), but to Maire, learning English is a more practical and meaningful response. For her, English opens the doors to America and the promise of material and economic advantage. She advocates a break with the prescribed, ceremonialised behaviour patterns, with the old ties of loyalty and authority, with the old sacral view of history. The values that derive from the traditional, backward-looking principle, the communal memory, only hinder progress. She complains about Manus's lack of any dynamic, practical sense:

You talk to me about getting married – with neither a roof over your head nor a sod of ground under your foot. I suggest you go for the new school; but no – 'My father's in for that'. Well now he's got it and now this is finished and now you've nothing.   (*SP*, p. 404)

There is a ruthless streak in Maire. She urges self-assertion and self-improvement, innovation and initiative, an elevation of the principle of merit above traditional, ceremonial principles. She has already befriended the English soldiers despite their mutual incomprehension and has managed to enlist their help with the hay; and, of course, she puts individual rights above traditional family and tribal bonds by entering upon an exogamous relationship with Yolland.

Hugh's comments on the difference between Irish and English languages and cultures would seem to conform to the traditional

Nationalist discourse. 'English', says Hugh, 'couldn't really express us' (*SP*, p. 399), but the play itself, written in English, memorably expresses distinctively Irish experience at a crucial point in its history. Gaelic culture and classical culture, Hugh says, make a 'happier conjugation' (*SP*, p. 399) than English and classical, but when he demands of his students the etymology of certain words, he is always using English, not Gaelic, words – 'baptise', 'perambulation', 'verecund', 'conjugation', 'acquiesced'. Indeed, the Irish language does not derive from Latin and Greek in the way English does. Hugh belittles English by saying it is suitable 'for the purpose of commerce' and that it makes poetry sound 'plebeian' (*SP*, p. 417). This, from the man who, himself, delights in the music of the English language and exploits its etymological and rhetorical richness to the full. He appears unbearably chauvinistic when he's talking to Yolland: 'No. I'm afraid we're not familiar with your literature, Lieutenant. We feel closer to the warm Mediterranean. We tend to overlook your island' (*SP*, p. 417), but he seems to be aware that he's delivering a clichéd racial polemic rather than offering a genuine insight, for the stage directions indicate that 'as the scene progresses, one has the sense that he is deliberately parodying himself' (*SP*, pp. 416–17).

Curiously, when Yolland expresses his enthusiasm for Irish language and culture, Hugh, instead of encouraging Yolland's Hibernophilia, takes a surprisingly critical view of the Irishry. He explains to Yolland how the richness of Gaelic language and literature is related to social deprivation and political powerlessness: 'Certain cultures expend on their vocabularies and syntax acquisitive energies and ostentations entirely lacking in their material lives' (*SP*, p. 418). Language offers the possibility of transcending a constricting and stultifying environment. Hugh might appear to be resuscitating the central concept of nineteenth-century Revivalists – the opposition of Irish imagination and spirit to the utilitarian and technocratic philosophies of rationalist England – but he refuses to let the old flattering self-image of the romantic Nationalists go unquestioned. He knows that language can offer consolation amidst desolation simply by distorting the truth: 'Yes, it is a rich language, Lieutenant, full of the mythologies of fantasy and hope and self-deception – a syntax opulent with tomorrows. It is our response to mud cabins and a diet of potatoes' (*SP*, pp. 418–19). Hugh wants to recall his people to the real world, even though he appreciates their motives for wishing to detach themselves from it: 'it can happen that a civilization can be imprisoned in a linguistic contour which no longer matches the landscape of . . . fact' (*SP*, p. 419). Hugh's focus for much of the play is on the past, on origins and etymologies, but he recognises that exclusive commitment to some primal ideal can be a form of imprisonment. Tradition, he sees, can only survive through translation. He replies to 'inevitabilities', not by escaping into romantic fantasy (like Jimmy Jack), not by intransigence (like Manus) and not by revolt (like the Donnelly twins, Doalty and Owen), but by seeking to adapt to change, by looking for ways to reconcile the traditional and the modern, emotion and reason, the intimate reality of the parish and larger perspectives that cut across time and place. He criticises Jimmy Jack for becoming 'fossilized', stuck in the past, in a version of reality which is hopelessly out of touch with the modern world, and applies the same criticism to Owen who, having repudiated his earlier collaboration with the Ordnance Survey as 'a mistake' (*SP*, p. 444) and thrown aside the Name-Book, champions the notion of a cultural permanence that should not be changed:

> OWEN: I know where I live.
> HUGH: James thinks he knows, too. I look at James and three thoughts occur to me: A – that it is not the literal past, the 'facts' of history, that shape us, but images of the past embodied in language. James has ceased to make that discrimination. . . . B – we must never cease renewing those images; because once we do, we fossilize.
>
> (*SP*, p. 445)

Owen's inflexible nationalism and Jimmy Jack's sexual fantasies are linked: neither man can see that he has committed himself to a fiction. For Hugh, the great challenge now is 'to learn those new names . . . we must learn to make them our new home' (*SP*, p. 444). The crucial recognition here is that 'home' isn't a given: it's 'made'. Spoken Irish–English, Hugh speculates, can become a creditable, identifiable linguistic medium – an idea that has Tom Paulin's support: 'A language that lives lithely on the tongue ought to be capable of becoming the flexible written instrument of a complete cultural idea'. Friel's work, which unselfconsciously makes use of authentic Irish–English vernacular, is enactment and proof of Paulin's theorising.

The need to learn the new names and make of them a new home represents a new awareness for Hugh, too, one which, we may suppose, the experience of the Ordnance Survey has brought him. Earlier in the play, he is not at all amenable to the idea of change. He refuses to take seriously the thought that Gaelic should give way to English. When Maire quotes the words of 'The Liberator', Daniel O'Connell, that 'The old language is a barrier to modern progress' (*SP*, p. 400), Hugh refuses to confront the challenge of reality posed by Maire, mocks O'Connell as 'that little Kerry politician' and, reaching for his hip-flask, simply changes the subject. His proud boast of how he had forced the authorities to agree that he should run the National School exactly as he had run his hedge school (that is, that instruction should be in Irish, not English) further reveals a deeply entrenched conservatism. Returning home after an absence of six years, his son Owen's first observation is that 'everything's just as it was! Nothing's changed' (*SP*, p. 403). Hugh is clearly not exempt from the dangers of 'fossilization' or 'self-deception' which he condemns in others. His authority on any subject is compromised by his comic pedantry which Friel exploits delightfully and by the fact that for most of the play he is under the influence of the liquor he has consumed in Anna na mBreag's – in the house of 'lies', where, significantly, he has been celebrating a *caerimonia nominationis* – the 'ritual of naming' (*SP*, p. 397) Nellie Ruadh's baby.

From the start, however, Hugh is not completely closed to the 'Other'. Contrasting with Manus's attitude when Owen announces that he is helping the Ordnance Survey, Hugh shows restraint and makes no comment. And contrasting with Manus's sullen reserve when Yolland is introduced, Hugh does not let prejudice interfere with the proffer of traditional Irish hospitality. He is 'expansive, almost courtly, with his visitors' (*SP*, p. 405) and extends a warm and generous welcome to the entire Ordnance Survey team. Where Lancey's oppressiveness makes rebels out of both his sons, it confirms Hugh in his belief in the need to adapt in order to survive, to abandon myth and come to terms with the implacable processes of history. He refuses the word 'always'. When Maire asks him at the end what 'always' means, he replies: 'It's not a word I'd start with. It's a silly word' (*SP*, p. 446). He agrees in the end to teach Maire English but cannot be sure that, having learnt the language, she will be any better equipped to 'interpret between privacies' (*SP*, p. 446).

Hugh is a large and complex creation. He would seem to voice Friel's acceptance of the English language, of the need for change and adaptability, while his regard for the archaic Latin and Greek languages and cultures demonstrates an equal concern with preserving continuity, the sense of the past, even in the midst of change. Jimmy Jack is the one who is completely lost to the past and whose hold on reality is, consequently, tenuous. But Hugh has the ability to *use* the past, as his closing translation from the *Aeneid* illustrates. He can use the past to enlighten present dilemmas and obtain a perspective on them. 'To remember everything is a form of madness' (*SP*, p. 445), he tells Owen, in direct echo of George Steiner. What Hugh recommends is a selective remembrance, one which allows for new versions of the past to emerge, for the reappearance of repressed forces which may have a potentially liberating effect in the reshaping of the present. There is no dogma, no commitment, that should not continually be subject to critique: 'My friend', Hugh says, 'confusion is not an ignoble condition' (*SP*, p. 446), a position which would seem to have Friel's endorsement, if we are to go by Hugh's symbolic elevation at the end when he ascends the stairs as he speaks. His knowledge of the classics gives him, not ready answers, but a civilized perspective on contemporary events. The curtain falls suddenly, unexpectedly, in the middle of his attempts to recall a passage from Virgil about the overthrow of 'Tyrian towers' by a race of Trojan blood. The episode is, characteristically, equivocal: is it the dispossession of the Irish or the overthrow of the English which Hugh is placing within a larger cycle of recurrence? The play ends with more questions than answers.

While focusing on the tragedy implicit in the loss of a language, Friel allows us to consider, through the character of Hugh, the desirability of a fusion of Gaelic and English traditions so that culture may be enhanced rather than strangled by violence or sentimentalised and cheapened as in *The Communication Cord*. When Maire recites the English place-names Yolland has taught her – Winfarthing, Barton Bendish, Saxingham Nethergate, Little Walsingham, Norwich, Norfolk – we are reminded that English history is also a history of invasion and assimilation. Change, Friel indicates, need not imply extinction, but possible enrichment.

Nevertheless, Hugh, who has the play's largest and most luminous insights, is, to the very end, subject to Friel's subversive irony. As with the Field Day project itself, Friel sees the virtue of retaining an element of healthy cynicism and avoiding any fixed position. So, not even Hugh is allowed to stand as a normative character. Rather, he is made to appear pathetically ineffectual, too comfortably removed from the turmoil of history. The last we see of him he is frozen in a posture of total stasis, isolated at the top of the stairs,

looking down upon the scene beneath him. In the midst of cata-
clysm, his is the crepitating, drunken, self-absorbed murmur worry-
ing over the exact wording of Virgil, reminiscing on the paralysing
effect of local attachment even in the days of lusty youth.

The romantic image of heroic young Irishmen marching off to
fight for freedom and suffer death for their country in 1793 – a year
that is central in Republican mythology – is undercut by Hugh's
painfully honest account of how, twenty-three miles away from
home, he and Jimmy Jack were so overcome by homesickness, they
had to return to Ballybeg:

> We were gods that morning, James; and I had recently married *my*
> goddess, Caitlin Dubh Nic Reactainn, may she rest in peace. And
> to leave her and my infant son in his cradle – that was heroic, too.
> By God, sir, we were magnificent. We marched as far as – where
> was it? – Glenties! All of twenty-three miles in one day. And it
> was there, in Phelan's pub, that we got homesick for Athens, just
> like Ulysses. The *desiderium nostrorum* – the need for our own. Our
> *pietas*, James, was for older, quieter things.   (*SP*, pp. 445–6)

Commitment to Republican activism, these lines imply, is a commitment to abstractions and goddesses, similar to Jimmy Jack's devotion to Pallas Athene, a departure from the actualities of love and
family.

We are forced to consider the possibility that Hugh's civilised,
classical balance, his serene, speculative, even-handed rejection of
anything in particular, may, in fact, be a recipe for political inertia
and, thus, for passive submission to the oppressor. The apocalyptic
temper that increasingly makes itself felt towards the end puts the
contemplative mode epitomised by Hugh under maximum pressure.

The characterisation of Hugh, in fact, recalls that of prior literary
fathers such as the notoriously irresponsible Michael James Flaherty
in Synge's *The Playboy of the Western World*, who absconds from
present crisis and spends most of his time getting drunk at Kate
Cassidy's wake (as Hugh is likewise claimed by an off-stage, drunken
festival) and the equally irresponsible Paycock in O'Casey's *Juno and
the Paycock*, whose drunken refusals to confront reality lead ultimately to the point where, having allowed everything to slip away
from him, he is unable even then to contemplate any more meaningful action than to slump into a self-pitying jeremiad about the terri-

ble 'state o' chassis' into which the world has fallen. Friel's Hugh has more dignity and more self-knowledge than either of these characters, but he is no more capable of positive action. There is available to him neither the heroic transcendence of the resolutely self-determining Christy nor the practical virtue exemplified by O'Casey's family-centred women. Through Hugh, Friel presents the contemplative alternative to political action; and the political action, although it takes place off-stage, in classical fashion, as it does in O'Casey, still exerts a dramatic force that should not be underestimated. Arguably, the violence is all the more troubling for remaining unseen.

What, crucially, Friel shares with Synge and O'Casey is a characteristic tragicomic dramatic structure which, by continually undermining itself, refuses any kind of fixity and finality. Like the great tragicomedians before him, Friel sets out to destroy complacency, to explore the possibility of crossing boundaries and occupying an interstitial space between the received discourses, a project which, as Jimmy Jack warns, is fraught with tension: 'you don't cross those borders casually – both sides get very angry' (*SP*, p. 446). Written at a time when 'truths' and 'causes' were plentiful commodities, when retrenchment was the order of the day, Friel's drama challenges the certainty of received opinions and attitudes, exemplifying Hugh's rejection of 'always'. The saddest loser in the play is Manus, the representative of the stubborn, unyielding attitude of the traditional Nationalist who will have nothing to do with England. Manus understands the Lanceys perfectly, he says; it's people like Yolland who 'puzzle' him. The inability to categorise unsettles Manus; the free, floating spirit, the potential exogamist, is truly alien to him. Manus, the one who is most headstrongly and glumly set against change, is the pathetic victim of his own inflexibility, ending up with no job, no girlfriend, no home, no destination and too self-absorbed even to appreciate Sarah's loyal, tender, potentially redemptive feeling for him.

Many critics are too keen to slot Friel into fixed positions and make his play yield up simple messages. Lionel Pilkington, for example, complains that Friel's attempt to show history as 'images of the past constructed in language' conflicts with the manner in which the play is presented: 'The play's naturalistic dramaturgy,' Pilkington avers, 'conceals the extent to which characters and action are fictional and constructed in language'.[26] Friel manages to convince that 'his version of nineteenth-century Irish history . . . is grounded, unproblematically, in fact'.[27] But, as the play's title announces, Friel *is* offering us versions, 'translations', and the consistent sign of the play's constructed and fictional nature is the representation of the original Gaelic order almost entirely in and through English. The play's supremely ironic form allows us to see not only the conflict between Gaelic-speaking peasants and English colonists, but also the outcome from a perspective a century and a half later: English has superceded Gaelic, but so successfully have the original Gaelic-speakers made English words their new home that even sophisticated literary critics can forget the sensational fiction on which the play rests – the illusion that we are hearing Gaelic when, in fact, it is English that is being spoken. Friel's is an exquisitely balanced performance, simultaneously emphasising disjunction *and* redemption, absence *and* presence, fragmentation *and* transformation, loss *and* triumph, tradition *and* modernism – the inevitable compromise of language, the pulse of life itself. While the play may certainly contain elements of nostalgic lament for the loss of the Irish language, it can also be viewed optimistically as representing Friel's imaginative alternative to the sterility of traditional and cultural Nationalism which, from the Young Irelanders to their present-day inheritors, insists upon the restoration of the Irish language as a prerequisite for national cohesion and renewal. While demonstrating our need to create enabling myths of ourselves, he also emphasises how those myths must continually be subject to critique if we are to avoid becoming fossilised.

THE THREE SISTERS

Field Day's second production was of Friel's 'translation' of Chekhov's *The Three Sisters*, which was premiered in the Guildhall, Derry, in 1981. To many reviewers, Friel's 'translation' was something of a curiosity and, certainly, the Irishman's decision to rework the great Russian dramatist's greatest play (begun in 1900 and first produced in 1901) raises some interesting questions. Why was Friel attracted to Chekhov? What special relevance, if any, did Chekhov's play have to the cultural project of the Field Day Theatre Company?

Friel tells us 'he simply sat down at his desk with six English versions in front of him',[28] one of them no doubt being the translation by Tyrone Guthrie and Leonid Kipnis, which was the text of the production that Friel saw take shape at the Tyrone Guthrie Theatre in Minneapolis in 1963. His own 'translation', Friel said, 'was undertaken primarily as an act of love and, since the only Chekhov translations available to the Irish theatre are American and English, in the hope that this translation may make the unique experience of Chekhov more accessible to Irish audiences'.[29] In an interview in *Magill* in December 1980, Friel explains further:

> I think that the versions of *Three Sisters* that we see and read in this country always seem to be redolent of either Edwardian England or the Bloomsbury set. Somehow the rhythms of these versions do not match with the rhythms of our own speech patterns, and I think that they ought to, in some way. Even the most recent English translation again carries, of necessity, very strong English cadences and rhythms. This is something about which I feel strongly – in some way we are constantly overshadowed by the sound of the English language, as well as by the printed word. Maybe this does not inhibit us, but it forms us and shapes us in a way that is neither healthy nor valuable for us.[30]

Friel insists that his translation was undertaken for dramatic, not political reasons: use of a specific idiom, he felt, could be crucially and subtly revealing of character.

And so we find no radical changes to existing translations in Friel's version. He largely contents himself with localizing some of the detail and colloquialising some of the language, and it was generally agreed that these undertakings were accomplished with tact and subtlety. However, there were those, in Ireland as well as England, who questioned the need for such an enterprise at all. *The Times* reviewer, for example, thought that 'Chekhov needs no special papers to take up Irish residence. He can be at home there in a standard translation',[31] while the writer in the *Irish Independent* proclaimed: '*Three Sisters* is a universal and timeless play of imperishable beauty, and it needs no colloquialized slant to enhance its level of acceptability.'[32]

There were perhaps deeper reasons why Friel was attracted to Chekhov's drama and wanted to work on it and play with it. For one thing, there is a notable affinity between the two writers, which manifests itself not only in a shared thematic interest, but also in terms of mood, character and dramatic technique. It is even possible to outline parallels in the social conditions out of which the two dramatists wrote. Elisaveta Fen, in her Introduction to the Penguin edition of Chekhov's plays, writes of the mood of 'disappointment and depression' in the Russia of 1880–1900 – 'the result of the failure of Alexander II's reforms to make a deep enough impression on the great, inert mass of the Russian population and its officialdom. Besides, these reforms were made largely sterile by the Reformer's successor'.[33] Politically, Fen says, the country was 'passing through a phase of reaction and retrenchment'. Economically, Russia at this time was 'undergoing a process of partial proletariatization as her impoverished peasants were being driven off the land into newly opened factories'.[34] This Russian disenchantment and frustration have their easily recognisable counterparts in the Ireland of the 1970s and 1980s. The continuing Troubles enforced a sense of impasse and endless malaise, a feeling of stagnation and depression. Economically, the North was in a state of recession, with unemployment at an all-time high. Politically, no progress seemed to be possible and the resulting vacuum was filled by the terrorists. In Ireland as a whole, the ongoing process of modernisation was attended by the usual traumas of dislocation and the break-up of traditional values.

Both playwrights are centrally concerned with the theme of 'replying to inevitabilities' and a very similar dramatic tension informs the work of both, a tension which stems from the recognition of the disparity between the reality of people's lives and the dreams by which they attempt to live. The playwrights accept both, seeing human life as the meaningful and at the same time pathetic, ludicrous and tragic attempt to bridge the gap. Chekhov's method of reply is perhaps in the end more thoroughly tragic than Friel's, reflecting, as Elsiveta Fen puts it, 'the mood of spiritual discouragement, helplessness before the overwhelming, impersonal forces of circumstance, an awareness of personal insignificance'.[35] At the centre of Chekhov's play is the poignancy of lifelong frustration, of unrequited love, of soul-destroying marriage, of partings without a hope of reunion. Friel, by contrast, considers the possibility of redefining traditional notions of both the perceiving subject and the received reality. He invokes the concept of 'translation', which is forward-looking as well as backward-looking, and he dramatises a process of transition in plays such as *Philadelphia*, *Aristocrats* and *Translations*. The future may be unknown, but at least change is possible. In *The Communication Cord* and *Dancing at Lughnasa*, spontaneous, genuine human feeling survives and Friel experiments with new ways of giving direct expression to it. Where Chekhov's play ends as it began, Friel includes the possibility of progression. Chekhov's drama of spiritual discouragement may thus represent for Friel a catharsis achieved by proxy, offering a similar kind of dramatic experience to that which is found in such doom-ridden plays of his own as *The Gentle Island*, *Freedom of the City* and *Living Quarters*.

The Three Sisters, like earlier Friel plays – *Philadelphia*, *The Loves of Cass McGuire* and *The Enemy Within* – is a play about exile, about life lived in difficult and uncongenial conditions. The situation of the three sisters is typical of Friel's families of frustrated and disappointed women in, say, *Aristocrats* and *Dancing at Lughnasa*. Like Kate, the eldest sister in *Dancing at Lughnasa*, Olga, the eldest sister in *The Three Sisters*, twenty-eight when the play begins, is a schoolmistress. Longing for a husband and yearning to return to Moscow, Olga by the end of the play becomes headmistress, which she never wished to be, and has moved away to live at the school. The second sister, Masha, is married to yet another schoolteacher – the worthy but ridiculous pedant, Kulygin. Masha married young and unwisely and has now fallen hopelessly in love with Vershinin, the new colonel of the local artillery, who alone makes her life bearable. By the end, however, Vershinin is also preparing to move away to another posting. The youngest sister, Irina, is celebrating her twentieth birthday, which is also the first anniversary of her father's death: the action of the play is quickly established within a context of life's transience. Irina, having proclaimed the therapeutic effects of work, gets a job in a post office and hates it, taking no consolation in the lap-dog attentions of her admirer, the Baron Tusenbach. The brother, Andrey, who dreams of becoming a professor at a Moscow university and a famous scholar ends up with no more exalted station than that of a permanent member of staff on the local county council, under Protopopov, his wife's lover. Trying to find a substitute for love in gambling, Andrey loses and mortgages the house to cover his gambling debts. The play's only winner would seem to be Andrey's wife, the odious, materialistic, vulgar Natasha who tyrannizes over the household, wanting to dismiss the old family retainer Anfisa, cancelling the visit of the mummers, ousting Irina from her room, cheating on her husband.

In flight from a harsh reality, the characters seek to escape into private worlds. For Andrey it is through his music, his books and his gambling; for others it is through work. The sisters, exiled in a nameless, drab, provincial town, look wistfully back to their Moscow childhood. This tendency towards fantasy or nostalgia is, of course, one that has been central to Friel's characterisation from the beginning: Columba finds respite from the harsh regime of Iona in idealised memories of his Irish childhood; Gar O'Donnell escapes from the stultifying world of Ballybeg into his New World fantasies; Cass McGuire retreats from disappointment into her 'rhapsody' of the past. The nostalgic yearning for a lost past or the dream of a Utopian future, Friel shows, is rooted deeply in the Irish communal consciousness. What both Friel's and Chekhov's characters conspicuously share is an inability to live in the present: either they keep looking back or looking forward.

The drunken, futile old doctor, Chebutykin, an old friend of the Pozorov family, is typical in his pathetic, hopeless longing for transformation:

> When I get my pension in twelve months time I'll come back to spend the remainder of my days with you. Straight back to the sun like a migrating bird. And I'll be so changed you won't know me. I'll be a quiet, benign (lifting his glass) and totally abstemious old gentleman.   (*TS*, p. 90)

Vershinin recognises how life is always being displaced into the past or the future. 'We Russians', he says, 'are a people whose aspirations are magnificent; it's just living we can't handle' (*TS*, p. 43). The tone and even the phrasing recall Hugh's candid recognition of communal illusion and unreality in *Translations* ('Yes, it is a rich language . . . full of the mythologies of fantasy and hope and self-deception – a syntax opulent with tomorrows. It is our response to mud cabins and a diet of potatoes; our only method of replying to . . . inevitabilities': *SP*, pp. 418–19). Both Vershinin and Hugh see the danger of living too much in a dream which only inhibits one's negotiations with the present reality.

But Vershinin himself constantly takes refuge from the living reality in visions of how beautiful life will become in the future. He speaks repeatedly of the possibility of transformation, social change, the importance of education and imagination in effecting that change, the need to work for a better life:

> in two or three hundred years time the quality of life on this earth will be transformed and beautiful and marvellous beyond our

imagining. Because *that's* the life man longs for and aspires to. And even though he hasn't achieved it yet, he must fashion it in his imagination, look forward to it, dream about it, prepare for it. But he can fashion it in his imagination and prepare for it only if he has more vision and more knowledge than his father or his grandfather. (*TS*, p. 27)

Vershinin's is an optimistic, dynamic, future-oriented view of life, urging recognition of the larger perspective and pattern. But his vision of a future in which everything will one day be transformed does not necessarily indicate a fundamental optimism on Chekhov's part, though this was what Soviet producers of the play wanted to emphasise. They sought to enlist Chekhov as a herald of their glorious revolution. But Chekhov was always careful to dissociate himself from all political 'tendencies':

The people I am afraid of are the ones who look for tendentiousness between the lines and are determined to see me as either liberal or conservative. I am neither liberal, nor conservative, nor gradualist, nor monk, nor indifferentist. I would like to be a free artist and nothing else. . . . That is why I cultivate no particular predilection for policemen, butchers, scientists, writers or the younger generation. I look upon tags and labels as prejudices.[36]

In the Introduction to his Methuen translation of the play (1983), Michael Frayn reminds us that there is no reason to suppose that Vershinin is Chekhov's mouthpiece, any more than, say, Baron Tuesenbach, who is just as sympathetic a character but who says the opposite to Vershinin, insisting that human life will never change. Or why should the neurotic, Byronic Solyony, the cynical critic of a corrupt society who identifies himself with the poet Lermontov, not be Chekhov's man? Or Chebutykin, like Chekhov a doctor, and proponent of the view that all is illusion and nothing really matters? Vershinin's optimism – 'life is going to get better and better and better and better!' (*TS*, p. 76) – as Frayn also remarks, is 'ironically undercut by the whole structure of the play'. Despite such assertions as Vershinin's, we see that nothing at all gets better in the course of the three year span of the play's action. Nothing essentially changes. Vershinin keeps reiterating his optimistic philosophy, obsessively, clearly only wishing to convince himself that life isn't as bad as his own present unhappiness might suggest it was. The pervasive mood of the play is a vast longing, accompanied by the demoralising suspicion that there is nothing that can be done. The possibility of meaningful action is constantly receding. The characters are unable to change or overcome their destiny. The sisters yearn for Moscow, but, like Beckett's tramps, do not go. There is an ironic disparity between speech and action, a central theme of Friel's plays, from *Philadelphia* to *Translations* ('Yes, it is a rich language . . . full of the mythologies of fantasy and hope and self-deception – a syntax opulent with tomorrows': *T*, p. 418), as indeed it is a central theme of the whole modern Irish theatrical tradition from Synge and O'Casey to Beckett.

The ending of *The Three Sisters*, like the ending of so many of Friel's plays, is richly ambiguous. Is Olga's last speech the message of the play, a message of determination and hope inspired by the sound of the music of the military band as the soldiers pull out?

> Just listen to that music. It's so assured, so courageous. It makes you want to go on, doesn't it? Oh my God! Yes, of course we will die and be forgotten – everything about us, how we looked, how we spoke, that there were three of us. But our unhappiness, our suffering, won't be wasted. They're a preliminary to better times, and because of them the people who come after us will inherit a better life – a life of peace and content and happiness. But our life isn't over yet. By no means! We are going to go on living. And that music is so confident, so courageous it almost seems as if it is about to be revealed very soon why we are alive and what our suffering is for.   (*TS*, p. 114)

As at the beginning so at the end, the sisters group together in a tableau and the whole play would seem to lead up to Olga's impassioned speech of courageous determination to face the future. But Chekhov doesn't end the play there. Into this static, ironical microcosm of life flows the neutral indifference of the quotidian. The music 'fades', Kulygin comes in with Masha's hat and coat and stands 'waiting with infinite patience' (*TS*, p. 114), glad to have his wife to himself again. Andrey, the would-be scholar, pushes the pram on to the stage. The useless old doctor sings to himself. Just as Olga's and Irina's 'great surge of joy' and 'passionate longing for home' (*TS*, p. 10) at the very beginning of the play are ironically undercut by remarks drifting in from Chebutykin, Solyony and the Baron ('Rubbish – rubbish – rubbish'; 'All words – all rubbish'; 'Talk

– talk – talk. Endless silly talk. That's all they do is talk': *TS*, pp. 10–12), so Olga's final resolve is ironically juxtaposed with Chebutykin's 'Matters sweet damn all . . . sweet damn all it matters' (*TS*, p. 114). This indifference of Chebutykin's runs deeply and pervasively through the play. Irina can not feel anything for the Baron whom she has agreed to marry the next day, Andrey doesn't care whether the mummers do or do not come. As Frayn notes, 'all attempts at forward motion – all the moves into the world of work, for instance – lead nowhere'. Irina's hopes of redemption by work are betrayed by the actual experience of it; Andrey's hopes of an academic career come to nothing; the sisters' hopes of Moscow are no closer to being realised at the end than at the beginning. *The Three Sisters* is a play not about the hopes of Vershinin or Olga or Andrey but, says Frayn, 'about the *irony* of those hopes – about the way life mocks them'. The only character whose hopes seem likely to be realised is Natasha and that is only because her hopes are so small and material – another baby, more dictatorial control over the household, Protopopov waiting in his troika. This is very different from Vershinin's vision of a life which will be 'transformed and beautiful and marvellous beyond our imagining'. The deepest irony of all, as Frayn concludes, is that it wouldn't make any difference if the big hopes *were* realized. Vershinin knows that if the sisters actually did live in Moscow they would soon not even notice that they had moved:

> I've just been reading the diary of a French cabinet minister that he wrote in jail – he was sentenced over the Panama Canal swindle. And he writes with such enthusiasm about the birds he sees from his cell window – birds he'd never even noticed when he was in government. And now he's out of jail he pays no more attention to the birds than he did before. Like you and Moscow: once you're living there, it'll mean nothing to you. Happiness? I don't believe in it. I don't believe it exists. Happiness is . . . a mirage.   (*TS*, p. 54)

This speech represents a momentary clouding of the vision of a future Utopian millenium which Vershinin elsewhere espouses with passion and eloquence. Vershinin, too, we see, cannot escape a sceptical and disconsolate pessimism, a corrosive disillusion. We recall Ben Burton's remark to Aunt Lizzy in *Philadelphia*: 'Ireland – America – what's the difference?' (*SP*, p. 64).

The Baron is the only character who momentarily lives the present moment rather than the mirage of a lost past or imagined future:

> And suddenly I feel elated – no, exalted! I love you! I love life!
> I love everybody and everything! Look at these fir-trees, those
> maples, those birches – I've never seen them before! Aren't they
> beautiful. (*TS*, p. 101)

The Baron notices the beauty in the world as if for the first time. The
irony is that he is at this point on his way to be killed. He knows he
is facing death: there is no future to distract him from the miracle of
the present. Hope cuts us off from the present moment, but we have
also seen that we cannot live without it. As Masha says: 'I think we
must have a faith, and if we haven't we must find one' (*TS*, p. 49).
Hope sustains as well as destroys.

It was noted in the discussion of some of Friel's best plays, for
example, *Faith Healer* or *Translations*, that it is impossible to find the
author in the characters. The dramatic technique involved here Friel
could well have learnt from Chekhov. It is one which, in seeking to
avoid all tendentiousness, collapses the barriers between author and
audience. The author enters his narrative*ous* an impresario of ironies. The scientist in Chekhov always demanded detachment and
objectivity. From the evidence of his own plays, we can see why Friel
would be attracted to Chekhov's restrained, open, sceptical mind
which was opposed to all kinds of fanaticism and emotionalism. In
Chekhov's drama every character, every attitude, is seen from a
variety of angles, the drama oscillating between hope and despair,
passion and ennui. Bleakness and cruelty are lightened by gentleness, affection, conscience. Chekhov stresses indifference, but
also work, duty, individual feeling. He finds consolation in ironic
humour.

A writer, Chekhov believed, should draw life as it really is, not as
he would like it to be. If he is to understand life, he should stop
believing what is said and written, and observe and meditate himself. The purposefulness in Chekhov's art, the keen moral sense, has
its counterpart in Friel's concern to make us think again and feel
anew. Both writers are dedicated to making the world more civilised, more enlightened and humane. Chekhov was a model of the
artist who could do all this without reference to party politics. Setting himself sternly against the herd instincts of fanatical nationalism, he insisted upon the primacy of the individual conscience. He
believed in evolution, not revolution. He was, to use F. L. Lucas's

word, 'a gradualist', with a deep sympathy for human beings, however misguided, silly or ineffectual they might be. Lucas characterises him as 'a good European liberal, with a dislike of nationalism, a loathing of despotism and no blind belief in Slavs, "noble peasants" or "the Russian soul"'.[37] This is echoed in the self-advertisement of the Field Day Company, dedicated to questioning the traditional perceptions which have straightjacketed Irish social life and private conscience alike. 'It is about time we put aside the idea of essence', Seamus Deane says, ' – that hungry Hegelian ghost looking for a stereotype to live in.'[38] In his tolerant understanding of human frailty and the pathetic illusions of mankind, Friel exhibits an unmistakably Chekhovian moral temper and concern. As well as that, both writers have the saving grace of humour, the consummate light touch. Theirs is an unflinching but generous perspective, appreciative of life's rich variety and mysteriousness. They give us the feel of life by showing us the balance of life, and this is why their artistic effects remain so elusive, so difficult to describe and explain. They are essentially poetic dramatists, concerned with unfolding an inner condition, expressing the paradox, the contradiction and incompleteness of experience, the confusion and complexity of motivation, the basic ambiguity of all human behaviour.

Thus, neither submits easily to the tyranny of a sequential and chronological structure, as the examples of *Philadelphia, Freedom of the City, Living Quarters* or *Faith Healer* would also illustrate in Friel's case. The drama is developed concentrically. Nothing much happens. The one sensational piece of action in *The Three Sisters* – the duel between Solyony and the Baron – takes place off-stage. But though nothing more happens, we recognise that we are seeing deeply into the inner life of personal relationships. The action moves in leisurely episodic swirls. The movement on stage, like the conversation, like the emotion, is drifting and loose, continually switching our attention from one group of actors to another in collage or cinematic fashion. As in Synge or O'Casey, structure and rhythm deny fixity and finality. The play typifies Friel's method of orchestrating a range of attitudes to create a complex poetic image rather than making a definitive statement.

Friel incorporates two new interludes of his own devising, two moments of potential 'blossoming' or 'quickening', of breaking out of the futility and ennui to experience freedom and flight. Significantly, these moments are also an escape from 'talk', the new, tentative self-expression taking the form of music and dance. Once 'talk' has been dispensed with there is the promise of intense communion with another. Fedotik and Roddy sing together to Roddy's accompaniment on his guitar, and the stage directions read:

> There is a sense that this moment could blossom, an expectancy that suddenly everybody might join in the chorus – and dance – and that the room might be quickened with music and laughter. Everyone is alert to this expectation; it is almost palpable if some means of realising it could be found. Vershinin moves close to Masha. If the moment blossoms, they will certainly dance. Fedotik moves close to Irina (to Roddy's acute annoyance); they, too, will dance.   (*TS*, p. 50)

But 'the moment is lost', Masha 'drifts away' from Vershinin, Fedotik 'moves away' from Irina and the characters once again retreat 'in vague embarrassment' (*TS*, p. 51) into their private worlds. A similar pattern of behaviour occurs a little later when the Baron plays 'The Blue Danube Waltz' on the piano:

> Masha dances by herself. As before there is the possibility that the occasion might blossom. But there is less possibility this time. (*TS*, p. 59)

The dictatorial Natasha enters and selfishly breaks up the carnival, forcing the derelict lives back into the dull, sluggish flow of provincial Russian life. But the movement towards finding a new expression for deep, repressed feeling, which is here dispelled for a second time, is eventually taken to its triumphant fulfilment in *Dancing at Lughnasa*.

THE COMMUNICATION CORD

'Rewriting', this central concept of Friel's drama of the 1980s and 1990s, includes not only 'rewritings' of the official, historical record (as in *Translations* and *Making History*, which follow on from earlier historical 'rewritings' such as we find in *The Enemy Within* and *Freedom of the City*, all of these plays recentring the concrete, individual reality that tends to be written out of the hagiography or the public record), it also includes the 'rewriting' of prior literary texts, both those of other writers (Chekhov, Turgenev, Macklin) and those which Friel has authored himself. Thus, *The Communication Cord* is, quite deliberately on Friel's part, a 'rewriting' of *Translations*, just as *Losers* had been a 'rewriting' of an early short story, 'The Highwayman and the Saint', or *Aristocrats* had reworked another early story, 'The Foundry House'.

The Communication Cord, the third Field Day production, premiered in Derry's Guildhall in 1983, was Friel's answer to those who accused him of idealising 'traditional' Ireland in *Translations*, of encouraging dreams of innocence, of secretly wishing to recall us to a sacred Gaelic Golden Time before the depredations of famine or the incursions of English colonial influence. The hedge school is replaced by a 'traditional' Irish cottage, which Friel describes as 'a reproduction, an artefact of today making obeisance to a home of yesterday' (*CC*, p. 11). Nora Dan is the only native of Ballybeg whom we meet, and, introduced as 'the quintessential noble peasant', she is then described as 'obsessed with curiosity and greed and envy' (*CC*, p. 21) and given a language which is a nauseating concoction of repetitive, sentimental obsequiousness. When one of the visitors addresses her as 'Mrs Dan' (*CC*, p. 21), she explains: 'Glory be to God, isn't that a good one! Sure I was never a missus in my life, Tim. I get the Dan from my father – that's the queer way we have of naming people about here'. The mystical *caerimonia nominationis* of *Translations* has degenerated into mere regional eccentricity. The intimate genealogy implicit in the names of Maire Chatach, Sarah John Sally, Jimmy Jack Cassie, Anna na mBreag, Doalty Dan Doalty and Nellie Ruadh is replaced by the irreverent nicknaming of Jack the Cod, Barney the Banks and Tim the Thesis.

The adventurer Owen of *Translations* is reincarnated as Jack, the opportunistic impresario of events in *The Communication Cord*. Jack uses his 'father's house' (*CC*, p. 17) as a love-nest and has agreed to 'lend' the cottage to his friend, Tim, so that Tim can impress his girlfriend's father, Senator Donovan, by pretending that he owns the cottage. Jack cynically persuades Tim of the advantages of duping the Senator: 'Daddy Senator suddenly realizes that there's more to you than the stooped, whingeing, trembling, penniless, myopic part-time junior lecturer without tenure' (*CC*, p. 21). The scholar and linguist, Hugh, has metamorphosed into Tim, who is researching 'Discourse Analysis with Particular Reference to Response Cries'

(*CC*, p. 18). Like Yolland, Senator Donovan feels he has entered a new 'order' of being in Ballybeg: 'This is what I need – this silence, this peace, the restorative power of that landscape' (*CC*, p. 30), though, of course, the Senator presumes that as a native who knows 'the language of the tribe' he has direct access to the 'private core'. The tragic love triangle involving Manus, Maire and Yolland degenerates into the riotous shenanigans of Jack, Jim, Donovan, Susan, Evette and Claire. Friel returns to the vein of broad, farcical satire which he worked in *The Mundy Scheme*.

The drama of ancestral piety has become the proper subject of farce, the conventions of farce allowing Friel to give full expression to the gullibility, the vacuousness and egregious foolishness of those who allow themselves to be seduced by the imagery of a sanctified past; and, also, to indulge a sensationally cynical view of the motives that lie behind the promotion of traditional Ireland. In the programme notes to the play, Seamus Deane offers this summary description of the kind of diptych represented by *Translations* and *The Communication Cord*:

> *The Communication Cord* is an antidote to *Translations*. It reminds us that farce repeats itself as history and that the bogus, the fixed, and the chaotic are features of our daily lives in the social and political world. Tragedy gives us perspective and ennobles our feelings by rendering them subject to forces we can recognise but never define. Farce shows everything in close-up; it is concerned to reduce, to expose, to humiliate, and at the same time, to rescue us, via laughter, from the heroics of failure.[39]

Farce proposes a closed, changeless world governed by rules which embody a mechanical, deterministic view of life. Language is a constantly shifting, nervous, sometimes hysterical attempt to rationalise the present, with Tim, supposed master of linguistics, translating events into ever more improbable narratives and histories. Friel's theatre – from *Philadelphia* to *Dancing at Lughnasa* – is characteristically a theatre of memory, a space for exploration. *The Communication Cord* demonstrates what it would be like if no break with present reality, no lyrical moment, no subjective fantasia was possible within the existing frame of history, and the 'dark and private places of the individual soul' remained forever repressed. In the emphatically male world of the play, women and words alike are simply commodities or counters to be ruthlessly manipulated. Jack, like Sir in *Living Quarters*, is the prime mover of events in the play. Sir has his ledger, Jack his 'timetable' (*CC*, p. 16) with which he sets about mapping out a plan for the afternoon, but with much less regard for the truth than Sir. Jack is a descendant of earlier playboys such as Gar, Shane, Casimir, Keeney and Skinner, but his playfulness betrays an exaggerated cynical and predatory instinct. He is also a lawyer and Friel's lawyers have generally tended to be unscrupulous manipulators and controllers. Play, we see, need not necessarily be a genuinely freeing, life-enhancing activity: it may just as well seek to bring into existence an alienating inversion of the true relation of things. Jack's 'map' of events deliberately sets out to distort the landscape of fact.

Communication has no more substance than the cottage. The 'suave tongue of Dr Bollocks' (*CC*, p. 16), breathless with adoration, exclaims a romantic dream which bears no relation to actuality: 'This is the touchstone . . . this is the apotheosis' (*CC*, p. 31). Jack savagely mocks the Senator's quasireligious language:

(In parody) This is where we all come from. This is our first cathedral. This shaped all our souls. This determined our first pieties. Yes. Have reverence for this place (Laughs heartily). (*CC*, p. 15)

Ultimately, Donovan is exposed. Finding himself chained to the cow post, he abandons his bogus language: 'This determined our first priorities! This is our native simplicity! Don't give me that shit! (*CC*, p. 70).

Dialogue frequently takes the form of an echo. Tim repeats Jack's well-rehearsed platitudes about the cottage. His words are echoed by both Claire and Donovan. Jack and Donovan repeat themselves when they are talking to different women. In Act II, for example, Jack's 'chat-up' speech to Susan ('Many, many years ago, Susan, you and I were fortunate enough to experience and share an affection that is still one of my most sustaining memories . . .' (*CC*, p. 67)), is a direct echo of an earlier speech to Claire, when he is trying to persuade her to leave the cottage and not complicate his plans. In Act I, when Donovan is trying to ingratiate himself with Claire, who is masquerading as Evette Giroux, he says: 'When you're as young and as beautiful as Madame Giroux, language doesn't matter, does it? Words are superfluous, aren't they?' (*CC*, p. 34) – and later repeats these words when he is talking to another Evette Giroux who is, in fact, an old friend: 'Not that language matters when you're as young and as beautiful as you are' (*CC*, p. 73). The echoic character of Donovan's and Jack's speech is used to expose them as pathetic philanderers, yet, ironically, Donovan's idea of the superfluousness of words, when it is taken up at the very end in a much more serious way by Tim and Claire, represents the play's culminating insight: 'All that stuff about units of communication. Maybe the units don't matter all that much' (*CC*, p. 85).

At times, speech degenerates altogether into absurdity and inconsequentiality:

DONOVAN: I envy you, Tim. You know that, don't you?
TIM: Yes.
DONOVAN: That's not true. I don't envy you. You know that, don't you?
TIM: Yes.

(*CC*, p. 31)

Characters are continually 'talking past each other' and what we hear eventually is a frenetic babble of French and German accents, both authentic and imitated, and various forms of Irish–English. Even the natural world protests: the chimney blow-downs symbolically blacken Tim's face and the play ends with the collapse of the 'traditional' Irish cottage.

The collapse of the cottage is the collapse of a false myth. Like *Translations, The Communication Cord* dramatises the dissolution of Irish culture, but where the former registers a powerful note of regret and resentment at the passing of an old order, the latter emphasises the farcical absurdity which can result from attachment to the past. In *Aristocrats*, after the collapse of the Big House, Friel looks forward to new possibilities beyond the bankrupt myth. Similarly, in *The Communication Cord* he includes an assertion of free will and the possibility of human dignity. In contrast with Donovan's strident rhetorical insistences, Tim and Claire's achievement at the end is the realisation of a muted presence, of authentic relation beyond the homogenising, reductive, stereotyping activity of the dominant social (dis)order.

Tim recognises a development in his own thinking about language. His initial thesis was that language was 'a ritualised act between people. . . . The exchange of units of communication through an agreed code' (*CC*, p. 84). By the end, he admits that he may have 'to rewrite' (*CC*, p. 85) a lot of this thesis in the light of his new experience. Words, he comes to see, may not matter all that much as counters or 'units' of currency. There is no reliable correspondence between the words the subject uses and what the subject intends. In view of the social and semantic contaminations of language, it may be better to trust to 'reverberations' and 'implicit' meanings rather than explicit messages:

> TIM: We're conversing now but we're not exchanging units, are we?
> CLAIRE: I don't think so, are we?
> TIM: I don't think we can be because I'm not so sure what I'm saying.
> CLAIRE: I don't know what you're saying either but I think I know what's implicit in it. . . . .
> TIM: Even if what I'm saying is rubbish?
> CLAIRE: Yes.
> TIM: Like 'this is our first cathedral'?
> CLAIRE: Like that.
> TIM: Like 'this is the true centre'?
> CLAIRE: I think I know what's implicit in that.
> TIM: Maybe the message doesn't matter at all then. . . . .
> CLAIRE: It's the occasion that matters.
> TIM: And the reverberations that the occasion generates.
>
> (*CC*, p. 85)

Friel is here exploring Bakhtin's ideas about the inherently 'dialogic' nature of language: it is grasped only in terms of its inevitable orientation towards another. Words are not fixed 'units', like signals, but active components of speech, modified and transformed in their meaning by the variable tones and nuances which they acquire in specific social conditions. The slipperiness of the 'units of communication' that Tim talks about is emphasised by the way lines keep recurring in the play: lifted from their original occasion, they are re-employed, often verbatim, to quite different purpose or effect, in another context. Language, the play shows through its echoic technique, is always caught up in definite social relations and these relations are in turn part of broader political, ideological and economic systems. Ultimately, Friel takes consolation in the phenomenological notion of the intending subject as the source and origin of all meaning. Public is still opposed by Private and whatever authenticity is to be found lies in the realm of Private feeling. The Private self now struggles towards an alternative, non-rational, non-verbal expression, moving from 'reverberations' to a newly discovered language of the body. Ultimately, Tim muses, 'Maybe silence is the perfect discourse' (*CC*, p. 86). Tim and Claire's wordless communion, enacted in a kiss, the first authentic human contact in the play, is the discovery of a radically subversive 'realism', which brings the cottage tumbling down: 'They kiss and hold that kiss until the play ends. As they kiss they lean heavily against the upright. . . . The upright begins to move. Sounds of timbers creaking' (*CC*, p. 86).

FATHERS AND SONS

Friel's next play, *Fathers and Sons*, failed to receive an Irish première. The play was too big for Field Day to do it and, instead, it opened at the Lyttleton Theatre, London, in 1987.

Another of Friel's literary 'rewritings', *Fathers and Sons*, after Turgenev's great novel of 1861, is a tragicomedy of age and youth, of the old order and the new, the conservative fathers and the revolutionary sons. Once again, Friel was drawn towards a controversial work, for *Fathers and Sons*, like *The Three Sisters*, had provoked stormy disagreements when it first appeared, drawing fire from both Left and Right. Readers were perplexed because of the difficulty of ascertaining Turgenev's attitude to his characters. Conservatives accused him of grovelling at the feet of Bazarov, while Radicals thought the novel a libel on the younger generation. Turgenev's attitude towards his protagonist was deliberately ambiguous. He said he didn't know whether he loved or hated his protagonist. In his diary entry for 30 July 1861 he recorded feeling 'an involuntary attraction for him'.[40] Yet admiration for the nihilist went hand in hand with a desire to preserve the values of art, love, family and private sensibility that the iconoclastic Bazarov rejected.

Living, as Turgenev had lived, in violent conditions, in a time of revolt and uncertainty, Friel doubtless felt that Turgenev's story of the tensions between tradition and modernity had a special relevance to the cultural crisis of contemporary Ireland. In Turgenev he found, as he had found in Chekhov, a model of the detached diagnostician who bravely resisted the call from the politically minded for polemic and propaganda. Turgenev's art famously rests on his ability to suppress his own opinions and to become the people he wrote about. Though coming from an aristocratic background himself, he didn't let a sense of caste or privilege interfere with his imaginative and dramatic project. His sympathetic powers are shown in his instinctive understanding of both 'fathers' and 'sons'. Friel responded to the writer who sought to maintain close contact with life and to represent it without philosophising about it. The artist who loved the play of human nature, who knew how to reckon with its foibles, its pride, its habitual prejudices, its affectations, all its tragic and comic susceptibilities was truly a kindred spirit. The world of the 'fathers' is a world of shared traditions and values, a hierarchical world of masters and servants who interact on a basis of benevolent patronage and feudal loyalty. At the centre of this world are the values of civilisation, continuity and ceremony. The concern with order, which Bazarov interprets as lack of passion, fear of risk, the craving for security, nevertheless has the advantage of being able to offer a sense of belonging, a sense of 'home'. Traditional morality does not lie in formulated code or explicit programme, but in a decorum of diffidence and mutual respect, a resistance to technocratic rationality, an ideal of wholeness in a hostile world. This image of tradition is the living expression of the play's total and governing (liberal humanist) attitude. The point of view of the 'fathers' controls our perception of events and it is enacted in Friel's sensitive preoccupation with the rich variousness of life, his devotion to a common humanity beneath social and political categorisation.

At first the Old Guard strikes us very much as it does Bazarov – a colourful gallery of ineffectual, self-absorbed eccentrics and absurdities. But it is not long before a richly attractive humanity asserts itself. Nikolai, for all his garrulous bumbling, knows how to preserve a happy family atmosphere and even Bazarov admits early on to being impressed by his decency and astuteness. Similarly, Uncle Pavel is no mere 'Tailor's Dummy' or 'decaying dandy' (*FS*, p. 17), as Bazarov says he is. Behind the air of haughty detachment lie a genuine nobility of spirit, a capacity for deep feeling and a concern for others which is intimately bound up with his personal sense of honour. At the beginning, Fenichka, the servant girl who is the mother of Nikolai's child, is uneasy in Pavel's company, but within the traditional class system there is room for mobility and social transformation. By the end of the play both Fenichka and Pavel have grown into a relaxed and intimate relationship with each other, though for Fenichka this acceptance is at the cost of her former close friendship with the other servants. Pavel, after the duel, handles the situation with admirable tact, always conscious of others' feelings. His delicacy spares both Fenichka and Bazarov any further unnecessary pain or indignity and he even finds a way to apologise to Fenichka: 'My mistake. I get things wrong, Fenichka. Sorry' (*FS*, p. 70). When Bazarov dies, Pavel is the one who recognises Anna's anguish and takes control of the conversation to help her towards the consolation that is available in 'routine, acceptance, duty' (*FS*, p. 87).

Friel's devotion to character and situation as felt experience, concrete life, is nowhere more strongly apparent than in his dramatisation of the scene where the Bazarovs mourn their dead son. Old Bazarov tries to put up a manly front to Arkady but breaks down uncontrollably; then, when his distraught wife enters, he finds the strength to support and console her. Holding each other, they sing a 'Te Deum'. The scene's closing tableau proclaims the continuity of their faith, the consolation that comes from their love for each other. That faith and that love are reasserted, not shaken, in the face of adversity.

The old order is characterised through a powerful, unsentimental portrayal of family life, wherein the values of loyalty, affection, trust, respect, are triumphantly affirmed. So sensitively and lovingly is that world revealed that it is hard to share Bazarov's desire to see it overthrown. Bazarov is a scientific, positivist hero who stands for the modern conscience. He is a realist, opposed to the superstition, the confusion and sentimentalities of the past which have hindered progress. Thus, his nihilism is not a simple negativity, but a necessary stage in the evolution of a 'remade' society: 'in our remade society the words stupid and clever, good and bad, will have lost the meaning you invest them with, will probably come to have no meaning at all' (*FS*, p. 26). 'Nihilism', Arkady explains, 'begins by questioning all received ideas and principles no matter how venerated those ideas and principles are. And that leads us to the inevitable conclusion that the world must be made anew' (*FS*, p. 10). If there are echoes here of the Field Day enterprise, the big difference is that Bazarov's *skepsis* is indiscriminate, calling for a wholesale destruction of the past, a *tabula rasa*. He refuses to allow for anything in the past that might be useful and worth preserving or reviving. The play dramatises the failure to bring the forces of tradition and modernity into any kind of meaningful dialectical rapport.

Bazarov's revolutionary commitment is also deeply compromised. A democrat, he nevertheless feels contempt for the people he champions. He loves a cause abstractly. He is portrayed as the extraordinary individual, the perennial spirit of revolt, rather than the representative of inexorable material forces. It is his savage egoism which is the driving force behind his iconoclasm. He has broken away from all that is commonly considered sacred and submits to neither Custom nor Law. He is his own Law. Devoted to what *is*, he dismisses poetry and art. Calling for the destruction of the old values, he is contemptuous of censure and praise alike and goes his own way against the odds, despising success and opinion, refusing to let anything, including love itself, distract him form his duty.

Friel follows Turgenev in opening up the man behind the carapace of his commitment. Thus, though Bazarov vigorously denounces Romantic fancy, he cannot help falling madly in love with the aristocratic Anna Odintsov who awakens his passionate nature. When he speaks of Nikolai's and Fenichka's love for each other, after his own rejection by Anna, he concedes the meaningfulness of words like 'blessed' and 'goodness' (*FS*, p. 56), which before he had mocked. Bazarov's discovery of 'a new vocabulary' (*FS*, p. 56) of love is, significantly, accompanied by music – Nikolai's playing of Beethoven's *Romance* – which signals and helps to enact a freeing of private feeling, a relaxation of the rational and ideological controls. At the end, when Bazarov leaves the Kirsanovs to go and help his father deal with the typhus epidemic, he is given to pause by the spectacle of the 'happy family group' (*FS*, p. 71) which gathers to bid him goodbye.

To the end, Bazarov remains outside society, alone and abandoned. Ordinary mortals feel uncomfortable in his presence. Death catches him unawares and he dies randomly in the service of the people whom he despises. Hostile critics took his untimely end as a final attempt by Turgenev to make his hero 'trivial' and to punish him for his nihilism. Bazarov at last admits his own defeat, concluding that Russia has no more need of nihilists like him: 'I am no loss to Russia. A cobbler would be a loss to Russia. A butcher would be a loss. A tailor would be a loss. I am no loss' (*FS*, p. 72). The moral grandeur of his death does not obliterate the fact that he was defeated in society. The conclusion would seem to point to the moral that happiness requires acceptance of life: those who reject it are defeated, though they may have the hope of final reconciliation.

The figure of the failed, despairing rebel is one which has traditionally haunted the Irish political imagination (in the form of, say, Hugh O'Neill, Wolfe Tone, Robert Emmet, Henry Joy McCracken or Parnell), not to mention Friel's own work (from Gar O'Donnell and Fox Melarkey to Skinner and Hugh O'Neill). Turgenev's Bazarov becomes more sympathetic in failure. He is rejected by Anna and, henceforth, his political drive loses power, the expression of his ideas becomes a function of his frustrated and impotent pride and he finds himself governed by the impulse of the moment, as when he accepts the duel or when he returns to Anna. In Friel's version, Bazarov is not the intensely divided protagonist of Turgenev's novel. He emerges from the duel with Pavel and his rejection by Anna as 'a fully mature young man' (*FS*, p. 66). He knows that Arkady will marry and tells him without rancour that he is not equipped for the 'harsh and bitter and lonely life' (*FS*, p. 67) of the nihilist. At the same time, he renews his own commitment: 'I am committed to the last, mean, savage, glorious, shaming extreme' (*FS*, p. 67), and claims that he has 'no regrets' about the failure of his relationship with Anna. The possible ironies behind all this are, unfortunately, not drawn out.

The flattening out of the character in the play is apparent in yet another way. In the novel, human actions are set against a large-scale backdrop of social upheaval and the massive, vibrant processes of nature, so that the human individual appears small and insignificant. The play, on the other hand, takes place entirely on a domestic level. There is little sense of larger social life – an historical perspective – which is what would be required to validate Bazarov's point of view.

The conflict between traditional values and revolutionary nihilism is contained throughout and finally resolved, within the controlling structure of classic realism. The play ends with two tableaux offered as complex, 'completed' images of the personal life, both reverberating against the earlier picture in Act I of the Bazarovs renewing love and faith in the shadow of grief and loss. In the first of the closing tableaux, Nikolai draws Fenichka to him and invites her to join him singing 'Drink to Me Only': she 'gives him an uncertain smile but does not sing' (*FS*, p. 95). Behind the happy picture of the union of young and old, peasant and aristocrat, is Fenichka's inability to profess love for Nikolai when pressed earlier by Bazarov, and her present awareness that even as Nikolai draws her to him, he is lost in the past, in memories of his first wife. In the second tableau, Katya moves beside Arkady, catches his hand and begins to sing: 'he does not sing' (*FS*, p. 95). In becoming the master of his father's estate, in agreeing to marriage, Arkady knows he has betrayed the nihilistic spirit and his promise to his dead friend.

Thus, Friel emphasises the paradoxes of existence. The play fuses motion and stillness, contradictory content and organic form. Self-contained and closed, the drama constitutes a pattern of knowledge which leads to a philosophy of detachment. All the play's parts are designed to work spontaneously for the common good, each in its subordinate place – a formal enactment of the ideal (liberal humanist) society. But to be that, the play must suppress anything that fundamentally threatens the ruling structure and cannot be resolved into a closed unity. In persuading us of its 'universal' or 'objectively realised' truth, it conceals its relation to social and political values. From the Bazarovian point of view, its appeal to the inner life would be seen as a recipe for political inertia and, hence, submission to the *status quo*, the play itself a monument to the impotent conscience of bourgeois society, gentle, sensitive and ineffectual.

MAKING HISTORY

Making History was first performed by the Field Day Theatre Company in the Guildhall, Derry, on 20 September 1988. Where *The Communication Cord* ended by positing a 'truth' before words, a 'truth' which nevertheless finds expression in spontaneous gesture and the non-verbal forms of communication, *Making History*, like *Freedom of the City*, emphasises the distortions to which the 'truth' is subject when it is implicated in language, and especially when the language that is used to frame it is in the hands of the politicians, the systems men, the myth-makers, the historians and the writers. After suggesting the desirability of cultural fusion of Gaelic and English traditions in *Translations*, Friel in *Making History* returns to the political theme of *Freedom of the City*, exploring the discrepancies between different discourses, once again exposing the fictional element in history. The intention is to shake the two divided and embattled communities in Northern Ireland into awareness that the myths and values to which they adhere are not absolute, but selective, atavistic histories which have only succeeded in imprisoning them in their respective bunkers and which cry out to be rewritten, translated into new forms.

History, we see, is made in two ways: first, by the men of action in the public world and, second, by the chroniclers and interpreters. What Friel emphasises is that there is no such thing as History, only histories. As Archbishop Lombard says:

> I don't believe that a period of history – a given space of time – my life – your life – that it contains within it one 'true' interpretation just waiting to be mined. But I do believe that it may contain within it several possible narratives: the life of Hugh O'Neill can be told in many ways. And those ways are determined by the needs and demands and the expectations of different people and different eras. (*MH*, pp. 15-16)

In the subtle texturing of his writing, in all kinds of echoes, correspondences and allusions, Friel keeps this notion of the relativity of truth constantly before us. Thus, to Hugh O'Donnell, Henry Bagenal, the Queen's Marshal and Hugh O'Neill's new brother-in-law, is 'the Butcher Bagenal' (*MH*, p. 13), while Mabel Bagenal reports to her husband that her brother calls O'Donnell 'the Butcher O'Donnell' (*MH*, p. 17). The whiskey Lombard holds up in his glass is either 'a lure to perdition' or 'a foretaste of immortality' (*MH*, p. 69). There is no absolute truth, no history which is entirely objective, no ideologically free zone. History, as Lombard insists, is something which is produced. Language *signifies* or represents reality, it doesn't simply *reflect* it. Histories are stories and the chronicler's first obligation, according to Lombard, is to write the kind of story which will help to shape his people's destiny in a desirable way. Lombard is clear about what his history of O'Neill should accomplish:

> Now is the time for a hero. Now is the time for a heroic literature. So I am offering Gaelic Ireland two things. I'm offering them this narrative that has the elements of myth. And I'm offering them Hugh O'Neill as a national hero. (*MH*, p. 67)

O'Neill resists Lombard's myth-making project, seeing himself engaged in a battle for the 'truth' (*MH*, p. 63). He insists on a complexity of identity which Lombard tries to reduce to the simplicity of 'national hero'. O'Neill pleads with this troublesome priest not to 'embalm' him in the 'pieties' of 'a florid lie' (*MH*, p. 63). He wants

Lombard to acknowledge his full humanity: 'The schemer, the leader, the liar, the statesman, the lecher, the patriot, the drunk, the soured, bitter émigré – put it *all* in' (*MH*, p. 63). When Lombard speaks of writing O'Neill's history, O'Neill corrects him by saying that it isn't his, but Lombard's history. For what is central to O'Neill is not necessarily central to Lombard's view of things. O'Neill recognises that Lombard is going to suppress the entire English dimension of his life and career, including the importance to him of Mabel Bagenal, O'Neill's English wife. Lombard tries to explain that since his subject is 'the big canvas of national events' (*MH*, p. 69) and not O'Neill's private life, Mabel is not a central figure in his (his)story. To O'Neill, however, his life is not purely a public life. And, anyway, not even his public life is as Lombard presents it – 'a man, glorious, pure, faithful' (*MH*, p. 71).

O'Neill is acutely aware of the divisions within him. His 'intelligence' comprehends and grudgingly respects the aristocratic English order epitomised by Sir Henry Bagenal. He has even fought alongside Bagenal against the rebellious Irish: 'Oh, yes, that's a detail our annalists in their wisdom choose to overlook' (*MH*, p. 27). Sir Henry Sidney, he declares, was 'the only father' he ever knew and he remembers with a special affection the formative years he spent in the splendid homes of Leicester and Sidney. His 'blood', on the other hand, comprehends and loves Gaelic Ireland. He has a 'grand accent', but at critical points his accent thickens and the sounds of his Tyrone origins break through. At first he does not share O'Donnell's and Lombard's jubilation when news arrives that Spain has agreed to help the Irish against England: 'O'Neill moves away and stands alone downstage' (*MH*, p. 31). Friel ironically juxtaposes the rising tide of anti-English feeling in O'Donnell and Lombard with O'Neill's nostalgic revery of his idyllic life in England. The day-dream dissolves in O'Neill's recollection of Sir Henry Sidney's drunken observation which branded the young O'Neill a 'fox' (*MH*, p. 35) (the name linking him with the earlier schizoid Fox Melarkey), someone different, someone not fully civilised, not fully to be trusted. The hurt of 'that single failure in years of courtesy' has stayed with O'Neill till now, when he is about to prove himself as unruly and treacherous as Sir Henry had speculated all Irishmen secretly were. With Sir Henry's slight still ringing in his ears, O'Neill represses his English attachments and briskly moves to draw up battle plans against the English.

The conflict, O'Neill opines, is 'between two deeply opposed civilisations' (*MH*, p. 28): 'Impulse, instinct, capricious genius, brilliant improvisation – or calculation, good order, common sense, the cold pragmatism of the Renaissance mind' (*MH*, p. 28). It is a conflict between ancient rituals and ceremonies on one hand and the modern European world on the other, between *pietas* and the demands of a rapidly changing world, between fossilisation and making new history. O'Neill can see the shortcomings and excesses of both sides. He can see that the English 'Renaissance mind' also produces 'the buccaneering, vulgar material code of the new colonials' and that the proud defiance of the Irish can be a suicidal lack of good sense. Maguire's stand against the English is a case in point, while that other Irish hothead, Hugh O'Donnell, is clearly lacking any of the seriousness of purpose that Skinner in *Freedom of the City* identified as a prerequisite of any meaningful opposition to the forces of imperialism. O'Donnell is an attractively warm, lively, reckless individual, but his childish enthusiasms and affections reveal a pitifully narrow view of events, a crippling parochialism. O'Neill, who has been trying to open his people to 'the strange new ways of Europe' (*MH*, p. 40) is exasperated by him: 'Even O'Donnell's enthusiasm worries me', says O'Neill, 'for him it's all a huge adventure – cattle-raiding on an international scale' (*MH*, p. 39).

O'Neill uneasily straddles both worlds. Mabel says he is something of an enigma to the Queen as well as to Lombard because he is 'English' as well as 'Irish': 'You're the antithesis of what she expects a Gaelic chieftain to be. That's your strength' (*MH*, p. 38). Yet O'Neill can be tempted to act with all the foolish rashness that he had criticised in Maguire and it is Mabel who tries to encourage him to be more calculating and more realistic. The world O'Neill inhabits is notoriously ruthless and unstable, a quagmire of shifting allegiances. A further lesson O'Neill learns from Mabel is that if the Queen decides to reinstate him in Ireland after the debacle of Kinsale, she will do so only because it suits her, not because she believes the words of his submission: 'Belief has nothing to do with it. As Mabel says, she'll use me if it suits her' (*MH*, p. 50). Lombard understands this devious public world better than O'Neill and one of the most difficult of all Friel's ironies is that it may well be the cold, slippery Lombard who represents Ireland's best political hope for the future.

To Lombard the key events in O'Neill's life are, first, his crowning at Tullyhogue. O'Neill recalls that the next month he was begging Elizabeth for pardon and points out that the crowning did nothing to unite the feuding Irish factions and bring about the foundation of an

Irish nation state, as Lombard implied it did. Second, the battle of
Kinsale, according to Lombard, was a magnificent, heroic event.
Again, O'Neill points out that the English routed the Irish forces in
less than half an hour, that the Irish 'ran away like rats' and that the
battle was a 'disgrace' to the Irish. Third, Lombard speaks of the
'tragic but magnificent exodus of the Gaelic aristocracy', while O'Neill
recalls that the Irish leaders, as they took flight for Spain, were
stoned by their own people for deserting them. Ironic juxtaposition
is a major compositional principle in this play about multiple identity, dual citizenship, conflicting allegiances. The culminating instance of this technique comes at the very end. Lombard reads from
his history which inscribes O'Neill, via a hieratic, Biblical language,
in a story of epic proportions. The hero of Lombard's fiction is
ironically juxtaposed with the drunken, broken, penniless wretch we
see before us, reciting his infamous submission to the Queen in
which he surrendered the last remnants of dignity and independence.

But neither discourse – neither Lombard's history nor O'Neill's
submission – tells the whole story. O'Neill is not the hero Lombard
presents and he is not either the pathetic capitulator nor the cynical
manipulator which his own submission might suggest. He over-
flows all the categories which others would try and force him into.
One of the general features of his speech – something which the
organisers and politicians such as Harry Hoveden and Lombard find
most irritating – is its waywardness and evasiveness. In conversation, O'Neill, like Hotspur, starts away and lends no ear unto the
purposes of state, refusing to be confined to any single, consecutive
line of thought. His speech indicates a desire to avoid history or 'fate'
and in this he is quite unlike Frank Hardy who, unable to live with
division, was impelled by his sense of fate to return 'home' and
discover there the ultimate quietus in death. Fatalism was the very
thing O'Neill criticised in Maguire, for it is a form of imprisonment,
a mindless acquiescence in enslavement. O'Neill is another character
plagued by 'the enemy within', but rather than adopt the myth of a
unified self, he claims the right to live authentically with doubt and
division. Resisting the role of volunteer in the service of any causes,
he insists on occupying the interstices between the public and private worlds. Where the version of the past contained in Sir's 'ledger'
in *Living Quarters* was a mysterious and apparently intractable 'given',
history is in the making in the later play and O'Neill heroically
resists to the death the preordained public role – the fate – which
Lombard would try to impose upon him.

Lombard's views may be given potent justification – there is plenty of evidence of Irish disunity, impracticality and hopelessness and there is plenty of evidence of English oppressiveness and preju- dice – but our sympathies are clearly with the anguished wreck of a man begging for 'truth' rather than the abstracted chronicler who ignores the private life in the interests of creating a desirable public image. There is something of Shakespeare's distaste for the 'politi- cian' in the characterisation of Lombard. There is, in fact, no more of a 'private' dimension to Lombard than there is to the public figures of the Policeman, Pressman or Priest in *Freedom of the City*. Ironically, Friel resorts to stereotyping in order to expose the stereotyper. While arousing our sympathy with O'Neill's stand against the stereotyping process, Friel himself dispenses with fully drawn characterisation when it would interfere with his own dramatic and ideological pur- poses. *Making History*, like *Faith Healer*, is a play about the fictional nature of 'truth', but the earlier play demonstrates a more effective blending of public theme and private feeling.

Indeed, O'Neill is the only character in the play to be drawn with any complexity. Of the other main characters, Hugh O'Donnell is simply a clown who sounds like Gar O'Donnell, though one must admire the assured way in which Friel extends the comic vernacular beyond the contemporary, parochial world in which it functions in *Philadelphia*, to deploy it now in a context of the great movements of sixteenth-century European politics in *Making History*.

The other major character, Mabel, is interesting at first. When she first comes to Ireland she finds it difficult to shed her English preju- dices. Irritated by her Irish servants, she finds herself shouting at them, 'Shut up out there! D'you hear me? Just shut up! If you want to behave like savages, go back to the bogs!' (*MH*, p. 20). Suddenly aware that her sister, Mary, has overheard her outburst, Mabel adds in an embarrassed gesture of conciliation: 'Just horseplay!'. But she can still say a little later, 'This is my home' (something which not even Gar O'Donnell could say), and proves that her loyalty to her husband is beyond question. After this, Friel has no further interest in her as a divided character.

The play's interest stems largely from the ideas it uses. Friel's characteristic dramatic territory has opened up remarkably to the sweeping winds of European history, and the play's final image of competing voices – Lombard's and O'Neill's negotiating history – is his most explicit representation of its contingent basis. Nevertheless, *Making History* works in a somewhat self-conscious way, its effects appearing rather deliberately organised, even somewhat contrived. We miss the layered, resonant quality of *Translations*.

5
Body
Foregrounding the Body: The Plays of the 1990s

'WORDS, WORDS, WORDS'

Underlying Friel's whole dramatic endeavour is a faith in the transcendental subject, a faith which links him with the great liberal humanist artists of the nineteenth century such as Chekhov and Turgenev whose artistic temperament is remarkably similar to his own and in whose artistic vision and technique he has shown a special interest. And it is this faith which distinguishes Friel from many modern theorists and philosophers of language and subjectivity. Catherine Belsey summarises the post-Saussurian view: 'It is language which offers the possibility of constructing a world of individuals and things, and of differentiating between them'.[1] Friel agrees that subjectivity is substantially constituted by language, but he refuses to accept that it is wholly a product of discourse. In Derrida's view, the individual is inscribed in language and a function of it; in Althusser's theory he or she is positioned and determined by illusory ideological processes; while according to Lacan, who adapts Freudian ideas, the individual is 'taken over' at the point of his or her insertion into language and society. For Friel, however, the individual is still essentially prior to his language, history and social conditions, *informed* by prevailing social and political values, but not simply a *symptom* of them. There is a 'second order' degree of responsibility for moral and political beliefs within the individual. Friel displaces subjectivity across a range of discourses but there is an ultimate authority for meaning in the centrality of the human subject – in intuition – as the source and author of meaning. If (in the early plays especially) Friel gives us the experience of 'subjection', he suggests that it is not inevitable. Plays such as *Aristocrats* and *The Communication Cord* tentatively, but explicitly, move towards the insight that we do not have to remain trapped in the 'given' network of linguistic and social relations. By being true to ourselves, to our own pre-verbal intuitions, we can take charge of our own destiny, assert our own intentions, recentre our own transcendent subjectivity and break out of the 'given' patterns and control systems. The fabulous kiss with which *The Communication Cord* ends inaugurates new possibilities, including the possibility of a new language of the repressed unconscious, a new language of the body. That closing embrace or the dancing in *Dancing at Lughnasa* reminds us that, as Raymond Tallis puts it, 'the fundamental reality, the reality from which all human lives begin and which no human life ever fully escapes, is the intercourse of one body (the human body) with other human and non-human bodies'.[2]

In *The Enemy Within* Columba must choose between his very human impulsions, and the spiritual need to attain transcendence. The physical and the spiritual, body and soul, remain unreconciled. Frank Hardy's 'performance' (an analogue to that of the artist), when it works, is an act of healing, offering, as Damian O'Hare observes (in 'The Theme of Faith in the Drama of Brian Friel', unpublished MA dissertation, University of Ulster, 1993), the truly 'holy' experience of making something whole. An itinerant travelling the Celtic margins and possessed of strange powers, Frank Hardy effects a rehabilitation of the body which in pagan religions did not suffer the kind of repression enforced by Enlightenment rationalism and Christianity. Friel's latest plays such as *Dancing at Lughnasa* and *Wonderful Tennessee* foreground the pagan consciousness of the body and, while sounding the characteristic Irish note of frustration and failure, nevertheless affirm a potential for wholeness.

In this chapter I shall begin by concentrating on Friel's development of a non-verbal language of gesture, movement and sound to give expression to the buried forces of the psyche. The Irish theatre tradition is one that is predominantly and self-consciously linguistic, epitomised by the figure of Synge's Christy Mahon who becomes a hero 'by the power of a lie'. The highly verbal character of the Irish tradition has often been remarked upon. 'The indigenous movement of verbal theatre,' writes Richard Kearney, 'boasts an august lineage extending from Goldsmith, Wilde, Shaw, Synge, Yeats and O'Casey to such contemporary dramatists as Murphy, Kilroy, Leonard and Friel. All these authors share a common concern with the play of language; they have created plays where words tend to predetermine character, action and plot'.[3] In Friel, however, there is a growing dissatisfaction with the inadequacy of words, an impatience with

their duplicity, especially when they are in the hands of the chroniclers and ideologues. As one of his characters in the unpublished
play, *A Doubtful Paradise*, exclaims: 'I'm sick and tired of words,
words, words . . . this madness'.[4] The feeling is akin to that which
Pinter describes:

> The strong feeling about words which amounts to nothing less
> than nausea. Such a weight of words confronts us, day in day
> out, words spoken . . . words written by me and others, the bulk
> of it a stale, dead terminology, ideas endlessly repeated and
> permutated, become platitudinous, trite, meaningless. Given this
> nausea, it's very easy to be overcome by it and step back into
> paralysis. I imagine most writers know something of this kind of
> paralysis. But if it is possible to confront this nausea, to follow it
> to its hilt and move through it, then it is possible to say that
> something has even been achieved.[5]

Immediately preceding this statement we find the following:

> I have mixed feelings about words. . . . Moving among them,
> sorting them out, watching them appear on the page, from this
> I derive a considerable pleasure.

'Mixed feelings about words': that is also Friel's attitude precisely. In
Friel, as in Pinter, we find the same tension between delight in
words, the love of a vivid, vital language on one hand and, on the
other, the nausea caused by contemplation of the vast mass of dead,
deceitful language which daily confronts us. Friel is continually
aware of the power of language to distort and lie as well as to
transform and heal. *Faith Healer*, he said, was 'some kind of metaphor for the art, the craft of writing . . . and the great confusion we
all have about it, who are involved in it'.[6] The 'weight of words' is
felt in many different ways, in plays as different as *Philadelphia*,
Freedom of the City, *Faith Healer*, *Making History* and *The Communication Cord*. But Friel also demonstrates a wish to go beyond or behind
what words can achieve and, like Pinter, to experiment with silences
and rhythmical speech in an effort to express the irrational, pre-
verbal level of being.

Friel, as Kearney says, is the exponent of 'a verbal theatre – albeit
in a highly self-questioning mode'.[7] His theatre is eminently verbal:
indeed, one of the criticisms sometimes levelled against it is that it

runs the risk 'of verbal overload, of becoming a series of oratorical "turns"'.[8] Yet, his work also shows an increasing interest in non-verbal consciousness and in devising means of expressing the deep rhythms of personality, the mysterious life of the spirit. His experiment with alternatives to 'a dead, stale terminology' culminates in *Dancing at Lughnasa*, which led the *New York Times* critic, Frank Rich, to the conclusion that the 'overwhelming power' of the play 'has almost nothing to do with beautiful words':

> It is typical of the play's own pagan force that that scene (the dance) seems to yank the audience into communion with its own most private and sacred things, at a pre-intellectual gut level that leaves us full of personal feelings to which words cannot be readily assigned . . . (The play) grabs the audience by expressing the verbally inexpressible in gesture and music.[9]

Rewriting history depends on the ability to access and reactivate repressed or submerged forces in history, to recentre what is marginal, to make the silences speak. In *Fathers and Sons*, Friel came up against the problem of incorporating the revolutionary 'Other' into the dominant bourgeois discourse. A much earlier drama of fathers and sons, *Philadelphia*, adopted a boldly experimental method of giving voice to the disruptive energies of the 'son' in the stifling, authoritarian world of the 'fathers'. Throughout his career, Friel has been interested in the experience which lies outside conscious control and the normal discursive modes. He explores 'hidden' or buried landscapes and cultures, what Heaney calls the 'outbacks of the mind',[10] 'the backward and abysm of mind and body',[11] which are variously figured as the 'Private' psyche of Gar O'Donnell in *Philadelphia*, the Viking past in *Volunteers* or the 'back hills' in *Dancing at Lughnasa*. Resisting the logocentric tendencies of classic realism which attempts to reduce the multiplicity and mystery of being to a single totalising perspective, he seeks to reinstate a sense of the alterity and ambivalence of meaning. Thus, he deconstructs linear non-contradictory consciousness in order to rediscover the essential strangeness of Being. Rather than simply recycling the old myths of the past, he wants to demystify the past in order to preserve its essential mystery and 'Otherness' for the present.

The experience of the 'strange' is available to those who, in Heidegger's words, seek to dwell poetically in the innermost and therefore unknown being of things. Friel seeks to evolve an appropriate language to give expression to that experience and in uncovering and giving voice to submerged psychic and cultural forces he pushes towards the limits of the representational means of realism. At the opposite extreme from a utilitarian, Lockean model of language as a map are the non-discursive, non-rational languages of gesture, music and dance. These are expressive means which have been present in Friel's drama from the beginning, although not fully exploited until *Dancing at Lughnasa*. As early as *Philadelphia* Friel was using a variety of musical effects for dramatic purposes. The very title of the play is taken from a popular American song and in the course of the play Gar sings snatches of it on several occasions to stiffen his resolve to leave Ballybeg. In his bedroom he stages imaginary ceilidh dances and Mendelssohn concertos, lyrical moments linked to music, a non-narrative, fluid medium, which leads to and inspires movement.

In the early plays such as *Philadelphia*, *The Loves of Cass McGuire* and *Aristocrats*, the music is not merely incidental, but plays a vital part in the exposition of the main themes; Yolland and Maire's kiss in *Translations* and Tim and Claire's embrace at the end of *The Communication Cord* speak volumes, inaugurating a new language of the body beyond the falsifying rituals of the word; in *The Three Sisters* the music creates, albeit only momentarily, a potent 'atmosphere' in which we have the feeling that anything could happen. *Dancing at Lughnasa*, however, makes music and dance the central subject and focus of the play. Where in *Philadelphia*, *The Loves of Cass McGuire* and *Aristocrats* the music is mostly a background effect, *Dancing at Lughnasa* (the title itself suggesting a crucial development) centres the actuality of performance, allowing us to see the very process of radical, if only momentary, character transformation through dance as it occurs.

These developments in Friel's career represent a challenge to and expansion of a predominantly verbal native theatre tradition. We must recognise, as well as the native verbal tradition, a broader context for his work – that of the great twentieth-century theatrical experiment in Europe and America associated with such names as Antonin Artaud in the 1930s and Jerry Grotowski and Peter Brook in the 1960s and 1970s.

Artaud reacted against a French theatre dominated by words, believing that rational language was unable to express a fundamental irrationality in human life. He compared the theatre to the Black Plague which, Artaud noted, often had the curious effect of causing the survivors, surrounded by death, to abandon all traditional rules and moral restraint and to launch themselves upon orgies of lust and greed. The plague released dark forces normally held in check. It revealed to people those acts of which they are capable and which they might otherwise have denied. To recognise the existence of these dark potentialities within us, Artaud believed, is the first step towards controlling them. Theatre, like psychoanalysis, has a cura- tive function. For Artaud, a theatre that is vital and useful should accomplish this by forcefully showing us what we are and teaching us that we live in an insecure world, continually under the shadow of death: 'the sky', he proclaimed, 'still can fall on our heads'.[12]

Artaud wanted to invoke a timeless, elemental power on stage, to 'transgress the ordinary limit of art and words' and 'magically to produce a kind of total creation *in real terms*, where man must reassume his position between dreams and events':[13]

> Theatre will never be itself again . . . unless it provides the audi- ence with truthful distillations of dreams where its taste for crime, its erotic obsessions, its savageness, its fantasies, its utopian sense of life and objects, even its cannibalism, do not gush out on an illusory, make-believe, but on an inner level.[14]

He envisaged a theatre of voices, gestures, music, of special sound and lighting effects: 'There must be poetry for the senses just as there is for speech, but this physical, tangible language . . . is really only theatrical in as far as the thoughts it expresses escape spoken lan- guage'.[15] The inner privacy can only be suggested poetically: 'Any true feeling cannot in reality be expressed. To do so is to betray it. To express it, however, is to *conceal* it. True expression conceals what it exhibits. . . . An image, an allegory, a form disguising what it means to reveal, has more meaning to the mind than the enlightenment brought about by words or their analysis'.[16] Artaud's theatre is not aimed at solving social or psychological conflicts, but sets out to express 'secret truths, to bring out in active gestures those elements of truth hidden under forms in their encounters with Becoming'.[17] He wanted to return theatre to its 'original purpose, to restore it to a religious, metaphysical position'.[18]

The great influence on Artaud was the Balinese dance drama which he saw at the Paris Colonial Exhibition in 1931 and which particularly impressed him because of its independence from a merely verbal language:

The Balinese theatre was not a revelation of a verbal but a physical idea of theatre where drama is encompassed within the limits of everything that can happen on stage, independently of a written script. Whereas with us, the lines gain the upper hand and theatre as we understand it finds itself restricted by them.[19]

Artaudian theatre evolves from what he called 'a musical condition'.[20] The theatre cannot analyse: it should be the 'double' of life – not of 'immediate, everyday reality . . . but another, deadlier, archetypal reality in which Origins, like dolphins, quickly dive back into the murky depths once they have shown their heads'.[21] Life is a kind of 'frail moving source forms never attain'[22] and the aim of theatre is to break through the forms of language in order to touch life. For Artaud, true reality is the life of our unconscious, pre-rational, dreaming minds; it is the reality of the illogical and archetypal. Theatre is essentially ritual; it is transformative, enacting a transition from one state of being to another. It should engulf the audience with a massive accumulation of effects, so that the spectators' response would be sensual and involuntary rather than detached and analytical.

Artaud's influence has been immense amongst those dramatists seeking alternatives to realism. Playwrights as different as Jean Genet and Peter Weiss are indebted to him and he has influenced the radically new theatre methods associated with Jean-Louis Barrault in France, Jerzy Grotowski in Poland, Peter Brook and Charles Marowitz in Britain and, in America, Julian Beck and Judith Malina's Living Theatre, Richard Schechner's Performance Group and Joseph Chaikin's Open Theatre.

Grotowski follows Artaud in seeking a return to the archetypal roots of drama, to a concept of theatre as a religious place, a place of ritual and magic, where man is passionately involved in the conditions of his existence and emerges purified from the experience. Stripping away all the non-essentials, Grotowski proposed what he called 'poor theatre' central to which was the 'holy actor',[23] the actor who through rigorous training reveals his most secret and painful self in the process of performance. The technique of the actor should aspire to the level of 'secular holiness':[24] 'One must give oneself totally, in one's deepest intimacy, in confidence, as when one gives oneself in love. Here lies the key. Self-penetration, trance, excess, the formal discipline itself'.[25] The actor is a kind of shaman or high priest who tries to subjugate and to fascinate, to charm away every possible rational defence which the spectator might cling to against the 'magic' of gestures and words. Grotowski, too, was influenced by Oriental art and mysticism, for he draws on techniques taken from Yoga, from Chinese classical ballet, from Indian Kathakali dance. In order to bring about this self-penetration within the audience, he says that the performance must involve a probing into the 'collective subconscious . . . the myths which are not an invention of the mind but are, so to speak, inherited through one's blood, religion, culture and climate'.[26] In this sense, his thinking is close to that of Artaud and Jung. The relation to the past, to myth, as outlined by Grotowski, is to be one of 'confrontation' rather than 'identification';[27] it is to be a 'collision with the roots',[28] an 'experience of common human truth' satisfying a need for both 'apotheosis' and 'mockery':[29]

A confrontation is a 'trying out', a testing of whatever is a traditional value. A performance which, like an electrical transformer, adjusts our experience to those of past generations (and vice versa), a performance conceived as a combat against traditional and contemporary values (whence 'transgression') – this seems to me the only real chance for myth to work in the theatre. An honest renewal can only be found in this double game of values, this attachment and rejection, this revolt and submissiveness.[30]

Grotowski's words are a curiously apposite summary of Friel's drama. Indeed, the kind of 'confrontation' with the past which Grotowski recommends is perfectly illustrated by Friel in, say, his use of the myths of the 'gentle island' in the play of that name or of the story of Hippolytus in *Living Quarters* or his dramatisation of the conflict between traditional and contemporary values in *Translations* and *Dancing at Lughnasa*. Grotowski's dialectical concept of theatre – theatre as 'a conjunction of opposites which gives birth to the total act'[31] – could find no more accomplished exponent than Friel. For Grotowski, as for Friel, art is what enables us 'to cross our frontiers, exceed our limitations, fill our emptiness – fulfil ourselves'.[32] However, seeking to dispense with the written text and to eliminate the barrier between actor and audience altogether, Grotowski eventually moved towards a form of collective activity which has been termed 'paratheatre' and 'active culture'. These terms refer to an activity that has its roots in drama, but does not result in a theatrical presentation before an audience. Grotowski's Polish Laboratory Theatre, we could say, exhausted the possibilities of conventional theatre form.

Friel is interested in 'holy theatre', but remains more acutely aware than Grotowski of what is theatrically feasible in a secular age which has lost its '"common sky" of belief"'.³³ The term 'holy theatre' is Peter Brook's.³⁴ He uses it to describe a theatre with a visionary, sacred aim, a theatre that stands opposed to the over-conventionalised, dull, commercial 'deadly theatre'.³⁵ Lamenting that 'we have lost all sense of ritual and ceremony',³⁶ Brooks honours Artaud, the prophet who raised his voice in the desert to proclaim 'a theatre working like the plague, by intoxication, by infection, by analogy, by magic; a theatre in which the play, the event itself, stands in place of a text'.³⁷ Under the influence of Artaud's 'Theatre of Cruelty', Brook instituted a group affiliated with the Royal Shakespeare Company to explore 'what a holy theatre might be' and experimented with ritualistic and orgiastic elements. In 1971 he presented *Orghast*, based on the myth of Prometheus. The performance took place in the ancient tombs of Persepolis for the Shiraz/Persepolis Festival of the Arts. For this production, Ted Hughes invented a new language, 'Orghast', made up only of sounds. The quest for a universal language of theatre was pursued in Brook's subsequent tour of West Africa, where it was soon apparent that African expectations were different from European. Brook returned to the RSC and Shakespeare, his work demonstrating that the basically verbal theatre still allowed for all kinds of experimental and ritual effects, while ensuring a measure of communication with the audience which might not otherwise have been attainable.

Like Artaud's, Friel's theatre is an essentially metaphysical theatre, concerned not only with questions of character and morality, but with the very nature of identity. Artaud's desire to present a 'deadlier, archetypal reality' is continued in Friel's concern to disturb the audience's composure and feeling of security and to invest his situations and actions with a universal resonance. Where Artaud found a model for his metaphysical theatre in the Oriental theatre of the Balinese dancers and in semi-primitive Indian ceremonials that he saw during a visit to Mexico, Friel draws on pagan African tribal ceremonies and Celtic religious festivals. Friel shares Artaud's, Grotowski's and Brook's concern to develop a theatre which will *be* an experience rather than merely represent or talk about one. The

Artaudian intuition of that 'frail moving source forms never attain' is echoed in Friel's sense of 'the burden of the incommunicable'.[38] And Artaud's call for a theatre 'bringing on trances just as the whirling Dervishes or the Assouas induce trances'[39] could be seen to be answered by the sisters' frantic dancing in *Dancing at Lughnasa*. Friel presents the effort to reanimate the world, just as Artaud's 'propose[d] something to get us out of the slump, instead of continuing to moan about it, about the boredom, dullness and stupidity of everything'.[40]

But of course Friel's theatre does not approach the radical transformations that Artaud, Grotowski and Brook called for in their visionary writings and sought to enact in their actual theatre practice. Friel doesn't set out to unleash some kind of collective delirium, he doesn't ask us to surrender critical judgment completely and his wariness about language doesn't amount to Artaud's, Grotowski's or Brook's more radical and irrational rejection of the Word. In Friel, the criticism of language is a theme, and he is interested in incorporating into his drama a more purely theatrical language of movement and sound, but there is no question of him seeking to exclude language or thinking that any alternative means of communication could ever entirely take the place of language. If Friel wants to expose his characters and his audience to what is 'strange' or 'Other' in themselves and in the culture, if he wants to rescue them from false familiarity and conventional stereotypes, to let the 'Other' speak, he also knows that the 'Other' can be a false projection too. Thus, the dancing in *The Three Sisters* and *Dancing at Lughnasa* is never free of comic irony and self-consciousness. Friel recognises that in seeking to dwell 'poetically' we may still find ourselves dwelling in illusion. The conflict between the desire for freedom and the need for rational control imparts to Friel's drama its distinctive tension.

L. R. Chambers, in an essay entitled 'Antonin Artaud and the Contemporary French Theatre', writes of Artaud: 'We have to understand that what Artaud wanted was a private theatre of his own, in which he himself would be at one and the same time actor and spectator'.[41] This indicates a tendency quite opposite to that which we find in Friel, for Friel emphasises a concept of theatre as 'public address'.[42] Artaud's only production in the style of his 'Theatre of Cruelty' was of Shelley's *The Cenci* which opened on 6 May 1935 before a familiar audience of Parisian sophisticates. It was received with only slightly less riotous protest than that which followed the

first production of Synge's *Playboy* at the Abbey in 1907. The play
closed after seventeen performances leaving Artaud in financial ruin,
artistically discredited and emotionally exhausted. The failure of *The
Cenci* ended Artaud's directorial ambitions. He never returned to the
stage, living out his tragic life in various mental institutions, afflicted
by delusions, drug abuse and finally cancer, which killed him in
1948.[43] The 'Theatre of Cruelty' had proved unworkable because he
had failed to consider his audience and what they would be prepared to accept. By contrast, Friel is a much more practical, much
less iconoclastic man of the theatre. He clearly sets out his views on
experimentation in 'The Theatre of Hope and Despair'. There he
declares his wariness of employing a too 'private' language which
would only result in him alienating himself from his audience. The
dramatist's first concern, he says, is 'to communicate with every
individual in his audience, but he can do that only through
the collective mind. If he cannot get the attention of that collective
mind, hold it, persuade it, mesmerise it, manipulate it, he has lost
everything. And this imposes strange restrictions on him'.[44] These
restrictions, Friel explains, are not shared by short-story writers or
novelists because they function 'privately, man to man, a *personal*
conversation'.[45] Seeing theatre as 'public address' rather than 'personal conversation', Friel believes it is therefore 'not as receptive to
new theories. It is more simple, more spontaneous'.[46] In order to
communicate and get his plays produced, the dramatist 'cannot
appear to exhibit the same outrageous daring that the painter shows.
. . . And therefore because of his indirection and his necessary cau-
tion and his obligatory deviousness he is never going to be an ultra-
modern, he is never going to be as apparently revolutionary'.[47] Where
Artaud, Grotowski and Brook aimed for a total, violent emotional
involvement of the spectator, Friel works more subtly. Continuing
the experiment with a non-verbal language, seeking to free his characters from a rational motivation and incorporating ritual elements
into his drama, he forces his audience to reconsider the value of the
aesthetic experience. But he recognises that his theatre belongs to a
different social context from primitive ritual in which the magic is
taken for real. He knows his theatrical 'illusion' cannot compete with
that. And so he aims for a dramatic synthesis in which music, space,
performance and language all have a part to play; a synthesis, too, of
Artaudian, Brechtian and traditional methods, as if in acknowledgement of the fact that life itself is an inseparable complex of impressions and judgements, illusion and disillusion.

DANCING AT LUGHNASA

In *Dancing at Lughnasa* (1990), the device of the boy/narrator allows memory to control and dominate the stage. Friel's dramatisation of nostalgic memory owes a good deal to Tennessee Williams's *The Glass Menagerie*, another play which is concerned with the tension between romance and reality. But whatever international influences there may be in *Dancing at Lughnasa* (Chekhov's and Lorca's ghosts are present too), Friel's concerns remain distinctively Irish – exploring the disposition for dreaming and mythologising which, as Hugh the schoolmaster in *Translations* explained to the Englishman Yolland, is a peculiarly Irish phenomenon. Williams's narrator is called Tom Wingfield, his name associating him with flight, as Friel's narrator, Michael, is also associated with flight through his interest in kites. Like Tom Wingfield, Michael may have escaped from a household of crippled women, but finds that he is still haunted by dreams and memories of twenty-five years ago. Past and present are virtually co-existent. The play consists of a series of vividly remembered scenes, at the centre of which is the dancing, stimulated by 'a dream music that is both heard and imagined, that seems to be both itself and its own echo' (*DL*, p. 71). As Michael explains, 'what fascinates me about that memory is that it owes nothing to fact . . . atmosphere is more real than incident' (*DL*, p. 71). By including Michael as narrator, Friel emphasises the constructed conditions of life. Michael is exploring his own memory and he admits its arbitrary nature: 'memories offer themselves to me' (*DL*, p. 70). The structure of the play is therefore associative rather than strictly logical. Various sources of 'derangement' coalesce in Michael's mind: Father Jack's 'return', the 'voodoo' of the newly acquired wireless, his father's first visit. The opening tableau which is lit up, bit by bit, in the inner stage of Michael's mind, presents the principal characters and highlights a sharp visual contrast between the five dowdy Mundy sisters (modelled on Friel's aunts who lived near Glenties in Co. Donegal) and the two men – the two 'fathers' – in the play. Father Jack, the sisters' brother, is a missionary priest who has been repatriated from Africa by his superiors after twenty-five years. He is wearing the uniform of a British army officer chaplain – a 'magnificent and immaculate uniform of dazzling white; gold epaulettes and gold buttons, tropical hat, clerical collar, military cane . . . he is "resplendent", "magnificent". So resplendent that he looks almost comic opera'. Equally bizarre is Michael's father, Gerry, a Spanish Civil War veteran, 'wearing a spotless white tricorn hat with splendid white plumage'. In Michael's imagination, Father Jack and Gerry have acquired a large and luminous presence in his memory of the drab, female world in which he was brought up.

As in so many other of his plays, Friel starts off with a highly conventionalised and repressed community, in this case the family of five spinster sisters, the youngest of whom, Chris, has a seven year old son, Michael. The tragedy of the five sisters and their brother is that they have lost touch with their deepest emotions. They are, to use a musical metaphor, out of tune with themselves. The play is highly reminiscent of Lorca's study of the tragic consequences of subordinating instinct to social codes or material interests in *The House of Bernarda Alba* ((1945). In this, Lorca's last play, dealing with the sexual and political repression of women in the villages of pre-Civil War Spain, he dramatises the bitter domestic infighting between five sisters and their domineering mother, watched over by their critical maid. The piece is, amongst other things, an eloquent attack on the old order. Lorca, like Friel, wanted to reform the theatre as well as society, combining the illusion of reality with an interest in poetic myth, fusing traditional and popular elements with original and cultured ones. Over Lorca's drama, as over Friel's, there broods a similar sense of tragic fate, the question of how far the characters are victims of dark, irrational forces, how far of a more prosaic and realistic determinism in the form of local custom and convention.

Friel's play is set in 1936, in the months when De Valera was drawing up his Catholic Constitution for a Catholic people. 'Will you vote for De Valera, will you vote?' sings Maggie to Rose's song about Abyssinia. These women are the victims of an oppressively Catholic ethos, shortly to be enshrined in a Constitution which recognised 'the Family as the natural primary and fundamental unit group of society' and 'the special position of the Holy Catholic and Apostolic Roman Church as the guardian of the faith professed by the great majority of its citizens'. Responding to a demand in the country at the time for traditional Catholic social teaching in matters of marriage and family law, the Free State outlawed divorce, contraception and abortion. De Valera's programme, writes Robert Kee, was characterised by a 'homely narrowness' and 'pious dogmatism':[48]

Conservative in social and economic outlook, paying limited attention to problems such as housing, slum clearance and social welfare in general, safely – some would say smugly – steeped in the orthodox moral and social teachings of the Catholic Church of that day, it offered little in the way of inspiration to the young. Emigration, so long held by nationalists to have been one of the evils of English rule and to have been caused by the lack of freedom, continued. A strict literary censorship banned at different times almost all the best moden writers, including Irish ones.[49]

Terence Brown refers to 'an almost Stalinist antagonism to modernism, to surrealism, free verse, symbolism and the modern cinema', which combined with 'prudery (the 1930s saw opposition to paintings of nudes being exhibited in the National Gallery in Dublin) and a deep reverence for the Irish past'.[50] Summarising the attitude of Irish writers' of the 1930s and 1940s, Brown continues:

> Instead of de Valera's Gaelic Eden, the writers revealed a mediocre, dishevelled, often neurotic and depressed petit-bourgeois society that atrophied for want of a liberating idea. O'Faolain's image for it, as it was James Joyce's before him, is the entire landscape of Ireland shrouded in snow: 'under that white shroud, covering the whole of Ireland, life was lying broken and hardly breathing.[51]

The repressive Catholic ethos may have helped to consolidate a sense of identity, but it certainly left little room either for modernism and cosmopolitan standards or for the instinctual needs of ordinary people or for the least remnants of 'pagan' tradition.

Kate, the eldest of the sisters in the play, is a teacher and the only wage-earner. Chris and Maggie have no income, while Agnes and Rose, who is 'simple', make a little money knitting gloves at home. Their clothes 'reflect their mean circumstances': Rose wears wellingtons; Maggie has large boots; Rose, Maggie and Agnes all wear overalls or large aprons. But vestiges of their femininity still shine through: the austerity of the furnishings is relieved by 'some gracious touches' – flowers, pretty curtains, an attractive dresser arrangement. The sisters are painfully aware that life is passing them by and that they are trapped in deadening routines from which no escape seems possible. Like Chekhov's three sisters dreaming of their 'Moscow', the Mundys are filled with an intense longing for a fuller life. Maggie speaks enviously of an old schoolfriend, the still 'bubbly, laughing, happy' (*DL*, p. 19) Bernie O'Donnell who is now

married to a Swede and is the mother of twins. Friel's elaborate
texturing of the drama amplifies the basic condition of the sisters'
lives. The exotic menu featuring 'Eggs Ballybeg' (*DL*, p. 62) which
Maggie conjures up is an amusing expression of the longing for
something different from the usual fare and is reminiscent of the
way Gar O'Donnell mocks S. B.'s dull routines by picturing his
father in such exotic roles as that of fashion model or FBI spy. For
Maggie, the ultimate delight is 'one magnificent Wild Woodbine'
(*DL*, p. 58). Smoking the cigarette would seem to be the only 'wild-
ness' available to these sadly wasted lives: 'Wonderful Wild Woodbine. Next best thing to a wonderful, wild man' (*DL*, p. 23). Any man
at all, Maggie says, would do her, adding, 'God, I really am getting
desperate' (*DL*, p. 62). The note of discontent is sounded in Chris's
opening line: 'When are we going to get a decent mirror to see
ourselves in?' (*DL*, p. 2), which recalls Christy Mahon's complaint
against 'the divil's own mirror we had beyond, would twist a squint
across an angel's brow'. Chris's call for change, for clearer self-
awareness, a more truthful self-image, is immediately countered by
Maggie who refuses to entertain the thought of discarding the old
mirror for fear of incurring seven years' bad luck. Thus, Maggie
reveals her own superstitious attachment to the *status quo*. Chris's
longing for escape from routine controls is further demonstrated
when she says that she 'just might start wearing lipstick' (*DL*, p. 3).
Agnes is the one this time who insists on the limits of freedom,
reminding Chris of the form Kate's withering disapproval would
take: '"Do you want to make a pagan of yourself?"' (*DL*, p. 3). The
characteristic pattern is established: tidal surges of desire welling up
within one or other of the sisters which are constantly checked or
diffused, sometimes good-humouredly or wittily, sometimes bitingly, sometimes sadly.

Kate is clearly the head of the family and, like Judith in *Aristocrats*
or Manus in *The Gentle Island* who preside over their respective
families, she is constantly and acutely aware that she is facing a
crisis, the challenge of having to adapt to change – Rose's awakened
sexuality, the loss of jobs and income, Jack's breakdown, eventually
Rose and Agnes's sudden desertion of the family to go and live in
England. More than anything, Kate fears the imminent disintegration of the family:

> You try to keep the home together. You perform your duties as
> best you can – because you believe in responsibilities and obliga-

tions and good order. And then suddenly, suddenly you realise that hair cracks are appearing everywhere; that control is slipping away; that the whole thing is so fragile it can't be held together much longer. It's all about to collapse. (*DL*, p. 35)

Kate objects to levity, playfulness and novelty for they are threats to her fragile order. The hair cracks, we recognise early on, are caused not just by external forces over which the sisters have no control, but by equally unruly forces within the family itself, within consciousness (even Kate's). The greater the effort of repression, it would seem, the stronger the insurrectionary pressures. The great merit of the play is the unmistakeable tension which we feel between the very human desire for order and stability and the equally strong desire for excitement and new experience. This tension has various forms. On one level, it is a struggle between Christianity and paganism, on another, it is the challenge offered to civilised value by an irruption of repressed libidinal energy, at yet another, it is the harrassment of the symbolic order of 'ordinary' language and fixed structure by a semiotic force outside language which disrupts all stable meanings and institutions.

Dancing is the play's central image for a contravention and violation of 'normal' reality. It is Friel's new expression of the secret life which before he had represented verbally (in the character of, say, Private Gar) but which we know in actuality never formulates itself in words, even in the mind. The dancing is the play's chief 'opening' activity which is disturbing because it represents a break in the acknowledged order, an irruption of the inadmissible within the usual routine, a ritualised suspension of everyday law and order. In the repressive climate of the 1930s, dancing was regarded with some suspicion as representing a species of moral decadence and a threat to the morals of the nation's youth. These puritanical attitudes were reflected in the Public Dancehalls' Act of 1953 which required licensing of dance-halls. This pleased rural businessmen and the clergy for it did away with open-air dancing at crossroads and dances held in private houses. But it was a measure which contributed to the dying out of many traditional customs, though ironically the government which enacted it was officially pledged to a revival of Irish folklore and Irish traditional music and dancing.

When Agnes suggests that the sisters all go to the harvest dance, Rose quickly launches into 'a bizarre and abandoned dance' (*DL*, p. 13) while Kate 'panics'. The word is derived from 'Pan', the personification of deity displayed in creation and pervading all things. Pan was the god of flocks and herds, of the woods and all material substances. Part goat, part man, he was renowned for his lustful nature. In reacting to the dancing as she does, Kate is reacting to the *id*, to the assertion of the spermatic principle, the free imagination, the buried impulse. She represents the repressive force of Christianity inhibiting full and free embracement of this primitive, pagan, secret life of Pan. 'Just look at yourselves!' she shouts at her sisters, 'Dancing at your time of day. That's for young people with no duties and no responsibilities and nothing in their heads but pleasure' (*DL*, p. 13). In Kate's eyes, dancing is 'pagan', associated with a kind of sexual freedom which contravenes her strict Catholicism: 'Mature women dancing? What's come over you all? And this is Father Jack's home – we must never forget that' (*DL*, p. 13).

Later, when Irish dance music comes over the radio, Kate's remonstrations are ignored by all the other sisters who, one by one, succumb to the music's strange enchantment. Friel comments that 'there is a sense of order being consciously subverted' (*DL*, p. 22). Their dancing, as Julia Cruickshank notes, is both an expression of individual identity and an affirmation of collectivity, the five sisters dancing as a family but still preserving their own distinctive personalities. Maggie's features 'become animated by a look of defiance' and she emits 'a wild, raucous "Yaaaah!"' (*DL*, p. 21). She draws her flour-covered hand down her cheek, patterning her face 'with an instant mask' (*DL*, p. 21). Described as a 'white-faced, frantic dervish', she is associated with the Ryangan natives amongst whom Father Jack has lived and who paint their faces with coloured powders and then 'dance – and dance – children, men, women, most of them lepers, many of them with misshapen limbs, with missing limbs' (*DL*, p. 48). Similarly, the Mundy sisters find momentary release from harsh reality in the ecstasy of the dance. Maggie is joined by a transfigured Rose, Agnes and Chris. Agnes moves 'gracefully, most sensuously' (*DL*, p. 21) while Rose dances wildly, her 'wellingtons pounding out their own erratic rhythm' (*DL*, p. 21). Eventually, even Kate, who has been watching the scene with unease, suddenly leaps to her feet, flings her head back, and utters a loud 'Yaaaah!' (*DL*, p. 22). Kate, the most repressed of the sisters, dances alone. Her dancing, we are told, is 'ominous of some deep and true emotion', but it is 'totally concentrated, totally private'. When the music stops, the sisters self-consciously and awkwardly recollect themselves, and the old routines are resumed.

Dancing would seem to be the expression of a distinctively female sexual energy which eludes a patriarchal, linguistic order:

GERRY: Do you know the words?
CHRIS: I never know the words.
GERRY: Neither do I. Doesn't matter. This is more important.

(*DL*, p. 33)

Gerry recognizes a natural subversiveness in femininity. He speaks of a difference between men's constant need for order and purpose in life and women's greater readiness to live without fixed division: 'Maybe that's the important thing for a man: a *named* destination – democracy, Ballybeg, heaven. Women's illusions aren't so easily satisfied – they make better drifters' (*DL*, p. 51). Gerry of course is a dancer too, but he's an exponent of *ballroom* dancing, a respectable, 'civilized' form of dancing which demonstrates the triumph of order and control. By contrast, the sisters' dancing is a regression to unchoreographed instinct, the unleashing of primitive, even savage, feeling. When Gerry dances, it is to 'Dancing in the Dark' (*DL*, p. 32), a Fred Astaire/Ginger Rodgers kind of number: when the sisters dance together, it is to '"The Mason's Apron" . . . very fast; very heavy beat; a raucous sound' (*DL*, p. 21), and they are transformed 'into shrieking strangers' (*DL*, p. 2) and 'white-faced, frantic dervishes' (*DL*, p. 21). In earlier plays we glimpse this notion of a fragile yet transgressive femininity. In *Philadelphia* and *Aristocrats*, it is set against the presence of a rigid, authoritarian father figure who inhibits free emotional expression. In both these earlier plays, the mother is a shadowy influence, symbolic of the free spirit that cannot ever be entirely extinguished. In *Philadelphia* she is 'small . . . and wild and young . . . and her eyes were bright and her hair was loose' (*SP*, p. 37); in *Aristocrats* she was 'absorbed into the great silence' (*DL*, p. 295). In *Freedom of the City* she is irrepressible Lily, whose inchoate, potentially subversive, vital, female energy declares itself within and against the imposed (male) ideological and linguistic structures symbolised by Derry's Guildhall.

Dancing has healing power. In Act 1, Maggie, after recalling painful memories of Brian McGuinness, a man whom she once was 'keen on' (*DL*, p. 20) but lost to an old schoolfriend, finds consolation and emotional release in the impromptu dance with her sisters which she initiates. Chris's dance with Gerry is what makes his leaving bearable: 'Just dance me down the lane and then you'll leave' (*DL*,

p. 33). This ritual of healing can be a communal experience. Jack describes 'children, men, women, most of them lepers, many of them with misshappen limbs – dancing, believe it or not, for days on end!' (*DL*, p. 48). Rose is transformed by her sexual experience in the 'back hills', amongst the dying embers of the Lughnasa fires: 'Indeed, had we not seen the Rose of Act 1, we might not now be immediately aware of her disability' (*DL*, p. 56).

The pagan connotations of the sisters' dancing is emphasised by relating it to the dancing which is a part of the festival of Lughnasa taking place in the 'back hills'. (*DL*, p. 16). The play, that is, concerns itself with the collective as well as personal memory. Just as the sisters' dancing expresses their individual private feelings so the dancing in the 'back hills' is the manifestation of a hidden, submerged culture which neither colonial influence nor Christian teaching has been able to extinguish. When Maggie and Rose first break into song – the appropriately exotic 'Abyssinia' song – and dance around the kitchen, Agnes's comments again playfully echo Kate: 'A right pair of pagans the two of you' (*DL*, p. 4). Rumours of what has been going on at the Lughnasa festivities infiltrate the Mundy household. Kate, the guardian of Christian value, is appalled when she hears the story of how a local boy has been badly injured when, during the drinking and dancing, he fell into the bonfire. Young Sweeney becomes her prime example of the dire consequences of yielding to 'pagan' and dissolute impulses and letting slip the properties of civilised order. The boy's name links him with the ancient Irish archetype of pagan disobedience and impiety, the legendary Sweeney who defied the Christian authorities and was punished by being condemned to fly around like a bird for the rest of his life. Young Sweeney is a denizen of the 'back hills', the *pagus*, the wilderness beyond the bounds of civilisation. It is to these same 'back hills' that the sinister Danny Bradley later takes Rose courting. Kate claims to know the people who live there: 'And they're savages! I know those people from the back hills! I've taught them! Savages – that's what they are! (*DL*, p. 17).

Any good reference work on Irish myth and legend will provide information about the meaning and origins of 'Lughnasa'. It was one of the four major pre-Christian, Celtic festivals, the others being Oimelc, Samhain and Beltaine. Basically a harvest festival, Lughnasa was celebrated for fifteen days in honour of the god Lugh, one of the most important Irish gods. In Peter Berresford Ellis' *A Dictionary of Irish Mythology*[52] we find that Lugh, cognate with Welsh Lleu and

Gaulish Lugos, was a sun god, known for the splendour of his countenance, and god of all arts and crafts. Over the years this mighty god's image diminished in popular folk memory until he was simply known as 'Lugh-chromain', which became Anglicised as Leprechaun. However, as Ellis points out, his name still survives in the place-names of many lands, not just Ireland: Lyons, Leon, Loudan and Laon in France, Leiden in Holland, Liegnitz in Silesia and Carlisle (Luguvalum in Roman times) in England as well as London which, like Lyons, was named the 'fortress of Lugh' – Lugdunum, hence the Latin Londinium. Egerton Sykes, compiler of *Everyman's Dictionary of Non-Classical Mythology*,[53] further informs us of how Christianity took Lugh's feast over as Lammas, the feast of first fruits, which is now commemorated by the August Bank Holiday. The name 'Lugh' survives in modern Irish in 'Lughnasad', the month of August. The element *nasad* in the name of the festival relates to words signifying 'to give in marriage' and Maria Leach, in the *Standard Dictionary of Folklore, Mythology and Legend*,[54] records a story of the festival of Lughnasad honouring the marriage of Lugh to the Sovranty of Ireland, a monstrous hag who was transformed into a radiant beauty. The hag – Ireland – was transformed by the caresses of the sun from the bleakness of winter into the floral splendour of spring – a version of the widespread myth of the union of sun and earth. Thus, Lughnasa is traditionally associated with sexual awakening, rebirth, continuance and it is significant that the date, 1 August, is exactly nine months, the normal period of gestation, before the great feast of Beltaine which celebrated the beginning of summer. These motifs of sexual awakening and magical transformation are central to Friel's play.

Friel's paganism links him with Synge who was also interested in exploring the possibility of Dionysiac comedy in which the instincts are given free expression. Synge, we may recall, revolted against the realism of Ibsen and Zola who dealt with 'the reality of life in joyless and pallid words'.[55] Instead, Synge wanted 'the rich joy found only in what is superb and wild in reality', an 'imagination that is fiery and magnificent and tender'.[56] He found this kind of imagination amongst the peasants of the west of Ireland. His distinctive 'Western World' is fantastic, romantic, both brutal and sentimental, both pagan and Catholic and, also like Friel's fictional world, one which oscillates between the mystery of poetic vision and the brutal realities of living, between dream and reality. But where Synge sought to replace the 'joyless and pallid' words of the realist with a language that was 'richly flavoured as a nut or apple',[57] Friel goes outside the native tradition of verbal theatre altogether, seeking to evolve new, non-rational forms through his experiments with pagan ceremony, music and a new wordless language of the body. Friel's transformations are only momentary, but they have a communal dimension which Synge's do not have. Where Synge dramatises a form of personal heroics, the achievement of the special individual, Friel's dancing at Lughnasa is much more democratic, being both an individual *and* a collective activity.

The dancing in the play is associated not only with the pagan festival of Lughnasa but also with African tribal rituals. As Cruickshank observes, the Celtic and Ryangan worlds are both small, neglected communities on the fringes of civilisation; both are ex-colonies, both are cultures rich in dance and ritual. Jack admires the Ryangan 'capacity for fun, for laughing, for practical jokes – they've such open hearts! In some respect they're not unlike us' (*DL*, p. 48). And so, like the Sweeney boy, Jack has 'gone native' (*DL*, p. 39), attracted by ancient ritual and wordless ceremony. Jack's lapse from Christian orthodoxy is synonymous with his loss of language ('My vocabulary has deserted me' (*DL*, p. 39)), the primary tool of the rational western mind. What Jack particularly values in Ryangan culture is the fact that there is 'no distinction between the secular and the religious' (*DL*, p. 48). The Ryangans allow the spiritual and the sensual to interpenetrate each other: 'almost imperceptibly the religious ceremony ends and the community celebration takes over' (*DL*, p. 48). Ryangan primitivism emphasises both the sensuous and the communal life. In Ryanga 'women are eager to have love children', Jack informs a horrified Kate (*DL*, p. 41) who earlier, we may recall, sought to discourage Chris's participation in the festival dance by reminding her of her maternal role: 'You have a seven-year-old child. Have you forgotten that?' (*DL*, p. 12). Like Father Chris, the returned missioner in the early play, *The Blind Mice*, Jack is forced to reassess conventional piety in the light of his experience of the 'alien' and the 'Other'. Repatriated to Ballybeg, he seeks to create a new, more congenial 'home' for himself than the one he has inherited. Michael remembers him as 'a forlorn figure . . . shuffling from room to room as if he were searching for something but couldn't remember what' (*DL*, p. 2).

The other rogue 'father' in the play is Gerry. He would seem to be descended from that earlier playboy–dancer–musical engineer, the insouciant Shane in *The Gentle Island*. Like Shane, Gerry brings music and dancing to a depressed, inward-turned family. Both are musical repair men: Gerry repairs the sisters' radio, Shane fixes up the old record player on the island. Like Shane also, Gerry is a dangerously disruptive influence who acts as a catalyst for many of the tensions that exist between the members of the family, especially when he shifts his attentions from Chris to Agnes at the end. He represents the intrusion of a kind of virile manliness into a predominantly female, celibate world. His presence awakens the sisters' repressed sexuality: seeing him approach the house, they all begin to prettify themselves in front of the mirror and watch his every move from the garden window with entranced curiosity. Gerry is an urban outsider (he speaks with an English accent) to the small, parochial world of the sisters, as much of a mystery man to the sisters as Synge's playboy was to the simple Mayo folk. Like Christy, Gerry offers to a repressed community the opportunity of release from routine, the experience of romance. For all his gift of the gab, he is the play's chief sponsor of 'wordless ceremony' (*DL*, p. 71), the one who carries Chris and, later, Agnes, beyond words: 'Don't talk. . . . Not a word' (*DL*, p. 32), he counsels, as he dances Chris across the garden. But his negative qualities are also clearly recognised – his irresponsibility and unreliability. Chris knows not to be taken in by him. She is realistic enough to see that however attractive her playboy may be, he is not to be trusted with her heart: 'Don't talk any more; no more words', she says to him, 'Just dance me down the lane and then you'll leave' (*DL*, p. 33). At the end, Michael finds out that even while Gerry was proposing to Chris, he already had a wife and son in England.

Not surprisingly, Kate is the most hostile critic of the jaunty, smiling, Gerry, the man who defies any easy categorisation and threatens confusion and disruption to her careful order. He has, she says, 'no business at all coming here and upsetting everybody' (*DL*, p. 24) and she preserves a chilly detachment, insisting on calling him 'Mr Evans' (*DL*, p. 24). She objects to him because 'he has no sense of ordinary duty' (*DL*, p. 34), he has run out on Chris and Michael. Kate even calls him a 'beast' (*DL*, p. 34), for with Gerry she is forced to confront the reality of the body. Slipping the leash of family responsibility, Gerry shows himself to be a shiftless, rootless individual with no secure sense of home or personal identity. Since leaving Chris, he has been a dancing instructor and is now a gramophone salesman and prospective international adventurer. Later, we hear that he became a 'dispatch rider' (*DL*, p. 50) in the Spanish Civil War, a fitting symbolic role for this restless individual whose function throughout the play is to facilitate the opening up of secret communications in and between the embattled sisters. Kate, the bastion of orthodox Christian value, reacts predictably to the news of Gerry's latest adventure, criticising all young Irishmen who go to Spain 'to fight for godless communism' (*DL*, p. 52). Gerry, with his stories of cows with one horn, and his talk of 'fabulous omens' and 'bad omens' (*DL*, p. 30) is another of the play's essentially pagan spirits.

However, Kate's attitude to Gerry is as ambivalent as her attitude to Jack. She is constrained to admit that Chris is transfigured in Gerry's company: 'And look at her, the fool. For God's sake would you look at that fool of a woman. (*pause*) Her whole face alters when she's happy, doesn't it? (*Pause*) They dance so well together. They're such a beautiful couple' (*DL*, p. 33). And, despite her fears of Gerry's sinister influence, she relents and tells Chris: 'Of course ask him in. And give the creature his tea. And stay the night if he wants to. (*Firm again*) But in the outside loft. And alone' (*DL*, pp. 25–6). Kate's speech summarises the tension in her between the desire for order and her natural womanly feeling.

In the play, dancing signifies a freeing of human behaviour from predetermining norms and motivations and an attunement of the individual to his or her deepest impulses, to the rest of the group and, ultimately, to the cosmic forces symbolically (and actually) transmitted through the music on the radio, 'Marconi's voodoo' (*DL*, p. 2). It is Gerry to whom the sisters turn when their radio keeps breaking down. He is the one who tries to fix their aerial so that they can tune in again to the 'dream music' (*DL*, p. 71). He is their link with the 'Other', with the world beyond their usual, stifling routines. He leads them out of themselves and helps them to discover the submerged parts of their own being. Not only is he a professional dancer, he is also one of the birdmen of the play, one of those adept at flying. Aloft in the sycamore tree tinkering with the radio aerial, he sways and sings, '"He flies through the air with the greatest of ease. . . . That daring young man on the flying trapeze"' (*DL*, pp. 52–3), while down below Agnes covers her eyes in terror, unable to watch the daredevilry of the dashing risk-taker, the 'clown' (*DL*, p. 54) amongst the branches. Gerry is linked with the ancient Sweeney and, by extension, with the young pagan celebrant from the 'back hills'. He is also linked with the boy Michael, another 'flyer', who throughout the play is engaged in making and trying to fly two kites. Michael's kites are decorated with grotesquely painted, savage faces, which recall the painted faces of Jack's Ryangan dancers. In the complex web of parallels and correspondences which we find in the play, there is a connection between flying, dancing and pagan ceremonial. All of these activities are forms of release from the tyranny of routine and the pressure of the fact. Recalling earlier 'flying' motifs – Cass's 'winged armchair' or Manus's 'airplane seat' – we remain uncomfortably aware that flying can all to easily become mere avoidance, delusion, escapism.

The play might seem to dramatise a gradual contraction of possibility, a gradual disintegration of the existing order. 'Lughnasa's almost over, girls. There aren't going to be many warm evenings left' (*DL*, p. 66), says Maggie, perceiving an end to the season of adventure and experiment. Rose's rooster, which has been associated with an exotic primitive ceremonialism, has been destroyed by the fox. Maggie's riddling wit, which so enlivened her exchanges with young Michael, at last fails her: 'I've a riddle for you. Why is a gramophone like a parrot? . . . Because it . . . because it always . . . because a parrot . . . God, I've forgotten' (*DL*, p. 70). As with Jack earlier, words let her down, but not as a necessary stage in the revitalisation or reordering of communicational structures. What Kate has always feared actually happens – the family breaks up. Agnes and Rose leave and when Michael catches up with them twenty-five years later, he finds that Agnes is dead and Rose is dying in a hospice for the destitute in Southwark. Dreamy Agnes and 'simple' Rose cannot survive outside the security of the family. Life in Ballybeg seemed to offer them less and less, but flight has not brought happiness nor fulfilment either. Michael rehearses the details of their sad end: how they moved about a lot,worked as cleaners of public toilets, factories, in the Underground; how there came a time when Rose could no longer find work and Agnes couldn't support the two of them. 'They gave up' (*DL*, p. 60). They took to drink and slept in parks, in doorways, on the Thames Embankment. Agnes died of exposure. Jack dies within a year of the events of the play 'and with him and Agnes and Rose all gone the heart seemed to go out of the house' (*DL*, p. 70). Maggie took on the tasks Rose and Agnes had done and 'pretended to believe that nothing had changed' (*DL*, p. 70). Chris spent the rest of her life in the knitting factory, hating every day of it. Kate's end is no happier: she has to take a job tutoring the children of Austin Morgan, the man whom she had once had 'a notion of' (*DL*, p. 10).

The play would seem to emphasise lost opportunities, tragic waste,

failure, a gradually diminishing life. And yet the feeling one is left
with is not at all as simple as that. The play doesn't end with the
narrator's blunt account of the ultimately tragic ends of the characters. Even knowing the destiny of his aunts, Michael remains 'fascinated' (*DL*, p. 71) by the hypnotic, magical power of memory. 'The
stage is lit in a very soft, golden light so that the tableau we see is
almost, but not quite, in a haze' (*DL*, p. 70). This is the space somewhere between the real world and fairy-land, where the Actual and
the Imaginary may meet. Life retains its aura of enchantment. The
play refuses pessimism. Unlike Maggie, Michael is conscious of
change – change for good as well as bad. He acknowledges the
sordid deaths of Agnes and Rose, but also registers the survival of
young Sweeney. In the closing tableau, 'the characters are now in
positions similar to their positions at the beginning of the play – *with
some changes*' (*DL*, p. 70). Michael's kites may never have flown in the
course of the play, but they are still 'boldly' displayed, the savage
faces on them 'grinning' (*DL*, p. 70) defiantly. One of the kites
stands between Gerry and Agnes, the other between Agnes and Jack,
for the failure of Agnes's flight has to be balanced by the perpetually
buoyant quality of Gerry's life and the freedom which Jack discovered. As Michael begins his final speech, Friel directs that the music
– 'It is Time to Say Goodnight' – should be 'just audible' in the
background. 'Everybody sways very slightly from side to side –
even the grinning kites. The movement is so minimal that we cannot
be quite certain if it is happening or if we imagine it' (*DL*, p. 71). Like
memory, our experience of the play itself is ambivalent. The liminal
movement and sound act to undermine our sense of a solid, fixed
reality. We are put in the position of Private Gar who, thinking of his
childhood fishing trip with his father, 'wonders now did it really
take place or did he imagine it' (*SP*, p. 89). Friel explores that space
between objective fact and subjective imagining, that 'limbo' in which,
as Michael puts it, 'everything is simultaneously actual and illusory'
(*DL*, p. 71). Michael's final speech powerfully asserts a ghostly presence, an 'atmosphere . . . more real than incident' (*DL*, p. 71), 'a
mirage of sound – a dream music' – which mesmerically leads people out of themselves, even out of the prison-house of language. The
play ends with Michael's vivid memory of 'dancing as if language
had surrendered to movement – as if this ritual, this wordless ceremony, was now the way to speak, to whisper private and sacred
things, to be in touch with some otherness' (*DL*, p. 71). In his opening
speech of the play, Michael speaks of a rite of passage, indicating

how, on one level, this is a play about growing up, about the transition from innocence to experience: 'I had a sense of unease, some awareness of a widening breach between what seemed to be and what was' (*DL*, p. 2). The stability and solidity of his childhood world have been disturbed: 'That may have been because Uncle Jack hadn't turned out at all like the resplendent figure in my head. Or maybe because I had witnessed Marconi's voodoo derange those kind, sensible women and transform them into shrieking strangers' (*DL*, p. 2). He comes to recognise a deep mystery in life. He has seen frustration, break-up, unbearable drudgery, failure, but he also becomes aware of a force for change which, though it may threaten the 'safe' world of childhood, is also the ground of hope and aspiration. His final tableau rearranges the opening one and the most abiding memory he is left with is of 'atmosphere', of 'dream music', 'dancing' – of a mysterious libidinal energy. The significance of this intuitive, illogical, level of experience is finally articulated verbally, in Michael's powerful, lyrical closing narration.

The play enacts an ideal balance – between narration and enactment, the rational and the irrational, language and music, the religious and the secular, past and present. To live in one sphere alone is inadequate. As Julia Cruickshank observes, Rose may be the one 'not educated out of her emotions', but she perishes away from the security of the family. On the other hand, Kate, the one most alarmed by instinct and irrationality, makes a strenuous effort to adapt and come to terms with Jack's 'nativism'. Michael can't help but be amused by her valiant struggle to accept. 'Startled', 'stunned' and 'shocked' as Kate is by the change in Jack, 'finally she hit on a phrase that appeased her: "his own distinctive spiritual search", "Leaping around a fire and offering a little hen to Uka or Ito or whoever is not religion as I was taught it and indeed know it," she would say with a defiant toss of her head. "But then Jack must make his own distinctive search"' (*DL*, p. 60). Ballybeg, too, is faced with the challenge of adapting to change in the form of the knitting factory. As in *Translations*, the community's survival depends on its ability to move with the times. Frank Rich, the influential – even feared – *New York Times* critic, commenting on the success of the Abbey Theatre production of the play at Broadway's Plymouth Theatre in October 1991, concluded his review with these words of appreciation of Friel's complex vision:

Even knowing that he (Michael) knows and what everyone knows about life's inevitable end, he clings to his vision of his childhood, a golden end-of-summer landscape in the production's gorgeous design, for what other antidote than illusions is there to that inescapable final sadness? *Dancing at Lughnasa* does not dilute that sadness – the mean, cold facts of reality, finally, are what its words are for. But first this play does exactly what theatre was born to do, carrying both its characters and audience aloft on those waves of distant music and ecstatic release that, in defiance of all language and logic, let us dance and dream just before night must fall.[5]

If in *Faith Healer* Friel takes us to the very edge of the postmodern Apocalypse, in *Dancing at Lughnasa* he recollects himself to affirm the vitality and dialogue of individual experience even when we are aware of what the future holds. Just as Chris's and Agnes's dancing is not simply socialised as Gerry's is, their story is not merely a chronicling of events. Like Father Jack's spirituality which cannot be held by the words of the Mass, it is fluid. The ultimate image of Friel's drama is of a space where 'language surrendered to movement' (*DL*, p. 71). The almost imperceptible fluidity of the play's closing tableau is a celebration of the power of theatre to renew and reveal, and a rejection of 'fossilised' history.

THE LONDON VERTIGO

Where *Dancing at Luhgnasa* affirms the possibility of self-transformation through an embracement of bodily experience and presents the 'lunacy' associated with 'Lughnasa' as a joyous, if momentary, experience of plenitude and freedom from oppressive religion and community, Friel, in his two succeeding plays, *The London Vertigo* (1990) and *A Month in the Country*, after Turgenev (1992), presents alternative views of the unconscious, of the bodily and the material, of desire, of the libidinal impulses. In *The London Vertigo*, the vertigo of the dance becomes 'the London vertigo' – a manic Anglophilia (matching the equally manic Hibernophilia which Friel excoriated in *The Communication Cord*); and in *A Month in the Country* it becomes the vertigo of love, love being an experience which carries people out of themselves and dissolves the boundaries between male and female, rich and poor, high and low, yet is the source of calamity, pain and confusion. Where the dance is irradiating, the 'London vertigo' is a foolish obsession and love a destructive passion. If *The London Vertigo* savagely mocks the very possibility of self-metamorphosis, *A Month in the Country*, allows the possibility but presents it as a release into 'catastrophe'.

After his most ambitious experiment in probing those realms beyond or before words in *Dancing at Lughnasaa*, Friel in *The London Vertigo* returns to his old theme of the problem of language out of which our reality is substantially constituted, to look again at the relationship between words (particularly the way they are spoken) and social power and between language and identity. He rewrites the story of Christy Mahon's positive self-metamorphosis through language, exchanging the conventions of romantic comedy which govern Synge's play for the conditions of farce.

More specifically and explicitly, *The London Vertigo* is a 'rewriting' of Charles Macklin's play, *The True-born Irishman*, which was first produced in Dublin in 1761 and then in Covent Garden, London, in 1767. Friel tells us that he was attracted to Macklin as a 'neighbour',[59] in both the geographical and the spiritual sense. Charles Macklin was born Cathal MacLaughlin, probably in 1699, probably in Culdaff in the Inishowen peninsula in Donegal. He was probably of poor peasant stock, though possibly descended from a leading old Irish family of Maclaughlins who lived in Inishowen. The details of his early life are not clear. We do know, however, that, seeking to make his way in the world, Macklin emigrated to England, having first learnt English (his first language was Irish), Anglicised his name and converted to Protestantism to escape the rigours of the penal laws. In London he became one of the most notable theatrical figures of his day, second only to Garrick, in an age of great British acting. He was also a playwright of considerable merit, *The True-born Irishman* being his only Irish play. Both the play and the author embodied many of the tensions with which Friel himself clearly felt a special affinity.

Macklin, having accomplished a quite astounding feat of emergence and self-metamorphosis for himself, satirises in his play the attempt of a Mrs O'Doherty to perform a similar transmogrification. Mrs O'Doherty, the wife of a wealthy Irishman, Murrough O'Doherty, during a visit to London for the coronation of George III, is smitten by the 'London vertigo' – 'a sudden and dizzy conviction that London is the very heart of style and wit and good fortune and excitement'.[60] On her return to Dublin, Mrs O'Doherty, now suffering from a kind of Pygmalion complex, changes her name to Mrs Diggerty and speaks in a ridiculous posh accent. As far as she is concerned, it is not only clothes which maketh the woman, but also French food, long-tailed horses, a title and – most fundamental of all – the language which she speaks. Where in *Translations* the pros and cons of adopting a new language are carefully balanced, here Mrs O'Doherty's replacement of her original language with another simply renders her a suitable case for the most savage satirical treatment. Mr O'Doherty, insisting on the importance of being earnest, sets out, with the help of his wife's brother, a Counsellor (that is, barrister) by the name of Hamilton, to restore the absurd Mrs Diggerty to sanity and decent Dublin domesticity.

The tension at the heart of *The True-born Irishman* is an opposition, recurrent in Anglo-Irish drama, between the provincial and the cosmopolitan, between the natural and the cultured, between the 'Irish' and the 'English' virtues. The play is bitingly anti-English, not only making fun of the pretentious aping of English manners and behaviour by Irish people but also touching on various unfair English practices affecting Irish prosperity. J. O. Bartley, in his introduction to a selection of Macklin's plays, ventures the opinion that 'the implications [of *The True-born Irishman*], though more superficial, are wider than those of Swift's nationalist writings; and though subordinate to the plot, and emerging as part of the presentation of character, . . . are real and revealing'.[61] It is generally agreed that O'Doherty, a part Macklin wrote for himself and played to great acclaim, was a mouthpiece for its creator's own views on Ireland, especially on the excesses of English colonialism and the corruption of politics in Ireland. O'Doherty, Bartley conjectures, is probably descended from a leading Donegal family who lived in Inishowen and were the overlords of the Maclaughlins from whom Macklin himself probably sprang. Bartley concludes:

> The choice of names is hardly likely to have been accidental when made by a MacLaughlin. There must be some identification here. Macklin, had circumstances been different, might have found himself in a position like O'Doherty's, from where to object to English manners and influences, and taxes, to dislike and distrust politicians, and to praise Irish traditions and the names surrounding them.[62]

All of the attractions of Macklin's play – broad and entertaining characterisation, vigorous dialogue, farcical satire, lively comic invention – are retained in Friel's. The changes that Friel has made – compressing the original three acts to one, reducing the cast from fourteen to five, vigorous pruning to produce 'a lean and less discursive text'[63] – all these changes were made with a view to increasing the play's attractiveness to theatre companies today and they are yet further demonstration of Friel's own assured theatrical instinct.

Macklin's true-born Irishman, Murrough O'Doherty, represents a departure from the conventional stage Irishman and an attempt at more realistic portraiture. Following the example of Ben Jonson, Macklin sought to incorporate into a basic humour type some sense of individual character. The estranged status of the provincial Irishman is used as an image of authenticity, but neither Macklin nor Friel resorts to sentimentalism in the depiction of his 'true-born Irishman'. Indeed, Friel finds Macklin's O'Doherty 'pompous and ponderous'[64] and it is interesting to note that many of Friel's changes to Macklin's play serve to diffuse further any idealising tendencies in the depiction of the 'true-born Irishman'.

For example, after Friel's O'Doherty echoes Macklin's in protesting to his brother-in-law about Mrs O'Doherty's desire that he should procure a title –

> She would have me desert my friends and sell myself, my honour and my country, as several others have done before me, so that she may sink the ancient name of O'Doherty in the upstart title of Lady Ahohill or Lady Culmore or some such ridiculous nonsense –

Hamilton replies in a direct address to the audience: '"Sell my country"! He really means it would cost him money!' (*LV*, p. 20). Hamilton's interjection, disallowing O'Doherty any idealistic, patriotic claims, imputes to him only a base materialistic motive and, coming at an early point in the play, inevitably colours the attitude we take to O'Doherty.

One of Friel's more notable excisions is a section in Macklin's play where O'Doherty lambasts 'courtiers', 'patriots' and 'politicians' and affirms the virtue of the unspoiled affections, common sense and the natural life. The passage, Bartley comments, would 'seem to express Macklin's own views':

> take this judgment from me then, and remember that an honest quiet country gentleman who out of policy and humanity estab-

lishes manufactories, or that contrives employment for the idle and the industrious, or that makes but a blade of corn grow where there was none before, is of more use to this poor country than all the courtiers, and patriots, and politicians, and prodigals that are unchanged.[65]

Friel is ready to suppress this affirmation of sympathetic quality in O'Doherty in the interests of producing a more dramatically piquant text that relies on 'showing' rather than 'telling'.

Also notable is the way Friel makes more use of O'Doherty's confidant, the barrister Hamilton, developing a much stronger dramatic relationship between the two characters, largely through emphasising O'Doherty's barely veiled contempt of his brother-in-law's supposed innocence. Thus, where Macklin introduces the business of renewing the leases in a simple expository way by referring to 'young Lord Oldcastle, who you know has a large estate in this country, and of whose ancestors mine have held long and profitable leases, which are now near expiring',[65] Friel is much less bland and seizes his dramatic opportunities. Exploiting Hamilton's role of one who, as befits a lawyer and an Ulster Scots–Irishman (which his name would suggest he was), is a bit of a precisian, he uses him to expose O'Doherty's corrupt middlemanship:

> O'DOHERTY: You know those huge estates owned by Lord Oldham?
> HAMILTON: On which your family for generations have had long and profitable leases?
> O'DOHERTY: The same. (To audience) Is the boob getting saucy?
> HAMILTON: And have sublet at enormous profit to much less fortunate Irishmen?
> O'DOHERTY: (To audience) Indeed he is!
>
> (*LV*, pp. 20–1)

Again, both Macklin and Friel have Hamilton express shock that O'Doherty would consider stooping to blackmail to obtain a good bargain from Count Mushroom in the business of the leases. Here is Macklin:

> COUNSELLOR: But, sir, I hope you won't accept of leases upon those terms.
> O'DOHERTY: O, I have no time to moralise with you on that point, but depend on it I will convince you before I sleep of the

propriety of my taking the leases: Lord, what signifies it; it is only a good bargain got from a foolish lord by the ingenuity of a knavish agent, which is what happens every day in this country, and in every country indeed.[67]

And here is Friel's much more dramatically pointed version:

HAMILTON: But, Murrough, you couldn't accept the leases upon those terms.
O'DOHERTY: Could I not? (To audience) And he's a barrister! Question is: How did the noodle ever qualify?

(*LV*, pp. 21–2)

By having O'Doherty mock Hamilton's moral squeamishness Friel strengthens the suggestion of O'Doherty's cynical ruthlessness and unscrupulousness.

Later, Friel's Mrs O'Doherty emphasises her husband's purely mercenary resistance to buying her a set of long-tailed horses and a title: 'You know it [the title] can be had! Just open your tight purse' (*LV*, p. 31). In Macklin's play, she complains to Lady Kinnegad about her husband:

MRS DIGGERTY: Aye, but he is as close-fisted as an old judge – Lord, he has no notion of anything in life, but reading musty books, draining bogs, planting trees, establishing manufactories, setting the common people to work, and saving money.
LADY KINNEGAD: Ha, ha ha! the monster![68]

In omitting this exchange, Friel again suppresses expression of O'Doherty's positive qualities.

At the end, Friel follows Macklin in allowing O'Doherty both a patriotic and a personal motive for revenging himself on Lord Mushroom, but quickly undermines any moral status O'Doherty might aspire to by having him include amongst his complaints against the English the objection that they are threatening Irishmen's monopoly on cuckoldry!

I'll make him smart. And smarter. Impudent rascal – to make a cuckold of an Irishman – take our own trade out of our own hands! And a branch of business we pride ourselves so much in, too. Why, sure that and the manufacture of linen are the only free trades we have. (*LV*, p. 37)

These spiralling ironies work to problematise the concept of 'true-born Irishman', stripping it of any unifying potential by turning it into an image of amorality and ruthless exploitativeness as well as of patriotic pride and provincial authenticity.

The most radical of the changes Friel has made to Macklin's play is his use of direct address to the audience. This is a Brechtian device, breaking the illusion of reality, reminding the audience of the fictional nature of what it sees and creating the distance to allow more critical evaluation of the action. Largely through the direct address to the audience, as we have seen, Friel develops the relationship between Hamilton and Mr O'Doherty; the technique also allows him to complicate the characterisation of Mrs O'Doherty and to develop his analysis of the problem of language.

Mrs O'Doherty is shocked into a resolve to mend her ways, but even as she assents to the good advice of her brother, she reveals an irrepressibly wayward and defiant side of her nature directly to the audience. When Hamilton, appealing to her mercenary instincts rather than her moral conscience, tells her that her husband is going to throw her out with only £100 a year if she doesn't reform, she is immediately filled with panic and, apparently, with remorse: 'I shall make no defence, brother. The story shocks me. Help me. Advise me'. But the direct address to the audience which follows lets us see behind the Public facade to the Private thought: '(To audience) Well, I'm caught, amn't I?' (*LV*. p. 34). Hamilton's advice that 'tears of repentance are the brightest ornaments a modern fine lady can be decked in' is met with her distinctly unrepentant aside: '(To audience) Wouldn't he give you an ache in the jerkin?' (*LV*, p. 35). Friel follows Macklin in allowing Mrs O'Doherty to reform, but then retreats from this comfortable resolution. There is the same refusal on Friel's part to indulge an easy sentimentalism in his treatment of Mrs O'Doherty as in his treatment of Mr O'Doherty. Friel keeps Macklin's concluding moralising pronouncement, but quickly dispels any sentimentalism by following the sententious language of the triplet with a further culminating intervention from the irrepressible Mrs O'Doherty:

O'DOHERTY: Indeed I think it's fairly ended.
            The coxcomb's punished;
            The fine Irish lady's mended.
            [*Suddenly Mrs Diggerty's head appears
            round the door.*]

MRS DIGGERTY: [*Winking broadly at the audience*]
     For the time being!   (*LV*, p. 45)

Friel thus incorporates into the play a further exploration of the
gap between 'Public' and 'Private' that has always fascinated him.
Ultimately, the 'London vertigo' includes a sense of the instability of
meaning, of self-division and the impossibility of closure. Friel complicates the traditionalist's warning against the excesses and absurdities of the modern 'English' world by adding his postmodernist
recognition of the primacy of the unconscious, of the bodily and the
material, of desire, of libidinal impulses. This results in a break with
the signifier, with representation, and the foregrounding of a set of
formalisms, in this case the conventions of farce, most notably the
use of direct address to the audience. Thus, Friel resists totality and
closure. Against Mrs O'Doherty's unself-conscious decadence Friel
asserts a positive decadence, a self-conscious awareness of our fictionalising powers and the provisionality of all meaning. Mrs
O'Doherty's closing line opens the possibility of further transgression of the play's dominant discourse and ideology.
     Macklin's Mrs O'Doherty is of course a patriarchal construction of
the feminine. She is in fact a particularly misogynistic version of
patriarchal ordering, based on masculine fantasies of the female
body – the myth of an unrestrained feminine libido that operates
independently of cultural codes, but which is ultimately subject to
the 'phallic' power to control or 'master' women and regulate female
sexuality within national, moral and economic structures. Friel, however, offers a kind of 'feminist' rewriting of Macklin's play, turning
Mrs O'Doherty into an 'Other' feminine that cannot be fully controlled within the terms of the phallic law. Refusing to expose itself
openly to public view, this 'Other' femininity mouths the words it
has been culturally assigned, but also unsettles orders of patriarchal
logic, unravelling the stories by which culture explains itself to itself.
The feminine confounds the structures of received narratives (Mr
O'Doherty's, Macklin's). Through the figure of Mrs O'Doherty Friel
asserts the presence of unruly feminine energies that refuse to be
repressed, a troublesome fluidity, a resistance to fixity and simple
categorisation. Through Mrs O'Doherty he mocks the whole metaphysical enterprise and insists on the priority of the body and the
concrete relationships of the historical process. Traditional essential-
ist ideas – including the concept of a racial essence, of 'the true-born
Irishman' or even of a coherent self – are thrown into question.

A MONTH IN THE COUNTRY

In his introduction to his version of *A Month in the Country*, Friel indicates his reasons for returning a second time to Turgenev. He sees Turgenev as the kind of writer who managed magnificently to turn to artistic account the difficult conflicts that threatened to overwhelm him in everyday life. 'For all his vacillations', Friel writes, 'the inner man, the assured artist, was organised and practical . . . he marshalled all these irreconcilables and put them to use in his work. Vacillation, the inability to act decisively, the longing to be other, to be elsewhere, became the very core of his dramatic action' (*MC*, p. 10). Friel could be describing his own dramatic interests, for self-division, the 'enemy within', the longing for 'Otherness' and the challenge of multiple possibility, are themes which he has placed at the centre of his dramatic action, from earliest plays such as *Philadelphia* and *The Enemy Within* through *Faith Healer* and *Translations* to *Dancing at Lughnasa* and *The London Vertigo*. Turgenev, Friel believes, 'fashioned a new kind of dramatic situation and a new kind of dramatic character where for the first time psychological and poetic elements create a theatre of moods and where the action resides in internal emotion and secret turmoil and not in external events. We now have a name for that kind of drama: we call it Chekhovian' (*MC*, p. 10). 'Metabiotic' ('a mode of living in which an organism is dependent on another for the preparation of an environment in which it can live' (*MC*, p. 10)), the term Friel uses to describe the relationship between Turgenev and Chekhov, could apply just as well to the relationship between Friel himself and these two great Russian writers. From them he learnt the potential of psychological and poetic drama which probed the fine, ever-changing nuances and scarcely perceptible vicissitudes of passionate feeling, reflected in dialogue of exquisite sensibility and the complex interplay of emotions. For *A Month in the Country* is a web of delicate patterns, like the lace-making Natalya refers to. It is a play of lyrical feeling, touched by nostalgia, set amongst the declining Russian aristocracy in a distant province. Like Chekhov and Turgenev, Friel is attracted to the country house setting, the atmosphere of delicate inertia and boredom, the longing for escape, as earlier plays such as *Living Quarters* and *Aristocrats* would also illustrate. *A Month in the Country* gives him another image of family, of a traditional order disrupted from within and on the brink of collapse, doomed to destruction by the forces of history.

The play presents a dark vision of love as 'madness' (*MC*, p. 81) and 'catastrophe' (*MC*, p. 94), an irruption of dangerous, irrational bodily energies. It is about the destruction of a quiet, rural idyll caused by the arrival of a young tutor, Aleksey. Aleksey acts as a catalyst, giving rise to the giddy 'madness' of love. Natalya, the twenty-nine year old wife of Arkady and mother of nine year old Kolya is, like Chekhov's three sisters, filled with a vast discontent and longing and, seeking escape from her pointless life and boring marriage, falls in love with fresh young Aleksey. Vera, Natalya's seventeen year old ward also falls in love with him. Aleksey, the simple, natural, vigorous, somewhat naïve university student is, in turn, overwhelmed by the strong, elegant, infatuated Natalya. The 'month' in the country is no lyrical escape but a deadly period of incubation in which the characters become the helpless, anguished victims of love's destructive contagion. Natalya jealously pursues Aleksey, destroying the happiness of her innocent ward whom she is willing to see married off to the pathetic fifty-seven year old land-owner Bolshintsov just so she will no longer be a rival. 'Unhinged' by both love and jealousy, Natalya bullies Vera, terrifies Aleksey, snaps at Lisaveta, deals with Schaaf (the German tutor) in a most capriciously high-handed manner, treats her besotted but platonic lover Michel with exaggerated suspicion and outrageous rudeness. She is unfair, unreasonable, unpredictable and unstable, veering wildly from one mood to another, abusing her power and position and revealing a quite shocking capacity for ruthless cruelty. Michel refers to her 'terrible disquiet' (*MC*, p. 59) and tells her that she acts as if 'possessed' (*MC*, p. 59), that she is 'pitiful' (*MC*, p. 59) in her infatuation. Vera calls her 'demented' (*MC*, p. 79): 'That's what love does: makes the unreasonable perfectly reasonable' (*MC*, p. 80). Natalya herself recognises that her life has 'lost all sense of balance' (*MC*, p. 67). The vertigo of love makes her behave in a way that appals even her, but she cannot help herself. She speaks of suffering 'a kind of temporary . . . derangement' (*MC*, p. 58) and confesses that she is 'just slightly demented . . . unhinged. . . . And dangerously irresponsible – giddy, heady, almost hysterical with irresponsibility' (*MC*, p. 58).

Aleksey also describes his feelings for Natalya as 'hysteria' and 'madness': 'A Chinese squib – a quick, blinding flash – then nothing' (*MC*, p. 100). Not long before he was speaking of her as the stable centre of a way of life which he found overwhelmingly impressive: 'At the centre of all this elegance and grace, there you were – the core, the essence, the very epicentre of it, holding it all in place' (*MC*, p. 82) – lines which echo Natalya's to Michel: 'When I'm with you I feel so centred' (*MC*, p. 29). But centres cannot hold in this play: Michel is as abruptly cast aside by Natalya in her single-minded pursuit of Aleksey as she is by Aleksey. Aleksey is gentle, friendly, easily upset, gauche, cocky. Like the boy narrator in *Dancing at Lughnasa* he is a kite-flyer. His innocent vitality, natural vigour and active personality contrast markedly with Michel's introspective brooding. As the catalyst who opens or frees the submerged, unruly forces of personality he is also opposite to the engineer, Arkady, who is symbolically constructing a weir, as if to stem the tide of human feelings and regulate the natural forces welling up within people. Friel cuts the references in Turgenev's play to such boyish activities as Aleksey's chasing squirrels, climbing trees, hunting wild birds and riding cows, but the young tutor in Friel's version is still a curious object of Natalya's amorous attentions. He is something of an ironic 'opener' or 'freer' catalyst, for the freedoms he stands for have a distinctly childish quality and he himself is much more at ease with Kolya and Vera than in the company of adults. The disruptive intruder, Aleksey, is a comic version of the rude and formidable Bazarov in *Fathers and Sons*. Both spring from the same social milieu, both are members of the new intelligentsia; both are self-made, socially sensitive, with a positive outlook, though Bazarov is more explicitly political in his orientations; both lack awareness of the irrational and betraying power of love. And our attitude to Aleksey is as ambivalent as it is to Bazarov, for Aleksey combines the limitations of the naif with the positive force of his status as the romantic embodiment of natural vitality.

In stark contrast, Michel's outward elegance masks a tired and cynical intellectualism which loses sight of the body and of nature – all that Natalya is desperately seeking to recover. She dreams of meadows and woods, the simple natural life and welcomes Doctor Shpigelsky with these words: 'You have the news of the countryside; bring some fresh air in here; cure us all; give us a good laugh' (*MC*, p. 24). Having led a life of privileged indolence she craves for direct sensuous experience, while all that Michel can offer her are symbols and allegories, an aestheticised 'Nature': 'You are so eloquent about "nature"', she says to him, 'But of course you're wrong. . . . Nature is blunt and crude and relentless. Nature cares about nothing except itself – surviving and perpetuating itself. Your exquisite nature is a savage' (*MC*, p. 43). Michel is a courtly figure out of the artificial world of *amour courtois*, the faithful devotee who suffers the pains of unrequited love, suddenly exacerbated by the thought that he is losing Natalya, not to her husband, but to 'that calf' (*MC*, p. 46) Aleksey. Anna suggests that it may be Michel's spirit of knightly nobility and romance which constitutes a moral centre: 'The people who offer their love without reservation, even though that love is never fully appreciated nor fully reciprocated, they are the fortunate ones' (*MC*, p. 107). However, our attitude to him is as ambivalent as it is to Aleksey. There is nothing attractive about Michel's permanent joylessness. When all the others move off to launch Kolya's new kite he is left alone, 'isolated, wretched' (*MC*, p. 49), unable to 'fly'. Failure in love leads inexorably to his bitterly demoralised conclusion that 'All love is a catastrophe . . . An endless process of shame and desolation and despair when you are stripped – you strip yourself! – of every semblance of dignity and self-respect' (*MC*, p. 94). In Turgenev's original version, Michel's cynicism is also dangerously subversive, for he tells Aleksey not only that all love is calamity but that independence is all that matters, that he must seize whatever pleasures life offers and that freedom is the highest value – sentiments which amount to a passionate denunciation of conventional social ethics, particularly of family morality, and which, not surprisingly, were cut by the Russian censors. If there was something of Turgenev in Aleksey as a member of the new classless intelligentsia and epitome of natural vigour, there was also no doubt something of himself in the figure of the pained and unsuccessful lover too. Isaiah Berlin, for example, suggests that Michel's situation was perhaps 'inspired by Turgenev's own ambivalent position in the household of the singer Pauline Viardot, whom he loved until the end of his life (his relationship with her husband was in some respects not unlike that of Rakitin and Islayev)'.[69]

The upshot of the month in the country is that Michel has to leave with Aleksey. Natalya's desperation recalls Pegeen's after the departure of her 'only Playboy' whom she did not have the courage to follow: 'And who is he to decide I haven't the courage to throw all this up and go with him!' (*MC*, p. 102), Nicola cries in a fit of angry self-recognition. She hasn't the courage and remains with her husband for whom she has respect but not love, facing total breakdown: 'Everything's in such a mess . . . I'm afraid I can't hold on much longer' (*MC*, p. 103). Vera's attempt at reassurance – 'everything'll soon be back to normal' (*MC*, p. 103) – only provokes the outburst that 'it's the normal that's deranging me, child'. Arkady, kindly as always, 'puts his arm around her' (*MC*, p. 103) and says soothing words, but she 'removes his supporting hand' (*MC*, p. 103) and the last we see of her is withdrawing to her room to lie down. There is an uneasy return to the *status quo*.

But what of the others? Vera's future lies with the moribund Bolshintsov. Arkady's jubilation at the end is treated with special irony, for he never knows the real reason for his wife's strange behaviour nor for Michel's and Aleksey's sudden departure. The only winners would seem to be the vigorous, positive, capable people – the servants, Matvey and Katya, (their relationship duplicating the age gap between Natalya and Aleksey; the ghostly influence of Katya's mother paralleling Anna's influence in Arkady's marriage); and the plain-speaking realists, Dr Sphilgesky and Lisaveta (whose prosaic, contractual relationship contrasts with the vertiginous swings in the central relationship between Natalya and Aleksey). The Doctor in the end gets his team of horses as a reward for engineering the sickening match between virginal Vera and the doltish Bolshintsov. The Doctor survives and prospers because he doesn't believe in love – and that is the basis of his self-justification to Vera: 'If I thought for a moment that love was a necessary – even a desirable – ingredient in these matters, then I'd say: pass this up. But since I don't . . . [*He shrugs*]' (*MC*, p. 99). Whatever success he enjoys is bought at the cost of the death of the heart. The play as a whole dramatises the pathetic, ghastly consequences of the failure of these people to reconcile heart and head, personal feeling with social and family responsibility, traditional value with the experience of the body.

The vertigo of love, we come to see, is but a condensed form of a more general disruption signalled by the pervasive instability of the relationship between words and the world to which they putatively refer. Thus, Friel develops a familiar theme of his own within the framework of Turgenev's drama. A gap opens up, in Beckettian or Pinteresque fashion, between speech and action. Natalya vacillates wildly between wanting Aleksey to stay and knowing he should leave:

And he's staying?
Of course he's staying.
But he really should go.
Should he?
Oh yes – he really must go.

Why must he?
Because if he stays, Natalya. . . . (*She hugs herself. Her face is alight*)
. . . if he stays . . . you are lost.

(*MC*, p. 72)

Even as Aleksey promises to leave 'Tomorrow', he 'kisses her and swings her round' (*MC*, p. 83) in a wild, ecstatic dance of freedom. Love unloosens the connection between speech and action, producing an ironic disjunction between them, pulling apart speech itself into violent self-contradiction. Natalya's insistence that Aleksey must leave 'Tomorrow' is immediately followed by 'And don't go, Aleksey – don't go – don't ever go' (*MC*, p. 83). At the end, perversely, her love can find expression only in words of hate: Aleksey's brief note saying 'Goodbye' provokes an unexpected vehemence – 'How dare he, the pup! The jumped-up, baby-faced pup! Who the hell does he think he is! . . . The bastard! [*About to break down*] Oh my God . . .' (*MC*, p. 102).

Friel exploits the character of Schaaf to make comic capital out of the inadequacies of language ('Hartz are trumpery' (*MC*, p. 17); 'With Lizaveta Bogdanovna ever again I refuse to couple' (*MC*, p. 22); 'The cat's gone! Who stole the cat?' (*MC*, p. 24)). Bolshintsov's attempts to learn a new language, the language of love, are equally comical in the scene where the Doctor rehearses him in lover's speech before he confronts Vera. Bolshintsov's final appearance, when he comes on and stands, face raised, smiling, listening to Vera's piano-playing, confirms our sense which the play gives us of the woeful inadequacy of words. To describe the beauty of the music, the spirit of Vera, Bolshintsov has but a single word, a pathetic cliché, to close the play: 'Nice . . . nice . . .' (*MC*, p. 109).

Arkady, too, is without words for either love or for his suffering when he thinks his wife is being unfaithful to him with Michel. It is left to Arkady's mother to speak for him and express his pain: 'I would like to know what passion is so magnificent it can justify this' (*MC*, p. 69). A little later he declares his own exasperation with the inadequacy of other people's naming when he shouts at Matvey for calling his weir a dam: 'Weir – weir – weir! Why is everyone so stupid. It's a weir – not a dam' (*MC*, p. 87); yet Arkady himself keeps misnaming Aleksey calling him Ivan by mistake. At another point, we find Vera pondering the adequacy of certain words: 'Esteem – affection – love . . . maybe they are synonymous; maybe they should be' (*MC*, p. 79). To Michel love is a 'game' (*MC*, p. 84), the language of love merely a means 'to dissemble' (*MC*, p. 84). He has learnt to distrust language ('All that inflated language, the emotional palpitations, the heaving passions'), yet cannot be content without it: 'We regret most of the things we say and we regret even more all the things we don't say; so that our lives just dribble away in remorse' (*MC*, p. 84). The Doctor makes a pretence of a vigorous, healthy language through the forced *jouissance* of his terrible punning and his insistence on constructing an elaborate fiction of himself in his absurd 'love-talk' to Lizaveta. The latest in a long line of Friel's masquers, role-players, jokers and playboys going back to Gar O'Donnell in *Philadelphia*, he tells her he is giving her 'Shpigelsky without the mask' (*MC*, p. 76), that she won't be marrying 'the laughing, fawning, ingratiating Shpigelsky. You're teaming up with the bitter, angry, cunning peasant' (*MC*, p. 76). But as Lizaveta recognises, the fiction of himself currently on offer cannot be the whole truth either. Identity will not be reduced simply to a 'Public' and a 'Private' persona.

Friel constantly reminds us of how words create worlds. In the first major interview between Natalya and Vera in Act 1, Scene 3 we see that Vera's ultimate statement of love for Aleksey is the result of a collaborative process in which, under pressure from Natalya's jealous prodding and probing, Vera actually talks herself into the admission of love, gradually creates the fact of love, brings to consciousness and formulates what before had existed only as a vague and fleeting feeling. Vera's innocence of Natalya's ruthless jealousy at this point, like Arkady's innocence of the true situation at the end of the play, illustrates Friel's delicately ironic method, which indicates a profound disturbance between depth and surface. The controlled and elegant surfaces of these characters' aristocratic lives are constantly being disturbed by irruptions of nervous outbreaks, quarrels, hysteria. But, as always in Friel, lying behind the disruptions and divisions, behind words, behind the mind/body split, is the ghostly presence of an aesthetic order and harmony symbolised by the music of the Irishman John Field which is threaded through the action.

The play is a curious, superbly satisfying mixture of opposites, a sophisticated recognition of the paradoxes of life. It is both funny and sad, romantic and realistic, and it is this comprehensiveness of vision that no doubt was one of Turgenev's major attractions to Friel.

WONDERFUL TENNESSEE

In his latest play *Wonderful Tennessee* (1993) – the title taken from a line in an American folksong 'Down by the Cane-Brake' – Friel extends his treatment of familiar themes, once again making music, song and dance central theatrical elements expressive of the transcendent impulse. This play also has its on-stage author and theoriser, Frank, who is writing a book on how European civilisation has depended on the measurement of time. The measurement of time, like language, works by dividing up and labelling the continuum of reality, abstracting it within a system of symbols and codes. In *Wonderful Tennessee* Friel once again explores the limits of language and rationality, probing dark, unruly, Dionysiac energies in the individual and society in a drama of classical tautness and Apollonian control. Pagan ritual, Celtic as well as Classical, underpins the dramatic action more comprehensively than ever. On the surface, it is a diffuse play in which there is hardly any action, and conversation is desultry. Its rhythm is the familiar, Chekhovian rhythm of vague desire. But it is in fact a very carefully and strictly structured play, with an elaborate pattern of recurring images and motifs, or, more precisely, repetitions-with-a difference. This kind of repetition emphasises at a local level the unity of life while simultaneously suggesting the constant presence of the 'Other', which is Friel's central theme. Objects, people, conversations are charged with meaning – though not always convincingly. The more ordinary they are, the greater the burden of significance, it sometimes seems, they are required to bear. The same weakness as was noted in connection with earlier plays such as *Volunteers* is discernible here: the disjunction between text and subtext, which produces a rather schematic quality in the drama. Text is manipulated rather too mechanically to disclose subtext. Consequently, 'deeper' meaning does not always appear to grow organically out of the unfolding situation as it does in the best of Friel's plays.

Long before we actually meet any of the six characters in the play, Friel powerfully establishes a primal reality against which all human endeavour and aspiration must be measured:

Silence and complete stillness.
    Then after a time we become aware that there are natural sounds: The gentle heave of the sea; a passing seagull; the slap and sigh of water against the stone steps. This lasts until we have

established both a place and an environment of deep tranquillity and peace. (*WT*, p. 11)

Then we hear the minibus approaching, then the singing, laughter and talking, 'discrepant and abusive in this idyllic setting' (*WT*, p. 11). We are three pages into the play before any human figure actually appears on stage: the real protagonist is the timeless, elemental world of nature pre-existing and long outlasting the human story. A magical, folkloric, sacred sense of place is challenged by a process of historical colonialism and encroaching modernity.

Once again, he focuses on a point of crisis, bringing his characters to the place at the very edge of the known world ('Next parish Boston, folks!: *WT*, p. 19) – Ballybeg pier – where they await the boat that will take them to Oileán Draíochta, the 'Island of Otherness; Island of Mystery' (*WT*, p. 28). Brought to this bridgehead into the Unknown, they are poised between the modern secular world and a strange, primeval zone of being. On one side is Charlie their bus driver, their last link with civilisation; on the other, Carlin, the enigmatic ferryman, who is supposed to take them to the island. The similarity of the two names Charlie/Carlin (Trish keeps confusing them) suggests the way 'home' and 'Other' inhere in each other – a Heideggerean sense of Being as a dialectical process towards 'home' through the 'unhomely' (that is, our experience of the 'Other') or a Freudian sense of the relation between the repressed unconscious and our common, conscious knowledge. 'I want to go home' (*WT*, p. 15), Berna and Trish complain when they first arrive at the pier; 'This is no mystery tour he's [Terry's] taking us on', says Frank a little later, 'he's taking us home!' (*WT*, p. 36).

The six characters in the play are brought to face Mystery, the 'Other', both sacred and demonic, in the world and in themselves. We view them at the point where their emphatically realistic, modern lives intersect with myth and legend. They are taken beyond the usual landmarks: the opening line is Trish's 'Help! We're lost' (*WT*, p. 11). 'Wonderful' is the recurring term that they use to describe the place; at the same time Angela can't believe that this very ordinary pier is the place they have been looking for and wonders 'What in God's name are we doing here?' (*WT*, p. 12), unwittingly indicating the fundamentally religious nature of their journey. Terry insists the island is 'everything you ever dreamed of' (*WT*, p. 13) and makes them take off their shoes as they are standing on holy ground. 'What Eden is this?' (*WT*, p. 68), Frank asks playfully. Even Trish comes to recognise the new kind of seeing which this place encourages: 'You'd think you could see *beyond* the horizon. It really is wonderful', her next line emphasising what is strangest of all – the understanding that the 'wonderful' resides in the ordinary: 'Oh my goodness . . . Ballybeg pier. In County Donegal' (*WT*, p. 21). The place they have come to is 'heavenly' (*WT*, p. 21), 'Arcadia' (*WT*, p. 19), the 'wonderful Tennessee' (*WT*, p. 45) of the song, where love and fulfilment are to be found. In *Dancing at Lughnasa*, the itinerant Gerry, uprooted from his local place, reflects: 'Maybe that's the important thing for a man: a *named* destination – democracy, Ballybeg, heaven' (*DL*, p. 51). 'Oileán Draíochta' also might have appeared on his list. As Terry says to Angela, pointing towards where the island is supposed to be, 'So. There we are. See it, Angela? Our destination' (*WT*, p. 27); and Angela echoes him a little later: 'There it is, friends – Oileán Draíochta, our destination! Wonderful – other – mysterious' (*WT*, p. 32). But it is also a wild and dangerous place – 'Bloody Indian territory' (*WT*, p. 19), a place of dark secrets and a bloody past of ritual sacrifice and atavistic killing. Trish thinks the island is ukulele-shaped, which would link it with George's music, but they cannot agree on what shape or size it is – it 'keeps shimmering' (*WT*, p. 28). Trish wants to know if it isn't 'a mirage' (*WT*, p. 29). In short, the island is unknowable, indefinable – 'Whatever it is we desire but can't express. What is beyond language. The inexpressible. The ineffable' (*WT*, p. 52). Its contradictoriness is continually stressed, for it is the place of the irrational, of 'The Passions That Refuse to be Domesticated. Nature over Culture! Instinct Over Management! . . . A Hymn to the Forces that Defy Civilisation' (*WT*, p. 38). The journey to the island is recognised as, amongst other things, a return to the Body.

Carlin never actually comes to take the group to the island of mystery. They remain on the mainland. Like the game which Angela invents to pass the time – pitching stones at an empty bottle ('It's called: how close can you get without touching it': *WT*, p. 67) – they must content themselves with circling, rather than penetrating, the heart of mystery. As if habituated to compromise, Trish says: 'I'm sure it's very beautiful out there. But I'd be happy to settle for this.' Unable to reach the island, they improvise a 'party' (*WT*, p. 32) on the pier. In Carlin's absence, George, who is a 'genius' (*WT*, p. 21) on the accordion, is their chief link with the 'Other'. He is a kind of presiding deity surrounded by his rout of votaries. Angela refers to him as 'Dionysus' and crowns him with a wreath of dried seaweed. Through his music, George leads the others out of their normal lives, as when they enter 'all doing a clownish parodic conga-dance, heads rolling, arms flying – a hint of the maenadic' (*WT*, p. 17) – a spectacle strongly reminiscent of the abandoned dancing of the Mundy sisters in *Dancing at Lughnasa*, or the wild behaviour of Lily and Skinner in *Freedom of the City*. In this respect, George is like Gerry, the music-maker and professional dancing-master in *Dancing at Lughnasa*, who encourages the Mundy sisters to dance; or like Skinner, who helps Lily to escape from conventional inhibitions, only George has got beyond words and discovered the much greater power of music in helping these city people towards a new freedom. George has been a member of a band called the Aeolians – an invocation of the Greek legend of Aeolus who was king of a floating island and god of the winds. The same attempt by a debased society to appropriate an original energy of a traditional pagan culture is seen in *Dancing at Lughnasa*, in the reference to Austin Morgan's store in the 'Arcade' (*DL*, p. 71). Maggie, we may also recall, loves to smoke 'Wild Woodbine' (*DL*, p. 23) cigarettes, and the music she and her sisters listen to comes from 'Minerva Gramophones – The Wise Buy' (*DL*, p. 28), the Roman goddess of wisdom appropriated by a technological, commercialised society.

George has been in another band called the Dude Ranchers, the name this time signifying the Americanisation of the native culture. The music George plays ranges widely from American folksong to Beethoven, English music-hall to hymns – again suggesting the evolution of a pluralistic, mongrel native culture. Not one of the items in George's eclectic repertoire is specifically Irish. Folk culture has been taken over by a 'popular' culture imported from England and America, to the point where the local has become the 'Other' rather than 'home'. The culture of the local has become colonised – the latest phase in the process of historical colonisation dramatised in plays such as *The Enemy Within*, *Translations* and *Making History*.

George is also like Father Jack in *Dancing at Lughnasa*. Both are destined to die; both constructed as 'outcast' figures, forms of 'Otherness', incarnations of the mythical spirit historically defeated, versions of the dying god (such as Dionysus). But where Jack's death-rite and the leave-taking of Rose and Agnes to London mean that 'the heart seemed to go out of the house' (*DL*, p. 70), in *Wonderful Tennessee* George's imminent decease actually galvanises the others to pledge their continued devotion to the pagan mysteries centred on Oileán Draíochta which they promise to revisit next year.

ANGELA [*Triumphantly*] Yes, we will! Next year – and the year after
that – and the year after that! Because we want to! Not out of
need – out of desire! Not in expectation – but to attest, to affirm,
to acknowledge – to shout Yes, Yes, Yes! Damn right we will,
Terry! Yes – yes – yes! (*WT*, p. 87)

The play is chiefly taken up with the characters' waiting. The
waiting for the boatman is reminiscent of Vladimir and Estragon's
waiting for Godot. Carlin, like Godot, is the external figure who
could transform their lives. Terry's persistent faith in the appearance
of Carlin – 'And there's still a good chance we'll make it – a very
good chance. Carlin *will* come. I honestly . . .' (*WT*, p. 46) – echoes
Vladimir and Estragon's exchange about the Two Thieves and the
chances of salvation. Like Beckett's tramps, Friel's three couples pass
the time playing games, singing and playing music, and telling
stories. The idea of 'story-time' – when each of the central characters
is formally called upon to tell a story – is a theatrical device which
Stewart Parker also uses in *Pentecost*, a play presented by Field Day
in 1987. Here, four people, cooped up in a house in Belfast during the
Ulster Workers' Strike of 1974 take their turn to tell their stories in
the hope of pushing their experience towards some kind of clarifica-
tion and closure. Parker refurbishes the story of Pentecost to assert a
faith in the original religious function of theatre, in its visionary
capability and pentecostal fire, against the contemporary annihilat-
ing suspicion of the word. The story-telling in Friel's play similarly
represents an effort to express a spiritual truth, to break the naturalistic surface and declare another order of being.

Berna tells the fantastic story of how a very ordinary house that
had been Jesus' home rose into the air and, like a 'floating island',
transported itself to Loreto, where it became a place of pilgrimage.
Berna likes the story because it is a shameless 'Offence to Reason'
(*WT*, p. 57), a 'stupid, futile defiance' (*WT*, p. 58). In her choice of
story, the solicitor trained in Reason reveals the secret of her self, her
yearning for an escape from Reason, her desire for Mystery. It's a
story which the others find disturbing. By contrast, Trish's story is
directly personal, telling of her wedding day. Terry says it's a 'boring' story, but Frank insists that well-known narratives are reassuring and therefore good to hear: 'All we want of a story is to hear it
again and again and again and again and again' (*WT*, p. 61). Trish's
story, however, turns out to be much less stable than expected. As it

is gradually taken over by Terry, Frank and Angela, new narrative lines are established and Trish's original story of her resentment at George for turning up late at the church is radically altered. The hidden truth of George's actions come to the surface: he was late because he had been away with his band trying to make enough money to give Trish and himself a good start in married life. The revised story heroicises George, confirming his love and commitment, turning complaint into celebration of human determination and endeavour. 'It was a wonderful day' (*WT*, p. 64), says Frank. Trish's story again dramatises the 'Other', the dissolving of fixed structures (narrative this time rather than architectural) so that new meaning can be produced.

Frank's story is referred to as an 'epiphany' (*WT*, p. 70). It is another revelation which leaves everyone 'speechless' (*WT*, p. 70). The 'Other' this time is represented by the dolphin which emerges from the veil of mist and the sea to perform a strange, 'disturbing' dance: 'Like a faun, a satyr, with its manic, leering face. Danced with a deliberate, controlled, exquisite abandon' (*WT*, p. 70). The dolphin, traditionally a symbol of love, here proclaims another disturbing reality lying beneath the complacencies of Frank's existence.

Terry tells two stories. The first is a reminiscence of a childhood trip to the 'Island of Mystery', which is largely composed out of elements of the others' stories. Like Berna's flying house, it is described as a 'floating island' which, according to legend, 'appeared out of the fog', until 'the fog devoured it and nothing was seen but the . . . tumbling of the dolphins' (*WT*, p. 29). Terry tells of a pilgrimage to this island that he made with his father; of their fasting the night before and their eating only bread and water while they were on the island. He tells of their prayers, of their walking round the 'beds' and picking up a stone from a mound of stones and placing it on top of the mound as they walked. He remembers his father filling a bottle with holy water and corking it with grass. And he remembers the 'votive offerings' (*WT*, pp. 30–1) – the 'bits of cloth' – left on the bushes. All these details, as we shall see, are returning but variable elements, parts of a larger pattern, figuring either in others' stories or in the actions played out on stage. Everything, in this play, is part of everything else.

Terry's second story tells of a another expedition made to the island by a group of fourteen drunken locals on their return from the Eucharistic Congress in Dublin. The story of how, amid much drinking, singing and dancing, one of the party, seventeen-year-old Sean O'Boyle, was ritually killed recalls the story of the Sweeney boy who falls into the fire and is badly burned during the Lughnasa festivities. In both plays, Christian ritual gives way to pagan ritual: the bishop swears his parishoners to secrecy about what they have done on Oileán Draíochta. Terry's island is not the 'Gentle Island' it first appears: it, too, is believed to be cursed. What has happened there is an 'Offence to Reason', an irruption of dark and dangerous instinct. As Frank says, 'We don't know the half of what goes on in the world' (*WT*, p. 75).

Angela's story broadens still further the archetypal basis of Friel's play. She tells of the Eleusinian Mysteries of ancient Greece – religious ceremonies which were held in honour of Demeter, the goddess of the harvest. These festivities also featured much drinking and dancing, and sacrifices were offered. The celebrants 'vowed never to speak of what happened' (*WT*, p. 84). Very deliberately, Friel, through these multiple echoes and parallels, relates the present to the past weaving his contemporary situation into a texture of ancient design.

What all the stories have in common is the challenge they present to the rational ideal. All of them work against any complacent understanding of the world. What becomes clear is that this is a play about the persistent, unquenchable longing for transcendence. After Terry tells his story about his childhood pilgrimage to the island with his father, he and Frank ponder the way the world has changed since then:

TRISH: But it's not a pilgrimage island now?
TERRY: No, no, that all ended years and years ago.
TRISH: Why?
FRANK: People stopped believing, didn't they?
TERRY: Nobody does that sort of thing now, do they?
(WT, p. 31)

The question marks at the end of Frank's and Terry's last two lines are telling: perhaps belief hasn't entirely disappeared from the modern, secular world. 'Believe me . . .' (*WT*, pp. 13, 15, 23, 41, 42) is Terry's refrain line in the play, a kind of Christ-like exhortation to faith. Faith clearly hasn't died completely, for the six characters have all assembled to go to the island with at least some vague intuition of the religious significance of their trip. Berna struggles to define the motive for coming to the island: 'To be in touch again – to attest' (*WT*, p. 31), she ventures, amidst Trish's flattening literalisms and while Frank hops around taking photographs:

> TRISH: Why did father go out there?
> TERRY: For God's sake, Trish! That was another age. To pray – to do penance –
> BERNA: To acknowledge – to make acknowledgement.
> TERRY: You had another word, Berna – to attest!
>
> (*WT*, pp. 32–3)

The sense we have here is of a struggle for a language – a language of devotion. What these characters notably lack is the dignity of a liturgy. Without a vocabulary of wonder, their speech declines into formula and cliché, as in Terry's exclamation in the second line of the above quotation, or the repetition of 'wonderful' throughout the play. They fall back on the words of popular song and on a fossilised kind of story-telling: 'You know that by heart' (*WT*, p. 29), comments Angela, after Terry relates the legend of the island; 'You know *that* by heart' (*WT*, p. 32), says Terry to Angela when she tells the story of Dionysus's capture by pirates. The only language of the 'Other' they know is that learnt by rote from stories in tourist pamphlets or classical textbooks. Berna absurdly uses a formal legalistic term to comment on her story of the flying house: it is an 'Offence to Reason'. Angela resorts to parody of an evangelical preacher in attempting to talk about the island mysteries. Trish's speech is particularly unable to accommodate the transcendental impulse. At the mention of the mysterious dolphins in Terry's, Angela's and Frank's stories all she can say is: 'Will we see dolphins; God, I love dolphins' (*WT*, pp. 29, 32); 'I love dolphins. I think they are terrific' (*WT*, p. 70). Trish's limitations irritate even the others, as when they first hear that Oileán Draíochta means 'Island of Otherness; Island of Mystery':

> TRISH: God, it's not spooky, Terry, is it?
> BERNA: Not that kind of mystery. The wonderful – the sacred – the mysterious – that kind of mystery.
> FRANK: Good girl, Berna.
> TRISH: All the same it's beautiful. . . . Isn't it?
>
> (*WT*, pp. 28–9)

None of the group (apart, perhaps, from George) can surrender readily to the 'Other', to 'passion' or 'instinct', without self-consciousness. Hence, the prominence of the parodic mode in their speech and behaviour. When they dance, it's a 'clownish parodic dancing'. There is never any on-stage moment of genuine 'releasement' or transcendence in which we can share, no exhilarating 'lift' out of the contingent. The transformational magic of the theatre which Friel so successfully exploited in *Dancing at Lughnasa* is not part of the theatrical experience in *Wonderful Tennessee*, where it is the yearning and struggle for transcendence rather than its achievement which occupy the play. These six modern-day, secularised pilgrims – self-styled 'bowsies' (*WT*, p. 35) – approach the ancient mysteries in a half-hearted, uncertain, sceptical manner. The dynamic of faith has degenerated, the rituals and observances have been debased. Angela jokes about how, under Terry's management, the island will become, not a site of pilgrimage, but a venue for bull fights, revivalist meetings and other spectacles. Their actions are a pathetic imitation of Terry's remembered boyhood pilgrimage, with its overtones of the Lough Derg pilgrimage as described by Carleton, Kavanagh, O'Faolain or Heaney. Where Terry remembers fasting, the six arrive with a hamper packed with all kinds of continental delicacies. The holy water is now a puddle where they obtain water to put into their whiskey. But a consciously religious sensibility persists: the scene where Terry is stripped of his shirt is a farcical interlude, but the shirt is left as a 'votive offering'. Frank places some scattered stones on top of the mound, remembering Terry's account of the manner of the praying as the pilgrims circled the 'beds' on the island, but he refuses any religious pretension: 'Simple domestic instincts . . .' (*WT*, p. 82). Angela dashes across to put out the fire that Trish is about to light, again remembering Terry's earlier remark that 'Fire dispels the enchantment – according to the legend' (*WT*, p. 29). Frank is writing a book developing an elaborate rational theory to dispel enchantment, but is compelled to acknowledge the limits of the rational ideal and consider the possibility that the best way to deal with mystery may be to accept it rather than try to explain it away:

FRANK: But there must be some explanation, mustn't there. The mystery offends – so the mystery must be extracted. [*Points to the island*] They had their own way of dealing with it: they embraced it all – everything. Yes, yes, yes, they said; why

bloody not? A rage for the absolute, Terry – that's what they
had. And because their acceptance was so comprehensive, so
open, so generous, maybe they *were* put in touch – what do you
think? – so intimately in touch that maybe, maybe they actually
did see.   (*WT*, p. 52)

Berna, it turns out, is the most deeply responsive to the spirit of
place. At one point she throws away her watch. The watch, as
Frank's book explains, is the means of measuring time within a
system of empiricist, Enlightenment thought. It is the symbol of the
technological world of scientific capitalism. Jack McNeill in *The Communication Cord* has a watch, which is the instrument of his highly
mechanical ordering of the world for personal advantage. In *Making
History*, O'Neill gives his wife, Mabel Bagenal, 'a new invention – a
time-piece you carry around with you. It's called a watch' (*MH*,
p. 19). The watch is the sign of a mechanistic and rationalist concept
of time, and in rejecting it Berna shows her desire to re-enter a
magical, pre-technological world.

   The ostensible reason for her dispensing with her watch is that
water got into it when, at the end of Act I, the deeply unhappy Berna
attempted suicide by throwing herself off the pier, an instance of the
perverse, self-destructive aspect of the irrational which we have
encountered before in Fox Melarkey and Frank Hardy. Act 2 opens
on the following morning: Berna has been rescued. If there is no
confident resurrectional motif pervading the play, we do recognise
that some kind of purification has taken place, something akin to
'the ritual purification in the sea' (*WT*, p. 83) which Angela describes
as forming part of the Eleusinian Mysteries, for Berna is less depressed and agitated, and, from this point onwards in the play,
becomes more immersed in the sacral sense of place, more evidently
in touch with the life-force, thereby attaining a renewed psychic
vigour.

   Broken, fearful and inhibited, heads 'full of rubbish. And panic'
(*WT*, p. 58), all the characters are nevertheless touched by mystery
and end up more than half-believing. They promise to return to the
island next year. Though in a literal sense they cut ridiculous figures,
Friel insists on larger contexts and perspectives than those of the
here and now, and manages to elicit the spectator's empathy rather
than any straightfoward judgmentalism. For these are temporal beings existing in an a-temporal state, restive, disquieted creatures

dimly seeking to acknowledge the life of the spirit and experience the Absolute in a deadeningly materialistic world.

'The wonderful – the sacred – the mysterious' has absorbed Friel from at least as far back as *Faith Healer*. Faith healing belongs to a folk, pagan tradition. Frank Hardy seeks to reactivate a sense of the wonderful, the sacred and the mysterious through incanting the Celtic place-names. He seldom visits England, he says, because of a notion 'that the Celtic temperament was more receptive to us' (*SP*, p. 332). The characters in *Wonderful Tennessee* similarly attempt to draw energy and ancestry from a Celtic sense of place. In the modern world, however, this can only be a very partial project because of the suppressions of the magical, pagan world-view by a secular age. Friel makes us vividly aware of the debasement of archaic, Celtic, pagan ritual, as Frank Hardy recalls the kind of places where he hoped to perform his healing:

> Maybe in a corner a withered sheaf of wheat from a harvest thanksgiving of years ago or a fragment of a Christmas decoration across a window – relics of abandoned ritual. Because the people we moved among were beyond that kind of celebration   (*SP*, p. 332)

– a sentiment which is echoed by Terry's 'Nobody does that sort of thing now, do they? (*WT*, p. 31). Frank's description of his audiences could equally well apply to the characters in *Wonderful Tennessee*: 'Abject. Abased. Tight. Longing to open themselves and at the same time fearfully herding the anguish they contained against psychic disturbance' (*SP*, p. 336). Like Frank Hardy's performances, the six characters in *Wonderful Tennessee* occupy a cultural space in which only a residual magical past survives. Looking out towards Oileán Draíochta, they tell their stories, attempting to invoke former presences, the spirit of place, as Frank Hardy does through chanting his place-names. All these characters want to awaken the cultural unconscious, to reactivate all that has been repressed by a secular age. Frank Hardy imagines a triumphant Irish homecoming:

> Toasts to my return. To Donal's finger. Toasts to the departed groom and his prowess. To the bride and her fertility. To the rich harvest – the corn, the wheat, the barley. Toasts to all Septembers and to all harvests and to all things ripe and eager for the reaper.

A Dionysian night. A Bacchanalian night. A frenzied excessive Irish night when ritual was consciously and relentlessly debauched. (*SP*, pp. 339–40)

The harvest festival imagery reminds us that Frank's homecoming was at the time of the Lughnasa celebrations (also the time of year at which *Wonderful Tennessee* is set). But Frank is forced to admit that 'There was no sense of home-coming. I tried to stimulate it but nothing stirred. Only a few memories, wan and neutral' (*SP*, p. 338). Frank's only 'genuine sense of home-coming' (*SP*, p. 376) is in the moment of death. A creative, healing ritualism has become debased into a perverse, destructive one. Frank's godlike capacities cannot survive in a modern, agnostic world. And neither can Grace, who dies a lonely, sordid death in the metropolis, cut off from her Celtic roots. The vision in *Wonderful Tennessee* is not so bleak: the spirit of rural Ireland may be languishing and deformed, but it hasn't wholly lost its powers to compel and perhaps even to renew. At the end, the earlier 'parodic conga-dance' is transposed into a kind of stately, immensely poignant devotional ritual – each of the characters slowly encircling the mound, lifting a stone, touching the votive offering, while humming to George's 'sacred' (*WT*, p. 88) music. The play's closing assertion of life, love, the Body comes from George and Angela, left alone on the stage, standing together in the shadow of death: knowing George will never be back to visit the island, she nevertheless begins singing 'loudly, joyously, happily' and he accompanies her 'with comparable brio' (*WT*, p. 90).

In Friel's last play, the six characters, shifting between the world of pagan mystery and their ordinary lives as solicitors, lecturers and writers, exhibit the dialectic between tradition and modernity which informs all Friel's plays. In *Faith Healer*, Grace comes from a middle-class family, her father a Northern Irish Judge; like Berna, she has been a solicitor herself. But, abandoning her orderly professional life, Grace has preferred an itinerant life with Frank in the Celtic outback, just as Berna is drawn towards all that constitutes an 'Offence to Reason', away from patriarchal authority. Frank Hardy's van and the minibus which carries the six characters from and to the city in *Wonderful Tennessee* are the symbols of a destabilising technological modernity. The minibus and the van, like Jack's motor-bike in *The Communication Cord*, or Michael's bicycle, Gerry's motor-bike, the car and the bus in *Dancing at Lughnasa*, emphasise the breakdown of the local centre. Similarly, Terry's hamper, packed with such delicacies as 'Venison and Apricot Compôte' (*WT*, p. 40), 'Honey Gateau' (*WT*, p. 40), 'Brandied Peaches and Romanian Truffles' (*WT*, p. 49), represents a reorientation away from a concept of local self-sufficiency.

Wonderful Tennessee is Friel's culminating statement of marginalisation or suppression of rural, pagan, oral tradition by an advanced modern material society which is literate and scientific, humanised and Christianised, and supported by the mass media of book, film, gramophone and radio. The characters have lost touch with their Celtic past. A whole cultural heritage has been suppressed in a process of Catholic and humanist colonisation. The bishop expressly forbids recognition or mention of the substratum of paganism in Irish life and the Irish psyche when he learns of the strange and violent goings-on on Oileán Draíochta. Puritan Ireland, Catholic as well as Protestant, has historically disapproved of dancing and festivity, viewing them as dangerously libidinous. Kate the schoolteacher in *Dancing at Lughnasa* who patrols the boundaries of respectable Catholic, middle-class morality, recognises the 'cracks' opening up in the Mundy household caused by the subterranean stirrings of a pre-industrial paganism: in *Wonderful Tennessee*, all the characters eventually show themselves to be susceptible to a pagan libido which threatens to disrupt a regimental, authoritarian social order. Though none of them is claimed so completely by paganism as Father Jack, or even (albeit momentarily) the Mundy sisters themselves, *Wonderful Tennessee* still dramatises the struggle for expression of a sublimated paganism. Friel's statement about *Dancing at Lughnasa* – that it is a drama 'about the necessity for paganism' – applies equally to *Wonderful Tennessee*. As Peter Breen has shown in a study of the discursive field of Friel's plays ('Place and Displacement in the Work of Seamus Heaney and Brian Friel', unpublished Ph.D. thesis, Warwick University, 1993), the reactivation of a ritualist, pagan past threatens or breaks down both the official Catholic nationalist and imperial English discourses enunciated by such representative historical figures as Columba (representative of a doctrinal Catholicism allied to a scribal technology imposed upon a non-literate, oral, Gaelic culture), Mary and Henry Bagenal (Protestant English planters motivated by a Renaissance rational humanism which demonises the Irish as barbarians), Captain Lancey (representative of a positivist English imperium engaged in politically occupying and discursively encoding Ireland within an English world-view), and Archbishop Lombard (framer of a tendentious modern bourgeois Catholic nationalism).

At the end of *Wonderful Tennessee*, when the minibus arrives to take the six characters back to the city, the stage directions read: '*The engine starts up. The singing and the engine compete. Both sounds are encompassed by the silence and complete stillness and gradually surrender to it*' (WT, p. 70). The two great human enterprises – the aesthetic ('singing') and the technological ('engine') – have to define themselves against, are finally swallowed up in, the primal, timeless, silence, which is the ultimate context within which all Friel's drama is played out.

Notes

Notes to Chapter 1: Introduction

1. Des Hickey and Gus Smith (eds), *A Paler Shade of Green* (London: Leslie Frewin Publishers, 1972), p. 221.
2. Ibid., p. 221.
3. Ibid., p. 221.
4. Ibid., p. 221.
5. Seamus Deane, 'Brian Friel', *Ireland Today*, 978 (1981), p. 7.
6. Brian Friel, 'Self-Portrait', *Aquarius*, 3 (1972), p. 17.
7. Ibid., pp. 17–18.
8. Emily Dickinson, Poem 11 in *Selected Poems of Emily Dickinson*, ed. James Reeves (London: Heinemann, 1988), p. 5.
9. Des Hickey and Gus Smith (eds), *A Paler Shade of Green*, p. 224.
10. Brian Friel, 'Self-Portrait', p. 21.
11. Brian Friel, in interview with Fintan O'Toole, 'The Man from God Knows Where', in *In Dublin* (28 Oct. 1982), p. 20.
12. Ibid., p. 21.
13. Ibid., pp. 22–3.
14. Ibid., p. 22.
15. Ibid., p. 22.
16. The remark is Hugh's in *Translations*, in *Selected Plays of Brian Friel*, ed. Seamus Deane (London: Faber, 1984), p. 446.
17. Brian Friel, 'Extracts from a Sporadic Diary', in *The Writers: A Sense of Ireland*, ed. Andrew Carpenter and Peter Fallon (Dublin: O'Brien Press, 1980), p. 42.
18. Ibid., p. 39.
19. Ibid., pp. 40–1.
20. Brian Friel, 'The Theatre of Hope and Despair', in *Everyman*, 1 (1968), p. 18.
21. Blurb on dustjacket of *Ireland's Field Day* (London: Hutchinson, 1985).
22. 'Preface', in *Ireland's Field Day*, p. vii.
23. Brian Friel, 'The Man from God Knows Where', p. 20.
24. Brian Friel, 'The Theatre of Hope and Despair', p. 22.
25. Richard Kearney, *Transitions: Narratives in Modern Irish Culture* (Dublin: Wolfhound Press, 1988), p. 123.
26. Frank O'Connor, *The Lonely Voice* (London: Macmillan, 1963), pp. 20–1.
27. Ibid., p. 18.
28. Ibid., p. 19.
29. Ibid., p. 41.
30. Ibid., p. 22.
31. Ibid., pp. 22–3.
32. V. S. Pritchett, 'Short Stories', in Eugene Current-Garcia and Walton R. Patrick (eds), *What is the Short Story?* (Glenview, Illinois and Brighton: Scott, Foresman and Co., 1974), p. 117.

33. Sean O'Faolain, *The Short Story* (Old Greenwich, Conn.: Devin-Adair Co., 1974), p. 30.

34. Ibid., pp. 31–2.

35. Robert Frost, 'To the People and the Press', in E. C. Latham (ed.), *Interviews with Robert Frost* (New York: Holt, Rinehart and Winston, 1966), p. 169.

36. Mikhail Bakhtin, 'The Problem of Text in Linguistics, Philosophy, and the Other Human Sciences: An Essay of Philosophical Analysis', quoted by Tzvetan Todorov, in *Mikhail Bakhtin: The Dialogic Principle* (Manchester: Manchester University Press, 1984), p. 68.

37. Jeremy Mortimer, quoted in BBC Press Service publicity leaflet for Brian Friel season on Radios 3 and 4 (31 Mar. 1989).

38. Brian Friel, 'Self-Portrait', p. 20.

39. Tyrone Guthrie, *A Life in the Theatre* (London: Hamish Hamilton, 1960), pp. 313–14.

40. Brian Friel, 'Self-Portrait', p. 20.

41. Richard Kearney, *Transitions*, p. 154.

42. Catherine Belsey, *Critical Practice* (London and New York: Methuen, 1980), p. 92.

43. Peter Messent, *New Readings of the American Novel* (London: Macmillan, 1990), p. 164.

44. Ibid., p. 164.

45. Ibid., p. 165.

46. Brian Friel, *The Communication Cord* (London: Faber, 1983), p. 18.

47. Mikhail Bakhtin, *The Dialogic Imagination: Four Essays*, trans. Caryl Emerson and Michael Holquist (Austin: University of Texas Press, 1981), pp. 262–3.

48. Brian Friel, 'The Man from God Knows Where', p. 23.

49. Ibid., p. 23.

50. Denis Donoghue, *We Irish: The Selected Essays of Denis Donoghue* (Brighton: Harvester Press, 1987).

51. Seamus Deane, 'Heroic Styles: The Tradition of an Idea', in *Ireland's Field Day* (London: Hutchinson, 1985), p. 58. Thomas Davis, 'Our National Language', in *Poetry and Ireland Since 1800: A Source Book*, ed. Mark Storey (London and New York: Routledge, 1988), p. 46.

52. Jean-François Lyotard and Jean-Loup Thébaud, *Just Gaming*, trans. Wlad Godzich (Minneapolis: University of Minnesota Press, 1985), p. 100.

53. Thomas Davis, 'Our National Language', in Mark Storey (ed.), *Poetry and Ireland Since 1800: A Source Book* (London: Routledge, 1988), p. 46.

54. See Richard Kearney, *Transitions*, pp. 158–60, where he lists key passages from George Steiner's essay 'Understanding and Translations', in George Steiner, *After Babel: Aspects of Language and Translation* (Oxford University Press, 1975), which served as a major critical and philosophical source for Friel's plays. Richard Pine adduces 'two further significant statements by Steiner': the first, from p. 58 of *After Babel*, concerns Steiner's description of an *'Ur-Sprache'* – 'a single primal language' which 'lies behind our present discord':

Being of direct divine etymology . . . the *Ur-Sprache* had a congruence with reality such as no tongue has had after Babel. . . . Words and objects dovetailed perfectly. As the modern epistemologist might put it, here was a complete point-to-point mapping of language onto the true substance and shape of things. . . . Thus, Babel was a second Fall.

This passage, says Pine, 'becomes the core of the map-making exercise in *Translations*'. The second statement is from Steiner's *In Bluebeard's Castle* (London: Faber, 1971), p. 21: 'Hegel could argue, with rigorous logic of feeling, that history itself was passing into a new state of being, that ancient time was at an end', which, Pine comments, 'becomes the philosophy of Yolland *père*'. See Richard Pine, *Brian Friel and Ireland's Drama* (London: Routledge, 1990), p. 246.

55. Brian Friel, *Translations*, in *Selected Plays*, pp. 418–19.
56. Patricia Waugh, *Practising Postmodernism, Reading Modernism* (London, Edward Arnold, 1992), p. 50.
57. Brian Friel, p. 416.
58. T. S. Eliot, *The Use of Poetry and the Use of Criticism* (London: Faber, 1964), p. 155.
59. Brian Friel, *Translations*, in *Selected Plays*, p. 446.
60. Ibid., p. 445.
61. Mikhail Bakhtin, *The Dialogic Imagination*, p. 271.
62. Peter Messent, *New Readings of the American Novel* (London, Macmillan, 1990), p. 209.
63. Ibid.
64. Ibid., p. 210
65. Mikhail Bakhtin, p. 23.
66. Ibid., p. 128.
67. Ibid., p. 127.
68. W. H. Auden, 'In Memory of W. B. Yeats', in *The English Auden*, ed. Edward Mendelson (London: Faber, 1977), p. 242.
69. T. S. Eliot, 'Religion and Literature', in *Selected Essays* (London: Faber, 1969), p. 393.
70. I. A. Richards, *Principles of Literary Criticism* (London, 1967). First published in 1924.
71. Cleanth Brooks, *The Well-wrought Urn* (London, 1949), p. 189.
72. John Crowe Ransom, *The New Criticism* (Norfolk, Conn., 1941), p. 54.
73. 'Preface', in *Ireland's Field Day*, p. viii.

Notes to Chapter 2: Subject

1. Fintan O'Toole, 'How Poetry Joins Dramatic Action', in *The Guardian* (29 Nov. 1991).
2. Ibid.
3. Brian Friel, quoted in Graham Morison, 'An Ulster Writer: Brian Friel', *Acorn* (spring 1965), p. 8.

4. See Seamus Heaney's essay 'The God in the Tree: Early Irish Nature Poetry', in *Preoccupations: Selected Prose 1968–1978* (London: Faber, 1980), pp. 181–9.

5. Hélène Cixous, 'The Character of "Character"', trans. Keith Cohen, in *New Literary History*, 5, ii (Winter 1974), p. 389.

6. Brian Friel, 'The Theatre of Hope and Despair', p. 20.

7. J. M. Synge, *The Playboy of the Western World*, in *The Plays and Poems of J. M. Synge*, ed. T. R. Henn (London: Methuen, 1963), p. 229.

8. Harold Pinter, speech to the Seventh National Student Drama Festival in Bristol, *Sunday Times* (4 Mar. 1962). Quoted in Martin Esslin, *The Peopled Wound: The Plays of Harold Pinter* (London: Methuen, 1970), p. 46.

9. Ibid., p. 44.

10. Brian Friel, 'Self Portrait', p. 18.

11. Samuel Beckett, *Waiting for Godot* (London: Faber, 1956), p. 94.

12. Samuel Beckett, *Endgame* (London: Faber, 1958), p. 53.

13. See Friel's use of the term 'supra-naturalism' in 'Extracts from a Sporadic Diary', in *The Writers: A Sense of Ireland*, ed. Andrew Carpenter and Peter Fallon, p. 42.

14. Brian Friel, quoted in Des Hickey and Gus Smith, *A Paler Shade of Green*, p. 224.

15. D. E. S. Maxwell, *Brian Friel* (Lewisburg: Bucknell University Press, 1973), p. 87.

16. Jonathan Swift, 'A Modest Proposal for Preventing the Children of Poor People from being a Burthen to their Parents or Country and for Making them Beneficial to the Public' (1729). Repr. in *The Portable Swift*, ed. Carl Van Doren (Harmondsworth: Penguin, 1984), pp. 549–59.

17. Robert Emmet led an abortive insurrection against English rule in Ireland in 1803 and his speech from the dock on the eve of his execution is a classic call for freedom. It ends with these words: 'Let no man write my epitaph: for, as no man who knows my motives dares now vindicate them, let not prejudice nor ignorance asperse them. Let them and me repose in obscurity and peace, and my tomb remain uninscribed until other times and other men can do justice to my character; when my country takes her place among the nations of the earth, then, and not until then, let my epitaph be written'. See Norman Vance, 'Text and Tradition: Robert Emmet's Speech from the Dock', *Studies*, 71 (1982), pp. 185–91.

Notes to Chapter 3: Text

1. See Jean-François Lyotard, 'Judiciousness in Dispute, or Kant after Marx', in *The Aims of Representation*, ed. Murray Krieger (New York: Columbia University Press, 1987), pp. 23–67.

2. Mikhail Bakhtin, 'Discourse in the Novel', in *Modern Literary Theory: A Reader*, ed. Philip Rice and Patricia Waugh (London: Edward Arnold, 1989).

3. Seamus Deane, *A Short History of Irish Literature* (London: Hutchinson, 1986), p. 246.

4. Michel Foucault, interview in *The History of Sexuality* (London: Allen Lane, 1979).

5. Ulf Dantanus, *Brian Friel: A Study* (London: Faber, 1988), p. 140. For detailed discussion of the early reception of *The Freedom of the City*, see Wolfgang Zach, 'Criticism, Theatre and Politics: Brian Friel's *The Freedom of the City* and its Early Reception', in *Irish Literature and Culture*, ed. Michael Kenneally (Gerrards Cross: Colin Smythe, 1992), pp. 112–26.

6. Ibid., p. 134.

7. Seamus Heaney, in interview with Seamus Deane, 'Unhappy and at Home', in *The Crane Bag*, 1 (1977), p. 67.

8. Seamus Heaney, 'Viking Dublin: Trial Pieces', in *North* (London: Faber, 1975), p. 23.

9. Philip Vellacott, 'Introduction', in *Euripides: Alcestis, Hippolytus, Iphigenia in Taurus*, trans. Philip Vellacott (Harmondsworth: Penguin, 1970), p. 18.

10. Robert Bagg, 'Introduction', in *Euripides: Hippolytos* (London: Oxford University Press, 1974), p. 10. Classical tragedy plays on the difficulty in determining the extent to which the tragic situation is brought about by divine or human cause. This difficulty is mirrored in the vacillations of the commentators. Thus, in a revised introduction to a 1977 edition of *Euripides: Alcestis, Hippolytus, Iphigenia in Taurus*, Vellacott explicitly contradicts the emphasis in his earlier commentary of 1970 (see note 9 above), taking a view that is much closer to Bagg's: 'The moral of *Hippolytus*, it is often said, is that you cannot fly in the face of Nature; that the person who tries to live without recognizing Aphrodite will come to a bad end . . . But such an account of the play is inadequate, and only partly true . . . Though Hippolytus' death may have been contrived at long range by Aphrodite, as she claims in the prologue, the subsequent action shows it as due to a series of four human errors: the Nurse's foolishness, Hippolytus' fanatical cruelty, Phaedra's indignant revenge, and Theseus' impatient yielding to an irritation and jealousy which has evidently been long restrained. Our interest in these errors obliterates any sense that matters are being divinely organized' (Philip Vellacott, 'Introduction', *Euripides: Alcestis, Hippolytus, Iphigenia in Taurus* (Harmondsworth: Penguin, 1977), p. 22).

11. Robert Bagg, 'Introduction', p. 11.

12. Brian Friel, 'Extracts from a Sporadic Diary', in *The Writers: A Sense of Ireland*, p. 40.

13. Seamus Heaney, 'Punishment', in *North*, p. 38.

14. Seamus Heaney, 'Viking Dublin: Trial Pieces', in *North*, p. 23.

15. See Catherine Belsey, *Critical Practice*, pp. 85–102.

16. Seamus Deane, 'The Literary Myths of the Revival', in *Celtic Revivals* (London: Faber, 1985), p. 30.

17. Brian Friel, 'Extracts from a Sporadic Diary', in *The Writers: A Sense of Ireland*, p. 42.

18. Ibid., p. 40.

Notes on Chapter 4: History

1. Seamus Deane, 'Heroic Styles: The Tradition of an Idea', in *Ireland's Field Day* (London: Hutchinson, 1985), p. 58.
2. Blurb on dustjacket of *Ireland's Field Day*.
3. Richard Kearney and Mark Hederman, 'Editorial', in *The Crane Bag*, 1 (1977).
4. Brian Friel, quoted in John Gray, 'Field Day Five Years On', *Linenhall Review*, 2, 2 (summer 1985), p. 7.
5. Ibid., p. 7.
6. Brian Friel, interview in *The Sunday Press* (30 Aug. 1981). Quoted in John Gray, 'Field Day Five Years On', p. 6.
7. Brian Friel, in interview with Fintan O'Toole, 'The Man from God Knows Where', p. 23.
8. Seamus Deane, *Ireland Today* (June 1985), quoted in John Gray, 'Field Day Five Years On', pp. 8–9.
9. Seamus Deane, quoted in John Gray, 'Field Day Five Years On', p. 8.
10. These are lines of John Wilson Foster writing about John Montague's *The Rough Field* which Edna Longley applies to *Translations*. See Edna Longley, 'Poetry and Politics in Northern Ireland', in *Poetry in the Wars* (Newcastle upon Tyne: Bloodaxe, 1976), p. 191.
11. Brian McAvera, 'Attuned to the Catholic Experience', in *Fortnight* 3 (March 1985), p. 19. Quoted in John Gray, 'Field Day Five Years On', pp. 7–8.
12. Brian McAvera, *Fortnight* 3 (March 1985), p. 20. Quoted in John Gray, p. 8.
13. Sean Connolly, 'Dreaming History: Brian Friel's *Translations*', in *Theatre Ireland*, 13 (1977), pp. 43–4.
14. Ibid., p. 43.
15. Ibid., p. 43.
16. Ibid., p. 44.
17. Ibid., p. 44.
18. J. H. Andrews, '*Translations* and *A Paper Landscape*: Between Fiction and History', in *The Crane Bag*, 7, 2 (1983), p. 122.
19. Ibid., pp. 120–1.
20. Brian Friel, 'The Man from God Knows Where', p. 21.
21. Brian Friel, 'Extracts from a Sporadic Diary', in *Ireland and the Arts*, ed. Tim Pat Coogan (London: Quartet Books, 1982), p. 58.
22. Ibid., p. 58.
23. Ibid., p. 60.
24. See Richard Kearney's remarks on 'The Conflict of Language Models (Ontology Versus Positivism)' in *Transitions*, pp. 155–7.
25. Michael Toolan, 'Language and Affective Communication' in *Cultural Contexts and Literary Idioms*, ed. Michael Kenneally (Gerrards Cross: Colin Smythe, 1988) p. 145.
26. Lionel Pilkington, 'Language and Politics in Brian Friel's *Translations*', *Irish University Review*, 20, 2 (autumn 1990), p. 292.
27. Ibid., p. 292.
28. Elgy Gillespie, 'The Saturday Interview: Brian Friel', in *The Irish Times* (5 Sept. 1981).

29. Blurb on dustjacket of Brian Friel's *Three Sisters* (Dublin: Gallery Press, 1981).
30. Brian Friel, interview with Paddy Agnew, in *Magill* (Dec. 1980).
31. Irving Wardle, 'Seeking a Sense of Ireland', review of Friel's *There Sisters, The Times* (5 Oct. 1981), p. 11.
32. Review of Friel's *Three Sisters, The Irish Independent* (10 Sept. 1981).
33. Elisaveta Fen, 'Introduction', in *Plays: Anton Chekhov*, trans. Elisaveta Fen (Harmondsworth: Penguin, 1968), pp. 8–9.
34. Ibid., p. 9.
35. Ibid., p. 9.
36. Anton Chekhov, letter to Alexei Plescheyev (4 Oct. 1888), in *Letters of Anton Chekhov*, trans. Michael Heim and Simon Karlinsky (London: Bodley Head, 1973), p. 109.
37. F. L. Lucas, *The Drama of Chekhov, Synge, Yeats and Pirandello* (London: Cassell and Co., 1963), p. 115.
38. Seamus Deane, 'Heroic Styles: The Tradition of an Idea', in *Ireland's Field Day*, p. 58.
39. Seamus Deane, 'In Search of a Story', programme note for *The Communication Cord* (Field Day Theatre Company, 1982).
40. Quoted in E. R. Sands, 'Introduction', in I. S. Turgenev, *Fathers and Sons: A Stressed Text with Introduction and Notes by E. R. Sands* (Cambridge University Press, 1965), p. x.

Notes on Chapter 5: Body

1. Catherine Belsey, *Critical Practice*, p. 4.
2. Raymond Tallis, *Not Saussure: A Critique of Post-Saussurean Literary Theory* (London: Macmillan, 1988), p. 64.
3. Richard Kearney, *Transitions*, p. 151.
4. Brian Friel, *A Doubtful Paradise.*
5. Harold Pinter, speech to the Seventh National Student Drama Festival in Bristol, *Sunday Times* (4 Mar. 1962). Quoted in Martin Esslin, *The Peopled Wound: The Plays of Harold Pinter*, p. 44.
6. Brian Friel, 'The Man from God Knows Where', p. 22.
7. Richard Kearney, *Transitions*, p. 154.
8. D. E. S. Maxwell, *Brian Friel*, p. 69.
9. Frank Rich, review of *Dancing at Lughnasa, The New York Times* (25 Oct. 1991), Section C, p. 1. Reprinted under the title 'A Rich Hymn to Friel', in *The Irish Times* (31 Oct. 1991).
10. Seamus Heaney, 'Kinship', in *North*, p. 42.
11. Seamus Heaney, 'Englands of the Mind', in *Preoccupations*, p. 150.
12. Antonin Artaud, *The Theatre and its Double* (London: Calder and Boyars, 1970), p. 60.
13. Ibid., p. 71.
14. Ibid., pp. 70–1.
15. Ibid., p. 27.
16. Ibid., p. 53.
17. Ibid., p. 51.

18. Ibid., p. 51.
19. Ibid., p. 50.
20. Ibid., p. 44.
21. *Artaud on Theatre*, ed. Claude Schumacher (London: Methuen, 1989), p. 98.
22. Ibid., p. 130.
23. Jerzy Grotowski, *Towards a Poor Theatre* (London: Methuen, 1969), p. 35.
24. Ibid., p. 34.
25. Ibid., p. 38.
26. Ibid., p. 42.
27. Ibid., p. 23.
28. Ibid., p. 22.
29. Ibid., p. 22.
30. Ibid., p. 122.
31. Ibid., p. 125.
32. Ibid., p. 21.
33. Ibid., p. 23.
34. Peter Brook, *The Empty Space* (Harmondsworth: Pelican Books, 1973), pp. 47–72.
35. Ibid., pp. 11–46.
36. Ibid., p. 51.
37. Ibid., p. 55.
38. Brian Friel, 'Extracts from a Sporadic Diary', in *The Writers: A Sense of Ireland*, p. 42.
39. Antonin Artaud, *The Theatre and its Double*, p. 63.
40. Ibid., p. 63.
41. L. R. Chambers, 'Antonin Artaud and the Contemporary French Theatre', in *Aspects of Drama and Theatre: Five Kathleen Robinson Lectures Delivered in the University of Sydney 1961–63* (Sydney University Press, 1965), p. 137.
42. Brian Friel, 'The Theatre of Hope and Despair', p. 19.
43. Artaud actually paid a visit to Ireland on 14 August 1937. He brought with him a magical stick which he believed had belonged to Christ, had been mentioned in the prophecies of St Patrick and he had owned himself in a previous incarnation. He visited the Aran Islands and on 8 September left Galway for Dublin, leaving behind him a drift of unpaid bills. He spoke very little English, which was probably just as well when he tried to wake the Irish up from their sleep of conformity by prophesying that Catholicism would be destroyed as idolatrous and the Pope would be condemned to death as a traitor. Proclaiming all law as criminal, he incited the Irish people to riot on the streets. After several brushes with the police, he was deported, arriving at Le Havre in a straight-jacket on 30 September 1937. See Ronald Hayman, *Artaud and After* (Oxford and New York: Oxford University Press, 1977), pp. 120–4. Ireland wasn't ready for Artaud in 1937 and ever since, with only a few exceptions, the modern Irish theatre hasn't shown itself ready either to take up the challenge of the continental avant-garde represented by such experimentalists as Artaud.

44. Brian Friel, 'The Theatre of Hope and Despair', p. 19.
45. Ibid., p. 19.
46. Ibid., p. 19.
47. Ibid., p. 19.
48. Robert Kee, *Ireland: A History* (London: Abacus Books, 1982), p. 223.
49. Ibid., p. 223.
50. Terence Brown, *Ireland: A Social and Cultural History 1922–1985* (London: Fontana, 1985), p. 147.
51. Ibid., p. 159.
52. Peter Berresford Ellis, *A Dictionary of Irish Mythology* (London: Constable, 1987), pp. 153–5.
53. Egerton Sykes, *Everyman's Dictionary of Non-Classical Mythology* (London and New York: J. M. Dent and E. P. Dutton, 1965), p. 129.
54. Maria Leach, ed. *Standard Dictionary of Folklore, Mythology and Legend*, vol. 2 (New York: Funk and Wagnalls, 1950), p. 652.
55. J. M. Synge, Preface to *The Playboy of the Western World*, in *The Plays and Poems of J. M. Synge*, ed. T. R. Henn (London: Methuen, 1963), p. 174.
56. Ibid., p. 175.
57. Ibid., p. 175.
58. Frank Rich, review of *Dancing at Lughnasa*, *The New York Times* (25 Oct. 1991), Section C, p. 1.
59. Brian Friel, 'MacLochlainn's Vertigo', introduction to *The London Vertigo* (Dublin: Gallery Press, 1990), p. 12.
60. Ibid., p. 10.
61. J. O. Bartley, 'Introduction', in J. O. Bartley (ed.), *Four Comedies by Charles Macklin* (London: Sidgwick and Jackson, 1968), p. 27.
62. Ibid., p. 28.
63. Brian Friel, 'MacLochlainn's Vertigo', in *The London Vertigo*, p. 11.
64. Ibid., p. 10.
65. J. O. Bartley, 'Introduction', *Four Comedies by Charles Macklin*, p. 87.
66. Ibid., pp. 88–9.
67. Ibid., p. 89.
68. Ibid., p. 103.
69. Isaiah Berlin, 'Introduction', in I. S. Turgenev, *A Month in the Country*, trans. Isaiah Berlin (Harmondsworth: Penguin Books), p. 14.

Selected Bibliography

PRIMARY WORKS

Published Plays

The Enemy Within (Newark, Delaware: Proscenium Press, 1975; Dublin: Gallery Press, 1979).
Philadelphia, Here I Come! (London: Faber and Faber, 1965: Farrar, Straus and Giroux, 1966).
The Loves of Cass McGuire (London: Samuel French, 1966; London: Faber and Faber, 1967; New York: Farrar, Straus and Giroux, 1967).
Lovers (New York: Farrar, Straus and Giroux, 1968; London: Faber and Faber, 1969).
Crystal and Fox (London: Faber and Faber, 1970), in *Two Plays* (New York: Farrar, Straus and Giroux, 1970).
The Mundy Scheme (London: Samuel French, 1970; New York: Farrar, Straus and Giroux, 1970 (in *Two Plays*).
The Gentle Island (London: Davis-Poynter, 1973).
The Freedom of the City (London: Faber and Faber, 1974; New York: Samuel French, 1974).
Living Quarters (London: Faber and Faber, 1978).
Volunteers (London: Faber and Faber, 1979).
Aristocrats (Dublin: Gallery Press, 1980; London: Faber and Faber, 1980).
Faith Healer (London: Faber and Faber, 1980; New York: Samuel French, 1980).
Translations (Faber and Faber, 1981; New York: Samuel French, 1981).
The Three Sisters (Dublin: Gallery Press, 1981).
American Welcome, in *Best Short Plays 1981*, edited by Stanley Richards (Radnor, PA: Chilton Book Co., 1981), pp. 112–14.
The Communication Cord (London: Faber and Faber, 1983).
Selected Plays, edited by Seamus Deane (London: Faber and Faber, 1984; Washington, DC: Catholic University of America Press, 1986).
Fathers and Sons (London: Faber and Faber, 1988).
Making History (London: Faber and Faber, 1988).
Dancing at Lughnasa (London: Faber and Faber, 1990).
The London Vertigo (Dublin: Gallery Press, 1990).
A Month in the Country (Dublin: Gallery Press, 1992).
Wonderful Tennessee (Dublin: Gallery Press, 1993).

Stage plays (Unpublished)

The Francophile, produced by Group Theatre, Belfast, 1960.
The Blind Mice, produced by Eblana Theatre, Dublin, 1963.

Radio Plays

A Sort of Freedom, BBC Northern Ireland Home Service, 1958.
To This Hard House, BBC Northern Ireland Home Service, 1958.
The Loves of Cass McGuire, BBC Third Programme, 1961.
The Founder Members, BBC Light Programme, 1964.

Radio Adaptations

A Doubtful Paradise (The Francophile), BBC Northern Ireland Home Service, 1962.
The Enemy Within, BBC Third Programme, 1963.
The Blind Mice, BBC Northern Ireland Home Service, 1963.
Philadelphia, Here I Come, BBC Third Programme 1965.
Winners, BBC Third Programe, 1968.
Faith Healer, BBC Radio 3, 1980.
Translations, BBC Radio 3, 1982.
Making History, BBC Radio 3, 1989.
Aristocrats, BBC Radio 3, 1989.

Television Adaptation

The Enemy Within, BBC, 1965.

Film Adaptation

Philadelphia, Here I Come!, 1970.

Screenplays

Three Fathers, Three Sons, RTE TV, 1964.
Farewell to Ardstraw (with David Hammond), BBC Northern Ireland TV, 1976.
The Next Parish, BBC Northern Ireland TV, 1976.

Short Stories

The Saucer of Larks (London: Gollancz, 1962; New York: Doubleday, 1962).
The Gold in the Sea (London: Gollancz, 1966; New York: Doubleday, 1966).
Selected Stories (Dublin: Gallery Press, 1979).
The Diviner: The Best Stories of Brian Friel (Dublin: O'Brien Press, 1982; London: Allison and Busby, 1983).

Non-fiction

'For Export Only', *Commonweal* (15 Feb. 1957), pp. 509–10.
'The Theatre of Hope and Despair', *Everyman* 1 (1968), pp. 17–22.
'The Future of Irish Drama: A Discussion between F. Linehan, H. Leonard, J. B. Keane and B. Friel', *The Irish Times* (12 Feb. 1970).
'Plays Peasant and Unpeasant', *The Times Literary Supplement* (17 March 1972), pp. 305–6.
'Self-Portrait', *Aquarius* 3 (1972), pp. 17–22.
'Extracts from a Sporadic Diary', in Carpenter, A. and Fallon, P. (ed.), *The Writers: A Sense of Ireland* (Dublin: O'Brien Press; New York: George Braziller, 1980), pp. 39–43.
'Extracts from a Sporadic Diary', in Coogan, T. P. (ed.), *Ireland and the Arts* (London: Quartet), pp. 56–61.
'Important Places', an introduction to Charles McGlinchey, *The Last of the Name* (Belfast: Blackstaff Press, 1986).

Interviews

'An Ulster Writer: Brian Friel' (Graham Morison), *Acorn*, 8 (spring 1965), pp. 4–15.
'The Saturday Interview: Brian Friel' (Elgy Gillespie), *The Irish Times* (5 Sept. 1981).
'The Man from God Knows Where: An Interview with Brian Friel' (Fintan O'Toole), *In Dublin* (28 Oct. 1982), pp. 20–3.

SECONDARY WORKS

Bibliographical and Biographical

Bigsby, C. W. E., *Contemporary Dramatists* (London: St James Press, 1977).
Hickey, Des and Gus Smith, *A Paler Shade of Green* (London: Leslie Frewin, 1972).
King, Kimball, *Ten Modern Irish Playwrights* (New York: Garland, 1979).
Mikhail, E. H., *A Research Guide to Modern Irish Dramatists* (New York: Whitston Publishing Co., 1979).
Mikhail, E. H., *An Annotated Bibliography of Modern Anglo-Irish Drama* (New York: Whitston Publishing Co., 1981).
Schlueter, June, 'Brian Friel', in Weintraub, S. (ed.), *Dictionary of Literary Biography*, vol. 13 (Detroit: Gale Research, 1982), pp. 179–85.

Books

Dantanus, Ulf, *Brian Friel: The Growth of an Irish Dramatist*, Gothenburg

Studies in English 59 (Atlantic Heights, New Jersey: Humanities Press, 1986).

Dantanus, Ulf, *Brian Friel: A Study* (London: Faber and Faber, 1988).

Maxwell, D. E. S., *Brian Friel* (Lewisburg, Penn.: Bucknell University Press, 1973).

O'Brien, George, *Brian Friel* (Dublin: Gill and Macmillan, 1989).

Peacock, Alan (ed.), *The Achievement of Brian Friel* (Gerrards Cross: Colin Smyth, 1993).

Pine, Richard, *Brian Friel and Ireland's Drama* (London and New York: Routledge, 1990).

Articles and Reviews

A. W., 'Introducing Brian Friel', *Acorn*, 14 (Nov. 1970), pp. 25–8.

Barnes, Clive, 'Brian Friel Writes of Current Troubles', *The New York Times* (18 Feb. 1974).

Bertha, Csilla, 'Tragedies of National Fate: A Comparison between Brian Friel's *Translations* and its Hungarian Counterpart, Andras Suto's *A Szuzai menyegao*', *Irish University Review*, 17, no. 2 (autumn 1987), pp. 207–22.

Billington, Michael, 'Friel Play', review of *The Freedom of the City*, *The Guardian* (28 Feb. 1973).

Birker, Klaus, 'The Relationship between the Stage and the Audience in Brian Friel's *The Freedom of the City*', in Harmon, M. (ed.), *The Irish Playwright and the City* (Gerrards Cross: Colin Smythe, 1984), pp. 153–8.

Boland, Eavan, 'Brian Friel: Derry's Playwright', review of *The Freedom of the City*, *Hibernia* (16 Feb. 1973).

Bordinat, Philip, 'Tragedy through Comedy in Plays by Brendan Behan and Brian Friel', *West Virginia University Papers in Philology*, 29 (1983), pp. 84–91.

Breen, Peter, 'Place and Displacement in the Works of Seamus Heaney and Brian Friel', unpublished Ph.D. thesis, Warwick University, 1993.

Brustein, Robert, 'The Dreaming of the Bones', review of *Dancing at Lughnasa*, *Theatre Ireland*, 29 (autumn 1992), pp. 49–51.

Brustein, Robert, 'Glossing over the Problem', review of *The Freedom of the City*, *Observer* (4 Mar. 1973).

Coakley, James, 'Chekhov in Ireland: Brief Notes on Friel's *Philadelphia*', *Comparative Drama*, 7, no. 3 (fall 1973), pp. 191–7.

Collective review of *The Communication Cord*, *Theatre Ireland*, 2 (Jan./May 1983) pp. 66–9.

Connolly, Sean, 'Dreaming History: Brian Friel's *Translations*', *Theatre Ireland*, 13 (autumn 1987), pp. 42–4.

Cronin, S., 'Storm over Friel play on Broadway', review of *The Freedom of the City*, *The Irish Times* (4 Mar. 1974).

Cruickshank, Julia, 'Brian Friel: Language, Music and Dance', unpublished MA dissertation, University of Ulster, 1991.

Deane, Seamus, 'The Writer and the Troubles', *Threshold*, 25 (summer 1974), pp. 13–17.

Deane, Seamus, 'Brian Friel', *Ireland Today*, 978 (1981), pp. 7–10.

Fenton, James, 'Ireland: The Destruction of an Idyll', review of *Translations*, *The Sunday Times* (28 Sept. 1980), p. 40.

Fitzgibbon, Emelie, 'All Change: Contemporary Fashions in the Irish Theatre', in Sekine, M. (ed.), *Irish Writers and the Theatre* (Gerrards Cross: Colin Smythe, 1987), pp. 33–46.

Fitzgibbon, Gerald, 'Garnering the Facts: Unreliable Narrators in Some Plays of Brian Friel', in Allen, M. and Wilcox, A. (ed.), *Critical Approaches to Anglo-Irish Literature* (Gerrards Cross: Colin Smythe, 1989), pp. 53–62.

Friel, Brian, John Andrews and Kevin Barry, '*Translations* and *A Paper Landscape*: Between Fiction and History', *The Crane Bag*, 7, no. 2 (1983), pp. 118–24.

Gaskell, J., 'Innocence Is No Defence Against the Bullet', review of *The Freedom of the City*, *The Daily Mail* (1 Mar. 1973).

Gray, John, 'Field Day Five Years On', *Linen Hall Review*, 2, no. 2 (summer 1985), pp. 4–10.

Grene, Nicholas, 'Distancing Drama: Sean O'Casey to Brian Friel', in Sekine, M. (ed.), *Irish Writers and the Theatre* (Gerrards Cross: Colin Smythe, 1987), pp. 47–70.

Seamus Heaney, review of *Volunteers*, *The Times Literary Supplement* (21 Mar. 1975), p. 306. Reprinted in Seamus Heaney, *Preoccupations: Selected Prose 1968–1978* (London: Faber and Faber, 1980).

Seamus Heaney, '. . . English and Irish', review of *Translations*, *The Times Higher Educational Supplement* (24 Oct. 1980), p. 1199.

Hobson, Harold, 'Divided Devotion', review of *The Freedom of the City*, *The Sunday Times* (4 Mar. 1973).

Johnston, Denis, 'Brian Friel and Modern Irish Drama', *Hibernia*, 7 (Mar. 1975), p. 22.

Kelly, S., 'New Friel Play at the Abbey', review of *The Freedom of the City*, *The Irish Times* (21 Feb. 1973).

Kiberd, Declan, 'Brian Friel's *Faith Healer*', in Sekine, M. (ed.), *Irish Writers and Society at Large* (Gerrards Cross: Colin Smyth, 1987), pp. 106–22.

Kretzner, H., 'Irish Heroes Who Never Come to Life', review of *The Freedom of the City*, *The Daily Express* (1 Mar. 1973).

Lambert, J. W., 'Plays in Performance', review of *The Freedom of the City*, *Drama* (summer 1973), pp. 14–16.

Leary, Daniel, 'The Romanticism of Brian Friel', in Brophy, J. D. and Porter R. J. (ed.), *Contemporary Irish Writing* (Boston: Iona College Press/ Twayne, 1983), pp. 127–42..

Levin, Milton, 'Brian Friel: An Introduction', *Eire-Ireland*, 7, no. 2 (summer 1972), pp. 132–6.

Lowry, B. 'Shades of Bloody Sunday in New Friel Play', review of *The Freedom of the City* (21 Feb. 1973).

McAvera, Brian, 'Attuned to the Catholic Experience', *Fortnight*, 3 (Mar. 1985), pp. 19–20.

McGowan, M. 'Truth, Politics and the Individual: Brian Friel's *The Freedom of the City* and the Northern Irish Conflict', in *Literatur Wissenschaft und Unterricht*, 12 (1979), pp. 287–307.

McMahon, Sean, 'The Black North: The Prose Writers of the North of Ireland', *Threshold*, 21 (summer 1967), pp. 158–74.

Marcus, Frank, 'On the Spot', review of *The Freedom of the City*, *The Sunday Telegraph* (4 Mar. 1973).

Maxwell, D. E. S., 'Imagining the North: Violence and the Writers', *Eire-Ireland*, 8, no. 2 (summer 1973), pp. 91–107.

Maxwell, D. E. S., 'Introduction to *The Enemy Within*', *Journal of Irish Literature*, 4, no. 2 (May 1975), pp. 4–6.

Miner, Edmund J., 'Homecoming: The Theme of Disillusionment in Brian Friel's Short Stories', *Kansas Quarterly*, 9, no. 2 (spring 1977), pp. 92–9.

Murray, Christopher, 'Irish Drama in Transition 1966–1978', in *Etudes Irelandaises*, Nouvelle Serie 4 (Dec. 1979), pp. 187–308.

Murray, Christopher, 'Recent Irish Drama', in Kosok, Heinz (ed.), *Studies in Anglo-Irish Literature* (Bonn: Bouvier Verlag Herbert Grundmann, 1982), pp. 439–43.

Neil, Ruth, 'Digging into History: A Reading of Brian Friel's *Volunteers* and Seamus Heaney's "Viking Dublin: Trial Pieces"', *Irish University Review* 16, no. 1 (spring 1986), pp. 35–47.

Nixon, K., 'A Trickle of Cheap Tears for *Freedom*', review of *The Freedom of the City*, *The Belfast Newsletter* (22 Feb. 1973).

O'Hare, Damian, 'The Theme of Faith in the Drama of Brian Friel', unpublished MA dissertation, University of Ulster, 1993.

O'Toole, Fintan, 'Friel's Lost Tribe', *The Sunday Tribune* (24 Mar. 1985), p. 20.

O'Toole, Fintan, 'How Poetry Joins Dramatic Action', *The Guardian* (29 Nov. 1991).

Pilkington, Lionel, 'Language and Politics in Brian Friel's *Translations*', *Irish University Review*, 20, no. 2 (autumn 1990), pp. 282–98.

Rich, Frank, review of *Dancing at Lughnasa*, *The New York Times* (25 Oct. 1991), section C, p. 1. Reprinted as 'Rich Hymn to Friel', in *The Irish Times* (31 Oct. 1991), p. 10.

Robbins, Ronald, 'Friel's Modern Fox and Grapes Fable', *Eire-Ireland*, 21, no. 4 (winter 1986), pp. 66–76.

Rushe, D., 'Friel's *Freedom* Ironic Commentary', review of *The Freedom of the City*, *The Irish Independent* (21 Feb. 1973).

Sheridan, Michael, 'Friel Play a Watershed in Irish Theatre', review of *Translations*, *The Irish Press* (25 Sept. 1980), p. 3.

Shulman, Milton, 'At the Royal Court', *The Standard* (28 Feb. 1973).

Simmons, James, 'Brian Friel, Catholic Playwright', *The Honest Ulsterman* (autumn 1985), pp. 61–6.

Timm, Eitel F., 'Modern Mind, Myth, and History: Brian Friel's *Translations*', in Kosok, Heinz (ed.), *Studies in Anglo-Irish Literature* (Bonn: Bouvier Verlag Herbert Grundmann, 1982), pp. 447–53.

Toolan, Michael, 'Language and Affective Communication', in Michael Kenneally (ed.), *Cultural Contexts and Literary Idioms* (Gerrards Cross: Colin Smythe, 1988).

Vance, Norman, 'Text and Tradition: Robert Emmet's Speech from the Dock', *Studies*, 71 (1982) pp. 185–91.

Wardle, Irving, 'The Freedom of the City', *The Times* (28 Feb. 1973).

Wardle, Irving, review of *Translations*, *The Times* (13 May 1981), p. 11.

Wardle, Irving, 'Seeking a Sense of Ireland', review of Friel's *The Three Sisters*, *The Times* (5 Oct. 1981), p. 11.

Winkler, Elizabeth Hale, 'Brian Friel's *Freedom of the City*: Historical Actuality and Dramatic Imagination', *Canadian Journal of Irish Studies*, 7, no. 1 (June 1981), pp. 12–31.

Winkler, Elizabeth Hale, ' "Eejitin' About": Adolescence in Friel and Keane', *Eire-Ireland*, 16, no. 3 (fall 1981), pp. 128–44.

Winkler, Elizabeth Hale, 'Reflections of Derry's Bloody Sunday in Literature', in Kosok, Heinz (ed.), *Studies in Anglo-Irish Literature* (Bonn: Bouvier Verlag Herbert Grundmann, 1982), pp. 411–21.

Zach, Wolfgang, 'Brian Friel's *Translations*: National and Universal Dimensions', in *Medieval and Modern Ireland*, edited by Richard Wall (Gerrards Cross: Colin Smythe, 1988), pp. 75–87.

Zach, Wolfgang, 'Criticism, Theatre and Politics: Brian Friel's *The Freedom of the City* and its Early Reception', in Michael Kenneally (ed.), *Irish Literature and Culture* (Gerrards Cross: Colin Smythe, 1992), pp. 112–26.

Parts of Books on Friel

Allen, Walter, *The Short Story in English* (Oxford: Clarendon Press, 1981).

Cairns, David, and Shaun Richards (ed.), *Writing Ireland: Colonialism, Nationalism and Culture* (Manchester: Manchester University Press, 1988).

Deane, Seamus, 'Brian Friel: The Double Stage', in *Celtic Revivals* (London: Faber and Faber, 1986), pp. 166–73.

Deane, Seamus, *A Short History of Irish Literature* (London: Hutchinson, 1986).

Fitz-Simons, Christopher, *The Irish Theatre* (London: Thames and Hudson, 1983), pp. 193–5.

Heaney, Seamus, *Preoccupations: Selected Prose 1968–1978* (London: Faber and Faber, 1980).

Hogan, Robert, *After the Irish Renaissance* (London: University of Minnesota Press, 1967).

Hogan, Robert, *'Since O'Casey' and Other Essays on Irish Drama* (Gerrards Cross: Colin Smythe, 1983).

Jeffares, A. Norman, *Anglo-Irish Literature* (Dublin: Gill and Macmillan, 1982).

Kearney, Richard, 'The Language Plays of Brian Friel', in *Transitions: Narratives in Modern Irish Culture* (Dublin: Wolfhound Press, 1988), pp. 123–60.

Longley, Edna, 'Poetry and Politics in Northern Ireland', in *Poetry in the Wars* (Newcastle-upon-Tyne: Bloodaxe Books, 1986), pp. 185–211.

McHugh, Roger and Harmon Maurice, *A Short History of Anglo-Irish Literature* (Dublin: Wolfhound Press, 1982).

Maxwell, D. E. S., *A Critical History of Modern Irish Drama 1891–1980* (Cambridge: Cambridge University Press, 1984).

Books Containing Useful Background Material

Andrews, J. M., *A Paper Landscape* (Oxford: Oxford University Press, 1975).
Artaud, Antonin, *The Theatre and its Double* (London: Calder and Boyars, 1970).
Bakhtin, Michael, *The Dialogic Imagination: Four Essays*, trans. Caryl Emerson and Michael Holquist (Austin: University of Texas Press, 1981).
Barthes, Roland, *S/Z: An Essay*, trans. Richard Miller (New York: Hill and Wang, 1974).
Bartley, J. O. (ed.), *Four Comedies by Charles Macklin* (London: Sidgwick and Jackson, 1968).
Bagg, Robert (trans.), *Euripides: Hippolytos* (London: Oxford University Press, 1974).
Belsey, Catherine, *Critical Practice* (London and New York: Methuen, 1980).
Brook, Peter, *The Empty Space* (Harmondsworth: Penguin Books, 1973).
Brown, Terence, *Ireland: A Social and Cultural History 1922–1985* (London: Fontana, 1985).
Brown, Terence, *Ireland's Literature: Selected Essays* (Mullingar: Lilliput Press; New Jersey: Barnes and Noble, 1989).
Chekhov, Anton, *Letters of Anton Chekhov*, trans. Michael Heim and Simon Karlinsky (London: Bodley Head, 1973).
Chekhov, Anton, *The Three Sisters: An Authoritative Text Edition*, trans. Tyrone Guthrie and Leonard Kipnis (New York: Avon Books, 1965).
Current-Garcia, and Walton R. Patrick (ed.), *What is the Short Story?* (Glenview, Illinois and Brighton: Scott, Foresman and Co., 1974).
Donoghue, Denis, *We Irish: The Selected Essays of Denis Donoghue* (Brighton: Harvester Press, 1989).
Dowling, P. J., *The Hedge-Schools of Ireland* (Cork: Mercier Press, 1968).
Eliot, T. S., *Selected Essays* (London: Faber, 1969).
Eliot, T. S., *The Use of Poetry and the Use of Criticism* (London: Faber, 1964).
Ellis, Peter Berresford, *A Dictionary of Irish Mythology* (London: Constable, 1987).
Esslin, Martin, *The Peopled Wound: The Plays of Harold Pinter* (London: Methuen, 1970).
Fen, Elisaveta (trans.), *Plays: Anton Chekhov* (Harmondsworth: Penguin Books, 1968).
Field Day Company, *Ireland's Field Day* (London: Hutchinson, 1985).
Forsyth, James, *Tyrone Guthrie* (London: Hamish Hamilton, 1976).
Grotowski, Jerzy, *Towards a Poor Theatre* (London: Methuen, 1969).
Guthrie, Tyrone, *A Life in the Theatre* (London: Hamish Hamilton, 1960).
Hayman, Ronald, *Artaud and After* (Oxford and New York: Oxford University Press, 1977).
Heidegger, Martin, *Being and Time*, trans. J. Macquarrie and E. S. Robinson (Oxford: Blackwell, 1967).
Hollingdale, R. J., *Nietzsche: The Man and his Philosophy* (London: Routledge and Kegan Paul, 1965).
Kee, Robert, *Ireland: A History* (London: Abacus Books, 1982).
Krieger, Murray (ed.), *The Aims of Representation* (New York: Columbia University Press, 1987).

Lavrin, Janko, *Nietzsche: A Biographical Introduction* (London: Studio Vista, 1971).

Leach, Maria (ed.), *Standard Dictionary of Folklore, Mythology and Legend* (New York: Funk and Wagnalls, 1950).

Lucas, F. L., *The Drama of Chekhov, Synge, Yeats and Pirandello* (London: Cassell and Co., 1963).

Lyotard, Jean-François, and Jean-Loup Thebaud, *Just Gaming*, trans. Wlad Godzich (Minneapolis: University of Minnesota Press, 1985).

Messent, Peter, *New Readings of the American Novel* (1990).

Nietzsche, Friedrich, *Ecce Homo: How One Becomes What One Is* (Harmondsworth: Penguin Books, 1979).

Nietzsche, Friedrich, *The Will to Power*, trans. Walter Kaufmann and R. J. Hollingdale (New York: Vintage Books, 1968).

O'Connor, Frank, *The Lonely Voice* (London: Macmillan, 1963).

O'Faolain, Sean, *The Short Story* (Old Greenwich, Conn.: Devin-Adair Co., 1974).

O'Faolain, Sean, *The Great O'Neill* (London: Longman, Green, 1942).

Rice, Philip, and Patricia Waugh (ed.), *Modern Literary Theory: A Reader* (London: Edward Arnold, 1989).

Schumacher, Claude (ed.), *Artaud on Theatre* (London: Methuen, 1989).

Steiner, George, *After Babel: Aspects of Language and Translation* (Oxford: Oxford University Press, 1975).

Steiner, George, *In Bluebeard's Castle* (London: Faber and Faber, 1971).

Storey, Mark (ed.), *Poetry and Ireland Since 1800: A Source Book* (London and New York: Routledge, 1988).

Sykes, Egerton, *Everyman's Dictionary of Non-Classical Mythology* (London and New York: J. M. Dent and E. P. Dutton, 1965).

Tallis, Raymond, *Not Saussure: A Critique of Post-Saussurian Literary Theory* (London: Macmillan, 1988).

Todorov, Tzvetan, *Mikhail Bakhtin: The Dialogic Principle* (Manchester: Manchester University Press, 1984).

Turgenev, I. S., *A Month in the Country*, trans. Isaiah Berlin (Harmondsworth: Penguin Books, 1981).

Turgenev, I. S., *Fathers and Sons*, a stressed text with introduction and notes by E. R. Sands (Cambridge: Cambridge University Press, 1965).

Vance, Norman, *Irish Literature: A Social History* (Oxford: Basil Blackwell, 1990).

Vellacott, Philip (trans.), *Euripides: Alcestis, Hippolytus, Iphigenia in Taurus* (Harmondsworth: Penguin Books, 1970).

Waugh, Patricia, *Practising Postmodernism, Reading Modernism* (1992).

Index